Labor
and Imperial Democracy
in Prewar Japan

D0153715

Twentieth-Century Japan:
The Emergence of a World Power

Irwin Scheiner, Editor

1. Labor and Imperial Democracy in Prewar Japan
   by Andrew Gordon

Labor
and Imperial Democracy
in Prewar Japan

Andrew Gordon

UNIVERSITY OF CALIFORNIA PRESS
Berkeley • Los Angeles • Oxford

The illustrations in the book are reprinted, by permission, from the following sources:

Ohara Institute for Social Research: figures 6, 7, 8, 9, 10, 13, 14, 16, 17, 18, 19, 20, 21, 22, 23, 24, 25, 26, 27, 28.

Senji gahō rinji zōkan: Tōkyō sōjō gahō (No. 66, September 18, 1905): figures 2, 3, 4, 5.

Tanno Setsu: Kakumei undō ni ikiru, ed. Tanaka Uta and Tamashiro Kikue (Tokyo: Keiso shobō, 1969): figures 12, 15.

Okamoto Kōji, *Gama shōgun: Minami Kiichi* (Tokyo: Privately published, 1971): figure 11.

Zusetsu: Shōwa no Rekishi (2): Minponshugi no jidai (Tokyo: Shūeisha, 1979): figure 1.

Chapter 2 draws on and reproduces material from Andrew Gordon, "The Crowd and Politics in Imperial Japan: Tokyo: 1905–1908," which first appeared in *Past and Present: A Journal of Historical Studies,* no. 121 (November 1988): 141–70 (world copyright: The Past and Present Society, 175 Banbury Road, Oxford, England).

University of California Press
Berkeley and Los Angeles, California

University of California Press, Ltd.
Oxford, England

© 1991 by
The Regents of the University of California

First Paperback Printing 1992

Library of Congress Cataloging-in-Publication Data

Gordon, Andrew, 1952–
    Labor and imperial democracy in prewar Japan / Andrew Gordon.
        p. cm.
    Includes bibliographical references.
    ISBN 0-520-08091-2
    1. Working class—Japan—Political activity—History—20th century. 2. Labor disputes—Japan—History—20th century. 3. Labor movement—Japan—History—20th century. 4. Riots—Japan—History—20th century. 5. Political participation—Japan—History—20th century. 6. Japan—Politics and government—20th century.
I. Title.
HD8728.G65   1990
322'.2'095209041—dc20   90-10872
                                                                                                            CIP

Printed in the United States of America
1 2 3 4 5 6 7 8 9

For Yoshie

Contents

Illustrations

Tables, Graphs, and Maps

xi

GRAPHS

MAPS

Abbreviations

NRN	Ōhara shakai mondai kenkyū jo, *Nihon rōdō nenkan* (1920–40)
NRUS	Rōdō undō shiryō iinkai, ed., *Nihon rōdō undō shiryō* (1959–75)
OISR	Ohara Institute for Social Research [Ōhara shakai mondai kenkyū jo]
ROS	*Rōdō oyobi sangyō* (1914–19)
TAS	*Tōkyō asahi shinbun*
TRTJC	*Tōkyō shi oyobi kinkō ni okeru rōdō tōkei jitchi chōsa* (1924, 1927, 1930, 1933, 1936)

Preface

This book is the unexpected product of a slight detour in my research about five years ago that took on a life of its own. I was studying the history of Japan's working-class movement with a relatively narrow objective: to produce a monograph on the working-class movement in the interwar era. I planned to combine my unpublished research on labor at the Ishikawajima shipyard and the Uraga Dock Company in the 1910s and 1920s with fresh study of smaller workplaces.

The point of departure was to have been the frequent nonunion disputes at heavy industrial worksites between the turn of the century and World War I, but I was aware that these years were also a time of numerous riots in Tokyo and other major cities and decided to investigate them briefly. The "brief" initial survey lasted several months. I was surprised to find the riots a source of insight into popular ideas and forms of action. The riots were not only related to the evolution of the labor movement; they also shed light on broader issues of political ideology and the changing structures of rule in Japan. As I tried to make sense of the riots and the "political crowd" in the early 1900s, I became increasingly frustrated with the broader interpretive framework for twentieth-century Japan's political history in which riots, unions, and labor disputes were part of a movement culminating in the "Taishō democracy" of the 1920s. Instead, I came to see these developments as part of the story of "imperial democracy" in Japan. The result is a book that, while it retains my original concern with the making of the worker's movement, also seeks to offer a fresh perspective on the broad sweep of twentieth-century history.

Along the course of this journey, I received important help from a large number of colleagues and friends, and one of the great pleasures of finishing this book is acknowledging their contributions. Sheldon Garon has been a friend and critic whose insights, doubts, and suggestions in response to numerous drafts of this project never failed to sharpen my sense of the problem. Gary Allinson, Albert Craig, Harry Harootunian, Gregory Kasza, Dirk Phillipsen, and Charles Maier all read the entire manuscript and offered valuable critical comments, while Chuck Bergquist, Alex Keyssar, Jim McClain, William Reddy, Miriam Silverberg, and Thomas C. Smith did likewise with portions of the work in progress. In Japan, Nimura Kazuo was an unfailing critic and host at the Ohara Institute of Social Research, whose staff also deserve special thanks. William Steele, Watanabe Etsuji, Suzuki Yūko, Nakamura Masanori, Utsumi Takashi, Nishida Yoshiaki, Hyōdō Tsutomu, Uekusa Masu, Nishinarita Yutaka, Watanabe Hiroshi, and Yoshida Kenji advised me on sources and engaged in spirited discussions of my interpretations as well. Peter Lange discussed the literature on European fascism with me. I was fortunate to have a superb research assistant, Uchida Sumine, to help collect and analyze the data on labor disputes in Minami Katsushika County. Connie Blackmore pitched in with critical typing help during a computer failure. While several of those mentioned in this paragraph will not agree with my interpretations of labor and imperial democracy, and while I take full responsibility for the result, good or bad, I am convinced that their generous critiques have made this a far better work than it would otherwise have been.

Funding for this project, provided by the Social Science Research Council (1983), the Department of Education Fulbright program (1984–85), and the Duke University Research Council (1987), allowed me the luxury of three trips to Japan to carry out the research. Duke's Research Council also supported further research and writing in the following years.

I dedicate the book to my wife, Yoshie. Together with Jennifer and Megumi, she has enriched my life in countless ways.

Introduction

In the first two decades of the twentieth century, crowds of city-dwellers took to the streets of Tokyo and launched the most vigorous urban protests yet seen in Japan. At least nine times from the Hibiya riot of 1905 to the rice riots of 1918, angry Tokyoites attacked policemen, police stations, and national government offices, smashed streetcar windows and beat the drivers, marched on the Diet, and stormed the offices of major newspapers. They destroyed public and private property, launching both symbolic and substantive attacks on the institutions of the established order of imperial Japan.

In the same years, wage laborers mounted new forms of protest in the workplace. In the handful of major factories, shipyards, and arsenals that made up the heavy industrial sector of the economy, a tradition of protest evolved before the advent of unions. Over 100 labor disputes took place in the heavy and textile industries during these years, with 49 of them concentrated at just nine major public and private enterprises between 1902 and 1917. Although unions led none of these disputes, a union movement did emerge in these same years; workers in Tokyo in 1912 created the major union federation of the imperial era, initially named the Yūaikai (Friendly Society). By 1916 they had built a solid foundation of about 20,000 members in the Tokyo and Osaka areas.

The crowd, labor disputes, and the early unions together constituted the lower-class, urban dimension to a movement for imperial democracy, with roots in the nineteenth century, which reached its peak between

1

1905 and 1918, but the actions of workers and urban crowds constituted just a portion of the movement as a whole. A host of other developments also mark off these decades from those that preceded and
followed, and thus define the movement. The Diet emerged as a central
component of the political order by the early twentieth century, contrary to the expectations of the oligarchic constitution-writers. The
Seiyūkai evolved into Japan's first stable political party between 1900
and 1913 under the adroit leadership of Hara Kei. A second, more
liberal, party then coalesced gradually out of a motley of anti-Seiyūkai
elements between 1913 and the 1920s (first named Dōshikai, then Kenseikai, finally Minseitō). Both inside and outside the Diet, a sustained
movement for expanded suffrage unfolded between 1897 and the adoption of universal manhood suffrage in 1925. Beginning in the late
1890s, both leaders of big business and struggling small-scale traders
and manufacturers joined a determined anti-tax movement; they met
with a measure of success in the repeal of the despised business tax in
1926. Several groups of women nurtured a precocious feminist tradition. Liberal, democratic, and (especially after 1917) socialist thought
flowered among intellectuals. And the liberal editorial stance of the
press reflected a widespread belief that the future would bring the further development of parliamentary government and a Japanese version of
democracy. Although only a minority in the West do so, most historians
in Japan now accept as common wisdom the proposition that a phenomenon they call Taishō democracy, including but not limited to these
developments, moved to center stage in the drama of Japanese history
with the Hibiya riot of 1905.[1]

In the pages that follow, I accept the fundamental premise that something new and important happened to the political and social order in
Japan after 1905 and seek to build upon it. By focusing on the history of
workers, the urban poor, and the urban crowd, I shall demonstrate that
a phenomenon better understood as imperial democracy grew out of a

1. Important studies of the history of Taishō democracy that begin the story in 1905
or earlier include Matsuo Takayoshi, *Taishō demokurashii no kenkyū* (Tokyo: Aoki
shoten, 1966) and *Taishō demokurashii* (Tokyo: Iwanami shoten, 1974); Eguchi Keiichi,
Toshi shoburujoa undō shi no kenkyū (Tokyo: Miraisha, 1976); Nakamura Masanori,
Emura Eiichi, and Miyachi Masato, "Nihon teikokushugi to jinmin: 9/5 minshū bōdō o
megutte," *Rekishigaku kenkyū*, August 1967; Shinobu Seizaburō, *Taishō demokurashii
shi*, vol. 1 (1954); and Miyachi Masato, *Nichiro sengo seijishi kenkyū* (Tokyo: University
of Tokyo Press, 1973). One English-language work whose contributors generally do see
Taishō democracy as a significant phenomenon is Harry D. Harootunian and Bernard
S. Silberman, eds., *Japan in Crisis: Essays on Taishō Democracy* (Princeton: Princeton
University Press, 1974).

profound transformation of the society. It was not limited to politicians, intellectuals, journalists, and the urban bourgeoisie. The process that generated imperial democracy touched the lives and drew upon the energies of common people throughout the nation.[2]

The first objective of this study, then, is to understand the political role that working men and women have played in twentieth-century Japan. I begin by reconstructing the process of movement-building by which some workers learned to carry out disputes and organize unions, pressing for better treatment in the workplace and improved status in the broader society, in some cases seeking a socialist transformation as well. Early chapters (2, 3) focus on two sources of the behavior and ideas that informed the subsequent building of a labor movement: the boisterous crowds of the riots of the early twentieth century and the nonunion labor disputes of these same years. The following chapters (especially 4, 6, and 7) zero in on labor in the east side of Tokyo, an area called Nankatsu, to see how unions developed and how the "dispute culture" of working-class Tokyo evolved.

Also part of the effort to understand labor's political role is the forbidding attempt to reconstruct the intellectual world of factory laborers. I wish to explore ways in which workers themselves envisioned the desirable future and perceived themselves as members of a factory work force and as participants in local and national communities. This attempt is forbidding because most documentary sources were left by observers—such as bureaucrats, journalists, or intellectual activists—who were not themselves part of the laboring community, and because movement historians have imposed their own notions of what a proper labor movement ought to have done upon workers who may well have had different ideas.

To arrive at a single "true" account of workers' consciousness is not possible, practically or epistemologically. Even so, we can attempt to look past the biases of elites seeking to control workers, activists seek-

---

2. It is important not to reduce "the people" or "the working class" to a monolithic whole whose ideas and energies are assumed rather than analyzed. I feel this treatment of "the people" to some extent characterizes, for example, the impressive work of Miyachi in *Nichiro sengo* and of Nakamura Masanori, Emura Eiichi, and Miyachi Masato in "Nihon teikokushugi to jinmin." Nakamura et al. recognize their lack of attention to the thought of the "people" themselves, noting that "it appears quite difficult to grasp awareness [*ninshiki*] of the people—that is, workers and the urban lower classes—other than by looking at their actions" (p. 14). Deducing thought from action is, indeed, one valid approach, but here I shall attempt also to look directly at what people said or wrote.

ing to mobilize them, and historians or social scientists seeking to understand them to let the actions and words of the workers speak to us in relatively direct fashion. At times it *is* possible to hear the workers' own voices, left to us in the form of speech transcripts or leaflets. We can never be absolutely certain that the rank and file shared the sentiments of these speakers or leaflet authors, but we can reasonably infer that they expressed common beliefs when we also have evidence that enthusiastic audiences heard these speeches or that hundreds of workers organized tenaciously to support the demands raised in a leaflet. Insofar as possible, I shall build the argument about workers' ideas from such documents, particularly in chapter 8.

This attempt to recreate a workers' culture requires that we avoid "culturalism" on the one hand and simplistic versions of either market or Marxist perspectives on the other. By culturalism, I refer to a perspective that extends far beyond academic discourse, dominating popular American conceptions of "the Japanese." In the worst incarnation of this view, a reified "Japanese culture," transcending history and defying analysis, predisposed the Japanese to endure, to cooperate, to deny self for the sake of the group, and to accept authority. Proof of the power of this culture is found in the facts that under 8 percent of prewar workers joined unions at the peak of the movement, that the left did poorly in the early elections after the establishment of universal manhood suffrage, that the women's movement fared poorly, and that the bourgeois political parties retreated in the 1930s. Such culturalism is afflicted with comparative amnesia; it conveniently forgets, for example, that unions in every comparable early industrial society, even Britain in the nineteenth century, were overwhelmingly minority movements.[3] Culturalist presentations of unique Japanese social patterns do not prepare us to recognize the cleavages and confrontations at the heart of modern Japanese history.

By simplistic market and Marxist perspectives, I refer to two unhelpful notions: the first, that the workers in Japan were an atomized body of profit-maximizing economic men seeking to survive in a competitive "modern" world; the second, that they constituted an increasingly

3. Gary Marks, *Unions in Politics: Britain, Germany, and the United States in the Nineteenth and Early Twentieth Centuries* (Princeton: Princeton University Press, 1989), pp. 10–11, finds that "workers who formed unions were a small minority in every Western society in the 19th century": about 12 percent in Britain in 1900, 5 percent in the United States and Germany.

homogeneous class, both cut off by capitalism from its past and being forged anew by capitalism into the vanguard of a progressive future. In actuality, their story involved efforts at collective action, false starts, defeats, and renewed struggles, and they were never so atomized as to lack community or so focused on economic gain as to lack concepts of justice. In addition, social class was not the only important unit of identification; workers identified and acted as members of the nation with an interest in furthering or sharing national glory, and as men or as women interested in improving their treatment and status in workplace, neighborhood, or national communities.

A second basic objective of this book is to connect the story of labor to a reinterpretation of the broader dynamics of Japanese political history from 1905 to 1940.[4] Most historians place the phenomenon called Taishō democracy at the center of their analyses of the broad sweep of prewar political history, although they disagree vehemently on its depth and significance. In fact, however, the phrase "Taishō democracy" is chronologically inaccurate and analytically empty. The name derives from the reign of the Taishō emperor, 1912–25, but in most Japanese accounts Taishō democracy began in 1905, six years before the Meiji emperor died, and it arguably lasted until 1932, seven years after the Shōwa era began. Of the twenty-seven years of Taishō democracy, thus defined, thirteen fall outside the Taishō era. The principal analytic significance to the fact that it was the Taishō emperor who presided over half this period lies in the contemporary belief that the death of the Meiji emperor marked the dawn of a new era.[5] The first year of Taishō indeed witnessed a major political crisis, but this "Taishō political change" was less a turning point or inaugural event in a new political era than one of several in a string of related upheavals dating from 1905. The main reason for the use of the Taishō label has been its dubious chronological convenience.

In addition, the concept of Taishō democracy has confounded efforts to deal with the complicated evidence concerning popular thought and behavior in prewar Japan. Many historians, in Japan some time ago and in the West more recently, have dealt with this complexity by depicting

4. Chapters 1 and 5 detail the framework of analysis that informs the rest of the study.
5. Natsume Soseki, *Kokoro* (Washington, D.C.: Regnery Gateway, 1957), pp. 245–46 and passim offers a moving example.

the era of party rule as a superficial flirtation with democracy.[6] Troubled by evidence of nationalism and support for imperialist expansion voiced in the early days by many Taishō democrats, by the ideological ambivalence of calls for popular sovereignty under the "absolutist" Meiji constitution, and by the surrender or conversion of both liberal and radical Taishō democrats in the 1930s, some historians have skeptically dismissed "Taishō democracy" as a shallow phenomenon. True Taishō democrats would have opposed imperialism and sought popular sovereignty. Support for imperialism and the sovereignty of the emperor become impurities or deviations that a true Taishō democrat should have resisted. Because there were few who boldly resisted in the 1920s, or resisted at all in the 1930s, Taishō democracy is seen as superficial.

I am, on the contrary, impressed by evidence that the popular movements of the early 1900s, led by politicians and the press, moved masses of people to act vigorously in pursuit of a shared, if ambiguous and contradictory, democratic vision. In this book I have thus sought to define an alternative framework that would both credit the depth and intensity of these ideas and help explain the eventual dissolution of the democratic movement and collapse of democratic rule.

Japanese historians, beginning with Matsuo Takayoshi, have generally ceased to dismiss Taishō democracy as superficial. Since the 1960s they have argued that the Russo-Japanese War and its aftermath in 1905 mark a watershed in the history of modern Japan. In this view, the Hibiya anti-treaty riot of 1905 ushered in the era of "Taishō democracy," a phrase its proponents use to indicate a profound break with the past, taking issue with the picture of Taishō democracy as a superficial movement of a few urban intellectuals and journalists. Yet the record of popular thought and behavior likewise confounds this analysis, which sees the riots of the early twentieth century as the first stage of a "Taishō democracy" in which a properly aroused populace should in theory have been both democratic and internationalist.[7] How does one

6. Matsuo Takayoshi (*Taishō demokurashii*) is one critic of those who dismiss Taishō democracy. See Harry Wray and Hilary Conroy, eds., *Japan Examined: Perspectives on Modern Japanese History* (Honolulu: University Press of Hawaii, 1983), pp. 172, 178, 193, for recent American dismissals or depictions of Taishō democracy as "limited."

7. See, for example, Matsuo Takayoshi, "Development of Democracy in Japan: Taishō Democracy, Its Flowering and Breakdown," *Developing Economies*, December 1966, pp. 615–16, where he writes that the key demands of Taishō democracy were for parliamentary principles and free speech; improved relations between workers and capitalists, tenants and landlords; and rejection of imperialism.

explain why the Tokyo crowds venerated the emperor and fervently
supported empire, yet rebelled violently against a government that did
the same, without dismissing the common people of the early twentieth
century in condescending fashion as mindless or manipulated? How
does one account for the persistent concern of workers to win the respect due the "people of the nation" (*kokumin*) in a framework that
expected laborers, as the key element in what should have been the
socialist mainstream of Taishō democracy, to transcend nationalism?

I side with those historians who take the Taishō changes seriously to
this extent: the year 1905 did mark a turning point; the Hibiya riot
reveals these changes were not limited to a narrow intelligentsia. I differ
in seeking a conception better able to encompass the richness and contradictions that marked social and political history after 1905. In sum,
while I, too, am troubled by the support so many Taishō democrats
offered for imperialism and by their respect for imperial sovereignty, I
feel that to consider these features as limits or impurities distorts the
experience and understanding of the historical actors themselves. It
places in opposition elements that many Japanese of the period considered an integrated cluster of ideas, which I describe as "imperial
democracy," rather than Taishō democracy.[8]

In addition to noting these problems with the phrase "Taishō democracy," I see a positive case for this different framework. The first
major gain of recasting the political ideas of this era, and the movement
to realize them in public life, as "imperial democracy" is that we shift
focus away from the "limits" or the "shallowness" of an ideal Taishō
democracy and highlight instead the "contradictions" at the heart of an
actual movement for change that was broadly based and profound. To
be sure, the terms *contradiction* and *shallow* are imposed by the historian, but some conceptual imposition is inevitable and necessary. The
notion of contradiction does greater justice to the dilemmas of workers,
party politicians, and bureaucrats, of ruled and rulers. The jarring

8. Carol Gluck makes a similar point in *Japan's Modern Myths: Ideology in the Late
Meiji Period* (Princeton: Princeton University Press, 1985), pp. 237–39, when she claims
that "parliamentary ideology is not synonymous with the political ideals evoked by the
words *Taishō demokurashii*." Her "parliamentary ideology" that "situated the practice
of parliamentary politics at the center and imperial authority at the legitimating
circumference" is roughly synonymous with "imperial democracy." (I say "roughly"
because I would distinguish the practical imperial democrats in the parties from the
movement's idealistic theorists, such as Yoshino Sakuzō, who remained lukewarm
about the ability of the existing parties to play the institutional role of mediators between popular and imperial wills.

juxtaposition of the two words points to the potentially contradictory goals of a movement and then a regime committed to both national glory and widened participation; when push came to shove in times of national crisis, this contradiction made the imperial democratic regime vulnerable to political attack, and it inclined the imperial democrats themselves to sacrifice democracy on behalf of empire.

Second, in contrast to the descriptive and inaccurate adjective *Taishō*, the term *imperial* indicates the dynamic links both backward and forward in time from the era of imperial democracy itself (1905–32). Looking backward before 1905, the core of the transformation of the Meiji era included not only the rise of capitalism but also the consolidation of imperial sovereignty and the beginnings of imperialism; the chapters to follow will show that these developments ironically prepared the ground for the democratic movements of the early 1900s, making untenable the closed political order envisioned by the oligarchs.

Looking forward beyond 1932, the difficulty of explaining the seemingly abrupt shift from "Taishō" liberalism to "Shōwa" fascism has troubled historians since World War II. By viewing the 1930s from the vantage of a 1920s structure of "imperial" rather than "Taishō" democracy, we are pointed toward clues to explain this trajectory. The effort to maintain both formal and informal empire generated resistance abroad, in particular from the Chinese, which weakened the legitimacy and prestige of civilian party rulers. We shall see that the rise of capitalism, furthered in part by the spoils of empire, generated resistance at home from increasingly assertive workers or tenant farmers; the resulting social discord likewise discredited the parties in power. At the same time, the attraction of imperialist expansion as a panacea and the imperial institution as a rallying symbol helped the military and a newly activist bureaucracy to present themselves as servants of the emperor and gain political ascendance.

Third, the concept of imperial democracy distinguishes the movements of the bourgeoisie, focused on their political parties, and the movements of workers or poor farmers, focused on unions and "proletarian parties," more effectively than the construct of Taishō democracy. As a catchall for a vast array of movements, "Taishō democracy" is far too inclusive; among those that Japanese historians have included are labor and tenant unions, as well as both the social democratic and bourgeois political parties. They have generally seen the social democrats as the "ought-to-be" inheritors of the movement, and have criticized the bourgeois parties as weak and willing to compromise principle for the sake of power.[9] We can better distinguish these strange bed-fellows by placing the bourgeois parties at the center of a drive in the early twentieth century for political change, the movement for imperial democracy, while recognizing their uneasy relationship with the popular energies that also fueled the movement. We may then consider the movements of workers, farmers, and intellectuals that emerged by the 1920s as often separate from, and sometimes opposed to, imperial democracy. This frees us from concern with the betrayal by the bourgeois parties of an all-encompassing "Taishō" democratic movement and shifts the focus instead to the contradictory pressures imping-ing upon these parties.

Thus, I propose the notion of a trajectory from imperial bureaucracy to imperial democracy to fascism as a framework better able to account for the evidence in the realm of labor history, as well as for the overall modern development of Japan through 1945. I do not tell the full story here; absent are farmers, and indeed all those outside the major cities, most of the story of women, of students, and of intellectuals. Ultimately, these histories, too, must be viewed in terms of this framework for it to prove truly useful, if only because the rulers who implemented the fascist program of the late 1930s had for some years seen these histories as connected. They perceived restive laborers as part of a general social crisis, defined as well by phenomena such as the popularity of Marxism among university students and the large population of cafe waitresses in the cities.

I offer this interpretation in the hopes of stimulating a critical rethinking of the Japanese historical experience in the twentieth cen-tury, once again problematizing the nature of democracy in prewar Japan and suggesting ways in which domestic social protest, in this case the building of a labor movement in places like Nankatsu, fit into the broader process of political evolution. I wish, that is, to understand the relationship between social class contention and changing structures of rule. In part 1, for example, I argue that explosive popular energies were contained within the movement for imperial democracy, that they threatened to break the bounds of the movement by 1918, and that this threat played a direct role in bringing Japan's first political party cabinet to power.

In part 3, especially chapter 9, I likewise argue that the intense con-

9. See Tetsuo Najita, *Hara Kei and the Politics of Compromise* (Cambridge, Mass.: Harvard University Press, 1967), pp. 205–8, for an important critique of these critics.

flicts in industrial neighborhoods such as Nankatsu helped create the environment of crisis that catalyzed the shift from party to military-bureaucratic rule, from imperial democracy to Japan's "imperial" version of fascism. Western historians who see "militarism" primarily as a response of the bureaucratic and military elite to international crisis too easily overlook both the obsessive fear of these leaders that domestic society was collapsing and their subsequent decision to have the state attempt the unprecedented task of reordering civil society. The alternative to overlooking this fear need not be a simplistic view of cause and effect in which the military is seen to take power to thwart a social revolution; rather, a complex relationship existed between social contention, elite and intellectual perceptions and fears, and changing structures of rule. Historians of Japan must be particularly sensitive to such relations because Japanese themselves in positions of local and national power have been intensely and precociously concerned to head off conflict, maintaining both harmony and their own privilege. Thus, episodes of turbulence well short of revolution can be responsible, largely or in part, for changes in policy or in the identity of rulers.

In the chapters that follow, I shall consider "imperial democracy" first as a movement for change, supported broadly in the society, and later as a structure and ideology of rule intended to cope with change. For the early imperial democrats, constitutional government and imperialism were inseparable. The latter did not limit or vitiate the former; it made it worth having. But as labor emerged as a social force in the 1920s, and crises at home and abroad during the Great Depression shook an order now dominated by the imperial democrats, the contradictions emerged. A structure of rule that justified party government and, in some cases, liberal social policies as serving the causes of social order and empire collapsed. In the regime that replaced imperial democracy, the rulers discarded democracy for the sake of empire and a renovated social order.

PART ONE

The Crowd and Labor in the Movement for Imperial Democracy, 1905–18

ONE

The Movement for Imperial Democracy

Imperial democracy had two incarnations. It began as a political movement. Later it became a system of rule.

When imperial democracy emerged as a movement for change in the
early twentieth century, its leaders contested for power with the Meiji
oligarchs. They raised a challenge to the ruling structure erected between the 1870s and 1890s, which we may call imperial bureaucracy.
In this prior system, civilian bureaucrats and the military ruled the nation on behalf of the sovereign emperor, and they bore no direct responsibility to the people, who were expected to support their policies
obediently.[1]

The imperial democratic movement had roots in an earlier challenge
to these imperial bureaucrats, the Movement for Freedom and Popular
Rights. The Popular Rights movement, however, dissolved by 1884 in
the face of both government repression and conflict between its own
dual strata of supporters, the ex-samurai and landed elite on one hand
and poor farmers on the other. In the early twentieth century, the imperial democratic activists emerged with greater force and staying power
to demand expanded suffrage, tax reduction, and respect for the electorate represented in the Diet. These causes of propertied, educated
men represented the formal vanguard of the movement for imperial

---

1. On "bureaucratic absolutism," roughly synonymous with "imperial bureaucracy," see Bernard Silberman, "The Bureaucratic State," in *Conflict in Modern Japanese
History*, ed. Tetsuo Najita and Victor Koschmann (Princeton: Princeton University Press,
1982), p. 231.

democracy, although as with the agitation for popular rights of the nineteenth century, they overlapped with lower-class protest.

The height of imperial democracy as a movement to gain access to political power came between 1905 and 1918. In this latter year, the formation of Hara Kei's Seiyūkai Party cabinet marked both a major success of the movement and a watershed in its transformation into a structure of rule. As party rule subsequently became almost routine, many of its advocates, now found in key bureaucratic groups as well as the parties themselves, sought further democratic reforms as the best means to control ongoing demands for participation and the radical movements of workers, intellectuals, and poor farmers. But the imperial democratic ideology that justified party rule was not a uniform conception. The two major parties, Seiyūkai and Minseitō, differed greatly in their vision of how much popular involvement, in how liberal and democratic a form, was desirable. From 1924 to 1931 the decidedly more liberal vision of the Minseitō Party and its bureaucratic allies, which would have granted significant autonomy to popular organizations, was dominant. But the critical difference of the parties over means should not obscure agreement on ends. They were united in a commitment to preserving a capitalist order in which their own position had been secured and an international order in which Japan's Asian hegemony was respected.

As a structure of rule, imperial democracy was centrally concerned to placate or control labor, for organized workers were among those who inherited and transformed the oppositional spirit of the earlier movement for change. During the depression the intense confrontation between imperial democrats in power and angry, but powerless, workers and farmers, fighting for both respect and their livelihoods, helped discredit imperial democracy as a system of rule and an ideology of control. The result, in the 1930s, was the eclipse of the parties, the repudiation of democratic ideas, and eventually the dissolution of the labor movement under a new regime.

THE ROOTS OF IMPERIAL DEMOCRACY

Imperial democracy was the unanticipated product of Japan's dramatic nineteenth-century revolution. The adjective *imperial* signals the relevance of two central features of this revolution: the oligarchs who created the constitutional order of 1890 through 1945 located political sovereignty in the person of the Japanese emperor; and they built Japan into an Asian empire through victories in war in 1895 and 1905. Put simply, by establishing an emperor-centered constitutional order, promoting a capitalist, industrializing economy, and leading Japan to imperial power in Asia, the imperial bureaucrats of Meiji unwittingly provoked the movement for imperial democracy.

FORGING A NATION-STATE

The Meiji leaders dismantled the socially stratified and politically fragmented Tokugawa order and drew upon Western models to build a unified state and society. At both elite and plebian levels of society, their initiatives stimulated the movement for imperial democracy. That is, as the imperial bureaucrats of the early Meiji decades legitimized and exercised authority, they offered a limited opportunity for popular participation; this provoked challenge by samurai, by landed local elites, and by poor commoners who joined the Popular Rights movement. Although the movement failed to win the liberal constitution it sought, the term *failure* is misleading. Its leaders survived and reemerged in the era of imperial democracy, in large part because the successful nation-building of the bureaucratic state created the conditions under which a challenge could be mounted.

The promulgation of a constitution and the convening of an elected Diet meant that Japan was a nation of subjects with both obligations to the state and political rights. Obligations included military service, school attendance, and the individual payment of taxes. Rights included suffrage and a voice in deciding the fate of the national budget. The fact that these rights were limited to men of substantial property is well recognized and, of course, important. Clearly the constitution was expected by its authors to contain the opposition. Nonetheless, to stress only the limitations placed on popular rights by the Meiji constitution is to miss its historical significance as a cause of future change: the mere existence of a constitutionally mandated, elected national assembly with more than advisory powers implied the existence of a politically active and potentially expandable body of subjects or citizens. Indeed, the decision of the oligarchs for a constitution was made in acute awareness that such a citizenry was in the process of forming itself and developing its own ideas about the political order. In 1881 Itō Hirobumi, the Meiji oligarch and architect of the constitution, received a letter from his trusted aide Inoue Kowashi: "If we lose this opportunity [to adopt a Prussian-style constitution] and vacillate, within two or three years the people will become confident that they can succeed and no matter how much oratory we use . . . public opinion will cast aside the draft of a constitution presented by the government, and the private drafts of the constitution will win out in the end."[2]

The creation of a constitutional polity also meant that Japan's political future could, indeed should, be conceived with reference to the so-called advanced nation-states of Europe and North America. As these nations generally offered a greater range of political rights to their citizens than did Japan, their role as models helped sanction the expansion of the electorate and other changes. The argument for democratic reforms gained force to the extent that the more democratic Western constitutional states appeared prosperous and successful in international competition.

The inauguration of electoral politics under the new constitution encouraged several new institutions and types of political activity, which played a major role in the history of imperial democracy. These included a vigorous partisan press, political parties, and other tools found in electoral political systems: rallies and speech-meetings (*enzetsu kai*), speaking tours (*yūzetsu*), and, later, demonstrations. Most of these preceded the constitution and helped the oligarchs see a need for it, for their first flowering came during the era of the Popular Rights movement. Even if new laws regulating the press, political parties, and political meetings restricted such activities, the constitution gave them an important new legitimacy.

By the late nineteenth century, hundreds of legal, open political rallies were convened each year in Tokyo alone. This was something new in Japanese history. Both leaders and most participants in the 1880s and 1890s were men of means and education, in the main landlords, capitalists, and an emerging class of urban professionals, in particular journalists and lawyers. Such men were to be the leaders of the formal movements for imperial democracy of the early twentieth century as well. But the simple emergence of such practices as assembly and speechmaking left open the prospect that other, less privileged individuals or groups would eventually seek to make use of them, and even in the 1880s the process of nation-building was beginning to transform Japan's popular political culture.

In 1860 the Dutch engineer Willem Kattendyke had lamented the parochialism of the Nagasaki merchant, concerned only with profit and

---

2. Richard Devine, "The Way of the King," *Monumenta Nipponica*, Spring 1979, p. 53.

willing to have his samurai betters take sole responsibility, credit, or blame for events in the political realm. According to his diary, Kattendyke had occasion to ask one merchant how the townspeople would defend themselves from outside attack. The merchant replied, "That's nothing for us to concern ourselves with. That's the *bakufu*'s business." In the 1870s and 1880s a patriotic German, Ernest Baelz, had described the lack of popular patriotism in Japan with distaste. As the Satsuma rebellion began late in 1876, he confided in his diary that "people in general have seemed to me extraordinarily indifferent, quite unconcerned about politics and such matters." On the occasion of the emperor's birthday in 1880, he wrote, "It distresses me to see how little interest the populace take in their ruler. Only when the police insist on it are houses decorated with flags. In default of this, house-owners do the minimum." And in 1873 Fukuzawa Yukichi had observed that the Japanese people had no sense of themselves as *kokumin*, which he defined to mean "a nation" in a marginal notation. This critical word, a compound that literally means "the people of the country," required such a gloss in the 1870s, for the Japanese political vocabulary did not yet include a widely accepted term for "the people" that connoted popular involvement with, or responsibility for, the affairs of the nation.[3]

By the early twentieth century, these formerly parochial, apolitical people, or their children, had a firm sense of themselves as members of the nation and were anxious to voice their political opinions on matters of foreign and domestic policy and insistent that they be respected. The Meiji observers just quoted, with an idealized view of the citizenry of Western nations as the base of comparison, probably exaggerated the apathy or passivity of the Japanese commoners of the nineteenth century. Peasant rebellions and urban riots were traditions to which these commoners had access, and the twentieth-century crowd and working class drew on them. Yet even the most radical or violent peasant upris-

3. Willem Johan Cornelis Ridder Huyssen van Kattendyke, *Uittreksel uit het dagboek van W.J.C. Ridder H. v. Kattendyke gedurende zijn verblijf in Japan in 1857, 1858, en 1859*, (The Hague, 1860), translated from the Dutch as *Nagasaki kaigun denshūjo no hibi* by Nagata Nobutoshi (Tokyo: Heibonsha, 1964), p. 55. Erwin Toku Baelz, *Awakening Japan: The Diary of a German Doctor* (Bloomington: Indiana University Press, 1974), pp. 21, 62. Keiō gijuku, ed., *Fukuzawa Yukichi zenshū* (Tokyo: Iwanami shoten, 1959), vol. 4, *Bunmeiron no gaikyō*, p. 154. For discussion of terms for "the people" and the absence of the word *kokumin* in late Tokugawa and early Meiji discourse, see Suzuki Shūji, *Nihon kango to chūgoku* (Tokyo: Chūō kōronsha, 1981), pp. 47, 52, and also Fukui Nanako, "One Aspect of Nakae Chōmin's Process of Thought," *Kansai daigaku bungaku ronshū* 37, no. 1 (December 1987): 53–54.

ings of the 1860s maintained a local political perspective; angry groups of peasants seldom went beyond attacks on the rich to attack the political order.[4] By contrast, the new political language of popular protest of the early twentieth century reveals a fundamentally national orientation. By 1905 the word *kokumin* had become as ubiquitous as the term for empire; both were watchwords of the movement for imperial democracy.

The great irony, of course, is that both terms achieved popularity as a result of nation-building programs dating from the 1880s, promoted by bureaucrats and private ideologues who feared that the "people" were insufficiently supportive of national goals.[5] They concluded that a new body politic, the *kokumin*, was needed in a new age.

At the heart of this elite program for nation-building was the promotion of universal education. The spread of literacy prepared the ground for the rise of imperial democracy; it resulted from the conscious decision of the "nation-builders" of the late nineteenth century that a powerful modern polity and economy required a literate populace. By the time of the Hibiya riots in 1905, over 95 percent of school-age boys and girls, in Tokyo and nationwide, were indeed going to school. This was a recent and dramatic change, for in 1892 just over half of the nation's school-age boys and girls actually attended classes.

Some have argued that such education, by promoting an emperor-centered ideology, produced nationalistic subjects respectful of the hierarchy of local and national leaders, from village heads to factory owners to bureaucrats, who derived authority from their identification with the imperial father-figure at the apex of the status hierarchy. This view, however, is far too simplistic. Meiji education surely promoted nationalism and support for the emperor, but the record of urbanites and workers in opposing their putative superiors shows that the success of the schools in also creating docile workers or subservient subjects was limited. Universal education provided the tool of literacy, and this could produce citizens who supported both the emperor *and* democratic reforms.

As these newly educated youths reached adulthood, during the first

4. Stephen Vlastos, *Peasant Protests and Uprisings in Tokugawa Japan* (Berkeley: University of California Press, 1986), chs. 7–8, and Patricia Sippel, "The Bushū Outburst," *Harvard Journal of Asiatic Studies* 37, no. 2 (December 1978), on the limited horizons of late Tokugawa collective action.

5. Carol Gluck, *Japan's Modern Myths: Ideology in the Late Meiji Period* (Princeton: Princeton University Press, 1985), p. 102 and passim.

two decades of the twentieth century, the revolution in basic literacy created a population of avid newspaper readers, which included the working poor in the cities. The images of the rickshaw puller and the prostitute waiting for their customers with newspaper in hand became a sort of literary conceit and a symbol of a new era. A May 1900 article in the *Chūō kōron* remarked that Japan had entered a new stage in the history of newspaper readership when the locus of readers "moved further downward into lower-class society, and one sees petty merchants, young students, rickshaw pullers waiting for customers, and the women of the brothels all with newspapers in hand."[6] This appears to be more than a titillating account for the middle-class readers of the respectable *Chūō kōron*. One early survey, in the socialist *Heimin shinbun* in 1904, described a slum tenement in Tokyo's Honjo ward with 150 residents in twenty-seven apartment units; they reportedly held twenty-eight newspaper subscriptions among them. The first larger, more systematic, surveys cover the tail end of the "movement" stage of imperial democracy. Four-fifths of 659 worker households on the working-class island of Tsukishima in the heart of Tokyo subscribed to newspapers in 1919. Eighteen percent of the subscribers took two or more papers. And three-fifths (61 percent) of the household heads in a perhaps more representative survey of 2,591 glass-factory workers in late 1920 were regular newspaper readers.[7]

The inexpensive antigovernment papers that took the lead in promoting the various causes associated with imperial democracy were particularly popular among the urban poor and the lower middle classes. The *Yorozu chōhō* was the best-selling and cheapest paper in Tokyo around the turn of the century, and its pages were filled with both jingoism and calls for a greater popular role in politics. In a sample of sixty-seven letters to the *Yorozu* in 1900, the newspaper historian Yamamoto Taketoshi found that workers, artisans, rickshaw pullers, or delivery boys sent almost one-third (twenty) of them.[8] Such evidence suggests that a newspaper-reading public, including many among the urban poor and workers, emerged in Tokyo and other major centers during this era of the urban riot and the rise of imperial democracy.

6. Yamamoto Taketoshi, *Kindai Nihon no shinbun dokusha sō* (Tokyo: Hōsei University Press, 1981) p. 129, quotes the May 1900 issue of *Chūō kōron*.
7. Naimushō eisei kyoku, *Tōkyō shi, Kyōbashi-ku Tsukishima ni okeru jitchi chōsa hōkoku* (1921), reprinted as Sekiya Kōichi, ed., *Tsukishima chōsa* (Tokyo: Kōsei kan, 1970), p. 158. Yamamoto, *Kindai Nihon no shinbun*, pp. 193, 224–26.
8. Yamamoto, *Kindai Nihon no shinbun*, pp. 95–101.

CAPITALISM

A second critical set of changes that forms the backdrop for the emergence of both the urban crowd and the working class in the early twentieth century was brought on by the rise of industrial capitalism in Japan in the late nineteenth century. We must note three important consequences.

First, the expansion of heavy industry, beginning in the interwar decade around the turn of the century, produced a growing class of wage laborers, who tended to cluster in the cities, Tokyo and Osaka in particular. While the industrial work force nationwide doubled in size between 1900 and the eve of World War I (which Japan entered on the Allied side in August 1914), from just over 400,000 to 853,000, the Tokyo work force tripled in these years, reaching 89,000 in 1914. Several large communities of factory laborers and the working poor emerged in the wards to the east and southwest of the imperial palace in Tokyo, to play major roles in the events described in this book.

Second, the growth in the industrial work force was more pronounced among men. Male workers, who accounted for just over half of Tokyo's workers in 1900, numbered 61,000, or 68 percent of the work force, in 1914.[9] The tendency of the men in the working class to remain wage laborers over the long run is reflected in surveys of the occupational backgrounds of workers. Whereas in 1917 just over one-third of the mainly female textile workers came to their jobs with prior experience as industrial wage laborers, nearly half of shipbuilders and 59 percent of machinists surveyed that year had been engaged in industrial wage labor in previous employment.[10]

Third, expansion of cities, of industry, and of commerce increased the size of the urban petite bourgeoisie. These men, only partially enfranchised, yet almost invariably taxpayers, were the owners of retail shops, wholesale enterprises, and small factories in modern or traditional industries. They and their employees were a prominent element in movements for imperial democracy, including the political crowd.

In Tokyo the expanded pool of workers lived in neighborhoods stretching in an arc from the east to the south of the Meiji emperor's residence, including Honjo, Fukagawa, Kyōbashi, and Shiba wards in

9. NRUS 10:108–13. Kanagawa-ken, rōdō bu rōsei ka, ed., Kanagawa rōdō undō shiryō: senzen hen (Yokohama: 1966), 1:1012.

10. Mori Kiichi, Nihon rōdōsha kaikyū jōtai shi (Tokyo: Sanichi shobō, 1961), pp. 249–50.

particular. In later years these neigborhoods would spread both further east into the villages of Minami Katsushika County (Kameido, Ōshima, Terashima, Sumida and Suna) and south into Ebara County (Shinagawa, Ōzaki, Kamata).

The residents of these neighborhoods were not only factory workers. Yokoyama Gennosuke's social reporting of the turn of the century lists a tremendous array of artisans in construction trades, traditional manufacturing, and new cottage industries such as wire umbrella making. These men and women, as well as the ubiquitous rickshaw pullers, who numbered upwards of 20,000 each in Osaka and Tokyo at the turn of the century, lived in the same neighborhoods as the wage workers in mechanized factories, both large and small. In Yokoyama's understanding, they were all part of the same "lower-class society," and their common involvement in the riots of this era argues in favor of his interpretation.[11]

An occupational survey of Tokyo in 1908 gives a rough indication of the numbers of wage laborers and the working poor.[12] About 40 percent of the employed population of the capital (712,000) were either owners or employees in factories, artisan shops, construction trades, needle trades, and other cottage industries. Another 11 percent engaged in transport trades (the rickshawmen had declined, but streetcar employees increased), and about 40 percent were engaged in commerce. The professional class of civil and military bureaucrats, doctors, lawyers, educators, and journalists accounted for just 9 percent of employment, a fundamental shift from the Tokugawa era, when roughly half the population of Edo and other castle towns were part of the samurai military and bureaucratic "service elite."[13]

Although poor city-dwellers, including artisans, were not new to Japan, and there is no clear evidence that these people were objectively worse off than in the past, the relative insecurity of the residents' livelihoods was probably something new. The livelihoods of shopkeepers, artisans, and wage workers of one sort or another were increasingly affected by the unfeeling rhythms of a capitalist economy in which new industries were constantly arising to threaten traditional (or just slightly

11. Yokoyama Gennosuke, *Nihon no kasō shakai* (1898; reprint, Tokyo: Iwanami shoten, 1949).

12. Tōkyō-shi, *Tōkyō-shi shisei chōsa shokugyō betsu genzai jinkō hyō* (1908). Unfortunately, this survey fails to distinguish between owners and employees, which limits its usefulness.

13. The expression is that of Thomas Huber in *The Revolutionary Origins of Modern Japan* (Stanford: Stanford University Press, 1981).

less new) occupations, even while they generated new jobs. The inauguration of streetcar service in the major urban centers of Tokyo, Yokohama, Osaka, and Kyoto meant the beginning of the end of the rick-
shawman's trade, which dated back only to 1870.[14] Lacking a study of
standards of living among the urban poor and workers between the
1870s and 1920s that would allow a firm statement, we shall proceed
on the assumption that the volatility of occupations and income, and
certainty of change, more than any absolute immiseration, was the key
new aspect to urban working-class life that lay behind the active role of
these people in both the rise of the urban crowd and the working-class
movement.

The thousands of owners of small manufacturing operations and
proprietors of small shops scattered throughout the city were also active
participants in the movement for imperial democracy beginning around
the turn of the century. Living in the same communities with the masses
of the working poor, these people were distinguished from their poorer
neighbors by ownership of some property and the consequent obligation to pay taxes, although their right to a voice in political affairs was
not always greater. By 1914, 46,950 members of this "non-privileged
bourgeoisie" in Tokyo had to pay the business tax alone, but only
4,000 of these taxpayers were of enough substance to be eligible to join
the Tokyo Chamber of Commerce. In 1908, 84,232 Tokyoites paid
over three yen apiece in total taxes, but only 46,781 qualified to vote in
prefectural elections.[15]

Taxation without adequate representation truly began to anger such
people in 1896 with the enactment of a business tax by the imperial
Diet. Over the following three decades, retailers and manufacturers
nationwide conducted a series of campaigns for reduction or repeal of
this extremely unpopular imposition, levied as a surcharge on sales,
numbers of employees, rent levels, and capital assets, rather than
profits. Various single-industry lobbies also petitioned for lower taxes

14. The rickshaw was invented in Japan in 1869 and first used commercially in 1870.
By 1878, 110,000 were in use in Japan, and the rickshaw also spread throughout Asia.
See *Nihon kindaishi jiten* (Tokyo: Tōyō keizai shinpōsha, 1978), p. 327, s.v. "jinrikisha."
On strikes by rickshawmen, see *Kanagawa rōdō undō shiryō*, pp. 79–82, and Koyama
Hitoshi, "1903 nen no Osaka no jinrikishafu no sutoraiki," in *Gekkan rōdō*, May 1979,
pp. 2–3. The effect of the new imperial order on old jobs was capricious; unprecedented
numbers of rallies and parades to celebrate Japanese victories during the Russo-Japanese
war brought on a tremendous boom in the centuries-old lantern-maker's trade, for participants would carry these cheap lanterns as they marched. See Sugiyama Tenpū, "Sakkon
no chōchinya," *Chūō kōron*, June 1904, p. 68.
15. Tōkyō-fu, ed., *Tōkyō-fu tōkei sho* (Tokyo, 1908), p. 1011.

in several sectors faced with additional sales tax burdens (woven textile manufacture, food oil, soy sauce, salt, sake, and sugar). This class of businessmen is important to our study precisely because of its permeable boundaries. During the riots and strikes of the first two decades of the twentieth century, the owners and employees in a fish market or a tailor's shop, as well as owners and workers in small factories, expressed common political attitudes of suspicion and opposition to the bureaucratic oligarchy.

IMPERIALISM

From the late nineteenth to the early twentieth century, Japan emerged as an imperialist power in Asia. This helped generate imperial democracy in at least three important ways. First, and most often noted by Japanese scholars, imperialism was expensive. The defense and expansion of Japan's foothold on the Asian mainland seemed to Japan's rulers to require continual expansion of the army and navy. The business tax of 1896 was one step taken to raise the money needed to maintain the incipient empire, but it was the Russo-Japanese War that brought the cost of war and empire home to thousands of Japanese. The war cost 1.7 billion yen, eight times the cost of the Sino-Japanese War. The oligarchs financed 80 percent of this with bonds, and they raised 52 percent of the bonds abroad, but the tax burden on city-dwellers also increased dramatically. In addition to the war bonds, the government levied special sales taxes on sugar, food oil, salt, tobacco, wool, soy, and sake. The proportion of all state revenue raised by such taxes nearly doubled, from 6.5 percent before the war to 12.6 percent by 1907, and the tax question became a main concern of the business community and the urban populace as a whole.[16]

Second, imperialism stimulated growth in heavy industries producing ships and weapons for the military, and the spoils of the Sino-Japanese War enabled the government to grant subsidies to the shipping and shipbuilding industry. It was in these expanding shipyards and arsenals that a tradition of nonunion protest over conditions and terms of work evolved between the turn of the century and World War I, concurrent with the activity of political crowds in major cities.

Third, imperialism had an impact on popular thought parallel to the backlash of the oligarchs' nation-building program. The Sino- and

16. Nakamura Masanori, Emura Eiichi, and Miyachi Masato, "Nihon teikokushugi to jinmin: 9/5 minshū bōdō o megutte," *Rekishigaku kenkyū*, August 1967, p. 5.

Russo-Japanese wars stirred tremendous popular enthusiasm, but support for empire did not translate into uncritical support for the government. Rather, it fostered the belief that the wishes of the people, whose commitment and sacrifice made empire possible, should be respected in the political process. In a concrete display of this link between imperialism and popular behavior, the numerous parades and demonstrations of the Russo-Japanese War (fig. 1) created a precedent and custom of popular gatherings for public, implicitly political, purposes; the Hibiya riot of 1905 was one unanticipated result. (The surge of outdoor gatherings in 1904–5 is shown in Appendix A.)

Officials, including the Tokyo police, saw potential danger in these war rallies. For several months in 1904 they banned privately sponsored rallies and demonstrations on the occasions of major war victories, but they had to back down in the face of popular anger. The *Yorozu chōhō*, perhaps the most vociferous champion of imperial democracy in its early days, saw the victory celebrations as "timely opportunities to expand popular rights" and create a politically active and involved citizenry. The political crowds that took to the streets in 1905 and after were to some extent an outgrowth of the wartime rallies.[17] One defendant in the 1905 Hibiya riot trial made this connection explicit. The judge asked Ōtake Kanichi why some rally organizers prepared large banners painted with slogans, written in difficult language, critical of the government. The intention, he replied, was akin to that behind the encouraging slogans on banners prepared for wartime troop send-off parades.[18]

The emperor-centered constitution, the rise of imperialism, and capitalism were thus driving forces behind historical change in modern Japan. This perspective does not mean that the rise of capital simply called into being the political superstructure of a constitutional, imperialist nation-state. In important ways economic development was the result of political initiatives, and the bureaucracy that took these initiatives also influenced the subsequent rise and fall of imperial democratic rule. Changes in the realms of polity, economy, and ideology were mutually reinforcing. As they unfolded, and the oligarchs were

17. Sakurai Ryōju, "Nichiro senji ni okeru minshū undō no ittan," *Nihon rekishi*, no. 436 (September 1984), pp. 71–82. For the *Yorozu* statement, see p. 80 n. 39.

18. "Kyōto shūshū hikoku jiken yoshin kiroku" 3:197. No publication information given. A copy of this printed four-volume set is available in the Waseda University Library. Hereafter cited as "Kyōto jiken."

able to stake a claim to an empire in Asia, these changes prepared the ground from which imperial democracy sprang.

The experience of wage laborers and the urban poor in the movements for imperial democracy of 1905 to 1918 is the concern of the remaining chapters in part 1. In them, we explore how these people responded to the political world and the world of work. Some of them eventually created a force independent of the bourgeois party movement. In so doing they catalyzed the transformation of imperial democracy from a movement of outsiders to a system of rule.

The working-class movement under the imperial democratic structure of rule is the focus of part 2. When workers emerged as an independent, organized force in the 1920s, a portion of them opposed the still insecure imperial democratic structure of rule. Others accepted this system and sought to raise their status within it. By the late 1920s it appeared that bureaucrats and party leaders were implementing a liberal version of imperial democracy that would have recognized and incorporated independent labor and lower-class elements. But this did not last.

Part 3 examines the crisis of the depression and the retreat of unions and the proletarian parties during the 1930s, when the imperial democratic regime collapsed. What happened in the 1930s had roots in previous decades, but from the perspectives of 1918, 1925, or even March 1931, when a labor union bill, a tenant bill, and female suffrage gained the approval of the lower house of the Diet, gradual gains for parliamentary politics and the labor movement were surely among the most striking features of Japanese history in this century. We must pay careful attention not only to the contradictions of imperial democracy, which issued in the retreat from democracy, the march to war, and the rise of a fascist regime by the late 1930s, but also to the profound changes that produced both the political crowd and a working-class movement.

TWO

The Urban Crowd and Politics, 1905–18

The period bounded by the massive Hibiya riot of 1905 and the nation-wide rice riots of 1918 is aptly dubbed Japan's "era of popular violence."[1] Tens of thousands of Tokyoites participated in nine instances of riot during these years (table 2.1). These outbursts were serious affairs; in the six major Tokyo riots, hundreds were injured and arrested, and at least twenty died. On four occasions cabinet changes took place largely or in part because of the riots.[2]

The 1905 Hibiya riot, in particular, had insurrectionary qualities. The peace settlement to the Russo-Japanese War had brought Japan neither reparations nor the expected territorial gains on the Asian mainland, and it stirred tremendous popular antagonism. The riot broke out when police tried to ban a rally at Hibiya Park on September 5, called to oppose the signing of the treaty in Portsmouth, New Hampshire. Rioting continued for three days, during which Tokyo was reported to be without an effective government. Surviving photographs of September 6 and 7 show dozens of people fishing lazily along the banks of the imperial palace moat, normally strictly forbidden terrain. Crowds destroyed over 70 percent of the police boxes in the city, and police records

---

1. The term is *minshū sōjō ki*, used, for example, by Miyachi Masato, *Nichiro sengo seiji shi kenkyū* (Tokyo: University of Tokyo Press, 1973), pp. 226–28.
2. Cabinet changes of January 1906, 1913, 1914, 1918. See Matsuo Takayoshi, *Taishō demokurashii* (Tokyo: Iwanami shoten, 1974), pp. 34–35, on the somewhat ambiguous 1906 case.

counted 528 rioters injured and 17 killed, in addition to over 500 in-jured policemen (figs. 2–5).[3] The news of the riot stimulated similar, although smaller, risings in Kobe and Yokohama, and it was preceded or followed by nonviolent rallies or speech meetings in hundreds of villages, towns, or cities in all but two of the nation's forty-four prefectures.[4]

This was the first of six major and three minor riots in the "era of popular violence." While table 2.1 reveals that the immediate causes of riot varied greatly, this surface diversity is misleading. Underlying patterns of ideas and action link these events, making them part of a distinct historical formation. They stood at the apex of a huge pyramid of collective action comprising in addition several near riots and hundreds of commonplace peaceful instances of assembly and action (see Appendix A).[5]

The assemblies and riots of this "era of popular violence," then, were central elements in the movement for imperial democracy. While the ideology and actions of the crowd were derivative to the extent that they were fashioned out of a context of meeting places, dates, a representative assembly, and a constitution bequeathed by the oligarchs, the participants in the riots unequivocally articulated a vision of the political order at odds with that of the elite. In the nineteenth-century oligarchic conception of "imperial bureaucracy," the people were to obediently support the policies of the emperor's ministers. In the popular vision of "imperial democracy," the ministers were to carry out policies reflecting the unified, *expressed* will of the emperor and the people. This vision affirmed both emperor and people as touchstones of legitimate rule, and it placed the glory of the empire among its foremost goals. It also left ambiguous the heart of the matter. What procedural means would ensure that policies did, in fact, honor both emperor and popular wills?

3. The Tokyo police were (and are) stationed in hundreds of tiny one- or two-room "boxes" scattered throughout the city. This ensured that the police were close to the people. It also made them vulnerable.

4. Okamoto Shumpei, "The Emperor and the Crowd: The Historical Significance of the Hibiya Riot," in *Conflict in Modern Japanese History*, ed. Tetsuo Najita and Victor Koschmann (Princeton: Princeton University Press, 1982). The above is drawn, in addition, from Nakamura Masanori, Emura Eiichi, and Miyachi Masato, "Nihon teikokushugi to jinmin: 9/5 minshū bōdō o megutte," *Rekishigaku kenkyū*, August 1967, and Morinaga Eisaburō, *Shidan saiban* (Tokyo: Nihon hyōronsha, 1972), 3:30–46.

5. For the conception of a pyramid of collective action, see Charles Tilly, *The Contentious French* (Cambridge, Mass.: Belknap Press, 1986), pp. 381–82.

TABLE 2.1   RIOTS IN TOKYO, 1905–18

Date	Main Issues	Secondary Issues	Site of Origin	Description
Sept. 5–7, 1905	Against peace ending the Russo-Japanese War	Against clique government For "constitutional government"	Hibiya Park	17 killed; 70 percent of police boxes, 15 trams destroyed; progovernment newspapers attacked; 311 arrested; violence in Kobe, Yokohama; rallies nationwide
Mar. 15–18, 1906	Against streetcar-fare increase	Against "unconstitutional" behavior of bureaucracy, Seiyūkai	Hibiya Park	Several dozen streetcars smashed; attacks on streetcar company offices; many arrested; increase revoked
Sept. 5–8, 1906	Against streetcar-fare increase	Against "unconstitutional" actions	Hibiya Park	113 arrested; scores injured; scores of streetcars damaged; police boxes destroyed
Feb. 11, 1908	Against tax increase		Hibiya Park	21 arrested; 11 streetcars stoned
Feb. 10, 1913	For constitutional government	Against clique government	Outside Diet	38 police boxes smashed; government newspapers attacked; several killed; 168 injured (110 police); 253 arrested; violence in Kobe, Osaka, Hiroshima, Kyoto

Date			Location	Description
Sept. 7, 1913	For strong China policy		Hibiya Park	Police stoned; Foreign Ministry stormed; representatives enter Foreign Ministry to negotiate
Feb. 10–12, 1914	Against naval corruption For constitutional government	Against business tax For strong China policy	Outside Diet	Dietmen attacked; Diet, newspapers stormed; streetcars, police boxes smashed; 435 arrested; violence in Osaka
Feb. 11, 1918	For universal suffrage		Ueno Park	Police clash with demonstrators; 19 arrested
Aug. 13–16, 1918	Against high rice prices	Against Terauchi Cabinet	Hibiya Park	Rice seized; numerous stores smashed; 578 arrested; incidents nationwide

THE CONTEXT OF RIOT

The people of Tokyo in the early twentieth century inhabited a world in transition; their assemblies and occasional riots reflected and furthered the trajectories from subject to citizen, wealth to capital, and isolation to empire. The constitution integrated the ancient imperial institution with the structure of a nation-state; it sanctioned political participation for some city-dwellers and stimulated demands for greater participation by those left out. Capitalism drew increased numbers of the working poor and wage laborers into the city, and it heightened the uncertain, dependent quality of their existence. The rickshawmen, who proliferated soon after the invention of that conveyance in 1869, and the streetcar, which attacked their livelihood when service began in 1903, were the most visible symbols of this transformation of the city. Not coincidentally, the former accounted for numerous rioters and the latter became one of the most common targets of angry crowds. Imperialism both elicited jingoistic calls for a strong foreign policy and exacted major sacrifices, in money and lives, from the populace.

Any social world, of course, is transitional, but the claim that the political crowd of 1905 to 1918 was transitional is more than a truism. One finds continuities between the thought and behavior of the crowd of this era and protesters of earlier and later eras, yet in key particulars the demarcation is sharp and clear between previous crowd actions, those of this era, and those that would follow. Continuities are visible in the ways crowd behavior and ideology echoed traditions of collective action of an earlier era. The "fair price" distribution of rice in 1918 closely followed the scripts of riots of late Edo times.[6] Direct attacks on the homes or offices of wrongdoers such as the rice merchants in 1918 and the streetcar company in 1906 harked back to Edo-era attacks on the wealthy. The theatrical quality of the events, the parody and inversion of symbols, and the echoes of festival celebration seen in the use of traditional drums to build atmosphere at a rally and the coincidence of riot and holiday would have been familiar to a Tokugawa peasant or town-dweller.[7] Finally, outside the realm of formal politics, the people

6. Edo was the pre-1868 name for Tokyo. It also refers to the Tokugawa era, 1600–1868, during which Edo was the capital of the Tokugawa shogun's government.

7. *TAS*, March 16, 1906, p. 6, for use of the drum. Herbert Bix, *Peasant Protest in Japan, 1590–1884* (New Haven: Yale University Press, 1986), p. 77, on echoes of Kabuki in villagers' conceptions of their protest.

of Tokyo had lived in a "spectating world" for over two centuries.[8] They had long been accustomed to gather in crowds, and authorities since the 1600s had associated even apolitical assembly with turbulence and immorality.[9] Traditional popular entertainments included puppet and Kabuki theaters, the more plebeian Yose variety halls, and sumo wrestling. As the high technology of the early 1900s created modern settings for mass entertainment, opportunities for, and interest in, leisure-time gathering and spectating increased. No fewer than fifty-one moving picture theaters opened their doors in Tokyo between 1909 and 1912.[10]

Despite continuities with the Edo era, the demarcation between the riots of the early 1900s and nineteenth-century crowd actions is unmistakable.[11] The rice rioters in Tokyo revealed a new national political awareness in their calls for the resignation of the prime minister. The widespread attacks on police boxes and government offices, such as on the Home Ministry in 1905, betray a similarly changed political sensitivity; rioters of the Edo era typically attacked merchant wealth, not samurai office. In terms of organization, the critical role of organized interest groups of politicians, lawyers, journalists, and small businessmen had no pre-Meiji precedent.

In addition, a temporal gap is clear. Before the 1905 riot, one must go back to the 1860s to find Tokyoites (Edoites at that time) engaged in citywide collective violence. In 1887 Popular Rights activists produced a flurry of rallying and demonstrating in Tokyo with the "Three Great Issues Petition Movement" for freedom of speech, lower taxes, and reform of the unequal treaties. These precisely anticipated the concerns of the post-1905 crowd and identify the incident as an early stage in the transformation of popular collective action and poli-

8. The phrase "spectating world" is from David Smith, "Tonypandy 1910: Definitions of Community," *Past and Present*, no. 87 (May 1980): 171. See Edward Seidensticker, *Low City, High City, Tokyo from Edo to the Earthquake: How the Shogun's Ancient Capital Became a Great Modern City, 1867–1923* (New York: Knopf, 1983), ch. 4, on popular culture in Tokyo of this era.

9. On the 250-year duel between the authorities and the Kabuki theatre, see Donald H. Shively, "Bakufu vs. Kabuki," *Harvard Journal of Asiatic Studies* 18, nos. 3–4 (December 1955).

10. On movies, see Yoshida Chieo, *Mō hitotsu no eiga shi* (Tokyo: Jiji tsūshinsha, 1978), pp. 72–74.

11. In formulating this distinction between Edo-era and twentieth-century collective actions, with the 1905–18 crowd in between, I was greatly aided by Tilly's formulation for France, where the mid nineteenth century was a transitional era between repertoires, with marked similarities to the Japanese sets. See Tilly, *Contentious French*, pp. 390–98.

tical ideas. But no major violence accompanied the agitation; the urban lower class, which joined in later riots, was neither sufficiently politicized nor yet of a size or concentration to produce major upheaval.[12]

The divide at the end of this era is also precise. After the rice riots of 1918, no more citywide riots took place. In the 1920s, assemblies were more numerous than ever, and clashes between police and demonstrators or striking workers were commonplace, but several aspects of the violence were different. First, the mobilization process was new; it involved workers acting through their own organizations. Second, the open conflict between bourgeoisie and proletariat was new. Third, the limited scope of the actions was different. Confrontations of workers with police and owners generally came only at the assembly site or picket line itself. Even at the peak of labor protest during the depression of 1927–32, no citywide scattering of attacks on merchants, streetcars, or the authorities took place.

Between 1905 and 1918 the crowd had a uniquely heterogeneous social base and voiced a distinctive ideology of populist nationalism. These social and ideological configurations behind the movement for imperial democracy were peculiar to this "era of popular violence." The willingness of respectable leaders to appeal to the crowd contrasts to Tokugawa protests and to the Popular Rights movement on the one hand and to the politics of the 1920s on the other. In the early 1880s the urban intellectuals, former samurai, and rural men of substance active in the Jiyutō or Kaishintō parties lost no time in condemning and distancing themselves from the poor commoners active in several violent uprisings. In the 1920s their successors fearfully sought to control, repress, or incorporate new working-class organizations. But between 1905 and 1914 the successors to the Meiji Popular Rights leaders, and in some cases the same people, took enthusiastically to the podium at huge rallies, and even applauded the violence of the crowd as a positive expression of the "healthy spirit of the people" (*kokumin no genki*). When such speakers were put on trial and asked, "Didn't you know that similar speeches have always led to riots in the past?" they would earnestly deny any intent to provoke a riot and defend the right to demonstrate in an orderly fashion.[13]

A changing political and economic context thus produced crowds

12. Inoue Kiyoshi, *Kaisei jōyaku* (Tokyo: Iwanami bunko, 1955), pp. 129–70, for more on this intriguing movement, which merits further study.

13. Hanai Takuzō hōritsu jimusho, ed., "Taishō 3 nen sōjō jiken kiroku" (n.d. [1914]), 3:58. Held in the library of the Tokyo Lawyers' Association.

whose members developed their own ideas about their changing world
and demonstrated "awareness" in various ways: in patterns of mobilization, composition, internal organization, in the choice of targets, of
sites and dates of assembly, and in the recurrent expression of key ideas
that moved diverse individuals to act in concert. While the high degree
of control maintained by a narrow elite that promoted capitalism and
created a modern nation has seemed distinctive to many historians of
modern Japan, the history of the crowd reveals a more complex, ironic
distinctiveness: elite control was limited, and the revolution from above
in fact fueled the popular response.

PATTERNS OF RIOT

The 1905 Hibiya riot inaugurated the "era of popular violence" with a
vengeance; it was the most intense uprising of the period. It also set a
pattern of mobilization, of crowd composition, and crowd structure
that was repeated and further elaborated in the ensuing events. Yoshino
Sakuzō was one contemporary who saw the riot as the first of several
related events. Before it, he wrote, "a few workers had on occasion
gathered in Ueno Park or Shiba Park, but that would be the beginning
and end of it. They left no lasting impact. The events of September 1905
were indeed the first time that the crowd acted as a political force."[14]

Eight of the nine riots listed in table 2.1 followed a similar three-stage
pattern of mobilization. In the first stage, organized political groups
would mobilize when an issue engaged their attention. Men in diverse
formal bodies of lawyers, journalists, businessmen, and local and
national politicians sought out like-minded groups, formed joint committees or federations, called meetings, adopted resolutions, and drew
up petitions and presented them to authorities. They used a sympathetic
press to publicize their cause.[15]

The locus of this activity varied with the issue. Diet politicians played
a major role in 1905. In 1906, when the issue was a proposal submitted
to the Tokyo City Council and Home Ministry to raise streetcar fares
from three to five sen per ride, opposition came from the ward councils
or ad hoc groups of councilmen in all fifteen of Tokyo's wards.[16]
Groups of lawyers (Hōritsu Club), journalists (Zenkoku kisha dōshikai), students, and politicians in the majority Seiyūkai Party coordi-

14. Yoshino Sakuzō, "Minshū no seiryoku," *Chūō kōron*, April 1, 1914, p. 87.
15. For detailed analysis of these groups, see Miyachi, *Nichiro sengo*.
16. Katsuragawa Mitsumasa, "1906 nen Tōkyō no densha chin age hantai undō," *Shirin*
68, no. 1 (January, 1985): 65–102, dissects the mobilization process in the streetcar case.

nated the "Movement for Constitutional Government" of 1913. They opposed Prime Minister Katsura's stubborn support for two new army divisions. In 1914 the scandal of corrupt arms dealing in the navy precipitated joint actions on the part of three overlapping clusters of organizations: the "Constitutional Government" groups of the previous year, supporters of a tougher China policy in the China Comrades Association, and opponents of the business tax, led by the National Federation of Business Associations.

In the second stage, organizers in each case reached out to the general public. They would call a series of speech-meetings (*enzetsu kai*) in any of several well-known halls, attracting from 100 to 15,000 listeners for a two- or three-hour series of speeches by heroes of the various popular causes. As the agitation of 1913 gained in intensity, for example, *eighteen* organizations joined to sponsor a January 12 rally in Tokyo, one of a month-long succession of almost daily indoor assemblies throughout the city.[17] The culmination of this second, still peaceful, stage, would be an outdoor assembly, labeled either a "people's" or a "citizens'" rally (*kokumin* or *shimin taikai*).

In the third stage, crowds turned violent. Riots began in the aftermath of rallies in Hibiya Park in 1905, 1906, 1908, and September 1913. In 1905 and twice in 1906 violence spread throughout Tokyo and lasted several days. In the evenings, crowds of 50 to 500 would coalesce at scattered locations downtown or in the "Low City," smash streetcars or police boxes, and dissolve. Rallies outside the Diet also turned violent and spread citywide (and to other cities) in February 1913 and February 1914.

Many other such gatherings, of course, did not end in violence, and the authorities often determined the outcome. The police ban on rallies at Hibiya Park and the Shintomiza Theater in 1905 infuriated those who came to protest the treaty, precipitating the riot. When the home minister rejected the unpopular streetcar fare increase proposed in March 1906, on the other hand, he quickly ended the rioting of that month, and his preemptive decision to deny a fare increase in 1909 avoided a repetition of the 1906 violence.

As this pattern repeated itself, the inhabitants of Tokyo came to recognize these three stages as a distinct process not previously part of the

17. Amamiya Shōichi, "Dai ichiji kensei yōgo undō," in *Nihon seiji saiban shiroku*, ed. Wagatsuma Sakae (Tokyo: Dai-ichi hōki, 1969), 2:13–16. Miyachi, *Nichiro sengo*, pp. 296–304.

life of the city. First came political organizing, followed by collective
assembly, and, finally, violent action. By 1914 the process was so familiar that Yoshino Sakuzō described it as "a sort of fad."[18]

Each of the riots involved a similarly diverse array of participants.
Impressionistic descriptions in the press and trial records drew on a
stock of social clichés in portraying the crowd as a motley of lower-class
city-dwellers, sprinkled with students and an occasional well-dressed
gentleman. On the day of the September 5 riot in 1906, the *Tōkyō asahi
shinbun* noted that the police had been alerted to keep an eye on "factory workers in each ward, as well as others such as rickshawmen and
so forth."[19] The rickshaw puller, in particular, stood in the eyes of
official and middle-class observers as an emblem of volatile poor
urbanites.

Japanese historians have compiled extensive lists of those arrested or
brought to trial, which in fact reveal the journalistic clichés to be close to
the mark. Table 2.2 summarizes the data available for those arrested or
tried for rioting in five of the incidents and offers a rough idea of how
the composition of the accused group compared to the population of
the city as a whole.[20]

The heterogeneity of those arrested is striking. The only major group
missing was the professional class of bureaucrats, doctors, lawyers,
journalists, and managers, the very people who had organized the
gatherings that ended in riot. Wage labor, broadly defined, was probably the major element in the political crowd, with artisans a leading
component in the early incidents, and factory labor more prominent by
1918, but the crowd drew from a broad range of lower- and some
middle-class urbanites: masters, artisans, and apprentices, shopkeepers
and their employees, factory wage workers, outdoor laborers, transport
workers, and students. With the exception of the students, Tokyo
crowds appear to have been not unlike the London or Parisian crowds

18. Yoshino, "Minshū," p. 87.
19. *TAS*, September 5, 1906, p. 6.
20. There is no occupational census ideal for our purposes. The 1908 survey used
here is the best available. Its main defect is the lack of any distinction in level within an
occupation. A textile worker and a textile factory owner would both be classed in the
"textile occupation." A rich merchant and his delivery boys would all be classified as
tradesmen, in the subcategory of "rice trade." But if we make the reasonable assumption
that wealthy owners of large establishments were a minority compared to both small
owners and employees in any one category, these figures can offer a rough indication of
the composition of the Tokyo working population. The figure of .8 percent unemployed
(5,534 of 712,215) is surely too low, reflecting official undercounting of this category.

of the eighteenth century: "the workshop masters, craftsmen, wage-earners, shopkeepers, and petty traders of the capital."[21]

The women of Tokyo were also conspicuous for their near total absence from the crowd.[22] Had women been prominent or even present during rallies and riots, they would have been noticed, for their actions would have been illegal. First the 1889 Law on Assembly and Political Societies and then Article 5 of the 1900 Public Order Police Law barred women from all forms of political participation, not only voting, but joining political parties, speaking at rallies, and even *attending* rallies.[23] On those occasions prior to these laws when women orators did take the podium, during Popular Rights rallies of the 1880s, the press took notice.

Despite the low profile of women in the riots, the forces producing imperial democracy did touch women and begin to reshape their social role and self-conception in these years. Consider this rare vignette, from the rally to demand a strong China policy of September 7, 1913. The main rally platform was set up at the balcony of the Matsumoto Restaurant in the center of Hibiya park, but a part of the overflow crowd converged on the bandstand located at the edge of the park, creating an unplanned second rally site:

> Suddenly Ōno Umeyo, a believer in the Tenri religion [one of several popular new religions founded in the Meiji era] and the 19-year-old eldest daughter of Ōno Shūsuke of the village of Tsukitate, Kurihara County, Miyage Prefecture, ascended the bandstand. She wore a tight-sleeved summer kimono with a purple-blue skirt and had a *hisashigami* hair style [a popular hair style of the period]. The crowd cheered and hooted: "Fantastic! Hurrah! A new woman!" and so forth. She raised her voice: "Truly it is the duty of the Taishō woman to save our comrades in China." With her eloquent words she cut a brilliant figure.[24]

21. George Rudé, *The Crowd in the French Revolution* (Oxford: Clarendon Press, 1959), p. 178. Or Nicholas Rogers, "Popular Protest in Early Hanoverian London," *Past and Present*, no. 79 (May 1978): 85.

22. No women were arrested in any of the riots. On the other hand, a special issue of a popular pictorial magazine of the time includes women in several drawings of the 1905 riots. In one, a kimono-clad woman is among two dozen rioters fleeing the police. In another, five Tokyoites sit reading an "inflammatory leaflet concerning the National People's Rally," a woman among them. And a young woman in school uniform is one of five people shown marching on the cover of the magazine. The matter of women's involvement in early twentieth-century political life needs further investigation. See *Tōkyō sōjō gahō*, no. 66, September 18, 1905 (subtitled in English *The Japanese Graphic*).

23. On the decision to ban women from politics, see Sharon Seivers, *Flowers in Salt* (Stanford: Stanford University Press, 1983), chs. 1–2.

24. *TAS*, September 8, 1913, p. 5.

TABLE 2.2   OCCUPATIONS OF PEOPLE ARRESTED OR
TRIED IN TOKYO RIOTS, 1905–18

| Occupation | Incidents | | | In 1908 Occupational Census |
	1905 and Sept. 1906	Feb. 1913 and Feb. 1914	1918	
Merchant/ tradesman	91 (28)	64 (30)	60 (24)	(41)
Artisan	82 (25)	27 (13)	22 (9)	(7)
Outdoor labor/ building trades	28 (9)	13 (6)	47 (19)	(6)
Transport [Rickshaw]	29 (9) [16 (5)]	10 (5) [3 (1)]	7 (3) [6 (2)]	(11) [(2)]
Factory labor	44 (14)	16 (8)	53 (21)	(14)
Student	10 (3)	41 (19)	10 (4)	—
Professional/ white collar	13 (4)	8 (4)	28 (11)	(12)
Unemployed	20 (6)	28 (13)	9 (4)	(1)
Other	10 (3)	7 (3)	13 (5)	(10)
Totals	327	214	249	712,215

SOURCES: 1905, 1906, and 1913 from Miyachi Masato, *Nichiro sengo seiji shi kenkyū* (Tokyo: University of Tokyo Press, 1973), p. 227; 1914 from Hanai Takuzō hōritsu jimusho, ed., "Taishō 3 nen sōjō jiken kiroku," vol. 1; 1918 from Inoue Kiyoshi, ed., *Kome sōdō no kenkyū* (Tokyo, 1960), 3:320–35; 1908 occupational census data from *Tōkyō-shi shisei chōsa shokugyō betsu genzai jinkō hyō* (Tokyo, 1908).
NOTES: Figures in parentheses are percentages. For 1905, sample is persons tried for rioting, excluding leaders of organizing committee. For 1906, those arrested and listed in *Tokyo asahi shinbun*, September 7–10, 1906. For 1913, those tried for rioting. For 1914, persons tried for rioting, excluding five leaders of the China Committee. For 1918, those tried for rioting. The merchant/tradesman category includes apprentices and employees. Owing to rounding off, column totals are not always 100 percent.

The reporter's introduction of the young woman as Uno's daughter and his attention to her clothes invoked familiar female social roles of obedient daughter and decorative object. But the positive crowd response and her own words show her to have been a participant in the making of the popular idiom of imperial democracy.

In contrast to these plebeian rioters, the leaders who founded political associations, drew up resolutions, joined in federations, spoke at indoor speech-meetings, and finally sponsored open-air rallies were educated men of substance: lawyers, journalists, Diet representatives, local politicians, or small businessmen. The relationship between such leaders and the rioters is controversial. It perplexed contemporary authorities, very likely aware of the latest European theories of "mob psychology," who could not decide whether the rioters were puppets of these gentlemen leaders or an uncontrollable mob.[25] Thus, Koizumi Kōsaburō, a judicial official who prosecuted the rioters, invariably sought "to find the conspirators or agitators . . . among the sponsors of the rally, but we always failed. There was never a case where the rally sponsors planned on a riot or violence. . . . As soon as the rally ended, the crowd was overtaken by a mob psychology, and transformed into a living thing." Despite the difficulty in identifying a group of leaders who manipulated the gullible masses, he rejected the possibility that the rioters themselves had conscious motives: "If we questioned those arrested in the act of violence, they could not explain it."[26]

The surviving trial records reflect such biases in conveying two contradictory impressions of the relationship of rioters to leaders: an image of the manipulated rioter and a picture of the inebriated, uncontrollable rioter. Both types are seen to be devoid of political consciousness.[27] Prosecutors directed most of their energy to interrogation of a handful of leaders charged with conspiracy, asking few questions of the hundreds arrested for common crimes of arson or property destruction.[28] We must credit most of the defendants with a good deal more political motivation than they admitted, for their most sensible defense was to play upon official prejudice, seeking lenience by disavowing political awareness and claiming simply to have been swept up in the excitement. Historians have echoed the prosecution view in stressing the role of "professional rooters" (*sōshi* or *ingaidan*) acting at the behest of party leaders to manipulate crowds, especially in 1913 and 1914.[29]

These dismissive and inconsistent conceptions are inadequate. From evidence culled primarily from the trial records of 1914, a more finely

25. Gustave Le Bon's *Psychologie des foules* (1895) was the classic European analysis of the time. The Japanese translation, *Gunshū shinri*, appeared in 1910.

26. Koizumi Kōsaburō, *Taishō hanzai shi seidan* (Tokyo: Daigaku shobō, 1955), pp. 79–80.

27. See Amamiya Shōichi, "Hibiya yakeuchi jiken," in *Nihon seiji saiban* 1:402–3, on the bias of the prosecution.

28. Thus, six of the eight volumes of preliminary interrogation for the 1914 trial (Hanai, "Taishō 3 nen sōjō") focus on five conspirators. The remaining two have brief interrogations of ninety-three individuals. The four volumes of "Kyōto jiken," from 1905, focus even less attention on the common rioters.

29. Takahashi Hikotada, "Ingaidan no keisei," *Hōsei daigaku shakai rōdō kenkyū* 30 (1984): 3–4, and Najita, *Hara Kei*, pp. 160–62.

grained picture of the structure of crowd action develops. On one hand, the national leaders were seldom found rubbing shoulders with the crowd; nor were they in tight control of what happened after rallies. But neither were leaders and crowd wholly unconnected, with the latter moved by a mob psychology unrelated to the issues of the day. A middle stratum of unofficial or semiofficial streetcorner leaders existed. Some of these figures had links to organized groups, but the ties could be tenuous. The crowd could sometimes on the spur of the moment press one of its number into action as a leader or a link between the Diet politicians and the populace. These subordinate leaders and activist followers possessed considerable political awareness. They bridged the gap between, and overlapped with, both professional political leaders and the stone-throwing rioters. Acting in significant measure on their own initiative, they invoked causes that apparently resonated with the sentiments of those in the crowd.

Diverse individuals mediated between gentlemen politicians and the rest of the crowd. One Kumatani Naoyoshi, a 31-year-old recent migrant to Tokyo, was one such subleader with relatively close ties to the leaders. An acquaintance of a leading member of the China Comrades Association, Kumatani helped out at six rallies in the seven days prior to the riot in February 1914, carrying flags and banners. Accused of urging on the crowd in front of the Diet, he admitted the basic facts of the accusation, but attributed his actions to intoxication with both sake and the spirit of the crowd.

The rice merchant Kawamura, a 39-year-old resident of Kanda ward, is an intermediate figure who had leadership thrust upon him. A close friend of several members of the Kanda ward assembly, and himself a member of a committee in the ward opposed to the business tax, he claimed to have gone to the Diet on February 10, 1914, at the urging of fellow committee members "to file an [anti-tax] petition as an individual." He bought several newspapers along the way, extra editions with reports on the Diet situation, and as he neared the Diet, a crowd gathered around him and urged him to "read them to us," which he did. Later that afternoon, he again read aloud upon request a report of events inside the Diet to a group of those on the outside.[30]

Kawamura's actions reveal the theatrical dimension to crowd actions

30. Hanai, "Taishō 3 nen sōjō" 7, sec. 2:112–14. These episodes reflect a shortage of the latest newspaper copies, and the interest among those gathered in up-to-date information, rather than widespread illiteracy.

throughout the center of the city during each riot. The chief of the Kōjimachi police station had described "people everywhere making speeches in the streets," during the 1905 riots; Kawamura's public readings were part of this phenomenon of streetcorner speechifying.[31] In addition, he nicely illustrates the overlap between issues and constituencies within the crowd: a merchant concerned with the tax issue mingled with a group ostensibly convened in anger at naval corruption and a weak foreign policy.

Kawamura belonged to a political organization, but other impromptu leaders held no formal affiliation; informed of the issues, they held strong opinions and sought to act on them. One defendant in 1914 was Takei Genzō, aged thirty-two, a tradesman who sold machinery of some sort. After "one glass of whiskey" (*wisukii*) during the afternoon of February 10, he made his way to the Nihonbashi area and delivered an impassioned impromptu speech to a crowd gathered there:

> Prime Minister Yamamoto took a commission. The *Maiyū* supports the government, so it takes a commission, too. I'm a former soldier, and we should all rise in anger now for the sake of the nation. The police are running dogs of the bureaucrats. We have to smash the police line and attack the *Maiyū* newspaper.[32]

Colorful leaders of the moment surfaced during other riots as well, such as Matsumoto Dōbetsu, a maverick activist who achieved brief prominence in 1906. He was head of a small group he called "imperial socialists" and had attracted some attention for carrying a black-edged "mourning flag" during the 1905 Hibiya protest. In 1906, despite personal and financial ties with other political leaders, his group acted separately from the larger federation of city and ward councillors, lawyers, and journalists who sponsored the citizens' rally (*shimin taikai*) at a rented hall on September 5, the anniversary of the 1905 riot, to protest the streetcar fare increase. Matsumoto sponsored a separate rally that same day in Hibiya Park, attended by several thousand.[33]

According to the *Asahi*, as well as the prosecution at his trial, Matsumoto asked the audience whether they wished to allow the Home Ministry more time to change its mind: "Should we wait quietly until

    31. "Kyōto jiken" 4:352.
    32. Hanai, "Taishō 3 nen sōjō" 8, sec. 3:39–40.
    33. Estimates range from 2,000 to over 10,000. See the account of Matsumoto's background and activities in Katsuragawa, "1906 nen Tōkyō," pp. 89, 92–97.

the 11th [the day before the increase was set to take effect], or should we do some smashing [*yakeuchi*]?" Some shouted back, "Let's do it tonight!" but the majority seemed inclined to wait, so Matsumoto led a group on what he later claimed was intended to be a peaceful march to the Home Ministry. It turned out differently. Some in the crowd began to stone streetcars. Every night until September 12, when heavy rains dampened popular enthusiasm, crowds of tens or hundreds, and in a few cases thousands, stoned streetcars and police boxes or substations at locations throughout the central and "Low City" wards of the city.[34]

Just as the involvement of those in this intermediate stratum varied significantly, so did that of the masses of people in the "audience." Many of the defendants in 1914 participated out of simple curiosity. A 19-year-old tailor, Kawazumi, made his way to the Shimbashi police station on the evening of the 10th and, he admitted, threw stones at it. Why? "Everyone was shouting 'Go to it! Go to it! [*yare, yare*],' so I did it with no special reason." Yet we dismiss such youths as mindless or apolitical at some peril. Kawazumi had been to a speech-meeting prior to the riot, belying this perhaps calculated self-portrait as a casual participant. Others like him in fact followed the progress of the event in the press. One Ōmoto, a 21-year-old employee at a fish market, attended the rally at Hibiya upon reading of it in the newspaper; he admitted to shouting epithets at the police and throwing his wooden clogs at them. Newspaper reports on the planned rally also drew Nakagawa Seiichi, an unemployed youth, to Hibiya. An 18-year-old lumberyard worker, Tanaka, was one for whom curiosity and excitement were the apparent main attractions. He had attended several speech-meetings because he found them "entertaining" (*omoshiroi*), and he went to Nihonbashi and joined in the stone throwing with a friend, who said it promised to be entertaining, as well. This aspect of the rioting highlights the theatrical dimension, but does not deny the political significance. As the broad meaning of the word *omoshiroi* suggests, the rallies were probably both "entertaining" and "interesting."[35]

For inhabitants of a spectating world, the political speech-meeting, the rally, and even the riot were inexpensive forms of popular entertainment (except for those arrested: one of the thirty defendants fined for

34. *TAS*, August 29–September 1906; *Chūō kōron*, October 1906, pp. 1–8; *Tōkyō keizai shinbun*, August 25, 1906, September 8 and 15, 1906; Morinaga, *Shidan saiban*, pp. 47–56; *Hōritsu shinbun*, October 15, 1906, pp. 24–25.
35. Examples from Hanai, "Taishō 3 nen sōjō," vol. 8.

rioting in Osaka in 1913 was overheard to remark, with a laugh, "Twenty yen for picking up one rock! That's an expensive stone."[36] Unlike Kabuki, variety theater, sumo wrestling, or moving picture shows, rallies offered the prospect of audience participation. This form of theater had its stars, the "gods of constitutional government," who addressed huge throngs; its supporting actors and bit players, such as Matsumoto Dōbetsu, Kawamura, and Takei Genzō; and its audience, whose members sometimes leapt onstage.

One further index of this quite natural range in degree of engagement is supplied by the judge in the 1914 trial, who asked forty-four of the ninty-three common defendants if they had ever attended speech-meetings prior to the rally. Despite tempting advantages to denying such political involvement, thirteen claimed they had, while thirty-one said they had not. The political crowd thus covered a broad spectrum in two senses: varied occupations and differing degrees of engagement with the issues. Its members were drawn from the full range of lower-to-middle-class urbanites. The official leadership consisted primarily of professional politicians, lawyers, and journalists. The intermediate strata and the mass of the crowd included youths seeking patronage and aspiring to a political career, concerned residents of local prominence, and many people simply curious or interested in joining what promised to be a good time.

POLITICAL THEATER

A coherent set of political symbols can be found in the theater of the Tokyo crowd. Tokyoites used a constellation of dates, assembly sites, and targets to articulate a political vision embedded in the urban popular culture of the early twentieth century. Theirs was a vision of an imperial democracy at odds with the ruling ideas of the bureaucratic elite, though to an extent derived from them.

The timing of crowd performances reflected both awareness of the broader context of nation-building and dissent from ruling definitions of the commoners' role in the political order. Seven of the nine Tokyo incidents listed in table 2.1 took place on or about one of two dates, September 5 and February 11.

The former gained significance as the anniversary of the Hibiya anti-

36. *Hōritsu shinbun*, April 20, 1913, p. 20.

treaty riot of 1905. The organizers of the streetcar fare rally of September 5, 1906, included leaders of the 1905 anti-treaty coalition, and they deliberately and successfully used this anniversary to draw attention to their cause.[37] The rally and assault on the Foreign Ministry of September 7, 1913, also took place on the Sunday nearest to the 1905 anniversary date. The *Asahi* the next day reflected the awareness of precedent in describing how the police, "considering the several past experiences," kept a low profile and did not excite a major riot.[38] Participants no doubt made the anniversary connection on their own when a dandy in a Western suit with striped pants, a glass of sake in one hand, a walking stick in another, identified in the *Asahi* simply as "an old political rooter [*sōshi*]," shouted from the speaker's platform, "Don't you know me? The patron saint of the riot!"[39]

The case of February 11 is more complex and interesting. The Meiji government in 1874 chose February 11 as the date on which to celebrate the accession of the (mythical) first emperor, Jimmu, in 660 B.C. and with it the founding of the nation and the imperial line. In 1889 the state chose this date to promulgate the Meiji constitution,[40] and in the contest between the state and various opposition groups with their own interpretations of the true nature of "constitutional government" in the years after 1905 both sides sought to wrap themselves in the flag and the aura of imperial sanction by making this date their own.

The participants in the crowd joined the battle by attending the rallies and occasionally rioting. Certainly the simple fact that February 11 was a holiday made it easier for people to gather, and February was a time when the Diet was almost always in session. But it seems no coincidence that the rallies and riots of 1908, 1913, and 1914 all took place on either February 10 or 11. The bureaucratic elite, for its part, entered the contest, and stimulated awareness of the date's importance, by sponsoring huge, tightly policed, and consciously nonpartisan celebrations of the twentieth anniversary of the constitution in Hibiya Park in 1908 and 1909 and by issuing an Imperial Rescript on Poor Relief on

---

37. *Chūō kōron*, October 1906, p. 7.
38. *TAS*, September 8, 1913, p. 5.
39. He called himself "Yakeuchi jiken no taishō kitenjin." I think the term *sōshi* in this context suggests an association with the Popular Rights movement. See drawing in *TAS*, September 8, 1913, p. 5.
40. On the importance of this symbolic date in the making of "Meiji ideology," see Carol Gluck, *Japan's Modern Myths: Ideology in the Late Meiji Period* (Princeton: Princeton University Press, 1985), pp. 85–87.

this date in 1911.[41] In both 1913 and 1914, however, with a wide array of antigovernment forces all planning their own rallies, there was no official celebration of the twenty-fifth anniverary, suggesting that the oligarchs had at least temporarily lost control of this symbolic date.[42] Leaders of the movement for universal manhood suffrage were subsequently among the most self-conscious in contesting for the ideological high ground. Beginning with the rally on February 11, 1918, which ended in minor violence, pro-suffrage rallies took place on this date yearly until 1923, and by 1920 suffragists had dubbed February 11 "Universal Suffrage Day."

The settings for the drama were predictable as well. Crowds returned consistently to a few favorite meeting places and persistently chose the same targets. Hibiya Park, of course, was the most important assembly site. By the occasion of the 1913 siege of the Foreign Ministry, the *Asahi* simply noted: "Hibiya Park is by now synonymous with the people's rally."[43]

It emerged as such out of the same critical dialectic of nation-building policy and popular response that built the importance of February 11 and sanctioned the general practice of popular assembly and political participation. In Edo, while temples or shrines had served as holiday gathering places, there were no *explicitly* public spaces that the townspeople could call their own. Designed around the turn of the century on a Western model, built by the government, and opened only two years before the 1905 riot, Hibiya Park was first used extensively during the Russo-Japanese War of 1904–5 for privately sponsored rallies to celebrate Japanese military success.[44] These gatherings helped

41. See ibid., p. 146, on the 1908 celebration, and pp. 49–60, passim, on the bureaucratic conception of the constitutional order as above politics. See *Jiji shinpō*, February 12, 1909, on the twentieth anniversary celebration of 1909, which featured Noh plays and music, but no speeches praising the constitutional political order. The repeat of the celebration in two years was because of the concurrent use of Japanese and Western counting customs. Nakamura Masanori, Emura Eiichi, and Miyachi Masato, "Nihon teikokushugi to jinmin: 9/5 minshū bōdō o megutte," *Rekishigaku kenkyū*, August 1967, p. 16, describe the 1911 rescript, in which the emperor donated 1.5 million yen to found a poor relief organization and called for further private donations.

42. The death of the Meiji emperor in June 1912 may also explain the absence of a 1913 celebration, but not the 1914 case.

43. "Kokumin taikai ni Hibiya kōen wa mō tsukimono de aru" (*TAS*, September 8, 1913, p. 5).

44. See Appendix A. See also Sakurai Ryōju, "Nichiro senji" on wartime victory celebrations in the park, and Seidensticker, *Low City, High City*, pp. 116–23, on the designing and building of the park.

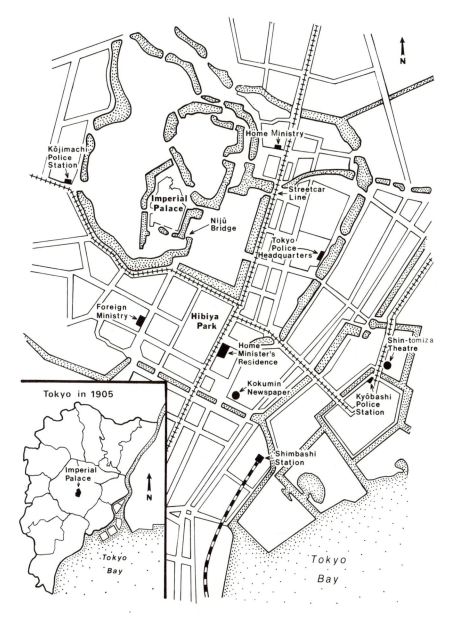

Map 1.   Central Tokyo in 1905

make the park a place of explicitly political significance that Tokyoites of all sorts felt *entitled* to claim as theirs, in opposition to the state. The riot of 1905 began when the police forbad an anti-treaty rally and barricaded the park. A crowd of 30,000, some shouting, "It's illegal [*fuhō*] to close the park!" overwhelmed the police, destroyed the barricades, and met anyway.[45] The disturbances of 1906, 1908, and 1918 also began with rallies in Hibiya.

This struggle over the use and definition of urban space is full of irony. The popular frenzy of support for both the Sino-Japanese and Russo-Japanese wars, and the resulting desire to gather to celebrate victories, was a product in part of the oligarchic policies of patriot-making. Yet even during the war with Russia the police had worried about the frequent, implicitly political gatherings for victory celebrations, but had failed to ban them effectively.

The struggle for Hibiya Park also neatly illustrates both the links and the tension between the concept of the legitimate polity promoted by Japan's rulers and the different vision of the urban populace. The government built the park as a symbol of the modernity and greatness of the new imperial capital and promoted it as a space for people to gather quietly in support of empire, emperor, and the ministerial servants of the emperor. People in the crowd, while concurring in support of both empire and emperor, disagreed both on the proper relation between the emperor, themselves, and the bureaucracy, and on the appropriate use of the park. They made Hibiya a symbol of their freedom to gather and express their political will.

A connection of more or less intimacy to this bureaucracy was unsurprisingly the thread that tied together all but one of the favorite targets of the crowd once it left Hibiya on a smashing spree. The Tokyo police, under the jurisdiction of the Home Ministry, was the institution least popular and most besieged. The hundreds of small, hard-to-protect two- or three-man "police boxes" scattered throughout the city were easy prey, and crowds stoned or burned them in five of the riots (1905, 1906, 1913, 1914, 1918). The Home Ministry itself was a second frequent target. During the violence of September 1905, the crowd directed its fiercest attack on the residence of the home minister, across the street from Hibiya Park (see map 1 and fig. 3). Ten thousand people surrounded the compound and set fire to parts of it.

45. According to police testimony. See "Kyōto jiken" 4:269, 283–84.

The police and the Home Ministry, both created by the oligarchs in the first decade of nation-building, stood as symbols of the larger political order and as the particular institutions most responsible for restricting the activities of ordinary people.[46] Yoshikawa Morikuni, one of Japan's first generation of socialists in the early twentieth century, witnessed an aged "jinrickshaw-type" ask one of the rioters to "by all means burn the Ochanomizu police box for me, because it's giving me trouble all the time about my household register."[47]

Other targets provoked enmity insofar as they were implicated in support of the bureaucratic system. These included progovernment newspapers, politicians, and political parties (usually Hara Kei and the Seiyūkai), the homes of the oligarchs, and, in September 1913, the Foreign Ministry.

The streetcar, which began service in 1903, the same year Hibiya Park opened, was a frequent target both for economic and political reasons (see fig. 5). It represented a direct threat to the livelihood of the capital's thousands of rickshaw pullers. Further, the fare increases proposed in 1906 and 1909 threatened to take substantial bites from the incomes of lower-class streetcar riders.[48] In addition, however, political issues fueled anger at the streetcar companies. Numerous resolutions of ward assemblies and other groups in 1906 criticized the highhanded, "unconstitutional" behavior of the Home Ministry and city council, and the intimate ties between Seiyūkai politicians on the council and the streetcar company. They blasted the selfish politicians and capitalists who "neglected the public good" and ignored the "will of the citizens" (shimin no ikō) in approving the increase.

The inversion or parody of procedures of the authorities and the appropriation of forms of parliamentary behavior recurred in the theater of the crowd. Inversion was seen in the 1905 demonstration, when the flags and banners were modeled on those used to send off troops just months earlier.[49] Many anti-treaty banners were designed as flags of

---

46. The Home Ministry was founded in 1873. The Tokyo police force was founded in 1874.

47. Takahashi Yūsai, *Meiji keisatsu shi kenkyū* (Tokyo: Reibunsha, 1961), 2:103. Takahashi, in the history sympathetic to the police and hostile to the socialists, concludes that Yoshikawa's testimony is reliable.

48. Even an increase of one sen per ride would have claimed an additional 2.5 percent of the average factory worker's monthly income of twenty yen, assuming two rides daily twenty-five days a month.

49. "Kyōto jiken" 3:197.

national mourning, mounted on large poles, the slogans framed with black ribbons. A portion of the crowd at Hibiya set off with these on a march toward the imperial palace, in effect offering "condolences" to the emperor on the failed policies of his ministers. This extraordinary symbolic act, implicating the emperor in politics, was too much for the police, who broke up the march.[50]

Appropriation is seen in the institution of the "people's rally" (*kokumin taikai*) itself, which typically followed a set pattern. First came a succession of speeches, presided over by a chairman (*gichō*), followed by passage (*kaketsu*) of a several-point resolution (*ketsugi*) drawn up by an organizing committee. In 1913 the sponsors distributed 50,000 copies of the resolutions adopted at the people's rally of September 7.[51] This was a popular reenactment of the form and vocabulary of the parliamentary procedure of the Diet, which may be read as a challenging assertion that the people had a place as participants in the process of government.[52]

A spirit of parody is found in the graffiti and the letters to the press at the time of the rice riot written in the mode of a Tokugawa peasant's defiant accusation of unjust officials.[53] It surfaced in the 114 comic haiku (*kyōku*) published as part of a contest sponsored by the nation's major journal for lawyers after the September 1906 riots.[54] But perhaps most creative was the flyer circulated anonymously on the eve of the anti-tax rally of February 11, 1908. An anti-tax movement of hundreds of business federations had begun the previous summer when the government, far from ending the unpopular new war taxes of 1904–5, proposed an increase in sales taxes on food oil, sake, and sugar. A national convention of the Federation of Business Associations (Jitsugyō kumiai rengō kai) called for a February 5 rally as the climax of this lobbying campaign, but the Diet approved the increase the day before the meeting with Seiyūkai support, and the five hundred conven-

---

50. Okamoto, "Hibiya Riot," p. 261.
51. *TAS*, September 8, 1913, p. 5.
52. For one of many examples of this appropriation of parliamentary language and form, see the description of an anti-tax "People's Rally" in Osaka in 1914 in *Tōkyō keizai zasshi*, February 14, 1914, p. 38.
53. Yoshikawa Mitsusada, "Iwayuru kome sōdō jiken no kenkyū," *Shisō kenkyū shiryō*, no. 5 (February 1939): 206–7.
54. The 114 entries are listed in *Hōritsu shinbun*, September 10, 1906, p. 27; September 15, pp. 22–23, September 20, p. 25, September 25, pp. 26–27, September 30, p. 27, October 5, p. 25, October 10, p. 26.

tion delegates could only vow to oppose pro-tax M.P.'s in the next election.[55]

The *Tōkyō mainichi* newspaper then reprinted on February 10 what it called an "inflammatory leaflet" of unknown origin that had been circulated throughout the city, calling for a rally in Hibiya Park on February 11. Police promptly arrested all known socialists in Tokyo. Several thousand people gathered at the Hibiya bandstand on the 11th, but no organizers were to be found. The *Asahi* reported that Matsumoto Dōbetsu attended, standing by quietly, slightly drunk. After several impromptu speeches denouncing the tax increase and demanding suffrage expansion, some in the crowd left the park and began to stone streetcars.[56] The flyer which drew this crowd to the park read:

ANTI-TAX INCREASE
PEOPLE'S RALLY [*Kokumin taikai*]
Hibiya Park, February 11, 1 P.M.

Admonitions to Attendees:

1. Do not bring any dangerous weapons.

2. Do not prepare oil, matches, or clubs.

3. Do not fight with the police.

4. Do not smash any police boxes.

5. Do not smash any streetcars.

6. Do not throw stones at the Diet building.

7. Do not attack pro-tax or Seiyūkai M.P.'s.

The style is that of the ubiquitous Edo-era injunctions to townspeople or villagers, typically mounted on a pole and planted in the ground for all to see and respect. The flyer teased the authorities and exhorted potential rioters precisely because its injunctions were an inverted list of the very actions most common in crowd incidents.[57] In the political culture of Tokyo in 1908, this document invoked for its readers an instantly recognizable pattern of crowd action. Their shared understanding of the symbols of political theater reflected the deep antagon-

---

55. The Seiyūkai did in fact lose three of its five seats in Tokyo in the next Diet election. Matsuo, *Taishō demokurashii*, pp. 53–62.

56. Leaflet in *Tōkyō mainichi shinbun*, February 10, 1908, p. 2. Also, *TAS*, February 13, 1908, p. 2. *Yorozu chōhō*, February 12, 1908, p. 3. *TAS* reported 10,000 attendees, thirty arrests; the *Yorozu* claimed 30,000 attendees, forty arrests.

57. Also of interest is the fact that the newspaper was willing to further the cause by reproducing the flyer rather than simply reporting its contents.

ism toward the bureaucratic elite on the part of Tokyoites excited by the political vision of imperial democracy.

THE IDEOLOGY
OF IMPERIAL DEMOCRACY

The constituent elements of the crowd had specific grievances. Workers and artisans were likely to care more about streetcar fares and rice prices than business taxes; the reverse no doubt held for shopkeepers and merchants. Yet, while the businessmen, lawyers, party politicians, and journalists each had separate formal organizations, they acted together in the mobilizing pattern that led to riot, and lower-class city-dwellers who were not part of any of these groups attended rallies that they organized.[58] Thus, despite the clear diversity of participants, leaders, and causes, the moments of common action and the repetition of key concepts and slogans reveal that a related cluster of issues and ideas created a new political space. In this space, disparate elements, which would later organize separately for differing causes, reacted together.

The participants in the political crowd responded to a set of surface issues that cohered both logically and in the identity of the activists. Scholars such as Miyachi Masato have carefully documented the overlap in the membership and leadership of those formal groups of lawyers, journalists, intellectuals, and politicians concerned with several related issues.[59] These imperials democrats supported empire abroad and economic justice and political reform at home. They were pro-emperor, pro-empire, *and* committed to elusive notions of constitutional government and popular involvement in politics. Individual voices differed; some accented the democracy, others the imperialism, but the goals themselves were logically related.

At the center was a simple notion. A strong modern nation required the active participation of a prosperous populace. This belief was the glue that held together the diverse issues that motivated the leaders and drew the crowds: imperialism abroad, lower taxes and economic relief at home, and greater popular involvement in a political process perceived as controlled by an arrogant or corrupt bureaucracy.

National leaders commonly linked these issues in public statements, as in the 1905 platform of the newly formed "National People's [*kokumin*] Club." This group of about 150 politicians, lawyers, and journal-

---

58. Miyachi, *Nichiro sengo*, pp. 209–14, on organizations of small businessmen.
59. Ibid., pp. 209–378.

ists, hoping to build on the political energies nurtured during the anti-treaty movement, proclaimed that constitutionalism and imperialism were the two great international trends of the day. Nations that followed them would prosper; others would decline. The twin goals "originate in popular awakening, stand on popular confidence, and are fulfilled through popular activity."[60]

The attitudes of members of the crowd are more elusive, but in newspaper accounts and those few trial records that allowed the plebeian participants to speak for themselves, both a set of three surface issues (economic welfare and justice, an aggressive foreign policy, and domestic political access) and a common, underlying political vision can be discerned.

Taxes and prices were the two recurrent economic issues. One or the other was prominent in the foreground or background of the riots of 1905 (new taxes to finance the war), 1906 (streetcar fares), 1908 (tax increases), 1914 (business tax), and 1918 (rice prices). Certainly the anti-tax movement, focusing mainly on the business tax and various retail sales taxes had greatest relevance for businessmen and merchants, who stood to lose most if taxes discouraged sales, but these sales taxes, as well as the unpopular travel tax, an imposition of one sen per ride on all streetcar, ferry, and trail travel, directly affected the populace as a whole.

Prices, on the other hand, were primarily the concern of the poor and working-class population. In urban and rural protest of the early to mid nineteenth century, the price and supply of rice had been at the heart of the popular moral economy.[61] Exchanges such as the following in 1914, between the judge and one Ōnishi Harukichi, a 55-year-old maker of wooden boxes, show the staying power of this concern of poor city-dwellers:

JUDGE: Which do you prefer, the bureaucracy or the Seiyūkai [Party]?
ŌNISHI: I don't know which I prefer, but with Mr. Katsura's cabinet, rice has just gotten more expensive, and with a Seiyūkai cabinet rice will be cheaper. That is the only reason the Seiyūkai is better.[62]

60. Ibid., pp. 253–54. The term *kokumin* is here translated as "popular." It was used four times in the sentence quoted.
61. Patricia Sippel, "The Bushū Outburst," *Harvard Journal of Asiatic Studies* 37, no. 2 (December 1978). Conrad Totman, *The Collapse of the Tokugawa Bakufu, 1862–1868* (Honolulu: University Press of Hawaii, 1980), pp. 216–24.
62. *Hōritsu shinbun*, no. 859, April 30, 1913, pp. 18–19.

Prices also upset people at the Shintomiza Theater at the start of the 1905 riot. Anger at the police, who banned the meeting, led to violence outside the theater, but the audience inside were also furious that organizers collected a "box lunch charge" at the entrance. Similarly, scuffling broke out at a speech-meeting of February 5, 1914, when some of those in a crowd of 2,500 protested collection of a ten-sen entry fee when big-name speakers failed to appear.[63] While this evidence is more suggestive than conclusive, Ōnishi's concern with prices was probably common.

But the numerous poor participants were not simply motivated by hunger and poverty, their anger manipulated by a politically attuned leadership. Foreign policy and domestic political issues, as well as prices, were important even to the poorer members of the crowd. Support for imperialism was a second tenet of the imperial democratic creed, one upon which all participants agreed. To honor the nation and the emperor, the crowd wanted Japanese hegemony in Asia and equality with the West. These goals were prominent in 1905, in September 1913, and in 1914. Few, however, were anxious to foot the bill for Japan's expanding empire. Spokesmen for the anti-tax forces skirted the issue by asserting that only lower taxes would produce the vibrant economy that would make Japan great.[64] To point out the contradiction between calls for lower taxes at home and costly empire abroad is simple enough (although the contradiction remained unresolved in late-twentieth-century America), but the logic of this populist nationalism had a certain elegant simplicity as well: only those neither politically nor economically oppressed could produce a strong nation.

Political reform was the third concern of those who joined the political crowds. Both actors and audience opposed the monopoly on political power held by bureaucrats from Satsuma and Chōshū. They sought a greater popular role in political affairs. Bureaucratic scorn for popular desires and the "unconstitutional" behavior of the political elite were major issues in 1905, 1906, 1913, and 1914. For the more pragmatic party politicians, constitutional government meant rule by cabinets drawn from the majority political party in the Diet. For many in the crowd, it had a rather different meaning, discussed below.

The overlap among these three concerns is most evident in the events of the Siemens Incident of 1914. As in a symphony with three entwined

63. "Kyōto jiken" 3:52; *TAS*, February 5, 1914, evening edition, p. 5.
64. See Eguchi Keiichi, *Toshi shoburujoa undō shi no kenkyū* (Tokyo: Miraisha, 1976), pp. 127–28, and Miyachi, *Nichiro sengo*, pp. 259–60, for examples.

motifs, the lobbying of numerous groups gradually built to the resounding climax of February 10. Organizers of the previous year's Movement for Constitutional Government had planned anti-tax rallies for January 6 and 14, before the catalytic news broke that high officers in the imperial navy had pocketed kickbacks from the German arms supplier. The China Comrades Association had also for months planned a series of rallies for an aggressive posture on the continent to coincide with the Diet session that winter. Similarly, the Tokyo Ward Council Federation and the National Federation of Business Associations, together with other groups, had planned a National Anti-Tax Rally in Tokyo for February 9, and the Business Tax Abolition League, composed of anti-tax members of the Tokyo City Council, was planning a rally on the 17th.[65]

In this context, the speeches at any one rally naturally referred to the entire set of current issues. Four days before the riot, at noon on February 6, over ten thousand Tokyoites attended an indoor "Rally of Federated National Comrades of Each Faction."[66] The title was cumbersome, but apt. Speakers, including imperial democratic luminaries Shimada Saburō and Ōzaki Yukio, attacked the government for endangering and sullying the honor of the nation, overtaxing the people, and handling finances poorly. Another huge indoor rally on the 9th sounded the same refrain. The streetcar companies reportedly feared vandalism after the meeting, while the police worried that the following day's rally at Hibiya Park might get out of hand. For both the attendees and popular leaders of these events, excessive taxes, a weak foreign policy, and corruption in high places were symptoms of a single illness, the lack of true "constitutional government."[67]

Voices from the crowd, recorded in the press and in trial records, spoke as well to a consistent set of underlying concerns, expressed in the diverse contexts of economic welfare, foreign policy, and domestic politics. Time and again people called for (1) fairness and respect for the public good, (2) freedom of action, assembly, and expression, (3) respect for the "will of the people," and, embracing all these, (4) "constitutional" political behavior.

65. Miyachi, *Nichiro sengo*, pp. 309–12.
66. "Kaku ha rengō zenkoku yūshi taikai."
67. *TAS*, February 1 through 10, 1914, reported on these and numerous related events. See Amamiya, "Kensei yōgo," in *Seiji saiban*, p. 21, for a contemporary observation that a similar mix of issues moved activists in 1913.

The failure to heed the public good and the favoring of selfish private interests were especially prominent concerns in 1906. Leaders of the movement against the fare increase commonly condemned the home minister for catering to private interests (*shiri*) at the expense of the public good (*kōeki*). When a crowd left one afternoon rally in March, it echoed this refrain, marching to the Ginza crossing, standing for ten minutes blocking two streetcars and shouting "Unfair increase! Ignores the public good!"[68]

The belief that the streets and public places belonged to the people was widely held. Members of crowds frequently coupled calls for freedom to assemble or demonstrate with a fierce antagonism toward the police. One policeman, stoned and beaten in 1905 for trying to prevent a crowd from carrying black-trimmed flags toward the imperial palace, claimed that people shouted at him, "This is not something the police should restrict."[69] Fukuda Torakichi, the chief of the Kōjinmachi police station, described in an affidavit the scene on September 5, 1905, in front of Hibiya Park, when a reporter for the *Yorozu chōhō* climbed atop an empty box near the south gate of the park and spoke:

> The government has taken unconstitutional actions and caused the police to close off this park, which is a place for us to enjoy freely. By what means can we guarantee our freedom? In order to make our demands prevail we must carry out a great movement. A treaty that could do honor to the lives of a hundred thousand people and the expense of two billion yen has been lost because of the present government.

These words, Fukuda claimed, greatly stirred the crowd. When police tried to halt the speech, people stoned them and attacked them with sticks and metal bars.[70]

Participants in later incidents frequently echoed the calls for freedom to assemble, speak, or act. A youth in 1911, angry at police interference during a rally to protest the terms of the municipal takeover of the streetcar service, shouted, "We have the freedom to criticize this failed

---

68. The Japanese version ("Neage futō, kōeki mushi") has a more rhythmic, chantable cadence. *TAS*, March 12, 1906, p. 6. The crowd here may be invoking Confucian notions of an official obligation to eschew private (*shi*) gain and serve the public (*kō*) good of the realm, but I would not exaggerate the particularity of the Asian ideological universe in this respect. In Western traditions crowds have also claimed to be acting for a higher public interest against selfish authorities concerned with private wealth. See Dirk Hoerder, "People and Mobs: Crowd Action in Massachusetts during the American Revolution, 1765–1780" (Ph.D. diss., Free University of Berlin, 1971), pp. 133–35.
69. For similar examples, see "Kyōto jiken" 2:210–11; 4:269, 284.
70. "Kyōto jiken" 4:353.

policy. The police action makes our blood boil."[71] Patrolman Watanabe Yokichi reported that a crowd of about five thousand marched in his direction during the Siemens riot in 1914. Urged by a gentleman in a rickshaw to move on the *Chūō* newspaper, the crowd seemed intimidated by the police blocking its way. Some threw pebbles in the direction of the police or the newspaper buildings, others yelled epithets at the police, and Watanabe reported that someone shouted, "Why are you blocking us? We have the freedom to pass through the streets. Why do you protect the newspaper company and not the people's rights?"[72]

The term *kokumin* and several words including the character *i* (will, intent), in particular *ikō* (intention) and *ishi* (will), were at the heart of the political ideology expressed in crowd actions. The very concept of *kokumin*, like Hibiya Park and the Founding Day of February 11, was another child of state-making policy that turned on the bureaucratic state. The campaign to create a new body politic had succeeded so well that in all the riots people in the crowd made claims that a legitimate political order must respect the will of the people, the *kokumin*.

The official leadership used these terms as early as 1905. Ōgawa Heikichi, an activist in the anti-treaty movement, explained to a judge that he joined in forming a political group called the Anti-Russia Comrades Society out of the need to express the "will of the people."[73] The numerous streetcorner leaders rising to speak on the spur of the moment also used this language. In 1905 one unidentified speaker climbed to the balcony of a small teahouse near the Shintomiza Theater, shouted that he was going to "express the will of the people," and delivered a speech (see fig. 2). Another unnamed figure spoke in the vicinity of the imperial palace, according to police testimony, saying: "We cannot accept this treaty. We must make the will of the people prevail."[74]

Those in the crowds of the Siemens riot of 1914 spoke or heard similar language. At Hibiya Park, one Oshimoto, an unemployed 24-year-old, with some connections to the China Association leaders, allegedly shouted that under an "unconstitutional cabinet that does not follow the will of the people, the police are repressing us."[75] Seto Motonori was a Jiyūtō Party activist as a youth in 1884, but he later became a

---

71. *TAS*, July 10, 1911, p. 5.
72. Hanai, "Taishō 3 nen sōjō," 4, sec. "ka": 11–12.
73. "Kyōto jiken," 1:25.
74. "Kyōto jiken," 4:55, 348. Also similar statements on pp. 18, 24.
75. Hanai, "Taishō 3 nen sōjō" 7, sec. 2:66–67. Oshimoto denied the remark, but even if he did not say it, the fact that the police would invent such comments indicates their ubiquity.

tailor, living in Tokyo with no formal political affiliation. On the afternoon of the riot, he scaled a large rock near Moto-toranomon and
addressed a group assembled there:

> Overthrow the Yamamoto cabinet! Yamamoto [Gonnohyōe] is a great thief
> who gained millions in riches through his "commission." Overthrow Yama-
> moto! We must sever Gonnohyōe's head from his body. That is my opin-
> ion. . . . We must either throw Yamamoto in jail or else I'll go take care of
> him and go to jail myself.

Why, asked the judge, did you say this? Seto replied: "Because it was
the will of the people. I had no choice."[76]

The final key adjective for the crowd in the movement for imperial
democracy was "constitutional" (*rikkenteki*). Both elusive and broad in
meaning, the word holds a key to understanding the critical difference
between politicians leading the Movement for Constitutional Government and the masses of people attending rallies or stoning streetcars.
For practical leaders of the political parties, constitutional government
by 1913 meant a system where the majority party in the Diet formed the
cabinet and carried out policy with the blessing of the emperor and the
support of the voters. For those in the crowd, and for some of those
popular leaders characterized by Tetsuo Najita as the "hards," the
phrase "constitutional government" did not seem tied to a particular
institutional arrangement.[77]

To the opponents of a fare increase in 1906, the behavior of Home
Minister Hara Kei and his Seiyūkai party allies in the city council was
"unconstitutional" because it opposed the popular will and injured the
public good of two million Tokyoites for the sake of the private gain of
the company.[78] An unidentified speaker addressing a crowd outside the
gate to Hibiya Park in 1905 made a similar point when he said: "Today
the police actions at Hibiya Park were extraordinarily unconstitutional.
They closed off the park, which should be free to all of us, and prevented us from voicing our demands."[79] Higuchi Eiichi, a 29-year-old
member of the Constitutional Youth Party, also used the word in
defense of freedom to assemble and express opinion. Prevented by

76. "Kokumin no ikō desu kara shikata nashi" (Hanai, "Taishō 3 nen sōjō" 7, sec.
2:124–25).
77. Tetsuo Najita, *Hara Kei and the Politics of Compromise* (Cambridge, Mass.:
Harvard University Press, 1967), pp. 105–6 and passim.
78. *Tōkyō keizai zasshi*, September 15, 1906, p. 38. *Hōritsu shinbun*, September 10,
1906, p. 27.
79. "Kyōto jiken," 4:355.

police from speaking to a crowd in front of the Diet, he claimed to have shouted, "Why are you doing this? Don't you know the constitution?"[80] And to the machine salesman Takei Genzō in 1914, constitutional behavior was simply the orderly, nonviolent expression of the popular will. Accused of urging the crowd to stone the police, he told the judge that, no, he had first told people they should take constitutional action and should not throw stones. After the police had drawn their swords, he still was a voice of reason, telling people to throw snowballs, for stones were dangerous.[81]

That a diffuse set of meanings attached to the term is not surprising. Vernacular reference to "constitutional" behavior has been wide-ranging in other contexts as well.[82] Its varied usage reveals that "constitutional government" encompassed that cluster of related values at the center of the imperial democratic ideology expressed by members of the Tokyo crowd: respect for the public good, freedom to assemble, and respect for the expressed will of the people.

Party government, therefore, was only constitutional to those in the crowd when they perceived it to support these values. Hara Kei and the Seiyūkai were the darlings of the crowd just once, in 1913, and this was a union of mutual suspicion and convenience. Seiyūkai domination of the Tokyo City Council was anathema to popular activists throughout this era; as home minister in 1906 Hara and his party were twice targeted as part of the unresponsive elite that ignored the will of the people, and in 1908 the tongue-in-cheek leaflet quoted earlier enjoined attendees at the rally in Hibiya Park on February 11 not to attack Seiyūkai Dietmen. For the young Oshimoto in 1914, the cabinet, which had been formed with the support of the Seiyūkai Party, was "unconstitutional" because it did not "follow the will of the people."

This is the heart of the matter. At the popular level, constitutional government was simply a political order in which the wielders of power favored the public good and respected the will of the people. It was also a polity where the wills of the emperor and the people were in harmony, with no selfish private or authoritarian bureaucratic interests standing between them, and where those in power furthered the greatness of the

80. Hanai, "Taishō 3 nen sōjō," 5, sec. "yo":20.
81. Hanai, "Taishō 3 nen sōjō," 8, sec. 3:39. For further vernacular uses of the term *constitutional*, see Gluck, *Japan's Modern Myths*, p. 243. Whether Takei or Higuchi were lying is not a critical matter, for there is no question that they said *rikkenteki* ("constitutional") in explaining themselves to the judge.
82. See Hoerder, "People and Mobs," pp. 115–17, on the issue of constitutionality in a student protest over rotten butter at Harvard in 1766.

nation and the welfare of the people. This view echoed pre-Meiji political concepts of the reciprocal obligations of ruler and ruled, but did not simply replicate such notions. In its vociferous defense of the right to assemble, and its ongoing calls for government serving the popular will on issues of national and international policy, the Tokyo crowd transcended the more localized, passive popular conception of Tokugawa times, where common people took action only when rulers failed to maintain a moral economy through benevolent intervention.[83]

This conception of constitutional government clearly offered an uncertain commitment to a parliament as the structural means to ensure representation of the popular will and unity of emperor and people. Yet despite this important qualification, its spirit was democratic in important respects. The crowd wanted a government that worked "for" the people in both foreign and domestic policies. Both speech-meetings and outdoor rallies symbolically affirmed government "by" the people, recreating parliamentary procedures and adopting resolutions directed at the relevant authorities.

An episode from September 1913 offers further dramatic evidence of the popular will to participate. In response to the murder of a Japanese national in Nanking, a rally at Hibiya Park called on the government to demand reparations of China and send troops to enforce this. Some of the thirty thousand reported in attendance marched on the Foreign Ministry and tried to force open its steel gate. Some stoned the few policemen on the scene; others shouted: "Why is the gate closed? It's the people's Foreign Ministry!"[84] The crowd then chose ten representatives "in dignified fashion," in the words of one impromptu leader. They were able to meet an assistant to the foreign minister and present their demands.[85]

The bold claim to possess "the people's Foreign Ministry," literally unutterable before the creation of the word *kokumin* itself, finally affirmed a species of popular sovereignty. The sovereignty issue is treacherous. In popular conceptions, constitutional government was not unambiguously "of" the people. Despite the fact that the crowd

83. See Vlastos, *Peasant Protest*, ch. 2, on the "political economy of benevolence," and chs. 7 and 8 on the local orientation of late Tokugawa rebellions.

84. "Kokumin no gaimushō da zo!" (*Jiji shinpō*, September 8, 1913, p. 8). Likewise, a speaker at the September 5, 1906, streetcar fare rally had stressed that the home minister was "the people's home minister, the citizen's home minister, not the home minister of a private corporation!" Katsuragawa, "1906-nen Tokyo," p. 96, cites press accounts.

85. *TAS*, September 8, 1913, p. 5; September 9, 1913, p. 5. *Jiji shinpō*, September 8, 1913, p. 8.

claimed the Foreign Ministry as its own, no one in it questioned the sovereignty of the emperor. The question itself verged on treason, and the Tokyo rioters were vociferously loyal. They insisted both that a proper political order honor the emperor, and that it operate for and by the people; their behavior and expressions implied a shared locus of sovereignty in a system of imperial democracy where "the trust [*goshinnin*] of the emperor is conferred directly on the decision of the majority. Therefore, constitutional politics is the politics of the unity of the ruler and the people. Now [1913] a wall stands between the emperor and the subjects, and the emperor's trust is not conferred directly on the decision of the majority."[86] The crowd collectively articulated this vision by customarily closing outdoor rallies with two cheers of "Banzai!" one for the emperor and one for the citizens.[87]

FROM CROWD ACTION
TO WORKING-CLASS ACTION

The 1914 riot was the last in which all elements in the chemistry of the crowd—the bourgeois leaders, the free professionals, the shopkeepers, their apprentices, artisans, and outdoor and factory laborers—reacted together. The next two Tokyo disturbances came in 1918. They were turning points in two related processes: first, the separation of the elements of the crowd; second, the transformation of imperial democracy from movement for change to structure of rule.

The relatively narrow scope of the violence after the suffrage rally of February 11, 1918, is one sign that actors and audience in the theater of the crowd were moving apart. Police clashed with rock-throwing demonstrators after an indoor rally to call for suffrage and commemorate the 30th anniversary of the constitution. Upward of a thousand people attended the rally, sponsored by leading politicians in the Kenseikai, and upon its conclusion the assembly began a march toward the imperial palace, ostensibly to bow to and cheer the emperor. Police dispersed the group, which was armed with small flags and at least one big drum, before it reached the palace. A spree of rock-throwing began, and seventeen demonstrators were arrested.[88]

Anticipating clashes typical of the 1920s, the violence in this case was

86. Miyachi, *Nichiro sengo*, p. 303; statement of the Greater Japan Youth Party, January 28, 1913.

87. That is, "Tennō banzai! Tōkyō shimin banzai!" Two examples are found in *Hōritsu shinbun*, September 10, 1906, p. 27, and September 15, 1906, p. 21.

88. *Tōkyō nichi nichi shinpō*, February 12, 1918, p. 5.

limited to the site of the rally and the route of the march. It primarily involved the police and the pro-suffrage demonstrators themselves. The suffrage movement of the following years certainly drew on patterns of action elaborated by the earlier crowd: the rally, the speech-meeting, the demonstration, the choice of a symbolic date, and rock-throwing clashes with police. And the common justification of suffrage as the only way to build a strong, unified Japan capable of taking the lead in Asia was in the best tradition of imperial democratic ideas.[89] But in the years after World War I, the working-class elements seceded from this movement for suffrage expansion, creating their own organizations with a different agenda.

The rice riots of the summer of 1918 provide further evidence of the separation of social and political groupings involved in earlier crowd mobilizations. They show that the urban poor could act without significant prompting from the educated leaders of the imperial democratic movement; in contrast to earlier incidents, rioters went into action with almost no preliminary buildup and very little direct or indirect encouragement from any formal "leadership" organizations.

The only relevant public act in Tokyo prior to the day of the riot was an ad placed in the *Asahi* on August 10, calling for an August 12 rally to discuss and protest the high price of rice. Police refused to grant a permit for the rally, although by evening a crowd of about 200 had gathered in Hibiya Park in any case. One metal worker stood on a bench, confessed that he was ill-educated and unable to give a proper speech, and called on someone else to speak, but nobody came forward. The crowd dispersed without incident when the park lights went out at 9:00 P.M.

At 6:30 the next evening, however, most of the 700 people attending a speech rally at Kanda Youth Hall, sponsored by thirteen assorted groups in favor of the dispatch of troops to Siberia, headed for Hibiya after the meeting.[90] By 7:00 P.M. a crowd of 700 to 800 had gathered in the park, and several individuals, including at least one factory worker, rose to give short speeches attacking the cabinet, the minister of agriculture, and the nouveaux riches (*narikin*). By 8:00 P.M. the crowd had swelled to perhaps 2,000, and when police tried to break it up, the riot began. Several groups ranging in size from 500 to 2,000 set off on a

89. Miyachi, *Nichiro sengo*, p. 341.
90. The Terauchi cabinet had made its formal commitment to join the anti-Soviet expeditionary force to Siberia on August 2.

series of destructive tours of the city, smashing storefronts of all types and attacking police boxes. Crowds also confronted rice merchants and enforced immediate "fair price" sales. Crowds throughout the city carried out the same range of actions on the following three nights (August 14–16), with at least nine instances of forced rice sales in Asakusa ward alone on the 14th. On August 16 a large shipment of rice reached the city, and the violence subsided over the next two days.[91] Prime Minister Terauchi and his cabinet resigned on September 29 and were replaced by Hara Kei at the head of Japan's first political party cabinet.

The formation of the Hara cabinet was a milestone in the transformation of imperial democracy into a structure of rule. Hara himself had always feared the people, even when he profited from their anti-oligarchic energies in the riots of 1913.[92] The independent actions of poor urbanites and farmers in 1918 decisively furthered the movement of Hara and his party from outsiders demanding power to insiders exercising it. As workers and the poor created their own organizations, the bourgeois leaders' awareness of the popular threat heightened. The more conservative of the imperial democrats, such as Hara, opposed further suffrage expansion and concessions to labor, while an emerging liberal grouping of imperial democrats primarily in the Kenseikai, with allies in the bureaucracy, came to justify suffrage expansion as a way for bourgeois political leaders to regain control of the people. Thus, in 1919 the Kokumintō Party supported universal suffrage as a "progressive solution to the problem of social order," and Takahashi Korekiyo, minister of agriculture in the Kenseikai cabinet that finally pushed the suffrage bill through the Diet in 1925, justified the measure as a political solution to head off "social problems."[93]

Not all of the leaders in the imperial democratic movement reacted in the essentially defensive fashion of these politicians or bureaucrats in later years. A lawyer named Fuse Tatsuji, to give just one example, had called for a hard line toward the Chinese in the rally of September 1913, but by the early 1920s he had become one of Japan's most prominent defenders of unionists, organized tenant farmers, and Koreans both in Japan and the Korean colony. His career typified an alternative re-

91. Inoue Kiyoshi and Watanabe Tōru, *Kome sōdō no kenkyū* (Tokyo: Yūhikaku, 1960), 3:286–308.

92. Najita, *Hara Kei*, p. 161.

93. Masujima Hiroshi, "Fusen undō to seitō seiji," in *Kōza Nihon shi: Nihon teikokushugi no hōkai*, ed. Nihon shi kenkyūkai (Tokyo: University of Tokyo Press, 1971), pp. 132, 145.

sponse of numerous lawyers, journalists, and intellectuals who resolved
the tension inherent in the movement for imperial democracy by
tempering or abandoning the imperialist rhetoric and broadening a
liberal democratic, or even socialist, commitment.[94]

Study of the riots clearly reveals that since at least the time of the
Russo-Japanese War, politically engaged Tokyoites included factory
workers, artisans, rickshaw drivers, shopkeepers, and clerks concerned
with national issues. It also makes clear that few of these individuals
possessed separate organizations or articulated a sense of themselves as
a separate constituency. Only toward the end of this era, in a process
described in the following two chapters, would Tokyo's workers begin
to organize effectively on their own and tentatively begin to articulate
their separate interests. In so doing, they initially built upon the vision
of imperial democracy put forward in crowd actions.

Thus, as imperial democracy became a structure of rule, numerous
new working-class organizations both drew on and transformed the
traditions developed by the political crowd between 1905 and 1918.
They often worked in tandem with activists such as Fuse Tatsuji, and
opposed the newly entrenched bourgeois parties. To build a workers'
movement, they used speech-meetings, rallies, and demonstrations, all
actions familiar to the workers in Tokyo even before Suzuki Bunji
founded the Yūaikai in 1912. Labor simultaneously transformed the
older movement by articulating an ideology that broke out of the imperial democratic framework. Symbolic of this, it now chose a new date,
May Day (first celebrated in 1920), to replace February 11 as the time
for its annual public demonstration.

94. On the split response of Tokyo lawyers, see Narita Ryūichi, "Toshi minshū sōjō
to minponshugi," in *Kindai Nihon no tōgō to teikō*, ed. Kano Masanao and Yui Masa-
mitsu (Tokyo: Nihon hyōronsha, 1982), 3:65–66.

THREE

Labor Disputes and the Working Class in Tokyo

Factory workers not only attended rallies and joined in riots from 1905 to 1918. Between 1897 and 1917 they elaborated two additional forms of collective action: the labor dispute and labor unions. The early evolution of labor disputes in Tokyo is the concern of this chapter; the emergence of unions is addressed in chapter 4, as our focus narrows to the workers of Nankatsu.

Riots, disputes, and union-organizing together constituted the working-class dimension to the movement for imperial democracy. The rise of industrial capitalism helped provoke and shape the riots, and of course it stimulated and shaped the way laborers undertook disputes and formed unions. Naturally enough, the forms of workers' action and the language and concerns of their protest had much in common with the actions and ideas of those in the crowd.

The increase in labor disputes after 1897 was surely an inevitable social concomitant to the industrial revolution. There were just 24,961 industrial wage workers (*shokkō*) in Tokyo in 1896; by 1917 the number had risen to 140,940.[1] The twenty-six years from 1870 to 1896 had witnessed only 15 labor disputes in Tokyo, while 151 such events took place in the twenty years from 1897 to 1917. Yet capitalist industry did not stimulate disputes or unions in a simple fashion. At least three important factors together mediated in the movement-building process

---

1. *NRUS* 10:108, 113.

by which workers articulated demands for change and organized to achieve them.

Gender was one of these. Textile mills were one of two great employers of wage labor in the nineteenth century, but in the case of the mill operatives, who were predominantly female, the division of gender intersected with that of class to inhibit their protests.[2] Nationalism was a second factor shaping workers' consciousness and behavior. Textile production, mining, and then heavy industry emerged as Japan became an empire, and as Japan's rulers promoted the idea that the nation's people, the *kokumin*, shared at least the burden of support for empire. As a result, a new desire to share in the glory of the imperial nation-state became an important element of workers' consciousness. At times, this gave workers a motive to protest their treatment and demand recognition of their sacrifice and effort on behalf of national goals. But capitalists who owned the factories, and the bureaucrats and politicians who controlled the government, could also claim credit for making Japan an Asian empire. When defense of empire seemed to demand belt-tightening and sacrifice, national pride could deflect labor protest. Third, attitudes and actions rooted in the precapitalist era shaped the collective actions of the first generation of factory labor in Japan. Especially in the newer industries, the concern of workers with their social status and treatment by superiors, which often took precedence over concern with wages, had roots in features of the preindustrial social landscape.

Thus, while the evolving institutions of capitalism certainly conditioned a labor response, so did the process of nation-building, the rise of imperialism, the tenacity of gender divisions, and the preindustrial experience of workers. The need for class solidarity and the means to achieve it were not equally self-evident to all workers on becoming factory wage laborers. Rather, workers gradually learned to carry out labor disputes of increasing sophistication. In so doing, they created important traditions of protest even before the advent of self-identified union organizers.

---

2. Textile and heavy industrial workplaces each accounted for eight of the nation's thirty largest industrial or mining employers in 1909 (the remaining fourteen were coal or copper mines), but while twenty-four disputes took place at the eight heavy industrial sites prior to 1917, just twelve took place in the textile mills. See Ishii Kanji, *Nihon keizai shi* (Tokyo: University of Tokyo Press, 1976), pp. 180–89 for the list of the thirty largest firms. The count of disputes is drawn from Aoki, *Nenpyō*.

LABOR DISPUTES

The first surge of dispute activity in Tokyo came in the aftermath of the Sino-Japanese War (1894–95), stimulated in large measure by war-induced inflation and industrial expansion. Table 3.1 presents dispute data for Tokyo in this era, showing that workers in the full range of wage employment undertook these actions.

The variety of industries, workplace sizes, levels of technology, and types of labor make generalization risky, but at least two trends are evident. On one hand, even in the 1890s, those who labored in traditional trades possessed considerable ability to organize and make demands of employers. Ship carpenters formed effective citywide unions in both Yokohama and Tokyo, drawing on Edo-era guild practices to carry out several well-organized strikes in the late 1890s, while men and women in trades from building tradesmen and fabric dyers to actors, geisha, and licensed prostitutes also undertook several dozen dispute actions in the late nineteenth and early twentieth centuries; together these constituted a distinct stream of collective behavior. Yet it appears that these artisan organizations were hardly involved in the imperial democratic movement and exerted little influence upon workers in newer industries.[3]

Second, independently of this first stream of collective action, a new tradition of protest, part of the working-class dimension to the movement for imperial democracy, evolved in the heavily capitalized large worksites of the industrial revolution: shipyards, railroads, machine and printing shops, textile mills. It was this latter stream of collective action that had most in common with the ideas and behavior of the crowd and that later merged with the union movement.

That Meiji-era disputes of artisans in traditional crafts had social roots in the Edo era will not surprise readers familiar with European labor history of recent decades. Work by historians E. P. Thompson, William Sewell, and numerous others has stressed the impact of pre-industrial traditions of collective action and concepts of rights and corporate organization upon the efforts of wage laborers in industrial

3. For a detailed discussion of the organizations and disputes of artisans in traditional crafts, see Sumiya Mikio, *Nihon chin rōdō shi ron* (Tokyo: University of Tokyo Press, 1955), pp. 34–35, 280–88, and Andrew Gordon, "Labor Disputes and the Emergence of the Working Class in Japan, 1897–1917" (Working Papers in Asian/Pacific Studies, Duke University, 1985), pp. 4–11.

TABLE 3.1   LABOR DISPUTES IN TOKYO, BY INDUSTRY, 1870–1916

	1870–79	1880–89	1890–94	1895–99	1900–1904	1905–9	1910–14	1915–16	All
Heavy industry	0	0	1	6	3	8	1	1	20
Printing, binding	1	1	1	7	4	9	3	0	26
Artisans	1	0	6	15	7	10	2	1	42
Textiles	0	0	0	2	2	4	3	0	11
Transport	0	2	1	5	5	2	4	0	19
Chemical (rubber paper, glass)	0	0	0	1	4	2	0	2	9
Shoes	0	0	1	0	1	2	2	0	6
Services	0	0	0	4	4	3	2	0	13
Other	0	0	0	2	4	8	5	5	24
Total	2	3	10	42	34	48	22	9	170

SOURCE: Aoki Kōji, *Nihon rōdō undō shi nempyō* (Tokyo: Shinseisha, 1968).

society.[4] The true puzzle in the Japanese case is the lack of evident influence of these disputes upon those in other sectors. The several cases where artisans successfully organized unions and carried out disputes in the late nineteenth century offered inspiration or practical models to very few laborers or masters in newer trades. Admittedly, these artisans practiced precisely those crafts with the poorest future prospects. Large ships would require less carpentry in the future. As Yokoyama Gennosuke noted in 1899, "Year by year imports of machinery are increasing, and for instance at the Ishikawajima shipyard there is now a wood-cutting machine that can do in an instant the work that would take an entire day for a strong sawyer."[5] But in England a century earlier workers had wrecked the machines that threatened their beliefs and destroyed their livelihoods, and the industrial working class drew on such traditions of resistance. Considering the Japanese case from a Europe-centered perspective, one would expect the nineteenth-century organizations of the ship carpenters or sawyers to mark a stage in the transformation and spread of earlier forms of organization or dispute action, and one would expect resistance to new technology that devalued traditional skills.

Neither of these expectations is born out. Perhaps we should reverse our comparative lens and view the English workers as the anomaly. When the Luddites smashed power looms, the triumph of capitalist industry in their own society, not to mention the entire Western world, was not complete. Their resistance and the attempt to maintain an older moral economy were not ridiculous in the context of their society and age. The Japanese sawyers may have seen no chance to resist change; in any case, I have found no reports of machine-breaking. In addition, the artisan tradition to which the Japanese had access appears to have been more limited, and far more dependent on the feudal political order, than that of the English.[6] Assertive, well-organized groups such as the

4. E. P. Thompson, *The Making of the English Working Class* (New York: Pantheon Books, 1963). William H. Sewell, Jr., *Work and Revolution in France: The Language of Labor from the Old Regime to 1848* (Cambridge: Cambridge University Press, 1980).

5. Yokoyama Gennosuke, *Naichi zakkyo go no Nihon* (1898; reprint, Tokyo: Iwanami shoten, 1949), p. 15.

6. Nimura Kazuo, "Kigyō betsu kumiai no rekishi teki haikei," in Ohara Institute for Social Research, *Kenkyū shiryō geppō*, no. 305 (March 1984): 12–14. The tentative tone of this paragraph reflects my belief that fresh study of artisan labor in the Edo and Meiji eras is needed to better explain the relatively limited artisan legacy to twentieth-century disputes and the union movement.

ship carpenters may have been the exceptions, and artisans' organizations in general were perhaps too weak to contribute, either directly or indirectly, to a new tradition of disputes or a union movement among wage laborers.

LABOR IN MACHINE FACTORIES AND SHIPYARDS

From the late nineteenth century through World War I, workers in and around Tokyo taught themselves how to conduct labor disputes. Their success varied from industry to industry, although in almost all cases one sees a trajectory from relatively scattered, poorly planned actions to more effective ones. Whatever the reasons, workers in so-called modern industries—textile mills, printing shops, railroad yards, arsenals, or Western-style shipyards—drew little evident strength or inspiration from the concurrent efforts of artisans. Their disputes, beginning after the Sino-Japanese War, thus constituted a new stream of labor action. Centered on the work group and workplace, rarely involving all the workers at an enterprise, and almost never led by unions, these actions reflected the concern of factory laborers with matters beyond wages: treatment, respect, and social status. In railroads, heavy industry, and printing, a few key worksites or companies were home to several disputes each, and these places served as centers where workers built a dispute tradition.

Workers in railroads and printing were among the most precocious, the former perhaps because of the early development of the industry, the latter probably because of their literacy. By the end of World War I, aggressive printing unions were initiating actions such as a five-day strike in August 1919 of 600 printers at sixteen Tokyo newspapers. The Tokyo streetcar conductors were able to mobilize 6,000 employees in an effective three-day strike in 1912. As early as the 1890s, railway conductors and locomotive engineers, as well as railway yard machinists, organized some of the most effective disputes of the preunion era. The most important of these railway disputes took place at the Japan Railway Company (JRC), the oldest and largest privately owned rail service in the nation, with lines running from Tokyo as far north as Aomori. The first JRC disputes came in 1892 and 1893. Workers demanded and won semiannual bonuses, previously given only to white-collar staff. A dispute of locomotive engineers in 1898 over similar issues developed into a strike and also ended in victory for the workers.

The final dispute, of machinists in 1899 and early 1900, collapsed in the face of the newly enacted Public Order Police Law.[7]

The railway workers at the JRC in 1898 and 1899 were remarkably successful in organizing support at the company's widely scattered stations and machine factories. The strike's leaders in 1899 were skilled, mobile machinists, who appealed to a deeply felt desire for social respect and self-improvement as they moved easily in and out of the various JRC factories and between the JRC and other public and private enterprises of the region. The machinists demanded more respectable titles and better treatment, on a par with the recently elevated locomotive engineers. In particular, they sought more rapid promotions, a program of semiannual pay raises and bonuses, and reform of a confiscatory savings plan.[8]

In spite of their strong organization, the machinists failed to win their demands. Managers were determined to strengthen control over the work force and prevent further militance. They fired several leaders of the movement, and when the Public Order Police Law took effect just as the demands were presented, the remaining leaders gave up the struggle.

Several important features of these disputes at the Japan Railway Company were to recur in shipyards and arsenals in subsequent years. No union led the 1892–93 or 1898 disputes, and in 1899 the workers themselves organized a dispute group first, and only then sought out the support of the Ironworkers' Union.[9] Also, the contrast between the limited, loosely organized actions of 1892–93 and the more sustained actions of 1898 and 1899 suggests that the railway workers learned over time to organize more effectively. Finally, respect, improved status, and an end to "discriminatory treatment" were critical issues for these men, as they pushed reluctant managers for titles connoting higher status and the bonuses and regular pay raises already offered white-collar officials and technicians.

The pride and comraderie of the locomotive engineers, masters of the great symbol of the modern age, may well account for their early initia-

---

7. Aoki Masahisa, "Nittetsu kikankata sōgi no kenkyū," *Rōdō undō shi kenkyū*, no. 62 (1979): 11–32.

8. Ikeda Makoto, "Nihon tetsudō kikaikō no tōsō," *Rōdō undō shi kenkyū*, no. 62 (1979): 60–61, 66–71.

9. Ibid., pp. 58–59.

tives. But the machinists at the Japan Railway Company built a similar organization and felt similar concerns. The railroad disputes foreshadowed the most sustained, portentous stream of labor activity in this era, that of the shipbuilders, machinists, and metal workers in heavy industry.

Throughout Japan, seventy-five disputes took place at heavy industrial enterprises between 1878 and 1916 (see table 3.2), and with the exception of five actions by ship carpenters in Tokyo and Yokohama, all in the 1890s, none of these involved unions. Disputes were particularly common in the largest shipyards and arsenals, which made use of the full variety of labor found in the heavy industrial sector: lathe work, machine finishing and assembling, metalcasting, boilermaking, ship repair, and ship assembly. As table 3.3 reveals, all but two of the thirteen major shipbuilders and arsenals experienced at least one dispute in this period. More interesting, well over half of all heavy industrial disputes took place in just ten of the largest enterprises.

The Mitsubishi shipyards in Nagasaki and Kobe, the Kawasaki shipyard in Kobe, the Uraga and Yokohama Dock Companies, the Kure and Yokosuka Naval Arsenals, the Osaka Ironworks, and, in Tokyo, the Koishikawa Arsenal and Ishikawajima shipyard accounted for forty-nine of the seventy-five disputes (65 percent). These enterprises produced social change as well as ships and cannon shells. They were sites where a self-conscious working class evolved and laid the groundwork for the far more numerous, better-organized disputes during World War I that began to produce a sense of crisis among Japanese elites.

Between the turn of the century and World War I, capitalist development both changed the scale and organization of heavy industrial workplaces and influenced workers' actions. Japan's emergence as an imperial power in Asia directly and indirectly channeled capital to heavy industry. The government founded the Yahata Steel Works with 600,000 yen from the massive indemnity from the Sino-Japanese War. This extraordinary influx of 360 million yen, 4.5 times the 1893 national budget, also enabled the government to enact subsidy programs in 1896 for the shipping and shipbuilding industries.[10]

10. One program subsidized the production of 267 ships, totaling approximately one million tons, by 1917; another encouraged rapidly expanding Japanese shippers to purchase new ships from domestic manufacturers. William D. Wray, *Mitsubishi and the N.Y.K., 1870–1914: Business Strategy in the Japanese Shipping Industry* (Cambridge, Mass.: Harvard University Council on East Asian Studies, 1985), pp. 304, 306, 458, 502.

TABLE 3.2   LABOR DISPUTES IN HEAVY INDUSTRY
NATIONWIDE, 1878–1916

Date	All Disputes	Strikes/Violence	Demands/Petitions
1878	1	0	1
1893	1	0	1
1897	8	4	4
1898	3	2	1
1899	0	0	0
1900	1	0	1
1901	0	0	0
1902	3	2	1
1903	2	1	1
1904	1	1	0
1905	2	1	1
1906	6	4	2
1907	13	8	5
1908	6	2	4
1909	3	2	1
1910	6	4	2
1911	2	1	1
1912	3	2	1
1913	3	1	2
1914	3	0	3
1915	1	1	0
1916	7	6	1
Total	75	42	33

SOURCE: Aoki Kōji, *Nihon rōdō undō shi nenpyō* (Tokyo: Shinseisha, 1968).
NOTE: No disputes in 1879–92 or 1894–96.

TABLE 3.3   DISPUTES AT MAJOR SHIPYARDS AND ARSENALS

Enterprise	Number of Employees (1909)		Disputes, 1897–1916
Kure Naval Arsenal	20,917	4	(1902, 1906, 1907, 1912)
Koishikawa Army Arsenal, Tokyo	12,561	4	(1902, 1906 [2], 1908)
Yokosuka Naval Arsenal	11,569	5	(1897 [2], 1907 [2], 1910)
Osaka Arsenal	8,075	0	
Sasebo Naval Arsenal	5,591	1	(1908)
Mitsubishi shipyard, Nagasaki	5,389	5	(1903, 1907, 1908 [2], 1913)
Maizuru Naval Arsenal	3,762	0	
Kawasaki shipyard, Kobe	2,640	3	(1907, 1908, 1914)
Osaka Ironworks	1,533	6	(1903, 1905, 1907, 1911, 1914, 1916)
Mitsubishi shipyard, Kobe	1,477	4	(1907, 1909, 1913, 1916)
Uraga Dock Company	1,346	6	(1905, 1907 [2], 1910, 1911, 1915)
Yokohama Dock Company	1,200	8	(1897 [3], 1898, 1907, 1910, 1911, 1916)
Ishikawajima shipyard, Tokyo	800	3	(1897, 1900, 1906)
Total		49	

SOURCE: Aoki Kōji, *Nihon rōdō undō shi nenpyō* (Tokyo: Shinseisha, 1968).

The resulting investment in more sophisticated technology in the shipyards put pressure on managers to control labor more effectively. They began to impose direct control over laborers whom they had previously managed through a system of internal contracting mediated by labor bosses or master workmen known as *oyakata*. This change came to different enterprises at different times between about 1900 and World War I. As it did, the independent *oyakata* were converted to, or replaced by, foremen integrated into a management hierarchy, and the common position of workers as wage laborers under the direct control of a company gradually became clearer.

From the time of the early surge of unrest at these worksites to the eve of World War I, heavy industrial laborers gained significantly in their ability to coordinate activities and carry out disputes. As they did so, workers in this technically advanced sector drew upon concepts with recognizably pre-Meiji antecedents.[11] In the actions of workers at the Uraga Dock Company around the time of the Russo-Japanese War, according to an *Asahi* reporter, a "time-honored sense of obligation [*giri*]" drew workers together in their occasional protests. The term for obligation, *giri*, had roots in the Tokugawa past, and it represented a critical social value. Its use suggested that feelings of solidarity among fellow workers set them in opposition to the company, even at this very early stage in the history of large-scale industry, when the company had only been operating for five years. Its use also reveals that "Japanese cultural values" could work to sanction resistance to authority.[12]

At the same time, the ability of workers themselves to *organize* on the basis of such feelings was little developed in these early actions. The work group and the workshop were the natural bases for their protest, including petitioning and selection of representatives. The typical use of a petition signed by all those in a workshop calls to mind the custom of the village petition, often the prelude to a peasant rising in the Tokugawa era. But workers made few advance plans, and these disputes usually involved only a portion of the company's workshops.

In addition, skillful managers could also seek to build from the value of *giri* a sense of obligation of worker to company, and, beyond this, to the nation. In the Uraga case, the navy was in fact a major customer, and managers readily invoked the glory of the empire to motivate the workers. When the company won an order for two naval ships in 1919, management issued a notice to all employees announcing that "the recent war has clearly shown that a nation's strength lies in its industry, and in the future we want you to consider yourselves not mere employees of a profit-making company but participants in a national enterprise."[13]

11. Although it is important to note that these concepts were not those of pre-Meiji artisans in particular, but rather more generally held social values.

12. It is interesting, as well, that this notion of obligation is seen to have been a key value promoting solidarity among opponents to the Narita airport in the 1960s and 1970s. See David E. Apter and Nagayo Sawa, *Against the State: Politics and Social Protest in Japan* (Cambridge, Mass.: Harvard University Press, 1984), p. 181: "It is this sense of obligation (*giri*) that was perhaps the most essential quality of the Hantai Dōmei itself."

13. See Andrew Gordon, *The Evolution of Labor Relations in Japan: Heavy Industry, 1853–1955* (Cambridge, Mass.: Harvard University Council on East Asian Studies, 1985), p. 112.

By the eve of the World War I boom, heavy industrial workers acted in concert with significantly more sophistication than a decade before. The case of laborers at one particularly well documented shipyard, the Uraga Dock Company, about fifty miles down the coast from Tokyo, demonstrates this nicely. The organizing abilities of workers at this yard clearly advanced between several disputes of 1905–7 and 1910–11. Business troubles put workers in a defensive position at the outset in both 1907 and 1910–11, but in 1910 they were able to win a pay raise, and they forced the company president to step down the next year. In contrast to disputes at Uraga in 1905 and 1907, where small work groups acted independently with little planning, workers discussed the wage issue in advance of the 1910 strike and made sufficient preparations to leave the shipyard en masse as soon as the wage demand was denied. They coped with police harassment by meeting in relatively small groups indoors in local restaurants or bars. Only on the first day of the strike did the police have an opportunity to disperse a large gathering of workers. Also, in 1910–11 virtually the entire work force joined the action.

By the time of a far more complex, lengthy, and contentious strike at Uraga in 1915, the shipbuilding workers possessed a sense of common interest transcending separate shop interests and setting the regular men against the company. The decision of several hundred workers to join the strike out of an obligation to fellow workers in other sections of the yard, even though they disagreed with them on the issue at hand, recalls the *Asahi* reporter's observation of worker solidarity and obligation a decade before. The difference between 1905 and 1915 at Uraga lay in the ability to act in concert on this incipient working-class consciousness.

The improving ability of heavy industrial workers to organize nonunion disputes is evident as well in the fact that only one of thirty-one disputes at the ten major heavy industrial sites before 1910, at the Koishikawa Arsenal in Tokyo in 1908, involved more than three-fourths of the work force, and this dispute did not develop into a work stoppage. Of the thirteen disputes at these sites between 1910 and 1916, in contrast, four involved almost all the workers at the enterprise.

In the incident at the Koishikawa Arsenal, as in so many others, issues of arbitrary or "inhuman" treatment were important to workers. As Katayama Sen described it in imperfect but effective English:

> Government arsenal has been treating its employees in the most cruel manner. They cannot go to the W.C. without a permission ticket during recess.

The number of the tickets is only 4 for a hundred workers, consequently some must wait five hours, which would be deplorable as well as detrimental to their health. Every and all little mistakes are fined at least 5 hours' earnings. They are fined 10 to 20 hours' earnings if they forget any thing their personal belongings. They are now limited to drink hot water in the meal time. It shows how they are treated in the arsenal, and being unbearable at the treatment, they 15,000 in number in a body petitioned the authorities for the immediate remedy with a tacit threat of a strike.[14]

LABOR IN TEXTILE MILLS

A dozen or so huge textile mills were the major employers of factory labor in Tokyo, and especially in the Nankatsu region, through the early days of World War I. About 75 percent of the workers were women. Male and female workers tended to act separately, and the gender division shaped their protests. At the same time, their demands and modes of organizing placed their actions in the mainstream of the new tradition of nonunion disputes in modern industry.

Considering their numbers, the centrality of their product in Japan's industrial revolution, and the fact that low wages and difficult working conditions placed them in perhaps the worst objective situation of any group of workers, disputes of mill workers were actually relatively infrequent. Before the 1920s most disputes that did occur were brief, with relatively little planning. The leaders were often the minority of male employees at a mill, and the preunion disputes rarely involved the entire work force. This was not for lack of numbers or grievances. In 1912 Tokyo's 36,750 textile workers accounted for 43 percent of all the city's wage workers. Of these, 76 percent (27,897) were women, and half of all textile workers were under twenty. In contrast to the average ten to eleven hours of work per day in the machine industry, twelve- to fourteen-hour days were common in the textile mills. Typical wages for textile women stood at twenty to thirty sen per day, and pay for the male textile workers ranged from thirty to fifty-five sen, both well below the range for machinists of forty-five to seventy-five sen per day.[15] In addition, the poorly ventilated mills produced tuberculosis at a rate that soon made Japan a world leader in this disease.

Several factors account for the apparent quiescence of the millhands. The young girls in the textile mills considered their employment a temporary stage, not a lifetime occupation. After the 1880s they usually

14. *Shakai shinbun*, March 8, 1908, p. 4. Katayama wrote this for the paper's column of English-language news briefs.
15. Tōkyō-fu, ed., *Tōkyō-fu tōkei sho* (Tokyo, 1912), pp. 150–51.

lived in dormitories and enjoyed virtually no freedom of movement. The men who led some textile disputes were commuters, who would have had difficulty planning concerted actions with the female majority in the dorms, but lack of interest in joint action was probably a bigger obstacle than the dormitories. Also, the fact that foremen were often men, while the rank and file were women, made less likely the cooperation of foremen and subordinates, so important in other disputes of the preunion era. Among the women themselves, rapid turnover inhibited the creation and passing on of their own tradition of resistance to factory bosses. They did compose and pass on songs about mill life that clearly reflect their creation of a factory culture of anger, despair, yet hope for a better life, but until the 1920s the most common form of protest produced by this culture was escape, not dispute.[16]

Despite these obstacles, textile workers did on occasion raise demands and organize disputes. In the 1880s and 1890s, before many companies had adopted the dormitory system and tightened control of the female workers, disputes of women alone were particularly frequent.[17] In the early 1910s, some of the first disputes even indirectly involving the new Yūaikai union, introduced below, took place in the textile mills of Minami Katsushika County.

In June of 1914, Tokyo Muslin, one of the oldest and largest mills in the city, and three other major producers decided to take joint action in the face of a depressed business climate. All four manufacturers cut back operations by half. Tokyo Muslin then fired 1,110 employees, both men and women, and cut pay roughly 40 to 50 percent for some of those remaining. But the action that truly angered the men who later came to seek Yūaikai mediation was the company's continued payment of bonuses to executives and dividends to shareholders (the other three companies all reportedly postponed or cancelled shareholder dividends). On the night of June 18, the 350 remaining male employees met in a public hall near the factory and drew up a petition to revoke the pay cut. The next day all 2,800 workers went on strike. Within two

16. In addition to the factors noted in this paragraph, a few textile owners or managers concerned with the cost of high turnover began to implement a range of so-called "paternal" practices in the early twentieth century, although I remain skeptical as to the effect of such policies on lowering the level of discontent. See Hazama Hiroshi, *Nihon rōmu kanri shi kenkyū* (Tokyo: Dayamondosha, 1969), ch. 3, esp. pp. 302–18. For a strong critique of scholars who dismiss out of hand the potential of textile women to act to change their situation, which translates several songs of the textile workers, see E. Patricia Tsurumi, "Female Textile Workers and the Failure of Early Trade Unionism in Japan," *History Workshop*, no. 18 (August 1984).

17. Tsurumi, "Female Texile Wokers," p. 16.

days the matter appeared settled, as the company promised to restore pay to existing levels by December. The men went back to work, but the 2,450 women were not satisfied. Their agenda was rather more basic. In a meeting between company executives and several female worker representatives on June 21, they demanded and gained a promise of shorter hours and better food.

Emboldened by these successes, the men at Tokyo Muslin decided to form a union. A group of 78 representatives of each work group again met at the nearby hall to draw up a union charter proclaiming their goals to be mutual aid, development of skills, and the progress of the company. When the company fired twelve union leaders on June 14 and ordered the others to disband their group or quit, a strike appeared imminent. Several dozen workers left their jobs on hearing this news, and the 242 union members assembled the next day, a holiday, in a hall in Kameido Park.

The union chairman addressed the gathering, with police observing. He claimed that women workers in the dorm were being beaten for stopping work in sympathy with the new union, and the group set a meeting for the next day. Before this took place, the chairman was arrested for allegedly implying in his speech that a riot might greet continued management repression. The workers' resolve quickly crumbled, and union members all signed pledges to disband their group and return to work.[18]

The issues that moved these men and women to act were of a piece with those provoking resistance in other new industries: job security, wage security, and fair treatment. The meeting in the park and alleged threat of a riot reveal overlap with patterns of urban crowd activity as well. In addition, however, the men and women acted separately, if sympathetically, in both June and July, and the concern with such basic human needs as edible food and sufficient rest, found among the women in this and other textile disputes, suggests that their point of departure was rather different from that of the men. Continued unrest in the textile mills, studied below, will show that neither the women nor the men were by nature uniquely susceptible to claims of paternal solicitude or incapable of opposing management. Yet not until the 1920s did the textile women begin to overcome both the obstacle of the dormitory system and the tendency of union organizers to ignore them. Eventually

18. *Yūai shinpō*, July 15, 1914, p. 4; August 1, 1914, p. 7; September 1, 1914, pp. 3–4; October 1, 1914, pp. 3–6.

they organized and pressed disputes in the textile mills of Tokyo, Osaka, and elsewhere over several years. This movement produced some of the bitterest, most electrifying labor struggles of the prewar era.[19]

THE LABOR DISPUTE
AS A NEW TRADITION

Precapitalist structures shaped the disputes of this era directly only when artisans such as the Tokyo ship carpenters drew on a Tokugawa heritage of craft organization. In disputes of railway workers, shipbuilders, and textile operatives in Nankatsu such craft traditions themselves had no evident impact, but industrial wage workers nonetheless both invoked "time-honored" concepts of loyalty and obligation and organized in a manner reminiscent of earlier generations of peasant protestors. The place of foremen as guarantors in the Uraga dispute of 1915 resembled that of village headmen, and observers at the time sometimes compared factory to village and foreman to headman.[20] Thus, in nonunion disputes, as in the urban riots, workers and other city-dwellers in some ways recreated traditions of the preindustrial past to protest and resist their degradation or impoverishment in a rapidly changing present. Many of those who manned the bureaucracy, invested in or managed factories, and dominated the political parties during these years and later also sought a usable past, invoking "tradition" to the different end of social control.

At the same time, and again as in the case of the crowd, new and changing structures of a capitalist economy, imperialism, and a national polity shaped these disputes. The story of industrial labor involved much more than a simple transfer of village traditions of either protest or obedience to the factory setting. The contrast between the disputes of the time of the Russo-Japanese War and those of the early years of World War I indicates that workers only gradually, over a decade of sporadic unrest, developed the ability to act on perceived common interest.

One influential element in the evolving capitalist structure was the managerial imposition of direct control over laborers. The shipbuilding workers revealed a sense of mutual obligation as early as 1905, but as the direct control exerted by the company increased they became more willing and able to act on their sense of common interest and raise

19. See chapter 9.
20. See *Shibaura seisakujo 65 nen shi* (Tokyo: Tokyo Shibaura denki kabushiki gaisha, 1940), pp. 38–39, for one example.

issues of "unbearable treatment." Before World War I, workers protested policies of direct control that restricted their freedom or relative
autonomy in the workplace. The Koishikawa Arsenal, for example,
was arguably the most hierarchic, tightly controlled worksite in the
nation.[21] At the arsenal, and at other industrial sites, workers reacted to
new management policies by organizing increasingly effective disputes.

Nonunion strikes and resistance to new management policy thus had
roots in the changing nature of social relations in the workplace and the
production process, as well as in preindustrial social values, traditions
of protest, and concern with social status. Separate actions at various
companies had similar goals of modifying coercive forms of control and
ending arbitrary treatment, and the several dozen disputes at major
heavy industrial firms between about 1900 and the middle of World
War I thus constituted an early stage in the construction of a working-
class movement in Japan.

The labor dispute and the political crowd became related parts of
Japanese urban and working-class culture in these early years of the
twentieth century. Several other important streams of thought and action emerged concurrently: the activities of union organizers and intellectuals such as Katayama Sen and Takano Fusatarō in the late 1890s,
socialists such as Kōtoku Shusui in the early 1900s, and moderate union
organizers such as Suzuki Bunji after 1912. As the following chapters
will show, during and after World War I the nonunion dispute tradition
and these other streams began to flow together, producing by the 1920s
a new urban culture of which the labor union and labor dispute were
integral parts.

21. Miyake Akimasa, "Kindai Nihon ni okeru tekkō kumiai no kōseiin," *Rekishigaku
kenkyū*, no. 454 (March 1978): 24–32, on labor management and worker response at
the Koishikawa Arsenal. On other enterprises, see Miyake Akimasa, "Nichiro sensō
zengo no rōdōsha undō: jūkōgyō daikeiei o chūshin to shite," *Shakai keizai shigaku* 44,
no. 5 (March 1979), and Nishinarita Yutaka, "Nichiro sensō zengo ni okeru zaibatsu
zōsen kigyō no keiei kikō to rōshi kankei: Mitsubishi zōsenjo no bunseki," *Ryūgoku
daigaku keizai keiei ronshū* 18, nos. 1–4, (June 1978–March 1979).

FOUR

Building a Labor Movement

Nankatsu Workers and the Yūaikai

As they set up temporary headquarters in local bars or restaurants, drew up demands, and met in public halls to elect representatives, the men and women who joined nonunion disputes proved able to organize themselves to increasingly good effect by World War I. But the absence of formal, permanent organizations—that is, labor unions—certainly limited their impact and potential gains.

Men in a few trades with preindustrial roots, such as the ship carpenters in the 1890s, had organized effective unions.[1] In addition, some heavy industrial workers in the 1880s and 1890s sporadically sought to create labor unions. In Tokyo the earliest such endeavor was the Union for Industrial Progress, founded in 1889 by a skilled master shipbuilder at the Ishikawajima yard and disbanded shortly thereafter. The more successful Ironworkers' Union, founded in late 1897, drew support from some of the same men and reached a peak of some three thousand members in a variety of heavy industrial trades at public and private firms throughout the Kantō region: lathe work, machine finishing, boilermaking, metalcasting, and wrought-iron work.[2] But the Iron-

---

1. Yokoyama Gennosuke describes the interesting attempt of the rickshaw pullers to organize a union that would have set terms of entry into the trade and controlled wage rates in his *Nihon no kasō shakai* (1899; reprint, Tokyo: Iwanami shoten, 1949), pp. 176–81. Translated by Eiji Yutani as "*Nihon no kasō shakai* of Yokoyama Gennosuke" (Ph.D. diss., University of California, Berkeley, 1985).

2. For a recent study of the Ironworkers' Union, see Stephen Marsland, *The Birth of the Japanese Labor Movement: Takano Fusatarō and the Rōdō Kumiai Kiseikai* (Honolulu: University Press of Hawaii, 1989). See also Andrew Gordon, "Workers, Managers, and

workers' Union collapsed in early 1900, in part because of repression under Article 17 of the Public Order Police Law of March 1900,[3] but primarily because the skilled leaders of working-class society at the turn of the century, the *oyakata* masters, were pushed by changing technology and management strategies to secure their own positions at the expense of building a movement. This led them to side with employers in some cases and to seek independent status as small factory owners in others. Working-class society in the late 1890s, at the start of the era of the nonunion dispute, did not offer the organizers of the Ironworkers' Union a solid base on which to build a sustained union movement.

THE WORKERS OF NANKATSU

Over the next fifteen years the context of labor activity changed significantly. New nonunion patterns of lower-class collective action emerged, and an ideology of imperial democracy spread among city-dwellers, including factory workers. In addition, managers revised their strategies of labor control as workplaces increased in size and complexity.[4] Together these changes enabled workers to organize with new vigor and commitment. As a result, the Yūaikai emerged in the period from 1912 until the end of World War I, and after the war, unions began to coalesce with traditions of nonunion protest. This halting process of movement-building is the concern of this chapter and several of those to follow.

To give focus to our inquiry, the men and women in the industrial neighborhoods of Nankatsu, who engaged our attention briefly as participants in the crowd actions and labor disputes of the early 1900s, will

---

Bureaucrats in Japan" (Ph.D. diss., Harvard University, 1981), ch. 3, and Aoki Masahisa, "Nittetsu kikankata sōgi no kenkyū," *Rōdō undō shi kenkyū*, no. 62 (1979): 11–32.

3. This law forbad "violence, threats, public defamation, agitation, or solicitation directed at others" for any of several purposes: encouraging *or* obstructing entry into an organization intended to take joint actions concerning labor conditions or pay; carrying out a joint work stoppage *or* a mass dismissal of workers; forcing the consent of "the other side" in regard to pay or labor conditions. The symmetrical treatment of workers and managers reflected the classical liberal European legal precedents from which the law was derived. In theory it limited employer organizations and restricted managerial coercion to the same extent that it constrained workers and their unions. Further, it did not outlaw unions as such, but forbad certain types of actions on their behalf. Given a more lenient interpretation in the 1910s and 1920s, the law offered unions a slight, but important, breathing space.

4. See Andrew Gordon, *The Evolution of Labor Relations in Japan: Heavy Industry, 1853–1955* (Cambridge, Mass.: Harvard University Council on East Asian Studies, 1985), ch. 2, on changes in labor-management relations with the imposition of direct management.

be the main characters. "Nankatsu" is the Japanese abbreviation for Minami Katsushika County, a sprawling district of both industrial neighborhoods close to the city and largely agricultural land to the east of the Arakawa drainage canal, but it was used colloquially by workers in the era under study to refer to the industrial sections. In this book, I follow this less formal practice and use "Nankatsu" or "Nankatsu region" to indicate the triangular region of factories and working-class housing bounded by Tokyo Bay, the Sumida River, and the Arakawa Canal. In administrative terms, this Nankatsu region includes the city wards of Honjo and Fukagawa, among the most densely populated sections of Tokyo, and the adjacent villages and towns of Minami Katsushika County (Sumida, Terashima, Azuma, Kameido, Ōjima, Suna, and Komatsugawa; see map 2).[5]

In the Edo era the wards close by the Sumida River had been home to several clusters of artisanal and commercial activity: dyeing, copperwork, and metalcasting in Honjo, and the lumberyards of Fukagawa.[6] In the late nineteenth century, the concentrated development of smaller factories continued in these densely populated inner wards, while a handful of large factories with several hundred employees each were scattered through Honjo ward. In addition, several of the nation's largest textile firms built major factories of several thousand employees each in the less crowded villages of Kameido, Terashima, and Azuma to the east. Kanebō and Tokyo Muslin built mills in 1889 and 1896; Fujibō, Nihon Bōseki, Tōyō Muslin, and Tokyo Calico followed between 1903 and 1908.[7]

Its great heterogeneity, and the great tragedy and drama that visited

---

5. In 1923 the population density of Honjo was 450 people per hectare, second only to Asakusa. Average density in the industrial sections of the county was only about 80 per hectare. Minami Katsushika–gun yakusho, *Minami Katsushika–gun shi* (1923; reprint, Tokyo: Meiji bunken, 1973), pp. 285–88. Although the concentration of factories and working-class neighborhoods in the region, the contemporary perception of "Nankatsu" as a coherent place, and the clear boundaries of river, canal, and bay justify the demarcation of Nankatsu described above, readers should be aware that the statistics used throughout the book must follow administrative boundaries used in official surveys that do not coincide precisely with our "Nankatsu" region. In particular, data for Minami Katsushika County cover the agricultural portions of the county to the east of the Arakawa Canal as well as industrial Nankatsu. However, the impact of these data on our picture of Nankatsu is negligible; the industrial areas of the county accounted for roughly 90 percent of factory laborers and labor disputes in the decades under study.

6. Sumiya Mikio, ed., *Keihin kōgyō chitai* (Tokyo: Tōkei shinsho, 1964), pp. 34–36.

7. Tokyo Muslin and Tōyō Muslin were two independent textile mills, but some confusion is forgiven. Contemporary observers mixed them up on occasion too! Both experienced major labor disputes at different times.

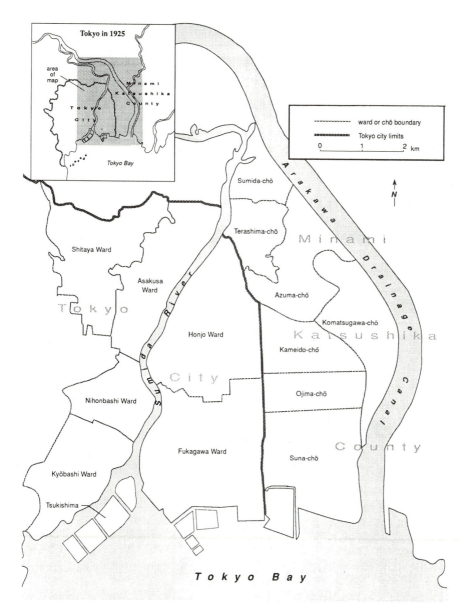

Map 2.   Nankatsu Region, 1925

it on occasion, recommend Nankatsu as a candidate for close study. By the Yūaikai era its factories ranged from Tokyo's largest textile mills and a few major machine or rolling-stock factories (the Hattori Watch Company, maker of Seikō watches; Hitachi; Japan Rolling Stock; and the Locomotive Manufacturing Company) to dozens of medium-sized firms producing rubber, soap, fertilizer, sugar, bicycles, machine parts, and more, to hundreds of tiny workshops of all types; its unions came to include every major prewar stream of organizing, beginning with the Yūaikai and branching out to include anarchist, moderate socialist, and communist unions, and even right-wing "anti-union" unions.

This area, in particular Honjo and Fukagawa wards, constituted the unromantic underside of Tokyo's "Low City," lovingly described by Edward Seidensticker in *Low City, High City*, his nostalgic tour of the capital in the early 1900s. These working-class wards lacked the entertainments and cultural energy of the heart of the Low City in Asakusa. A character in one of Nagai Kafū's stories, wandering through a Honjo neighborhood, offers an outsider's lyrical perception of the grimy landscape of the working-class wards in 1909:

> They walk[ed] toward the Ryūganji [Temple] along the Oshiage Canal. In the low noonday tide, the muddy bottom of the canal lay bare to the April sun, and gave off a considerable odor. Industrial soot floated down from somewhere, and from somewhere came the noise of industrial machinery. The houses along the way were on a lower level than the road. Housewives in the dark interiors, busy at piecework of various sorts to round out family budgets, and indifferent to the warmth of the spring day, were quite exposed to the passing eye. On dirty boards at the corners of houses were pasted advertisements for medicine and fortune tellers, and scattered among them were notices that factory girls were needed. . . .
>
> . . . The earth was dark and damp, the streets were narrow, and so twisted that he expected to find himself up a blind alley. Mossy shingled roofs, rotting foundations, leaning pillars, dirty planks, drying rags and diapers, pots and cheap sweets for sale—the dreary little houses went on in endless disorder, and when on occasion he would be surprised by an imposing gate, it would always be a factory.[8]

Nagai's (and Seidensticker's) appreciation, even with its stark imagery of darkness, dreariness, disorder and monotony, aestheticizes the unpleasantness and thereby probably distances and obscures it from

---

8. Edward Seidensticker, *Kafū the Scribbler: The Life and Writings of Nagai Kafū, 1879–1959* (Stanford: Stanford University Press, 1965), pp. 212–13, 214–15.

TABLE 4.1 FACTORIES IN THE NANKATSU REGION AND ALL TOKYO, 1907–12

Factory Size	1907	1912
Nankatsu Region		
50–99 workers	26	39
100+ workers	27	49
Total	53	88
All Tokyo		
50–99 workers	105	137
100+ workers	84	128
Total	189	265

SOURCE: Keishichō, *Keishichō tōkei sho,* 1907, 1912.
NOTE: Nankatsu region = Honjo and Fukagawa wards and Minami Katsushika County.

the reader. Nagai, after all, was a visitor to Nankatsu when he wrote this story in 1909; he lived rather more comfortably in the "High City" of the western suburbs. The perspective of the resident was different. The 1923 *Gazetteer of Minami Katsushika County* lamented the "tremendous impact" of air, water, and noise pollution generated by untreated industrial waste, indiscriminate dumping, unmuffled machinery, and loud factory whistles. Although workers depended on the factories for their livelihoods, residents and workers occasionally appealed to local authorities in ad hoc groups or through their new unions for relief from the noise or odor of a particularly offensive worksite.[9]

Nagai's description of Nankatsu dates from the early years of a surge of industrial growth in the capital. The factory labor force in Tokyo roughly tripled in the years between the turn of the century and World War I, reaching 90,000 men and women by 1914. Their workplaces, as Nagai noted, were often imposing brick structures standing well above a surrounding sea of one- or two-story wooden tenements and smaller shops, and they were changing the urban landscape. Table 4.1 shows the rise over this timespan in the number of medium- and large-scale enterprises in the Nankatsu region. Most growth, at least among larger factories, came after the Russo-Japanese War.

9. *Minami Katsushika–gun shi,* pp. 430, 441. For a protest several years later against a rubber factory causing sleeplessness and illness to residents, see *Rōdō shūhō,* November 28, 1922, p. 3.

THE YŪAIKAI

In Nankatsu and throughout the Tokyo environs, the Yūaikai enjoyed
far greater success than the Ironworkers' Union of a decade before. This
was not simply because of the charisma and organizing acumen of
Suzuki Bunji, although by all reports the man cut an impressive figure.[10]
Suzuki founded his "Friendly Society" in a church basement in central
Tokyo late in 1912 with thirteen artisans and factory workers, and by
1915 he had built an organization of some fifteen thousand dues-paying
members. Renamed the Dai Nihon rōdō sōdōmei (Greater Japan General Federation of Labor) in 1919, the union was to survive until 1940,
making it by far the longest-lived labor organization in prewar Japan.
(I shall refer to the renamed group by its abbreviated label, Sōdōmei.)

How can we account for the emergence of the first stable organization of wage laborers at this particular moment in Japanese history?
The economic and political transformations discussed in chapter 1—the
rise of the nation-state, capitalism, and empire—fueled the movement
for imperial democracy and allowed the political crowd to emerge.
They also led to both quantitative and qualitative changes in Japanese
working-class society that help explain the contrast between the abortive organizing efforts of the late nineteenth century and Suzuki Bunji's
more successful attempt.

First, the rapid spread to the workers and others among the urban
poor of education, literacy, and the habit of newspaper reading was
a product of nation- and empire-building policies that allowed the
Yūaikai leaders to communicate with their members more effectively
than their predecessors in the Ironworkers' Union had done.

Second, Japan's position as Asia's only imperial power helped transform the economy and urban society in the first two decades of the
century, providing a new social base for the success of the Yūaikai.
From the time of the Ironworkers' Union to the era of the early Yūaikai,
Tokyo's factory labor force tripled, from about 30,000 to 90,000.
Thus, when the Yūaikai first came to the region, Nankatsu was already
a growing manufacturing center of over 1,000 factories, with about
40,000 men and women in a diverse array of chemical (rubber, soap,
fertilizer), machine, and textile enterprises. Given such an industrial
base and the nation's established export routes, Japan rushed to fill the
vacuum created by Europe's wartime retreat from economic competi-

---

10. For a biographical treatment of Suzuki in these years, see Stephen Large, *The Rise
of Labor in Japan: The Yūaikai, 1912–1919* (Tokyo: Sophia University, 1972).

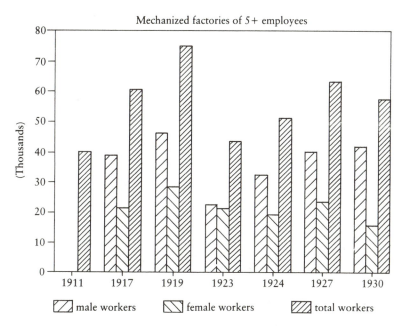

Graph 4.1.   Factory Labor in the Nankatsu Region

SOURCES: Data for 1911 from *Minami Katsushika–gun shi* (1923); for 1917–30 from Tōkyō-fu, *Tōkyō-fu tōkei sho*. Statistics are for December of each year. The 1923 data were compiled just three months after the earthquake.

NOTE: Nankatsu region = Honjo and Fukagawa wards and Minami Katsushika County.

tion in Asia, and the urban work force further grew in numbers, density, and diversity. Nankatsu became one of the nation's major industrial centers, and by 1919, at the peak of the war boom, its labor force had swollen to over 74,000 men and women (see graph 4.1). The economic and social environment could hardly have been more favorable for the fledgling Yūaikai.

As before, many of these workers were recent migrants to the city, but several significant shifts in the composition of the work force took place during and after the war.[11] First, the proportion employed in textile mills declined sharply, even though the absolute number rose, for the number and percentage working in the heavy and chemical industries increased far more rapidly (see graph 4.2). Other changes followed

11. Well over half the residents in the industrial wards of Nankatsu County were migrants in the early 1920s. *Minami Katsushika–gun shi*, p. 295.

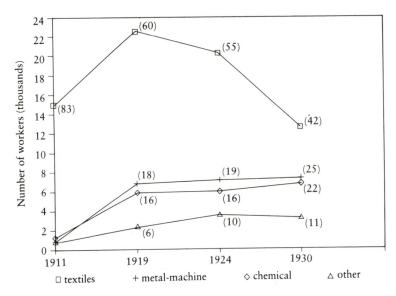

Graph 4.2. Wage Labor by Sector, Minami Katsushika County, 1911–30

SOURCES: Data for 1911 from *Minami Katsushika–gun shi*; for 1919 and 1930 from *Tōkyō-fu, Tōkyō-fu tōkei sho*; for 1924 from *Tokyo kōjō yōran*.

NOTES: The 1919 data are slightly inflated, as they count workers in factories with fewer than five employees. All other data are for factories of five or more employees. The figures in parentheses are percentages of workers in each sector.

from this sectoral shift. Reflecting the basic gender division along sectoral lines, the increase in employment from 1911 to 1917 primarily represented a rise in the number of male workers. Finally, in contrast to textiles, a relatively larger percentage of the machine, metal, and chemical workers came to work in smaller places, and most of the factories founded during and after the war were relatively small (tables 4.2 and 4.3). The relative weight of workplaces with fewer than 500 employees essentially doubled between 1911 and 1924 (table 4.3). By 1919 the workers of the Nankatsu region labored in nearly 2,000 factories, and only 76 of these employed over 100 workers.[12]

These demographic changes provided a firmer base for union organizing. The women in the large textile mills, however great their discontent, were banned from political activity, confined to dormitories, and often ignored by male activists. This had hindered (but ultimately

12. *Keishichō tōkei sho*, 1917, pp. 206–17.

TABLE 4.2   SIZE OF MINAMI KATSUSHIKA COUNTY FACTORIES
OPERATING IN 1925, BY YEAR OF FOUNDING

Number of Employees in 1925	Year Founded		
	1906–13	1914–19	1920–25
5–29	43 (58)	107 (75)	268 (85)
30–99	14 (19)	24 (17)	36 (11)
100–499	11 (15)	9 (6)	10 (3)
500 +	6 (8)	2 (1)	1
Total	74	142	315

SOURCE: Tōkyō shiyakusho, ed., *Tokyo kōjō yōran*, 1925.
NOTE: Percentages are given in parentheses. Owing to rounding off, column totals are not always 100 percent.

would not prevent) actions more sustained than the occasional disputes described above. Workers in the heavy and chemical industries, by contrast, drew on a more powerful preunion tradition of protest; thus, as their numbers and relative weight increased during the war, the Yūaikai gained support.

Two further developments help explain the emergence of organized labor in Tokyo at this particular moment. First, managers continued to impose more direct control in the workplace. In response, the foremen in new company hierarchies of control often retained a sense of themselves as leaders in working-class society, a fear of losing that position, and a suspicion of company promises to reward them for loyal service. They viewed the Yūaikai as a source of support, much as they had viewed the Ironworkers' Union. On the other hand, thousands of regular workers now felt themselves to be wage earners in the direct employ of large companies, rather than apprentices or journeymen serving *oyakata* masters. An increased "worker consciousness," an awareness and resentment of a new status as ill-treated, ill-paid, insecure members of a large, profitable enterprise, motivated many to support the Yūaikai as a potential ally in improving their status within the company or in the broader society.

Second, factory workers were part of a broader urban political culture that changed considerably between 1900 and 1912. As participants in the crowd actions of these years, factory workers were among those laying claim to the political status and rights of *kokumin*. The insistence that the political elite respect "the will of the people" and demands that

TABLE 4.3   WAGE LABOR BY ENTERPRISE SIZE AND INDUSTRY, MINAMI KATSUSHIKA COUNTY

Sector	1911		1924		1930	
Textiles						
5–29	383	(3)	293	(2)	1,068	(9)
30–99	218	(2)	168	(1)	1,093	(9)
100–499	—		305	(2)	435	(3)
500 +	14,312	(96)	19,408	(96)	9,931	(79)
Total	14,913		20,174		12,527	
Machine and Metal						
5–29	184	(21)	1,670	(24)	1,936	(27)
30–99	117	(13)	1,711	(24)	2,111	(29)
100–499	589	(66)	2,289	(32)	2,245	(31)
500 +	—		1,428	(20)	935	(13)
Total	890		7,098		7,227	
Chemicals						
5–29	380	(31)	1,946	(33)	1,772	(27)
30–99	500	(41)	1,180	(20)	1,815	(27)
100–499	341	(28)	2,204	(38)	3,097	(46)
500 +	—		549	(9)	—	
Total	1,221		5,879		6,684	
All Industry						
5–29	1,232	(7)	4,681	(13)	6,063	(20)
30–99	1,035	(6)	3,505	(10)	6,285	(21)
100–499	1,307	(7)	6,074	(17)	6,515	(22)
500 +	14,312	(80)	22,396	(61)	10,866	(37)
Total	17,886		36,656		29,729	

SOURCES: 1911 from *Minami Katsushika–gun shi* (Tokyo, 1923); 1924 from *Tōkyō kōjō yōran* (Tokyo, 1925); 1930 from Tōkyō-fu, *Tōkyō-fu tōkei sho* (Tokyo, 1931).
NOTES: Figures in parentheses are percentages. Owing to rounding off, column totals are not always 100 percent. Also, since the category "Other," given in graph 4.2, is omitted here, the three industry totals do not add up to the "All Industry" total.

the managerial elite respect the will, or the humanity, of workers were related elements of popular social consciousness in the early years of imperial democracy.

Coupled with the workers' persistent desire for social status and respect, these changes led both foremen and rank-and-file workers in Tokyo, Osaka, and then other cities to join forces in the Yūaikai. They overcame the obstacle of the Public Order Police Law to seek improved status, security, and respect in a hostile society.

THE LOCALS IN NANKATSU

The early Yūaikai sunk roots in neighborhoods of the Tokyo working poor that stretched in a semicircle around the imperial palace from Ebara County and Shiba ward to the southwest, through the central ward of Kyōbashi, then across the Sumida River into Honjo and Fukagawa wards and the villages of Minami Katsushika County (see map 2). Suzuki Bunji recruited many of the earliest members from several large machine and electrical equipment factories close by the union headquarters in Shiba.[13] The basic unit of organization was the local, further divided into chapters (10 or more members; dues ten sen per month). When a chapter reached 100 members, it would split off to form a new local.

Workers from the industrial neighborhoods of Nankatsu to the east of the Sumida River began to join the Yūaikai late in 1913. About 200 people attended the founding ceremony of the area's first Yūaikai local in October 1913, and this Kōtō (literally, east of the river) local boasted 110 dues-paying members by year's end. For roughly one year this was the only local in the area, and the group barely survived. Paid-up membership fluctuated between 50 and 100 per month.[14] Then in 1915 and 1916 the Yūaikai entered a period of sustained growth in Nankatsu. The Honjo local spun off from the Kōtō group in February 1915, with a

13. By late 1913 these included Shibaura Engineering Works (five chapters), Tokyo Electric Company (four), NEC (three), and Ikegai Iron Works (three). *Yūai shinpō*, January 13, 1913, p. 8. *NRUS* 3:437–39.

14. The back pages of each semimonthly issue of the *Yūai shinpō* (renamed *Rōdō oyobi sangyō* [*ROS*] in 1915) printed "Local News," including statements of income. Unless otherwise noted, the issues from the relevant months are the sources of this and the following figures on membership, meeting attendance, founding dates, and so forth. The Kōtō local note in the June 15 issue, p. 8, for example, remarks on the need to collect unpaid dues. Only five and six yen were coming in each month, and the local owed twelve yen in *Yūai shinpō* subscription fees to union headquarters. By September (*Yūai shinpō*, September 1, 1914, p. 8) it appears the union had weathered the storm, and membership stood at about 100.

grand founding ceremony attended by 1,500; the Ōjima chapter attained local status in July; over 1,000 people attended an inaugural ceremony for the Fukagawa local in January 1916; and several hundred joined the festivities for the Azuma local in April. Other chapters at several points reached local status between 1916 and 1918, but these five locals remained the largest and most active Yūaikai centers in the region until the union's reorganization along industry lines in 1919 and 1920.

Significant numbers of female textile workers began to join the Honjo and Azuma locals beginning in late 1916. Yūaikai bylaws at the time of its founding did not mention gender. Any "person" could join on the introduction of two members, although the omission of gender probably reflects the assumption that the only relevant people were men. Revised bylaws in August 1913 created a separate category of "auxiliary member" for women.[15] The contingent of women in Honjo exceeded 100 by November 1916, and the union began to hold some separate events for the female members. A joint Azuma-Honjo rally drew 240 women from the Kanebō, Fujibō, and Tokyo Muslin mills in February 1917, and 110 women attended a "tea meeting" of the Azuma local in January to hear a talk on the path for women to achieve "self-awakening."

The Honjo, Azuma, and Fukagawa locals were the most successful in the region, each enlisting over 100 new members, men and women, in active months. By June 1916 the Yūaikai national membership stood at 15,000, with 4,275 in Tokyo. By year's end about 1,000 of the Tokyo members, and eight of thirty Tokyo locals, were from Nankatsu, making it the second major center of Yūaikai strength after the Shiba-Ebara region to the south of the imperial palace.

The men and women who signed on, and paid monthly dues of roughly one hour's pay for an average worker, came from dozens of factories. The fifteen largest enterprises in Nankatsu employed between 500 and 4,500 each; these included nine textile mills, a railroad-car manufacturer, a rubber factory, two metal processors, the Tokyo Gas and Electric Company, and the Hattori watch factory, forerunner to Seikō. Table 4.4 shows that the early Yūaikai enjoyed greatest success at these plants, building considerable strength at nearly half of them by

15. *Yūai shinpō*, August 3, 1913, p. 8. In 1917 women protested this arrangement and became regular members. E. Patricia Tsurumi, "Female Textile Workers and the Failure of Early Trade Unionism in Japan," *History Workshop*, no. 18 (August 1984): 26 n. 74.

TABLE 4.4   YŪAIKAI PRESENCE IN NANKATSU REGION
FACTORIES, 1914–17

Size	Number of Factories with Union Presence (a)	Total Number of Factories in 1917 (b)	Percentage of Factories with Union Presence (a/b)
5–49	14	1,852	1
50–99	4	56	7
100–499	17	61	28
500 +	7	15	47
Unknown	3		
All	45	1,984	2

SOURCES: Union presence from the "Union News" (kaihō) column in each issue of Yūai shinpō and Rōdō oyobi sangyō, 1914–17. Total number of factories of fifty or more employees from Keishichō, Keishichō tōkei sho, 1917, pp. 206–17. Total for all factories of five or more employees from Tōkyō-fu, ed., Tōkyō-fu tōkei sho (Tokyo, 1917), p. 449. The 5–49 category is the difference of these two. The three unknown factories are mentioned in "Union News" in abbreviated form, making it impossible to ascertain whether they are listed in the Keishichō volumes.
NOTE: Nankatsu region = Honjo and Fukagawa wards and Minami Katsushika County.

1917. The data in table 4.5 also indicate that the union organizers gradually moved from this nucleus into smaller factories in 1916 and 1917, eventually gaining some support at roughly one-third of all Nankatsu firms with 100 or more workers, and at a sprinkling of the smallest workplaces.

This pattern reveals that men and women at the largest, relatively impersonal factories were most receptive to the union message. In these places a system had for some time been emerging in which foremen, as the lowest-ranked members of the management hierarchy, exerted direct control over wage laborers, but study of the early Yūaikai reveals little evidence of sharp tension between such foremen and their charges. In fact, these foremen, uneasy in their new roles, were among those most drawn to the Yūaikai, whose early leaders were slow to confront their bosses when compared to the nonunion men in the shipyards and arsenals. They mounted no overt challenge to, or criticism of, managerial authority, and Suzuki Bunji was careful to gain management support for, or understanding of, his activities before approaching the workers in a plant. The spread of the Yūaikai in Nankatsu was thus accompanied by no increase in labor disputes. Indeed, table 4.6 shows

TABLE 4.5   YEAR OF FIRST MENTION OF UNION
PRESENCE IN NANKATSU REGION FACTORIES, BY SCALE

Size	Year First Mentioned				
	1914	1915	1916	1917	All
5–49	1	3	2	8	14
50–99	2	0	1	1	4
100–499	2	1	13	1	17
500 +	0	7	0	0	7
Unknown	0	2	1	0	43
Total	5	13	17	10	45

SOURCES: "Mention of union presence" refers to the first reference to union members at a given factory found in the "Union News" (*kaihō*) column in *Yūai shinpō* and *Rōdō oyobi sangyō*, 1914–17. Factory size was determined from listings of all factories of fifty or more employees in the relevant volumes of Keishichō, *Keishichō tōkei sho* (Tokyo, 1914–17). Factories mentioned in the "Union News" column but not found in the *Keishichō* list are assumed to have had fewer than fifty employees.
NOTE: Nankatsu region = Honjo and Fukagawa wards and Minami Katsushika County.

that the factories in the region, both those with and those without Yūaikai members, were more peaceful during the 1911–15 span of early Yūaikai activity than before.

THE ORGANIZERS

The men who joined Suzuki's Friendly Society during its first few years and became organizers and leaders in their own right were primarily workers of humble origin. Not until the end of World War I did university-educated activists enter and help transform the union, so the early Yūaikai appears to have reflected the values and discontents of the workers themselves.

In 1923 Uchida Tōshichi became chairman of the newly founded Tokyo Metalworkers' Union, one of the strongest unions of the interwar era, with numerous locals in Nankatsu by the late 1920s. His route into the Yūaikai illuminates the nuts and bolts of union-building. Uchida came from a family of tea merchants in Saitama Prefecture, neighboring Tokyo. He began his life as a factory worker in 1908, at twenty-two, after an unpleasant stint as an apprentice in a rice broker's shop. When Suzuki founded the Yūaikai, Uchida was employed at the Mita Naval Arsenal, within walking distance of union headquarters. Upon reading

TABLE 4.6   LABOR DISPUTES IN THE NANKATSU REGION, 1891–1917

	Artisan	Transport	Textile	Machine & Metal	Chemical	Print	Other	All
1891–95	1	0	0	0	0	0	0	1
1896–1900	3	0	4	1	0	2	0	10
1901–5	0	1	2	0	2	0	0	5
1906–10	3	0	0	3	1	1	1	9
1911–15	0	1	3 (3)	2	0	0	0	6
1916	0	0	0	2 (2)	0	0	0	2
1917	0	1	2 (1)	2 (2)	1 (1)	0	0	6
Total	7	3	11	10	4	3	1	39

SOURCE: Aoki Kōji, *Nihon rōdō undō shi nenpyō* (Tokyo: Shinseisha, 1968).
NOTE: Figures in parentheses are the number involving Yūaikai mediation and/or involvement by Yūaikai members. Nankatsu region = Honjo and Fukagawa wards and Minami Katsushika County.

of the group in the newspaper, Uchida sought out Suzuki, told him that he believed in the need to organize workers for the good of society, and joined the Yūaikai. As he recalls his state of mind at the time, the arbitrary, capricious nature of direct managerial control at the arsenal, where he had been working for five years, fueled his determination to organize a union chapter there:

> I was psychologically on the verge of exploding. The arsenal was rigidly stratified and those on the bottom stayed on the bottom. There were many wrong and unfair practices [such as bribes to influence promotions and raises]. . . . At that time pay raises were given twice a year, but gift-giving had great influence, and since I believed in a world where one depended on one's skill and was rewarded for one's efforts, I was truly discontented.[16]

Uchida threw himself into organizing activity with vigor, first enlisting the aid of two or three friends, and then approaching the other workers. "After the arsenal closed each day, I would try to persuade the workers to join, walking along with them from the factory to the streetcar or riding together with them." Uchida enjoyed fair success, soon recruiting fifty workers into a new arsenal chapter of the Yūaikai.[17] Reflecting upon his activities years later, he remarked, "We [organizers] were all highly skilled workers. If not led into it by the truly skilled workers in a factory, the rest of the workers wouldn't follow and join the labor movement."[18]

Skill and experience were critical factors enabling Uchida and other early leaders to command an audience. Many of the first Yūaikai organizers were foremen or skilled men with considerable status in the workplace. If one such man signed on, he could quickly bring his subordinates into the union. Managers sometimes tolerated, but rarely encouraged, membership in the Yūaikai. Their concurrent policies of direct control aimed to draw these men into a company hierarchy, but the pages of the Yūaikai journal offer considerable evidence that skilled workplace leaders felt a need for the external resources of the Yūaikai.

One Kamimatsu Yūji joined the # 5 chapter of the Honjo local in August 1915, "bringing with him numerous fellow workers at Takada Shōkai's Yanagishima factory." Foremen at the Tokyo Gas Company were reported to be one major source of support for the Fukagawa local

---

16. Uchida Tōshichi, *Jinsei 50 yo nen* (Kawasaki: Privately published, 1950), p. 40; see ibid, pp. 1–26 for biographical information.

17. Ibid., p. 42.

18. Uchida Tōshichi, "Tekkō rōdōsha to shite," *Rōdō undō shi kenkyū*, no. 31 (May 1962): 14.

in July 1916, while a December local notice congratulated two members of this same local for promotion to the rank of subforeman. In some cases the line between company foreman and independent master worker was blurred, as when Nagano Tokujirō, a union official in the Kōtō local in September 1916, left his job for a new post at the Ōji Paper Company, taking with him over ten other members. The critical difference between this case, and similar instances of mobility among skilled masters in the Ironworkers' Union almost twenty years earlier, was the fact that Nagano and his followers reportedly maintained their union commitment at their new workplace.

Many rank-and-file members joined at the simple urging of a friend or a foreman. Encouraging members to bring their friends into the union was one of the most effective organizing techniques.[19] In such cases, the new member would not have the well-defined motives of a man like Uchida, who sought out Suzuki on his own. This was true of Saitō Tadatoshi, a migrant from northern Japan with no particular interest in the Yūaikai when he came to Tokyo in 1914. He began working at the Takeuchi Safe Company in Honjo ward and attending night school.

> The teacher at the school told me to join, and also Aihara Motojirō, staying with me at the boarding house, was a member. [In 1914] I entered the Yūaikai more out of obligation [giri] toward him than anything else. My interest in the Yūaikai rose after I joined. I became more aware of the relationship between the user and the used, and the fact that by [our] keeping silent, wages would not go up. Also, we could not get anywhere without bargaining on the basis of unity.[20]

Within a few years Saitō's insight into the need for unions developed into a determination to work for radical social change. His tremendous curiosity and desire for advancement were typical of numerous leaders of working-class origin. Saitō attended courses at various night schools between 1914 and 1919, and joined a political study group organized in 1919 by some young university graduates who sought to "go to the people" and change society after World War I. Uchida Tōshichi took similar zeal in a different direction, studying metalcasting after hours with a master metalworker, preparing for the day when he might set up on his own.[21] And Hirasawa Keishichi, one of the most energetic of the

19. Large, Rise of Labor, p. 44, credits Watanabe Tōru with this observation.
20. Interview with Saitō Tadatoshi, June 3, 1979.
21. Gordon, Evolution of Labor Relations, pp. 85–86, for details.

early Yūaikai leaders, who brought the union message to the factories of Ōjima in Minami Katsushika County, aspired to a career as a writer as well as a worker.

Hirasawa's saga recapitulates much of the story of labor in Nankatsu from 1916 to 1923. Born in 1899 in Niigata Prefecture, well north of Tokyo, he moved to the provincial city of Ōmiya at the age of eleven, and, after finishing higher elementary school, entered the Japan Railway Company's Ōmiya factory as a trainee. Proud of his new skills, and interested in studying, he and some friends subscribed to a magazine for youth published by Ōzaki Yukio, a charismatic popular hero and leader of the parliamentary forces in the movement for imperial democracy. The group met regularly to discuss the magazine, and they occasionally contributed letters to it and other magazines.[22]

Hirasawa left Ōmiya in 1910 when he was drafted. Upon finishing his military service, he worked at two railroad factories before moving to Ōjima, finding a job at the Tokyo Spring Company, and joining the Kōtō local of the Yūaikai in September 1914. He claims to have joined in search of a forum where his literary activities could help enlighten fellow workers. His first contribution to the union journal came in December 1914. Within a few months he was a director of the Ōjima chapter, and he was the principal force responsible for recruiting about 150 members by June 1915, at which point the chapter was upgraded to the Ōjima local.[23] In his path of entry into the Yūaikai, he thus shared the curiosity, idealism, and determination that marked Uchida, Saitō, and numerous others, and he had absorbed the political concerns of the movement for imperial democracy. His writings and speeches leave important clues as to the appeal the Yūaikai held for these organizers and for the workers who heeded their exhortations and joined the union.

THE APPEAL

Both union activities and the words of the union members indicate that the simple promise of recognition, respect, and community lay at the heart of the Yūaikai appeal. For fledgling organizers such as Uchida Tōshichi, this recognition also bolstered their position as community and workplace leaders.

22. On Hirasawa, see Matsumoto Gappei, *Nihon shakaishugi engeki shi* (Tokyo: Chikuma shobō, 1975), pp. 357–66; on this genre of magazine, see Earl Kinmoth, *The Self-Made Man in Meiji Japanese Thought* (Berkeley: University of California Press, 1981).
    23. Matsumoto, *Nihon shakaishugi engeki shi*, pp. 367–72, 381–83.

One simple form of recognition was the practice of listing all new members in the union magazine. In busy months this list covered three to five pages, densely printed in eleven rows per page, with thirty-five or more names to a row. Several additional forms of recognition were accorded the active new recruit. Local members selected officers at a ratio of roughly one officer per twenty-five members; by July 1915 the Honjo local had thirty-five members on its executive committee, and in March and April 1916 twenty-eight members in the Fukagawa local held posts of official responsibility in the local.[24] In addition, all those who recruited over five new members the previous month received special praise at both local "tea meetings" and larger speech-meetings, as well as in the magazine. Finally, all members were welcome to take the stage at union gatherings and offer a "five-minute speech." By 1915 these had become a regular, popular feature of union meetings. Standing before several hundred workers on a podium flanked by the union flag and perhaps a large stand of flowers, with the omnipresent police observer in the wings, this must have been a heady experience, confirmation of the importance, prestige, and danger of the union undertaking to both speaker and audience.[25]

Respect, as well as recognition, came in a variety of forms, each certainly minor in isolation, but of powerful cumulative effect. Kawasaki Jinichi, then a 15-year-old working at a rubber factory in Kameido, first heard Suzuki Bunji speak one evening in 1915 at a Nankatsu elementary school (see fig. 9). Nearly fifty years later, he recalled the deep impression made by the sight of Suzuki arriving together in that still rare conveyance, the automobile, with none other than Shibusawa Eiichi, Japan's premier industrialist-financier. Suzuki took to the podium, described the Yūaikai, called on people to join, and then shook hands with each new member. Impressed by this display, and "feeling perhaps if I joined my life would get easier, but without any particular understanding of labor unions," Kawasaki signed on.[26] Other leading figures of the business and bureaucratic establishment frequently accompanied Suzuki and spoke to the workers in these early years.

The Yūaikai worked to improve the place of workers in the local community by establishing special relations with area merchants. In

24. The term for officer was *kanji. ROS*, March 1916, p. 53; April 1916, p. 55.
25. For a photograph of one such meeting of a Honjo local, see *ROS*, November 1915, p. 93.
26. "Jun rōdōsha kumiai—Nankatsu rōdō kai oyobi kameido jiken," *ROS*, May 1963, p. 35.

June 1916 a Dr. Miura offered a discount to all members of the Kōtō
local in good standing (but he asked that they try not to bring nonunion friends and relatives for the same low price). Members who quit
factory jobs to open their own businesses—a barbershop in Honjo or a
general store in Fukagawa—would offer discounts to fellow unionists.
By 1916 thirteen stores in Fukagawa offered shoes, milk, clothing, sake,
hardware, and more at reduced prices to Yūaikai members.

The varied union gatherings also affirmed a place in the community
for Yūaikai members whose economic insecurity and low workplace
status offered little sense of self-importance and belonging. One of the
three main types of assembly was the "tea meeting," a relatively informal gathering combining socializing and local business. Union officers
met for monthly business meetings as well, and on major occasions such
as the inauguration of a new chapter or local, or the visit of a major
speaker, the union held a larger "ceremony," attended by hundreds,
perhaps as many as two thousand, members and residents. Such meetings grew out of the tradition of urban political assembly of the early
days of imperial democracy. They were among the first attempts of
workers to convene their own assemblies, thus marking the beginning
of a process whereby wage laborers came to constitute themselves as a
distinct, organized component of the urban populace. In the Nankatsu
area alone between 1915 and 1917, the Yūaikai held at least eighteen
meetings attended by over five hundred people.[27]

Numerous letters to the Yūaikai magazine attest to the importance of
respect, recognition, and community to the union's active members.
Their claim was simple: workers were human beings and deserved the
respect due dignified members of society.

Thus, one member in 1914 wrote that "society treats [workers] as
diseased, pitiful slaves of money, lacking in self-respect, learning, or
common sense," while another expressed his outrage at the arrogance
and cruelty of a supervisor who without notice lengthened the work
day, thus making it impossible for him to attend his night school class.
He lamented that "if Japanese industry does not respect the character of
its workers, it will not progress. Treated as beasts, we will become
beasts. Treated as gentlemen, we will become gentlemen. So long as

27. For these mettings, see *Yūai shinpō*, 1915–17, passim. The largest drew approx-
imately 2,000. For interesting detail on meetings and other union activities in Honjo, see
Sally Ann Hastings, "The Government, the Citizen, and the Creation of a New Sense of
Community: Social Welfare, Local Organizations, and Dissent in Tokyo, 1905–1937"
(Ph.D. diss., University of Chicago, 1980), ch. 5.

supervisors or capitalists look at workers as dumb puppets, as living machines, will any man of spirit or courage long remain a worker?"[28]

These letters expressed forcefully the desire for social respect and dignity. At the same time, they betrayed the self-doubt and sense of inferiority of those denied such respect. The first writer also admitted there was "a grain of truth" to social prejudice against workers. The second was less equivocal; he concluded his letter: "Only the inferior remain as workers." Yet a third writer to the *Yūai shinpō* echoed this refrain in June 1914:

> Of course we are not satisfied with the treatment given to Japan's workers. Yet the fact that many workers want to shift to some other work as soon as possible, the fact that few are committed to raising their status as workers, indicates that there are still people whose self-awareness is low. We must not accept this.[29]

In the speeches and plays of Hirasawa Keishichi, one finds some of the most eloquent expressions of the Yūaikai message, as well as important evidence of the overlap between the political or social consciousness of workers and that of the urban populace, or *kokumin*, as a whole (see fig. 10).

By all accounts a formidable presence on the podium, Hirasawa spoke with fervor and pride of his skills as a worker in a "five-minute speech" to the Ōjima local in 1915:

> Friends! Look at this arm [*ude*]! It is the arm of a worker in 1915. Until now this arm has met only misfortune, but it is no longer an age of misfortune. In a little while, the time will come when the Japanese nation will be unable to survive without this arm, without its work.

The word *ude*, arm, also has the meaning in Japanese of "skill," as in the expression common among workers, "to polish one's skills."[30] Hirasawa's powerful invocation of this idea earned him the nickname "Look-at-this-arm Hirasawa."

His statements suggest that at this early stage in the history of organized labor, Hirasawa, who certainly spoke for the Yūaikai leadership and probably for the mass of workers until at least 1917, saw no need for radical or aggressive action to bring recognition to the worker. His speech continued:

28. *Yūai shinpō*, April 15, 1914, p. 5, and June 1, 1914, p. 5.
29. *Yūai shinpō*, June 1, 1914, p. 5.
30. The expression was *ude o migaku*.

In the West are cases where the free people deposed and crucified their king. . . . The Japanese people are not like that. Japan is a constitutional polity. Is this because the people spilled their blood and killed the king? Because of the nature of the Japanese polity, the capitalists will awaken before the blood flows; considering our national polity, there is no need to struggle, and our future is not dark.[31]

In the early Yūaikai era, Hirasawa articulated a working-class consciousness in the mainstream of the ideas of the imperial democratic movement. He linked the idea that all Japanese people were members of a special polity, equal before the emperor, with the idea that the nation's insecure, abused, and exploited workers could legitimately unite to assert their worth, raise their status, and change the attitude of employers. In a melodramatic early play of 1915, *Struggle, Harmony, or Surrender?* a union member, whom we may take to be Hirasawa, intervenes in a dispute between a seemingly corrupt foreman and an angry worker. The unionist lectures the two on the need for harmony, but also speaks of the need to struggle to change all those, capitalists or workers, engaged only in the narrow pursuit of "personal profit and self-interest."[32] Hirasawa's conception was similar to that of Suzuki Bunji himself in these years, when Suzuki sought and gained support of some of the leading industrialists in the nation. Neither man felt workers to be a separate interest locked into inevitable battle with capitalists. In another early play, *Four Eyes*, set in a Nankatsu metal factory in 1917, a sympathetically portrayed worker, who refuses to join what he sees as an ill-advised strike, addresses the issue of how workers are to secure their dignity:

> The Japanese blood is not fit for shouts of socialism. . . . The time has come for the Japanese people to take back their souls as Japanese. The enemy of Japan's worker is not the government or the capitalist. Japanese workers should not act as workers. We should act as humans and people of the nation [*kokumin*].[33]

By 1916 workers in the industrial neighborhoods of Tokyo, and Yokohama and Osaka as well, were sufficiently committed to the Yūaikai message to sustain an organization of roughly 20,000 men and women, whose leaders and local activists were themselves almost all

---

31. Matsumoto, *Nihon shakaishugi engeki shi*, p. 387, cites *ROS*, July 1915.
32. The phrase, used also in popular criticism of bureaucrats and the streetcar companies in 1906, was *shiri shiyoku*.
33. Matsumoto, *Nihon shakaishugi engeki shi*, p. 406.

workers.[34] In Nankatsu the union had recruited members at over half the largest firms and one-fourth of those with 100 to 500 employees.

We must not exaggerate the stability of this young organization or the transformative thrust of its ideology. Dues-paying membership fluctuated from month to month in most all locals. The number of new members listed in the union magazine between its founding and 1917 far exceeded the 20,000 members still enrolled in 1917. In addition to the five successful Nankatsu locals created between 1915 and 1917, three others held opening ceremonies only to fold within several months. When a company, such as Tokyo Muslin in 1914, decided to oppose the Yūaikai, it had little trouble repressing the union or coopting its leaders.[35] And Hirasawa's call for action as humans or members of the nation, not workers, is striking. He rejected the concept of workers as an independent social force; they were part of the broader body politic demanding respect and participation in the imperial constitutional order.

Yet the growth of these years was a considerable achievement. As an unprecedented period of industrial expansion gained steam in 1916, the Yūaikai foothold expanded rapidly. Reluctance to oppose managers receded in the union locals, and the transformative element in Yūaikai thinking (that workers and capitalists must change, or be changed) overpowered the moderate exhortation to patience and cooperation. The union rank and file, it appears, were quicker than the leaders to see the contradiction between the original union goals of respect, improvement, and higher status for workers, undeniably radical in the context of Japanese society in 1915, and the limited range of actions proposed to achieve them. Even before the "external" stimuli of the Russian Revolution, the culmination of World War I in a victory for democracy, and the influx of intellectual activists into the union movement, such workers were beginning to seek new means sufficient to attain their ends.

Thus, Yūaikai members were involved either as mediators or leaders in six of Nankatsu's eight labor disputes of 1916 and 1917, and a number elsewhere as well. At the Mitatsuchi Rubber Company in Honjo, for example, 44 percent of the 855 employees carried out a four-day strike in February 1917. As with so many of the era's disputes, a desire for basic social respect motivated these workers. In addition to a 30 percent wage

34. The most accurate total for this period is from the April 1917 issue of *ROS*. National membership was 22,187 (1,549 women). About 3,000 were from the Nankatsu region, including 750 of the women members.
35. This case was described in chapter 3.

increase, they sought construction of a dining hall and a changing room, and three months' severance pay for all those with three years' seniority who left the company or were fired. Finally, they demanded that the body checks given to all employees upon leaving work be conducted inside the company gounds, out of public sight, rather than in front of the company gate. Suzuki Bunji entered as a mediator because a large group of Mitatsuchi workers were Yūaikai members, and he secured a 10 percent pay increase. Suzuki also negotiated a 10 percent raise for the 338 male workers at the huge Fuji Gas Spinning Mill in Honjo (2,154 employees) later in the year. A Yūaikai member and officer in the Honjo local led this well-disciplined six-day strike, during which the workers assembled daily on the grounds of a temple near the factory.[36]

The strikes at Mitatsuchi, Fuji, and elsewhere in the region resembled the preunion disputes found elsewhere between 1905 and the early days of World War I in important ways. They invariably began with the discontents generated by a particular workshop or "natural" subgroup, such as the men at the spinning mill, rather than with demands raised by a union local. An effective action would spread to other workshops, and some would finally draw in almost the entire yard. The difference between the disputes of the late war years and earlier ones lay in the facts that some workers were union members, and that the Yūaikai, not the local police or ad hoc groups of foremen, acted as mediators. As a result, the resolutions were more favorable to the workers than in most earlier incidents. Although not yet in the forefront of strike activities, the Yūaikai leadership was willy-nilly becoming involved in local disputes. The nonunion tradition of disputes to resist company policy was beginning to coalesce with union organization.

WORKERS AND THE MOVEMENT
FOR IMPERIAL DEMOCRACY

The movement stage in the history of imperial democracy in Japan extended from 1905 to 1918. The boundaries are neatest in the case of the political crowd, for the Hibiya and rice riots were unmistakable watersheds. The point of departure for the labor dimension to imperial democ-

36. For Mitatsuchi, see *TAS*, February 28, 1917, and Aoki Kōji, *Nihon rōdō undō shi nenpyō* (Tokyo: Shinseisha, 1968), p. 174. For Fuji Gas, see Hastings, "Government, Citizen, Community," pp. 166–67. For a similar incident at Yokohama Dock Company in 1916, see *ROS*, September 1916, pp. 217–18, and *Jiji shinpō*, August 16, 1916, p. 6. See also Gordon, *Evolution of Labor Relations*, pp. 78–79, for the demands raised in this Yokohama Dock incident.

racy is less clear-cut. Both heavy industrial disputes and early union activities date from the 1890s, and the Russo-Japanese War stimulated further dispute activity; the turn of the century is an approximate marker of the starting point. The sharp rise in disputes of 1917 through 1919 and the proliferation of labor union organization in 1919, however, mark a turning point with clear links to the boundary constituted by the rice riots.

Two features distinguish the era of the movement for imperial democracy from both the previous years and those to follow for the urban lower classes: they were socially defenseless and politically powerless. First, bureaucrats and politicians, while expressing new concern with the emerging "social problem," did not intervene to buffer the social impact upon workers of urbanization and industrialization until World War I and after. Bureaucrats first discussed social policy in the 1880s, and the Diet approved a factory law in 1911, but the law did not take effect until 1916.[37] The first municipal programs of poor relief and social welfare came in 1911, but these efforts were tentative and limited until the establishment of both the city of Tokyo's Municipal Social Bureau in 1919 and the Home Ministry's Social Bureau in 1920.[38] As both industrialization and urbanization began to remake the Japanese social landscape from the 1880s through World War I, factory workers and the urban poor were left to fend for themselves or depend on the purported benevolence of their betters.

Second, the political rights of lower-class city-dwellers, tenant farmers, and some of the middle class of small business operators, ranged from limited to nil. Yet such people were well aware that while they shouldered considerable political obligations, only the urban and landed bourgeoisie played leading political roles in the constitutional order. Taxation and military service were the two obligations whose burdens increased sharply with the Russo-Japanese War, and a shrill, populist, nationalistic press with a message accessible to increasing numbers of literate city-dwellers helped bring home to the populace the disjunction between obligations and rights, between uncomplaining sacrifice on the one hand and limited participation on the other.

Working people in the cities were thus offered neither social and eco-

37. The key provisions protecting women and children in the textile mills were deferred until 1926.
38. Hastings, "Government, Citizen, Community," ch. 1.

nomic protection by the state nor political means to protect themselves during this era of industrial revolution and the consolidation of a nation-state. In this context, the Yūaikai letter writer's 1914 call to "raise [our] status as workers," Hirasawa's insistence that workers were above all humans and *kokumin*, and the ubiquity among crowd activists of the notion that "constitutional government" meant freedom from police harassment and respect for the "will of the people" emerge as related popular conceptions. They all grew out of a sense of alienation or antagonism on one level (the street) directed toward the bureaucracy and Seiyūkai mainstream by the politically aware members of "lower-class society," and on another level (the workplace) expressed by workers toward their supervisors. These demands, and the underlying anger that produced them, constituted the proletarian dimension to the movement for imperial democracy.

As early as the 1890s anticipatory fear of precisely such demands and protests had generated apocalyptic visions of social disorder among bureaucrats, businessmen, politicians, and social policy intellectuals. These men saw the Japanese future mirrored in the experience of the advanced capitalist societies of Western Europe and North America. Their metaphors were medical, and the infected carriers were foreign, as they spoke of the prospect of "extreme social illness much like that which befell England at the beginning of this century" and the need to "solve this problem before it develops and save ourselves from the fate of Europe."[39]

As imperial democracy in fact developed into a multiclass political movement, its bourgeois leaders echoed these fears with increased intensity. Hara Kei and his party stood with the crowd just once, in the winter of 1913, when the Seiyūkai seemed to be taking a firm stand against Katsura and the oligarchs, in a union of mutual suspicion and convenience. Hara reveals in his diary entry on the day of the riot of February 10, 1913, that he and his erstwhile rival Prince Katsura stood together in their fear of a dangerous lower-class dimension to the movements for imperial democracy. He reported that Katsura was finally moved to resign by accusations of responsibility for the spectacle of "mounted troops trampling the crowd" outside the Diet. Hara then commented: "If he still refuses to resign, I think a practically revolution-

39. Obama Ritoku, *Meiji bunka shiryō sōsho* (Tokyo: Kazama shobō, 1961), 1:38, 65.

ary riot will occur."[40] Hara shared Katsura's horror at the thought of such an event. He attributed the crisis to "Katsura's mistaken policy and the gradual change in popular thinking since the Russo-Japanese War," and he did not simply seek cabinet posts for his party in the days after this riot; his diary also reveals concern that any new cabinet be capable of ending the disturbances.[41]

Despite Hara's fears, actual cases of "social illness" itself were not particularly threatening until the end of this era; the crowd acted in effect to further the political goals of established party leaders, and the proletarian stream of social and political action remained subsumed under the movement for imperial democracy. Crowds did not possess their own organizations; they took to the streets only after the formal groups of businessmen, journalists, lawyers, or politicians had charged the atmosphere with petitions, speech-meetings, and agitation in the press. Their riots never became "practically revolutionary." In addition, the dozens of disputes at major shipyards, arsenals, and factories between 1900 and 1917, while important as precursors to the events of the 1920s, posed only a mild threat to managerial authority and constituted no threat to the state, and through 1917 the Yūaikai spoke of cooperation with capitalists, engaging bureaucrats and businessmen as advisors. Japan's first socialists were also active in these years, and they located themselves outside the mainstream of the imperial democratic movement by opposing the Russo-Japanese War, but their popular following was quite small.

In sum, the unpropertied, less-educated elements in the movement for imperial democracy were not powerful, coherent, or independent enough to win recognition and extended rights as the price for social peace, and they were not threatening enough to prevent many party politicians from seeking advantage from the energy of street politics. As the bourgeois gentlemen of the late Meiji period led the movement for imperial democracy and slowly gained a share of power, the vast majority of workers and poor urbanites acted politically within the ideological and organizational framework of that movement. Poor and middle-class urbanites periodically took to the streets with their discontent; workers in shipyards and arsenals organized numerous disputes with

---

40. Hara Kei, *Hara Kei nikki* (Tokyo: Fukumura shuppan, 1965), 3:288.
41. Ibid., pp. 290–92. Similar concerns moved Hara during the 1914 riots. See pp. 388–91.

increasing effect; and by the middle of World War I, thousands of
Tokyo workers had joined the Yūaikai.

   The subordinate role of the unpropertied began to change toward the
end of World War I. The implicit alliance of bourgeois and proletarian
elements in the movement for imperial democracy dissolved, as workers
began on their own to combine previously separate actions: union organizing, the nonunion dispute tradition, and the speech-meetings, rallies,
and demonstrations of the political crowd. The separation of bourgeois
and proletarian elements and the elaboration of varied forms of popular
action among workers are revealed in a variety of events, beginning in
1918. On one hand, the relatively liberal politicians of the Kenseikai
Party continued to push the "Movement for Constitutional Government" until the enactment of universal manhood suffrage in 1925, but
lower-class urbanites no longer rioted after their rallies. Conversely, the
rice riots in 1918 differed from earlier incidents in the striking absence
of preliminary agitation by bourgeois political leaders, and in 1919 the
Yūaikai, renamed Sōdōmei, began to lead labor disputes. In 1920 political party supporters and the leaders of labor organizations began to
convene separate rallies. The parties continued to rally for universal suffrage, while unions gathered to demand repeal of laws which repressed
labor. Unions in 1920 also organized the first May Day celebration
in Japan, claiming their own separate symbolic day (see figs. 6 and 7).
   The rice riots were the greatest of these events signaling a new, more
polarized political configuration and autonomy for lower-class action,
even if the role of the unions was minor. In the cities the rioters heard
speeches condemning the Terauchi cabinet. That this riot finally propelled Hara Kei into the prime minister's office to preside over Japan's
first party cabinet was no accident. This chain of events brings us back
to this book's main theme, that social conflict and working-class action
were central causes of change in modern Japanese history. It reveals the
dynamic link between the emergence of workers or poor farmers as a
social force to be feared and the ascendance of imperial democracy as a
structure of rule: this popular explosion pushed Hara Kei, that most
cautious and equivocal of imperial democrats, decisively into the ruling
alliance. Yamagata Aritomo, a man not given to displays of emotion or
fear, was "terribly upset" by the rice riots, according to a visitor to his
Odawara retreat that August, and he had no choice but to turn reluctantly to the once-upstart commoner Hara as the only man who could

control the masses.[42] But in 1918, on the eve of the era of imperial democratic rule, the means to control the masses were far from evident or agreed upon, and the organization of workers or farmers was in its infancy.

42. The phrase was *ippō narazu yūryō* (*Hara Kei nikki* 4:431). Yokota Sennosuke, a trusted ally of Hara's, was the visitor. He conveyed this impression to Hara in a telegram. See also Masumi Junnosuke, *Nihon seitō shi ron* (Tokyo: University of Tokyo Press, 1968), 4:244–45.

1.   Victory parade during the Russo-Japanese War, 1904 or 1905.

2. Speech from the Shintomiza Theater balcony during the Hibiya riot, 1905.

3. Crowd storming the home minister's residence during the Hibiya riot, 1905.

4. Crowd fleeing police during the Hibiya riot, 1905.

5. Crowd destroying streetcars during the Hibiya riot, 1905.

6. Speaker at a 1926 May Day demonstration.

7. Arrest of a participant at a 1926 May Day demonstration.

8. Recipients waiting at soup kitchen, 1931 or 1932, Fukagawa.

9.   Suzuki Bunji addressing the Yūaikai's fifth anniversary convention in 1916.

10.   Commemorative photo of delegates to the 1916 Yūaikai convention. Hirasawa Keishichi is eighth from the left in the front row. The female delegate represents a Tokyo local of textile workers.

11.   Minami Kiichi in front of his factory in 1921.

12. Watanabe Masanosuke and Tanno Setsu in the mid 1920s.

13. Honjo ward in the aftermath of the 1923 earthquake.

14. Family members and friends of victims in the Kameido incident gathered outside Kameido police station in early September 1923.

15. Commemorative photo at a memorial service for Kameido victims in February 1924.

Labor under Imperial Democratic Rule

FIVE

Imperial Democracy as a Structure of Rule

The social turbulence and the political challenge to oligarchic authority raised by the movement for imperial democracy was dramatic. The oligarchs of Meiji, still active in the early twentieth century, viewed representative institutions and popular participation in politics with suspicious acceptance in some cases and clear hostility in others, yet their policies had set in motion forces they could neither ignore nor repress. A new bourgeoisie of capitalists and "free professionals" (lawyers, educators, journalists) in the cities, closely allied to a rural elite of men mixing roles as landowners, political leaders, investors, or entrepreneurs, led the imperial democratic movement for respect and empire abroad, party government at home, and economic justice for the taxpayer of the new capitalist order. The upper level of the new Meiji school system was the crucible in which these men both formed a collective sense of themselves and developed commonality with a new, more systematically trained and recruited, generation of bureaucrats as well.[1]

By 1918 imperial bureaucracy had gradually given way to imperial democracy as the structure and ideology of rule. The increased prominence of representative institutions, and the emergence of democratic intellectual voices were dominant political developments, and a Japanese species of bourgeois parliamentary rule continued for most of the following fourteen years. In this new era, the imperial democratic *move-*

1. Donald F. Roden, *Schooldays in Imperial Japan: A Study in the Culture of a Student Elite* (Berkeley: University of California Press, 1980).

ment dissolved. Its leaders, men like Hara Kei, Katō Kōmei, and Inukai Tsuyoshi, changed from outsiders seeking to gain a share of power to insiders exercising executive power in consultation with bureaucrats, proposing and passing laws, and seeking to maintain a social hierarchy in which their position had been secured. They sought to build institutions that would contain further change and articulated an ideology to promote political and social order.

To be sure, the parties never displaced the oligarchy or the bureaucracy. The triumph of Hara's politics of compromise produced an amalgam: an increasingly and uneasily partisan bureaucracy, increasingly bureaucratic parties, and a less obstreperous military. In contrast to the narrower earlier ruling structure of bureaucrats, generals, and admirals, former samurai all, the imperial democratic structure both served and included new groups with considerable power: businessmen, landlords, and professionals. The higher schools and the university would mold this elite; the Diet would be the primary arena to adjust the relation of its component parts. Most members of this expanded group of rulers, including the formerly leading bureaucrats and military men, came to believe that national strength and economic success required the cooperative participation of plural segments of a broadened elite.

THE CONSERVATIVE VERSION OF IMPERIAL DEMOCRACY

The Seiyūkai and Kenseikai/Miniseitō parties contesting for power in the era of imperial democratic rule agreed only on its broad ideological strokes: that a parliamentary order with a degree of popular participation would best serve national strength, social order, and the personal interest of party members; or, conversely, that these causes would not be served by narrow bureaucratic rule or simple repression and paternalism. Beyond this, as Sheldon Garon has forcefully shown, the two parties differed significantly and consistently on the crucial matter of how much popular participation would best serve the existing order.[2]

The boundaries of legitimate participation were thus not fixed, and they expanded over time. It is in contention over these boundaries that we find the critical connection between the story of labor in places such

---

2. Sheldon Garon, *State and Labor in Modern Japan* (Berkeley: University of California Press, 1987).

as Nankatsu and the history of national politics. As the working class emerged as a major social force after World War I, the men of substance, education, and status who had led the imperial democratic movement and now dominated the new structure of rule fought intense battles over how to maintain the system. They disagreed over whether imperial Japan should be a democracy for men of capital and landed property only, or whether national power and social order would best be secured by making Japan a more open democratic society for all men, and perhaps even for women.

Both these avenues were explored in the 1920s. The imperial democrats in power between 1918 and 1932 produced two sets of ideas and policies, one conservative and one distinctly more liberal. The former program is associated in the political world with the Seiyūkai Party, in power from 1918 to 1922 and 1927 to 1929, and with bureaucrats in the Ministry of Agriculture and Commerce; its primary practitioners in the economic world were managers of large-scale heavy industry. The Seiyūkai program dominated national policy in the immediate wake of World War I, and beginning in 1919 some industrial managers began to revise strategy toward labor. The liberal version of imperial democracy was the product of rising young Home Ministry bureaucrats and politicians in the Kenseikai/Minseitō Party. They, too, first articulated their program in the early postwar years and found some support in the business world. Their version was uneasily ascendant for most of the period between 1924 and 1931.

The Seiyūkai cabinets of 1918 to 1922 articulated the conservative vision of imperial democracy. In the labor field, Hara Kei's home minister, Tokonami Takejirō, introduced several related new social policies in 1919, all aimed at restoring social order and harmony. He and Hara committed Japan to participate in the International Labor Organization. He reinterpreted the ambiguous anti-strike, anti-union clauses of the Public Order Police Law by directing local police to tolerate "peaceful" unions and strikes, and arrests under the law declined from 1919. Tokonami was the central figure in founding the Kyōchōkai (Harmonization Society), an officially supported think tank charged with studying and solving social problems, in particular labor-capital conflict. Business leaders resisted the Kyōchōkai at first, afraid that to recognize the problem officially would only intensify it, but corporate sponsors gradually came round. They added 6.8 million yen to the initial government endowment of 2 million yen, and for two decades the Kyōchōkai played a major role in coordinating labor policies of the bureaucracy and the business world.[3] In 1920, to deal with unemployment and other social problems, the Home Ministry also created a Social Bureau which it substantially upgraded in 1922, giving it broad responsibility over labor problems. In these same years, several municipal governments, including Tokyo, also created their own Social Bureaus.

Tokonami went beyond studying the problem and expanding the bureaucracy. To revive in the workplace what he claimed to be a unique Japanese spirit of cooperation and obedience, he instructed the police to encourage "vertical" company unions and block horizontal worker groups. Despite early skepticism on the part of some capitalists, these became a critical element in the labor policy of many large firms in the 1920s. In a similar spirit, Tokonami drafted a Works Council Bill in 1919 that would have created mandatory councils of workers and managers in all enterprises of over fifty employees, but in the face of widespread criticism from business groups opposed to any compulsory program, Hara withdrew it.[4]

While all these steps sought to calm labor unrest without recognizing an independent labor interest, they do reveal a new elite perception found even in the Seiyūkai: to tame aggressive labor required positive policy as well as repression.[5] No previous government, after all, had encouraged worker organizations of any sort.

This new orientation to social policy and the populace extended beyond labor matters. Yokota Sennosuke, a leading Seiyūkai M.P. and a confidant of Hara Kei's, believed it necessary to pay careful attention to public opinion, contending that politics in the new era must be "rooted in the people [minponshugi] and tackle social problems."[6] The Hara government also set up a committee in the Agricultural Ministry in 1920 to investigate reform of tenant farming. It produced Japan's first draft of a law establishing rights to tenancy, but in the face of fierce landlord opposition, the Seiyūkai shelved the draft.[7]

The social and political program of the Seiyūkai included a limited, but important, reform of the prohibition on female participation in

---

3. See William Dean Kinzley, "The Quest for Industrial Harmony in Japan: The Kyōchōkai, 1919–1946" (Ph.D. diss., University of Washington, 1984).

4. Garon, State and Labor, pp. 47–54, for detailed analysis of these policies.

5. Ibid., p. 49.

6. Eguchi Keiichi, ed., Shimupojiumu Nihon rekishi: Taishō demokurashii (Tokyo Gakuseisha, 1976), p. 129, quotes Yokota.

7. Ann Waswo, Japanese Landlords: The Decline of a Rural Elite (Berkeley: University of California Press, 1977), pp. 118–23.

both political assemblies and associations. In late 1919, a group of women in Tokyo founded the New Women's Society and began a vigorous signature drive against the prohibitions. Several months later, in March 1920, the Seiyūkai for the first time came out formally in favor of ending the prohibition on female freedom of assembly (but not association). This limited revision passed the lower house in the following Diet session of 1921, although opposition in the House of Peers defeated the reform. Finally, a bill to allow freedom of assembly passed both houses in 1922. Women were free to attend and speak at political meetings, and to demonstrate, but they could not join political organizations or vote. However limited, the change did offer new legitimacy to female political action. Women's movements for further political rights, as well as female labor actions, intensified through the rest of the decade.[8]

A broad array of initiatives thus constituted the conservative program for imperial democracy. Cautiously and slightly, it broadened the scope of legal participation in national politics and recognized a place for controlled labor participation in the workplace. Hara supported a lowered property tax qualification for suffrage in 1919, but he consistently opposed universal suffrage for males in these years: "It is too soon. Abolition of property tax [voting] restrictions with intent to destroy class distinctions is a dangerous idea. I cannot agree."[9] Further, by insisting that the government would appoint even the "labor representative" to the International Labor Organization, by supporting councils and vertical unions while refusing any recognition of more autonomous labor activity, the Seiyūkai denied any notion of labor rights.

In fact, after Hara acted swiftly and severely by using troops to put down a major strike at the Yahata steel mill in 1920, even Yamagata sighed in admiration: "Hara is truly remarkable! The streetcars and steel mills have settled down. Hara's policies are remarkable."[10] In this democracy for the landed elite and the bourgeoisie, the state bureaucracy, in accordance with the will of the major party in the Diet, was to encourage a refurbished corporate paternalism and ensure it by repression of independent unions when necessary. Conservative imperial

8. Yoshimi Kaneko, *Kindai Nihon josei shi* (Tokyo: Kagoshima shuppan kai, 1971), 2:141–52, has a detailed account of the reform movement and government policy.

9. Ibid., p. 146, quotes Hara.

10. "Dōmo Hara wa erai. Densha mo seitetsujo mo osamatta. Hara no yariguchi wa erai." Masumi Junnosuke, *Nihon seitō shiron* (Tokyo: University of Tokyo Press, 1968), 4:366.

democrats expected that by involving workers in company-sponsored organizations, they would restore harmony to the workplace and to industrial society at large.

REFORMS IN THE WORKPLACE

A complementary strategy of conservative reform emerged at the company level beginning in 1919, in particular among employers in heavy industry. In the realm of rhetoric, the tone of management paternalism shifted in subtle fashion to speak of a more equal partnership of managers and workers.[11] In practice, the creation of factory councils was one important new departure. In typical councils, equal numbers of elected worker and appointed management representatives met periodically to discuss matters ranging from wage levels and employee welfare facilities to productivity.[12] Councils were always advisory, with agendas controlled by management. Subsequent to their widespread adoption at the nation's major heavy industrial firms, disputes in fact dropped sharply in number, suggesting that the councils were part of an effective new strategy.[13]

Councils of the postwar decade were found mainly at large firms in heavy industry engaged in either arms production, shipbuilding, metal processing, or machine engineering, and 87 percent of them were created between 1919 and 1921.[14] These were precisely the workplaces, dominated by relatively skilled, better-paid males, where the preunion disputes had been most numerous, where the labor movement of World War I and just after was strongest, and where the economic future appeared to lie. The councils were clearly a response of managers in this critical sector to labor demands for respect and greater equality of treatment. In addition, these large, capital-rich firms could afford to create specialized labor or personnel sections to study the latest foreign mod-

11. Andrew Gordon, *The Evolution of Labor Relations in Japan: Heavy Industry, 1853–1955* (Cambridge, Mass.: Harvard University Council on East Asian Studies, 1985), pp. 114–15.
12. Examples in Nishinarita Yutaka, "Rōdō ryoku hensei to rōshi kankei," *1920 nendai no Nihon no shihonshugi* (Tokyo: University of Tokyo Press, 1983), pp. 201–5.
13. For elaboration of this point, see Gordon, *Evolution of Labor Relations*, pp. 231–35.
14. Nishinarita Yutaka has found that forty-eight enterprises in heavy industry nationwide created councils between 1919 and 1928. The high point in the movement to found councils came in 1921, when twenty-seven were formed. Of the forty whose size can be determined, exactly three-fourths were in firms employing over 500 workers. This represented close to half of all factories in the nation of this size. Nishinarita Yutaka, "1920 nendai Nihon shihonshugi no rōshi kankei: jūkōgyō rōshi kankei o chūshin ni," *Rekishigaku kenkyū*, no. 512 (January 1983): 2.

els, be they institutions of "welfare capitalism" in the United States or the works councils of Great Britain.

This managerial response represented a conservative incarnation of imperial democracy at the level of the firm. That is, while managers expressed a new spirit of respect for labor and offered somewhat greater equality of treatment, they did not recognize unions or the rights of labor. Further, the new equality in rhetoric and practice was just one part of management strategy. While some leading employers, including the military arsenals, which had roughly 70,000 employees in the early 1920s, tolerated union activity, the majority of large firms remained steadfast in refusing to recognize unions as legitimate bargaining partners. Blacklists and union-busting were as important as councils in most major firms.

While this strategy served management well in the long run, success came only after years of determined implementation. Ironically, in the early postwar era the proponents of councils and the new paternalism did not appear to be on the right track. This was a time of polarization and contention in large factories, and by 1922 or 1923 a union-led spirit of confrontation was spreading to smaller workplaces as well. Significant elements in a growing labor movement repudiated both imperialism and parliamentary democracy and sparked a search for alternative programs to reinforce imperial democratic rule.

THE REPUDIATION
OF IMPERIAL DEMOCRACY

Some postwar leaders of the labor movement built a radical political movement in the 1920s that repudiated capitalism, imperialism, and parliamentary politics. The following three chapters will explore the evolution of this movement and the ideas of its participants. At the outset, we may briefly note the sharp ideological challenge to imperial democracy articulated by vocal elements in this movement. Events such as the founding of the Japanese Communist Party in 1922 of course indicate the emergence of workers and intellectuals with a radical agenda, but the communists only made major gains in the union movement after 1924. The first signs of working-class opposition to imperial democracy came in the campaign for expanded suffrage after World War I.

In 1919 labor unions were still acting in concert with party politicians leading the suffrage movement. The "people's rallies" (*kokumin taikai*) for universal suffrage in the winter of 1919 drew throngs of up to 50,000. At its 1919 convention the Sōdōmei adopted a resolution in support of universal suffrage for men. For the Sōdōmei, the right to vote ranked formally with the rights to live, to organize, and to strike as one of the "Four Rights of Labor."[15]

The turning point came in 1920. Part of the labor challenge was a repudiation of Japanese imperialism and militarism, symbolized by the decision of the Sōdōmei to drop the word "Greater" from its name (Greater Japan Federation of Labor). The Sōdōmei turned against the Siberian expedition that began in 1918, and in 1923 it called for self-government in Korea. In a similar spirit, an article in one union magazine supported the cause of female labor in Korean rubber factories, and a plaintive piece in another in 1922 lamented that children at play shouted "Soldiers, soldiers!" at a procession of workers carrying union flags en route to a rally.[16] Labor groups in 1920 continued to support suffrage, organizing the National Federation of Labor Organizations, with thirty-five member groups, to lead the labor push for the vote.[17] The suffrage movement of the winter of 1920 probably exceeded that of 1919 in scale and intensity, with rallies and demonstrations in both Ueno and Shiba parks almost daily from February 11 through the 22nd.[18] In mainstream rallies, led by party politicians, the older vocabulary of the political crowd dominated. When police tried to apprehend a student leader of a crowd outside the residence of Prime Minister Hara Kei on February 22, he allegedly shouted, "Under constitutional government, what business do you have kicking a child of the emperor?" and "There's no law against the people [kokumin] trying to meet the prime minister." One of the lawyers who defended the forty-two people indicted for rioting after this incident had himself been a defendant in the Siemens riot of 1914.[19]

But for the first time, workers began to hold separate rallies. Their emphasis was different. At Hibiya Park on Suffrage Day / Founding Day, February 11, 1920, posters read, "Our enemy is the capitalist" and "Destroy the zaibatsu." At Shiba Park on the same day, the Kantō

---

15. Masujima Hiroshi, "Fusen undō to seitō seiji," in *Kōza Nihon shi: Nihon teikokushugi no hōkai,* ed. Nihon shi ken kyū kai (Tokyo: University of Tokyo Press, 1971), p. 131.

16. See *Rōdō kumiai,* August 1923, p. 11, and *Rōdō,* September 1922, p. 7, for these examples.

17. Miyachi Masato, *Nichiro sengo seiji shi no kenkyū* (Tokyo: University of Tokyo Press, 1973), pp. 371–72.

18. Morinaga Eisaburō, *Shidan saiban* (Tokyo: Nihon hyōronsha, 1972), 3:125.

19. Ibid., pp. 127–29.

Labor Alliance of twelve groups rallied 10,000 supporters. Reporters noted a flag with the slogan "From slavery to humanity." Labor and mainstream suffrage groups clashed over the importance of demanding abolition of Article 17 of the Public Order Police Law, the major law hampering union organizing.[20] Three months later organized labor began the tradition of rallying and demonstrating on its own day when a spirited gathering of 10,000 workers at Ueno Park marked Japan's first May Day.[21]

This separation gradually turned toward antagonism, as leaders in the labor movement claimed suffrage was no longer an important goal; they rejected the tactic of using the vote as a means to longer-term revolutionary mobilization. Fierce disputes over the suffrage plank in the union platform disrupted Sōdōmei conventions of 1920 through 1922. The Kantō delegates generally opposed the call for suffrage; they viewed direct action and a general strike as primary labor tactics. Supporters of a parliamentary strategy barely survived this challenge in 1921, and the following year the radical wing prevailed. The convention deleted calls for universal suffrage from its platform.[22]

The mainstream suffrage campaign continued from 1922 to 1924, when a coalition cabinet centered on the Kenseikai came to power. This finally pushed a bill for universal manhood suffrage through the Diet in 1925, but popular involvement in the suffrage rallies had gradually diminished, and most labor organizations were indifferent or opposed. On Founding Day in 1922 suffrage advocates and labor unions squabbled over access to Shiba Park. The labor group claimed it had registered first but eventually gave way; well-known M.P.'s Ozaki Yukio and Kōno Hironaka addressed a suffrage rally of 10,000 attendees in the park.

In the tradition of the post-1905 crowd, some popular enthusiasm for such gatherings was still evident: after one mainstream rally in 1922 a crowd of 5,000 marched to the law office of the Seiyūkai Party president, who opposed the bill, and smashed his windows with a hail of stones. The seventeen people arrested offer an occupational portrait of the urban crowd of the day: identifiable occupations were two machinists, one printer, three petty tradesmen, one furniture maker, two mailmen, three office workers, and one day laborer.[23] Yet organized work-

---

20. *TAS*, February 12, 1920, p. 7.
21. *NRN* (1921), pp. 30–31.
22. Masujima, "Fusen undō," pp. 135–36.
23. *TAS*, February 12, 1922, p. 3.

ers had met separately the previous evening at Kanda Youth Hall to debate the relative importance of expanded suffrage and parliamentary action, and the Sōdōmei had held a separate rally on the 11th, where speakers focused on the need for unemployment relief and even supported arms limitation as a policy to aid the unemployed.[24]

The same pattern of separate gatherings repeated itself the following two years, and the suffrage rallies declined in size and intensity. Only 2,000 gathered for Suffrage Day at Ueno Park in 1923. The scene at the gate captured the growing distance between common Tokyoites and the suffrage groups. Organizers charged a hefty fifty-sen admission fee (about one-third of a day's pay for a typical young male worker). "Let us in for free!" crowds at the gate shouted, pelting the guards with snowballs. The major rally of the 1924 campaign was also low-key and small, with 5,000 attendees, compared to the gatherings of 10,000 to 50,000 common in earlier years. In both 1923 and 1924 the Sōdōmei and other labor groups sponsored various separate rallies on Founding Day as well as May Day.

IMPERIAL DEMOCRATS RESPOND

Saitō Tadatoshi, one of the early Yūaikai activists introduced above, was the main speaker at one gathering of 1,800 workers on Founding Day in 1923. The scene at the gate was emblematic of a ubiquitous elite conception of the worker as outlaw, whether en route to the company or acting in a public arena: the police subjected all entrants to body checks, and several scuffles with plainclothesmen occurred.[25] Thus, while paternal programs in the conservative version of imperial democracy extended a measure of recognition and respect to compliant workers within big firms, bureaucrats, party leaders, and managers agreed that independently organized radical workers were truly dangerous outlaws. In matters great and small, in policies of symbolic or substantive impact, the police in particular, as the front-line representatives of the state for common city-dwellers, hammered this point home. A twenty-year history of antagonistic relations with the urban poor set the stage for the tense, occasionally violent, dealings of the police with organized labor.

Police sensitivity to all forms of anti-system expression was acute. Revolutionary songs were a threat to social order, and police repeatedly

24. *TAS*, February 11, 1922, p. 5; February 11, 1922, evening edition, p. 2.
25. For an account of this scene, see *TAS*, February 12, 1923, p. 2.

warned strikers in the early 1920s not to sing forbidden lyrics. Workers sometimes dealt with this attention by joking about it. A labor magazine described a spirited Machinists' Federation rally of 5,000 members in Honjo on Suffrage Day / Founding Day of 1923. A befuddled country cop, called in for riot duty that day, could not discern whether a certain song qualified as revolutionary. "Isn't this a revolutionary song?" he asked his captain. Told that it indeed was, he swaggered over to the workers and ordered them to stop singing.[26]

Any man or woman who even suggested a radical critique of the economic and political structure of imperial Japan in a public forum, or who listened to such a message, did so in a context that made the outlaw status of the critique unmistakable. A policeman stood or sat at the side of the stage at all labor gatherings (see fig. 19). His role was not passive. When speakers skirted the boundaries of legitimate discourse, he issued a warning. When they crossed the boundary, he stopped the speech. If other speakers continued to spout blasphemy, he halted the meeting, if he dared risk the ire of the audience. These events were theatrical, even light-hearted, as some observers noted, but the jokes about country cops and laughter at speech-meeting theatrics suggest that workers used humor to cope with the troubling, omnipresent restrictions on what they could say and, by implication, think about the legitimacy of the existing social order.[27]

In the spring prior to the Ishikawajima strike, a staff member of the Kyōchōkai transcribed the addresses at a rally of the Sōdōmei's Electric and Machine Workers' Union at Kanda Youth Hall, attended by 800 people. Police halted fifteen of the twenty-two speeches. The record of this meeting pinpoints the radical keywords in the forbidden critique. The offending utterances were:

1. *Capitalists* are . . . [speech halted]

2. We workers first *must destroy* . . . [halted]

3. *The only course is* to build the road to freedom with our own strength . . . [halted]

4. We have absolutely no freedom. At dawn I had a dream. I was advancing down the road to freedom carrying a sword, when I fell into

---

26. *Rōdō shūhō*, February 13, 1923, p. 2.
27. For a description of the light-hearted aspect, see Murashima, *Rōdō sōgi*, p. 147–48.

a deep crevice. This is *a crevice that captures* those who speak the truth
...[halted]

5. It is just *too irrational* for members of our own class [i.e., the police] to stand above us and repress us...[halted]

6. As Lenin said, "Those who do not work *will not eat*...[halted]

7. To discover how, and with what, *to destroy this system* is our objective...[halted]

8. In order to live we must *finally destroy* the present system ...[halted]

9. Together with all of you, I will devote all my strength to *the destruction* of everything...[halted]

10. We *must destroy* capitalism...[halted]

11. In order to live we must attack capitalism at its roots; we *must entirely destroy* the existing social order...[halted]

12. One after another the speakers have been *unjustly halted*... [halted]

13. *We must struggle against* those who oppose us...[halted]

14. For example, *a revolution*...[halted]

15. The labor movement must move *to end the plunder* of capitalists...[28]

This catalog of forbidden phrases neatly delineates the boundaries imposed by the imperial democratic state on the opposed vision of radical labor: not only were acts of violence, destruction, or revolution unspeakable; in addition, the institutions of capital and the state (the police) could not be blamed for the plight of the workers.

THE LIBERAL VERSION
OF IMPERIAL DEMOCRACY

In a broad context of elite agreement on these outer limits of acceptable opposition, the conservative conception of imperial democracy articulated and implemented by Hara and Tokonami gave way to a significantly more liberal set of elite social policies beginning in 1924. This is made quite ironic by the fact that the labor-management strategy in big

28. Kyū-kyōchōkai, *Tōkyō-fu ka no rōdōsha dantai* (1921), held at OISR. Staff report of March 1, 1921, titled "Rōdō mondai daienzetsukai gaiyō." I have underlined the final several words of the original phrasing of each speech.

business that had emerged after World War I finally began to bear fruit in these very years. It suggests there was a significant disjunction between bureaucratic and party policy toward labor on one hand and managerial policies in the factory on the other.

At the heart of this management strategy lay the promotion of factory councils and a more substantive paternalism. By the end of the decade, managers had ousted organized labor from the nation's major heavy industrial worksites, and significant nonunion protest virtually disappeared as well. Dispute actions at the eleven leading shipyards and arsenals declined dramatically (table 5.1). They together experienced an average of ten labor disputes annually between 1917 and 1921; by the end of the decade, less than one dispute each year took place in these same workplaces. Just seventeen major disputes took place in enterprises with over 1,000 employees nationwide between 1929 and 1932, despite mass dismissals of white- and blue-collar workers in dozens of large factories. Only two of these disputes came in the heavy or chemical industries; the remainder took place in textile mills, coal mines, or among transportation workers.[29] Factory councils, in-company education, corporate welfare programs, careful hiring policies, firing of activists when possible, and the opposition in some cases of rightist groups within the factory had destroyed the union movement in this sector.[30]

Even so, many bureaucrats and party politicians doubted the relative quiet in the large workplaces would last. They were skeptical that factory councils and refurbished paternalism, coupled with ongoing official hostility to unions, would solve the labor problem, and they feared a revival of unrest when economic conditions again favored labor. Further, they could see that success even among larger firms was greatest in the huge state arsenals and private shipyards. Labor activism continued in major textile mills and a number of substantial machine, electrical, and metal firms, as well as in smaller factories in the metal, chemical, and food-processing sectors, and the tone of this activism was becoming increasingly radical.

As the labor movement expanded in this uneven fashion, bureaucrats

29. Hyōdō Tsutomu, "Shōwa kyōkō ka no sōgi," in *Nihon rōshi kankei shiron*, ed. Sumiya Mikio (Tokyo: University of Tokyo Press, 1977), p. 128.

30. Gordon, *Evolution of Labor Relations*, ch. 5, is a detailed study of the ousting of organized labor from large firms in the Tokyo-Yokohama area. The data in table 5.1 may exaggerate the decline in disputes slightly, since it is easier to document a dispute that occurred than it is to be sure that none took place. A survey of the several sources most likely to record dispute activities for the period from 1927–32 turned up only the three cases noted in the table. It is possible a few disputes were overlooked.

TABLE 5.1   LABOR DISPUTES AT MAJOR HEAVY INDUSTRIAL SITES, 1897–1932

	1897–1916	1917–21	1922–23	1924–26	1927–29	1930–32
Kure Naval Arsenal	4	3	0	0	0	0
Koishikawa Army Arsenal, Tokyo	4	10	1	0	0	0
Yokosuka Naval Arsenal	5	0	0	0	0	0
Sasebo Naval Arsenal	1	1	0	0	0	0
Mitsubishi						
Nagasaki yard	5	10	0	1	0	0
Kobe yard	4	4	0	1	0	0
Kawasaki shipyard, Kobe	3	3	1	1	0	0
Osaka Ironworks	6	7	1	0	0	0
Uraga Dock Company	6	4	1	1	1	1
Yokohama Dock Company	8	4	3	3	1	0
Ishikawajima shipyard, Tokyo	3	6	2	3	0	0
Total	49	52	9	10	2	1
Total annual average	2.5	10.4	4.5	3.3	0.67	0.5

SOURCES: Aoki Kōji, *Nihon rōdō undō shi nenpyō* (Tokyo: Shinseisha, 1968); *Shakai undō tsūshin*; *Shakai undō ōrai*; *Shakai seisaku jihō*.

in the Social Bureau of the Home Ministry and urban politicians in the Kenseikai/Minseitō Party championed a liberal incarnation of imperial democracy with increasing vigor. Between World War I and 1923 they had already developed an instrumental vision of social policy with a conscious kinship to Britain's "socially minded" liberalism of the late nineteenth century, but they lacked the political clout to implement it. Through national health insurance, a stronger factory law, unemployment insurance, and a union bill, they aimed to incorporate labor and stabilize the social order.[31]

Under the conservative version of imperial democracy of the Seiyūkai Party cabinets of 1918–22, and the nonparty Katō Tomosaburō cabinet that followed (June 1922–September 1923), this platform remained on the drawing table. The postearthquake, nonparty cabinets of Yamamoto Gonnohyōe (September 1923–January 1924) and Kiyoura Keigo (January–June 1924) then began tentatively to implement it at the behest of Home Ministry bureaucrats. In June 1924, when a coalition party cabinet returned to power, the Kenseikai Party and its allies in the Home Ministry pressed several dramatic new initiatives. Despite major failures in the legislative area, and a two-year return to Seiyūkai rule (1927–29), administrative practice did change in important ways. The period 1924–31 witnessed the uneasy ascendance of the liberal version of imperial democracy.

Soon after the earthquake, the Sōdōmei began unprecedented cooperation with the bureaucracy. Suzuki Bunji took a post in the Provisional Office for Earthquake Relief, and his union functioned as a semiofficial job exchange, providing relief work to its members. In October the Yamamoto cabinet announced support for a universal manhood suffrage bill. In February 1924, as organized labor in Nankatsu began to revive, the new Kiyoura cabinet announced that henceforth the "labor representative" to the ILO would indeed be chosen by workers.[32] In addition, the Kyōchōkai in 1924 for the first time supported "sound" unions as a moderating force for industrial peace. Finally, the Social Bureau began to consult with moderate union leaders concerning draft legislation; by the late 1920s Suzuki Bunji, Abe Isō, and others were serving on official advisory bodies.[33] The major force

---

31. Garon, *State and Labor*, pp. 62–68.

32. The electorate would be workers in unions with over 1,000 members.

33. Andrew Gordon, "Business and Bureaucrats on Labor," in *Managing Industrial Enterprise: Essays in Japanese Business History*, ed. William Wray (Cambridge, Mass.: Harvard University Council on East Asian Studies, 1989), p. 66.

behind these changes was a group of middle-level bureaucrats in the Home Ministry, aided in the ILO case by demands from the ILO itself that Japan reform its selection procedure.[34]

These policies granted a new legitimacy to labor, just as conservative opponents in the Ministry of Agriculture and Commerce and the military had feared. In the pithy metaphor of Commerce Ministry bureaucrat Yoshino Shinji in 1925, the state should not support unions because unions would not stop at moderation, "just as a cart cannot stop rolling down a hill."[35] But these policies also exacerbated tensions among labor movement leaders, just as the Home Ministry's labor policymakers had hoped. Moderates in the Sōdōmei, impressed by these state initiatives, moved away from the antiparliamentary stance that had dominated the union in the early 1920s. In February 1924 the Sōdōmei annual convention "changed direction," replacing its revolutionary platform with a call for parliamentary action, for pragmatic union-building, for collective bargaining, and for economic gain. The result was the rupture of the national movement.

A liberal state policy became the explicit order of the day under the Katō cabinet. After passage of universal manhood suffrage in 1925, the Kenseikai (soon renamed Minseitō) in 1926 called for "universal suffrage for industry": a union bill, a labor disputes conciliation bill, and the repeal of Article 17 of the Public Order Police Law. The union bill died in committee in 1926 because of opposition from bureaucrats in the Agriculture and Commerce ministries, the Seiyūkai Party, and the majority of business federations, but both the conciliation bill and the repeal of Article 17 became law.[36] These two measures amounted to the tacit recognition of labor's right to organize and to strike. By creating a legal structure of dispute conciliation, the state implied the prior legitimacy of dispute actions. In addition, in April 1926 the home minister directed prefectural governors to respect the spirit of the labor union bill, despite its defeat in the Diet. The cabinet also implemented the Health Insurance Law and Factory Law Revision, both passed in 1922 but delayed owing to lack of appropriations and opposition in the Privy Council.[37]

While the majority of industrialists, especially in zaibatsu firms, consistently refused to accept unions as bargaining partners who could help preserve social stability and insisted they would handle labor in the

34. Garon, *State and Labor*, pp. 89–98, for detailed study of these steps.
35. Yoshino Shinji, *Rōdō hōsei kōwa* (Tokyo: Kokumin daigaku kai, 1925), p. 14.
36. Garon, *State and Labor*, pp. 123–30.
37. Ibid., p. 130; Gordon, *Evolution of Labor Relations*, pp. 210–11.

factory without interference, a significant minority of employers' associations and employers, primarily in sectors dominated by smaller firms, did support the liberal version of imperial democracy. Several industrial associations supported the union bill of 1925, including the Tokyo Federation of Business Associations. In 1925 this group unequivocally asserted that "we believe that a labor union law, the healthy development of labor organizations . . . will not only bring good fortune to the workers but will consolidate the foundation of our industry."[38]

The labor initiatives centered on the "suffrage for industry" program were part of a broader set of relatively liberal reforms. The best known, of course, was universal male suffrage, approved by the Diet in 1925. Parallel to the attempted labor reforms was proposed legislation to protect the rights of the increasingly organized and contentious tenant farmers. In 1924 the Katō cabinet won passage of a "Tenant Dispute Mediation Law," and over the next sixteen years nearly two-thirds of all recorded tenant disputes were mediated under this law.[39] The Minseitō also supported a "Tenant Law" in the late 1920s.[40] Recognizing the formidable obstacle posed by the conservative peers, but afraid of alienating them, Katō cautiously pushed to reform the House of Peers and reduce its power, without success.[41] In the international realm, Foreign Minister Shidehara was sufficiently conciliatory toward China and willing to cooperate with the Western powers to earn for his programs the label "Shidehara diplomacy," what one historian has called "go-slow imperialism."[42]

The Minseitō also supported further broadening of political and civil rights for women. Women's groups pressed for three major reforms: the right of political association, the right to vote, and the right to hold regional or local public office.[43] On several occasions after 1924, indi-

38. See Nishinarita Yutaka, "Ryōdaisenkanki rōdō kumiai hō an no shiteki kōsatsu," *Hitotsubashi kenkyū nenpō: keizaigaku kenkyū*, no. 28 (April 1987): 79–93, for the most detailed account of industrial support. Quotation is from p. 91.

39. *NRN*, 1925, pp. 509–13; Richard Smethurst, *Agricultural Development and Tenancy Disputes in Japan, 1870–1940* (Princeton: Princeton University Press, 1986), p. 355.

40. Ronald P. Dore, *Land Reform in Japan* (New York: Oxford University Press, 1959), p. 82.

41. Peter Duus, *Party Rivalry and Political Change in Taishō Japan* (Cambridge, Mass.: Harvard University Press, 1968).

42. John W. Dower, *Empire and Aftermath: Yoshida Shigeru and the Japanese Experience, 1878–1954* (Cambridge, Mass.: Harvard University Council on East Asian Studies, 1979), p. 85.

43. This last, termed *kōminken* in the prewar legal system, was initially (1888) limited to male property owners paying over two yen in land taxes annually. With universal male suffrage, this right was also extended by the Diet to all males over the age of twenty-five.

vidual Diet members submitted legislation for these reforms that won Lower House approval but failed in the House of Peers, and the Minseitō Party itself gradually moved toward support for this program. In 1929 the prime minister (Hamaguchi), the foreign minister, and the home minister held an unprecedented official meeting with leading female suffragists and asked their support for the government's retrenchment policies. Women's groups interpreted this get-together as recognition that females had joined the body politic of *kokumin*. The Minseitō then introduced legislation for female suffrage and civil rights, which passed the Lower House in 1931, only to once more fail in the Peers.[44]

While the Seiyūkai opposed all of these measures, the two major parties and their bureaucratic allies shared substantial common ground. On the most general level, "imperial democracy" represented a broad consensus within party and bureaucratic elites in the 1920s. The imperial democrats in power not only concurred in supporting empire, emperor, and the capitalist foundation of society; they also agreed on the desirability of parliamentary government to secure these ends. They were of one mind as well on who the outlaws were. The relatively liberal Katō administration, which promoted universal male suffrage, also pushed the Peace Preservation Law through the Diet, unequivocally marking the elite's boundary for tolerable political thought and action: attack on the emperor system was a capital offense under the law, while repudiation of the "system of private property" was punishable by up to ten years in jail.[45]

The crucial point is simply that different elite conceptions of the means to these very general common ends were extremely important. The Kenseikai initiatives that unfolded in the years following the earthquake had a major impact. Although it followed the Seiyūkai in outlawing the revolutionary left, the Kenseikai nonetheless created a new context in which implicitly legitimate union activity surged among both men and women despite its failure to write many proposals into law, despite challenges to the liberal program from within the elite, and despite the fact that the police at the local level did not always follow central instructions. Historians of this period have not generally accepted this position. They have often dismissed both government so-

44. Yoshimi, *Kindai Nihon josei shi*, pp. 159–63.
45. See *Musansha undō torishimari hōki sūchi* (Kyoto: Kyōto kyōsei kaku, 1931), p. 26, for text and analysis of this law from the left.

cial policy of the 1920s and labor organizing as superficial: after all the union bill failed; the Peace Preservation Law in a sense offset suffrage expansion and the abolition of Article 17; gains for women were slight; and even in the new environment, union strength never topped 8 percent of the work force. Although recognizing that "much remains to be studied in the period," Peter Duus concluded in 1968 that "it is difficult to discern any large political or social changes wrought by the parties, even the reform-minded Kenseikai," and a more recent summary of American scholarship on Japan claims "the more [scholars] examine the nature of Taishō democracy, the more shallow they find it to be."[46]

Such dismissal overlooks both the several elements in the liberal program that did become law and the significant degree to which a determined bureaucracy could enforce even draft legislation through administrative practice. Neither does this dismissal account for the story of labor in Nankatsu from 1918 through the depression. Though laborers had their own goals, they were aware of the larger context. Some workers and movement leaders boldly attacked both empire and parliamentary democracy, while others took positive cues from the rhetoric and practice of imperial democracy, especially in its liberal incarnation. Building from a substantial base of organizing expertise and sentiment for change, both types built a movement of greater significance than national statistics on union membership suggest. A primary concern of the following chapters will be to understand the relationship between elite programs of imperial democracy and the thought and behavior of Nankatsu's workers.

46. Duus, *Party Rivalry*, p. 248. Harry Wray, "How Democratic Was Taishō Democracy?" in *Japan Examined: Perspectives on Modern Japanese History*, ed. Harry Wray and Hilary Conroy (Honolulu: University Press of Hawaii, 1983), p. 172.

SIX

Nuclei of the Workers' Movement

In the years after World War I, three previously separate streams of action, which had begun to overlap during the war, converged in the workers' movement. Radical intellectuals inspired by the revolution in Russia, moderate Yūaikai reformers of both working-class and intellectual background, and impatient workplace activists began to work together. The lines between these groups were sometimes blurred, and their alliance was sometimes tense. But their efforts produced one of the three most turbulent periods of working-class conflict in Japanese history.[1]

The postwar era was a heady time for union activists. Experimenting with a variety of ideological stances and organizational forms, they saw themselves riding the wave of a progressive future. The social upheaval in the major workplaces was serious, and unions scored notable gains despite their outlaw status in official eyes: labor organizations proliferated in Nankatsu and throughout the city; disputes touched the lives of far more than the nominal union membership; and labor efforts culminated in two intense waves of unrest, one in the summer of 1919 and another, a shocking nationwide series of shipbuilding strikes, in the summer and fall of 1921.[2]

---

1. I identify these as 1919–21, 1929–31, and 1945–53.
2. The citywide surge of strikes in late July 1919 included ten disputes in Nankatsu, which began between July 21 and 31. These ten days accounted for 29 percent of all Nankatsu disputes that year. Data from Aoki Kōji, *Nihon rōdō undō shi nenpyō* (Tokyo: Shinseisha, 1968).

TABLE 6.1 NUMBER OF FACTORIES, BY SCALE AND
SECTOR, MINAMI KATSUSHIKA COUNTY, 1922

	< 10 Workers		10–49 Workers		50+ Workers		Total
Textile and dyeing	54	(50)	41	(38)	14	(13)	109
Machine and metal	93	(49)	73	(38)	24	(13)	190
Chemical	90	(38)	114	(49)	30	(13)	234
Food	2	(14)	7	(50)	5	(36)	14
Other	26		19		5		50
Nankatsu total	265	(44)	254	(43)	78	(13)	597
All Tokyo total	859	(40)	1,011	(47)	291	(13)	2,161

SOURCE: *Minami Katsushika–gun shi* (Tokyo: 1923), pp. 457–58.
NOTE: The survey date was May 1922. Figures in parentheses above are percentages. Owing to rounding off, row totals are not always 100 percent.

By the mid 1920s, unions were an important resource for urban wage workers in Nankatsu and other industrial neighborhoods. The working-class movement had emerged out of the movement for imperial democracy to become an independent social force, which challenged the premises of imperial democracy as movement leaders repudiated the link between Japanese imperialism and a democracy they came to conceive in democratic socialist or antiparliamentary terms. At the same time, a careful dissection of the structure of labor organizations, and the aspirations of the Nankatsu workers in this and the following chapters reveals a divergence between the way movement leaders and the rank and file of workers conceived the purpose of collective action. Recognition of this complexity will help us understand the impact and the fate of the workers' movement during the depression and in the 1930s.

Labor activity in the early postwar years nationwide and in Nankatsu continued to center upon such workplaces as the larger shipyards, arsenals, machine and metal shops, and textile mills. These heavily capitalized and relatively tightly managed sites had been the locales of earlier nonunion disputes, as well as the early pockets of Yūaikai strength (both analyzed in part 1). However, the industrial base of Nankatsu diversified during and after the war to include an increasing number of smaller workplaces in the machine, metal work, and chemical industries, while the proportion of the work force in large textile mills declined (see graph 4.2).[3] By 1924 the combined proportion of employment in the former three industries in greater Nankatsu stood at 35 percent, up from just 12 percent before World War I. Table 6.1 makes clear that the vast majority of these workplaces in Nankatsu in 1922 were quite small. Eventually, to a slight degree before the earthquake and more dramatically after 1923, labor activity spread to the small- and medium-scale segment of Nankatsu's denser, more diverse postwar industrial structure.

UNIONS: BEYOND THE YŪAIKAI

Until the end of World War I, the relatively narrow ideological boundaries of the Yūaikai encompassed virtually all labor organization in Tokyo. In the years after 1918 both the organization and ideas of the labor movement diversified dramatically. The Yūaikai leaders reorganized the union along industrial instead of regional lines, and a number of unions either split off or emerged independently. These unions shed the earlier Yūaikai reluctance to strike. In addition, the union leadership changed as a new generation of radical young intellectuals, inspired by the Russian Revolution and the slogan "To the People," joined existing unions or founded independent ones, marking the start of a long, often stormy, relationship between worker and intellectual activists.

The period is complex because ideological tensions cross-cut organizational ones. Advocates of revolution clashed with supporters of reform. Demands for immediate change countered calls to transform society gradually. Union leaders and members had to choose between alignment with the Yūaikai or nonaffiliation, between area-, industry-, or enterprise-based organizations, between Bolshevist and anarchosyndicalist philosophies, and between groups led only by "pure" workers and those with intellectuals in key positions.

The most effective organizations built upon workshop and factory units. Beyond this level, unions joined forces in a variety of loose umbrella federations, and it was both in and between such federations that ongoing ideological battles were fought. Through these actions at the union's local and central levels, working men and women carved out a sphere of labor activity separate from, and often opposed to, that

---

3. The term *chemical* in contemporary statistics included ceramics, paper, leather, explosives, oil-refining, pharmaceuticals, rubber, celluloid toys, soap, dyes, and fertilizers.

of the bourgeois parties, and articulated an alternative vision for the future. It is the task of this chapter to analyze this process of movement-building.

THE TRANSFORMATION OF THE YŪAIKAI

In the immediate postwar era, the Yūaikai in Nankatsu retained its vitality and continued to grow. The union penetrated at least seven additional factories in 1918 and five in 1919. In the summer and fall of 1918 the Yūaikai also began its slow, uneven transition from "regional" to "industrial" organization by founding the Tokyo Metalworkers' Union and the Yūaikai Textile Workers' Union. The Metalworkers' Union made limited gains in Nankatsu, but by the spring of 1920 the textile union claimed 1,850 members in the Fujibō mill alone, as well as strength in several other Nankatsu mills.[4] The Yūaikai also founded the Rubber Workers' Union, centered on the large Mitatsuchi Rubber Factory, in March 1920; at its peak, this claimed over 1,000 members in three Nankatsu locals.[5] These industrial groups coexisted with older regional locals for at least two years, for local leaders apparently disagreed on the desirability of splitting effective existing regional groups along industrial lines.

In 1919 the Yūaikai renamed itself the Greater Japan General Federation of Labor (Dai Nihon rōdō sōdōmei, abbreviated to Sōdōmei). Some of the Sōdōmei regional locals remained for a time among the union's most energetic, including five such groups in Nankatsu. In February four of these joined forces in an important area federation of local unions, the Jōtō Federation, and in the summer of 1919 Hirasawa Keishichi became its chairman. He had quarreled with the increasingly influential intellectuals in the Yūaikai headquarters, who ousted him as editor of the Yūaikai monthly. Under Hirasawa's energetic leadership, the federation quickly developed into a center of social activity and study for the workers of the Nankatsu area.

The Jōtō Federation sponsored a library, a debating society, a health clinic, an arts and culture club (serving as outlet for Hirasawa's plays), a Labor Problem Research Group, and legal aid and job introduction services. In addition, it mediated in several major labor disputes in the area, including an action at the Ōshima Steel Company, an employer of 500 and one of the largest factories in Nankatsu, in which 150 union mem-

4. *Rōdō*, June 1920.
5. *Rōdō*, May 1920, p. 22.

bers won several concrete reforms, while also calling for "recognition of the character/dignity of workers."[6]

The federation seems to have attracted strong local interest and support. Fragmentary evidence reveals that one thousand people attended a federation speech-meeting in March 1919 at a Kameido elementary school; members of the federation bought 550 copies of the February issue of *Labor and Industry*; and by August the rented headquarters of the federation served as a labor club, hosting different activities each night of the week, ranging from singing to Japanese chess (*shōgi*) to discussions of labor problems.[7]

Through these activities, Hirasawa and his associates were creating one of the several nuclei of working-class activity that emerged in Tokyo and other major cities just after World War I. In 1919 and 1920 the Sōdōmei's dues-paying membership in Nankatsu easily exceeded 3,000 men and women, and in the turbulent year of 1919 the Yūaikai led or supported nine of the thirty-seven labor disputes in the Nankatsu region.

HIRASAWA KEISHICHI AND THE PURE LABORERS' UNION

The intellectual odyssey of Hirasawa Keishichi paralleled a broader shift in the workers' movement. He gradually moved to a more radical critique of Japan's capitalist society, advocating direct action and confrontation with factory managers. He also created, in the Pure Laborers' Union and a cluster of related groups, a second core of working-class activism in postwar Tokyo.

Hirasawa's shift lagged slightly behind that of the union movement's intellectual activists, and his angry relations with these men resulted in one of the first major splits along the worker-intellectual axis.[8] The direct cause of the split was the sharp critical reaction of intellectuals Asō Hisashi and Tanahashi Kotora, as well as of workers' leader Watanabe Masanosuke, to Hirasawa's alleged compromise of labor interests in two disputes of 1919. As union representative, Hirasawa had accepted the firing of two militant union members in settling a dispute at the Hitachi company's factory in Kameido. When the Sōdōmei con-

---

6. "Jinkaku shōnin," *ROS*, July 1919, p. 42.
7. Matsumoto, *Engeki shi*, pp. 389, 467; *ROS*, February, March, June, and August 1919 columns on local activities.
8. The division of people here into categories of "intellectual" and "worker" is a structural one, not a judgment on their quality of mind. Intellectuals are in general those with university education.

ducted an internal investigation of his conduct, the insulted Hirasawa, along with several leaders of area locals and several hundred members, left the union. In December 1920 he and his supporters officially launched the "Pure Laborers' Union" (*Jun rōdōsha kumiai*).

Ironically, Hirasawa's moderate, nonconfrontational conception of union activities then began to change, as the new union responded to increasingly assertive demands from the rank and file. The organization followed a trajectory toward direct action and syndicalism, while it continued to oppose the increasingly Bolshevist leadership of the Sōdōmei.[9]

Workers at three of Nankatsu's largest metal and machine producers provided most of the support for the Pure Laborers' Union: Japan Casting (240 employees), Ōjima Steel (900), and the Train Manufacturing Company (950). Hirasawa and his supporters chronicled the union's activities in several publications, part of a new and vigorous, if often ephemeral, working-class press in Tokyo.[10] By April 1921 the union had six locals. By the end of 1921 the Pure Laborers' Union had lost one local and added four others. At its high-water mark, the union drew support from several smaller factories and probably enrolled over 1,000 members.[11] Yet maintaining morale and membership proved more difficult than building it, and by 1923, after considerable upheaval and several unsuccessful disputes, an independent survey reported just 230 members in twenty locals, a federation of small cells scattered over numerous factories.

The Pure Laborers' Union, together with several allied institutions created in these years by Hirasawa or his associates, served for a few years as one center in the halting creation of a local working-class culture. The philosophy of the union drew upon Hirasawa's rhetoric of several years earlier, but it very clearly transformed his message. In a June 1921 editorial one of Hirasawa's co-organizers claimed that workers had a mission to create a new society, separate from capitalist society and opposed to its values. In this effort, the support and instruction of intellectuals was acceptable, but all basic decisions were to come from "pure workers." Only workers would be allowed voting

9. Matsumoto Gappei, *Nihon shakaishugi engeki shi* (Tokyo: Chikuma shobō, 1975), pp. 391–92, 560–64.

10. These included *Shinsoshiki* (New Organization), *Rōdō kumiai* (Labor Union), *Rōdō shūhō* (Labor Weekly), and *Rōdō shinbun* (Labor Newspaper).

11. See *Rōdō undō shi kenkyū*, no. 36 (May 1963): 37–38, and *Shinsoshiki*, June 1921, pp. 18–19, on organizational development.

membership in the organization. Taking a cue from Hirasawa's exalta-
tion of the worker's arm (*ude*), he claimed that "our arms are the
emblem of our union, our strength, pride, and asset."[12] One year later,
the allied consumers' "Cooperative Society" (*Kyōdōsha*) echoed and
extended this message:

> — We will not tolerate exploitation. We will resist the commercial system.
> — The bourgeois commercial system is deformed. We will destroy it.
> — Ours is an autonomous workers' consumer cooperative that will not only
>   destroy the old society; with our ideal of a new society, we will construct
>   a new society.[13]

Hirasawa found a strong ally in the summer of 1920 in the person of
Okamoto Torikichi, an unconventional man who gave up a secure position as a white-collar "salaryman" to work full time promoting social
reform. In 1919 he had founded the "Constitutional Enterprise Association" in Nankatsu, issuing an appeal for workers to form their own
"constitutional" institutions within the present society, with the goal of
eventually replacing it.[14] As headquarters, Okamoto opened the Ōjima
Labor Hall in August 1919, and that October he began publication of
the movement's journal, *New Organization*.

Upon its founding in 1920, the Pure Laborers' Union worked in
concert with Okamoto, using the Ōjima Hall as a meeting place and the
pages of *New Organization* for publicity. Hirasawa was apparently sufficiently drawn to Okamoto's message to be willing to overlook the
latter's white-collar background. Between 1920 and 1923 the two col-
laborated in the founding of several allied institutions in Nankatsu,
conceived of as building blocks of a new society. By 1921 the cluster of
associated workers' groups in the area included a labor bank, the consumers' cooperative mentioned above, a cultural academy, a workers'
theatrical group founded by Hirasawa, and a second labor hall in the
working-class neighborhood of Tsukishima, on the edge of Nankatsu.
These groups were active and solvent at least until 1923. The cooperative reported sales of 6,000 yen and a profit of 663 yen in its first five
months of operation, the labor bank reported 3,600 yen in deposits
soon after its founding, the cultural academy claimed seventy students
enrolled in its night classes on political science, mathematics, Japanese

12. *Shinsoshiki*, June 1, 1921, p. 17.
13. Matsumoto, *Nihon shakaishugi engeki shi*, pp. 569–70.
14. For Okamoto's biography, see *Nihon shakai undō jinmei jiten*, ed. Shiota Shōhei
(Tokyo: Aoki shoten, 1979), p. 133. Matsumoto, *Nihon shakaishugi engeki shi*, pp. 544–
45.

literature, English, and current events by June 1921, and Hirasawa's theatrical troupe by this time boasted a 500-seat theater.[15]

Okamoto saw the business enterprise as a basic unit of society and called for a constitutional order within it in which workers and capitalists were equals. Labor unions were to be recognized in each enterprise, and profits were to be shared. By supplying needed goods, the enterprise served the *kokumin* as well as the world; an enterprise run only for the sake of a capitalist's profit ignored the people.[16] In Okamoto's view, constitutional enterprises could make profits so long as the workers shared in them. The factory, he proclaimed, was an intermediate unit of society, between family and nation; at all three levels, equality and freedom were to be the basis of the new society.[17] The leaders in this movement offered a labor-centered elaboration of the idiom and ideology of the movement for imperial democracy. Their program was anchored in the concepts of nation and constitution, and it repudiated neither the emperor nor capitalism. Rather, it carved out a central place for wage workers as a separate group among the nation's people and sought to reform capitalism to offer respect and security to these people.

The active membership in the half-dozen groups that made up Hirasawa's movement barely exceeded one thousand at its peak, but the impact of these groups on the larger community was considerable. Hirasawa and his colleagues supported workers in prolonged disputes at Japan Casting, Ōjima Steel, and the Train Manufacturing Company in 1921, 1922, and 1923 respectively, although the Pure Laborers' Union did not initiate the actions. Rather, Hirasawa negotiated on behalf of the workers and the Ōjima Labor Hall served as strike headquarters, while Hirasawa's group helped with publicity and organizing rallies. Formal membership figures for the Pure Laborers' Union are, therefore, only a partial indication of its significance. Even if only a minority at a factory were committed to the Pure Laborers' Union and his movement to the extent of paying monthly dues, the local unions, with support from Hirasawa's headquarters, could mobilize the majority in a confrontation. The Ōjima and Tsukishima labor halls became more or less permanent "dispute headquarters" for area workers, whether part of the union or not, two of several nuclei of organizational expertise to which workers could rally.

---

15. *Shinsoshiki*, June 1, 1921, pp. 20–27.
16. The term was *kokumin o mushi.*
17. *Shinsoshiki*, October 1, 1919, pp. 1, 3–6.

INTELLECTUALS AND WORKERS IN NANKATSU

The forging of links between radical intellectuals and worker activists was an important new trend of the early postwar era. Although Hirasawa's group responded with antagonism, the interaction was more fruitful in other cases. In Nankatsu, two study groups in particular played a crucial role in cultivating additional nuclei of militant union leaders and social activists.

One centered on the celluloid worker Watanabe Masanosuke, and its fate intersected tragically with that of Hirasawa Keishichi in 1923 (see fig. 12). This was the Nankatsu Labor Association (Nankatsu rōdō kyōkai), an outgrowth of a smaller study group of former student radicals and workers founded in 1922. By the summer of 1923, thirty to fifty workers attended meetings of the group. Several of its leaders, the charismatic Watanabe chief among them, had joined the recently founded Japanese Communist Party. In addition, the association was beginning to take on characteristics of a labor union. It offered support to disputes taking place in the area, and set up three locals in Nankatsu to organize workers at targeted factories.[18]

The Tsukishima Labor Discussion Association, formed in 1919, was a second early point of intersection between intellectuals and wage workers in Tokyo. This organization was a product of the complex interaction between imperial democratic rulers seeking to study and contain social problems, intellectuals intent on radical social change, and workers anxious to improve their place in society. In October 1918, as part of his new social policy, Home Minister Tokonami in the recently formed Hara cabinet commissioned Takano Iwasaburō, a Tokyo University economist, to undertake a socioeconomic survey of a working-class neighborhood in Tokyo. The government hoped to identify the objective conditions that it felt lay behind labor unrest.[19] Takano chose the island of Tsukishima as a neatly circumscribed site for the survey, and on the advice of his colleague Yoshino Sakuzō, he enlisted the services of several members of the Shinjinkai, an organization of student radicals centered on Tokyo University, to aid him. These youths also used the survey to contact and educate workers; as an adjunct to

18. On the Nankatsu Labor Association, see "Zadankai: Junrōdōsha kumiai, Nankatsu rōdōkai, oyobi Kameido jiken," *Rōdō undō shi kenkyū*, no. 36 (May 1963), and Tanno Setsu, *Kakumei undō ni ikiru*, pp. 9–12.

19. See Sekiya Kōichi, ed., *Tsukishima chōsa* (Tokyo: Kōseikan, 1970), introductory essay by Sekiya on background to the survey.

the survey office, they set up the Tsukishima Labor Discussion Association as well as a consumer cooperative. At weekly meetings, the Shinjinkai activists held forth on Marxism, the economics of wage labor, and the nature of capitalist society. The gatherings helped convince several worker attendees, already involved in union or dispute activities, to make a lifelong commitment to the social movement. One of these, Saitō Tadatoshi, was the young machinist noted in chapters 4 and 5, who had joined the Yūaikai at a teacher's behest in 1914. He emerged as a leader of the Ishikawajima Shipyard union, whose 1921 dispute is chronicled below.[20]

FACTORY UNIONS

The unions of this era organized themselves almost exclusively into local units composed of workers at a single factory, and many groups explicitly restricted membership to those at a single workplace. The experience of labor at the Ishikawajima shipyard nicely exemplified the new trend toward factory unions. The shipyard straddled the edge of Nankatsu, with one factory in Fukagawa ward and the main yard just across the Sumida River on the island of Tsukishima. In the wake of two bitter, divided strikes in 1919, workers here gradually overcame divisions between the two major categories of worker, the shipbuilders and metalworkers in the shipbuilding division and the machinists and finishing workers in the machine division. They eventually founded the Machine and Shipworkers' Union (Zōki senkō rōdō kumiai, or Kōrō) in the summer of 1921, in large measure owing to the energetic leadership of Saitō Tadatoshi. The unwieldy name reflected the difficult birth of this group, which engaged in a major dispute shortly after its founding and became one of Tokyo's strongest unions in the early 1920s.

The strikes of 1919 reveal that the Ishikawajima workers were building permanent institutional structures on the basis of workshop solidarity, "strike committees" independent of unions, demonstrations, and rallies, all features of the nonunion mode of labor organizing. Obstructing effective further organization and action were divisions of ideology, reflected in the presence of four formal workers' organiza-

20. On the discussion group and Saitō's activities, see Kanagawa-ken, rōdō-bu, rōsei-ka, ed., *Kanagawa-ken rōdō undō shi: senzen hen* (Yokohama: Kanagawa-ken, 1966), p. 254, and Komatsu Ryūji, *Kigyō betsu kumiai no seisei* (Tokyo: Ochanomizu shobō, 1971), p. 179. Information also from the author's interview with Saitō Tadatoshi, June 2, 1979.

tions within the yard by December 1919 and divisions of trade and temperament manifested in the continued separate actions and opposed positions of machinists and shipbuilding workers.[21]

A threat to the job security of all the workers in 1921 eventually catalyzed the creation of a single union joining almost all men in the yard. The war boom came to an abrupt end in March 1920, and Ishikawajima responded by firing 367 "temporary" metalworkers one year later, in March 1921. Foremen of the old school then began to work together with union men such as Saitō to create an all-company union over the following months. As Saitō recalls:

> Takayama [Jiroichi] was a very emotional, passionate person, a real *oyabun* [crew boss] type. There were lots like that [among the boilermakers] because the work truly was done on a group basis with strong foreman leadership. They had responsibility for group job contracts. They took care of their followers. They were truly essential people, especially in the shipbuilding section. Without them we couldn't have organized the union. In the machine section, workers were better educated. They were also leaders in the union, but their vital role was in organizing, reconciling things within the union.[22]

By June the machinists and shipbuilders together had organized a preparatory group, which circulated a petition throughout the shipyard in support of a new Ishikawajima union. The nascent group received encouragement from nearby labor organizations including factory unions at the Mita Naval Yard and Niigata Ironworks. By July 14, 1,400 of about 3,000 workers had committed themselves to the union. A formal ceremony inaugurating Kōrō was held on July 24.[23]

Virtually all other important unions in Nankatsu were organized along factory lines as well. Even in Hirasawa's union, formally an inclusive group open to all "pure laborers," most locals were based on individual factories; the workplace, rather than trade or neighborhood, was the building block for the group. As at Ishikawajima, the emergence of a dominant single union in a factory was often the denouement of sharp contention within the workplace. This was the case at two major rolling stock producers in Nankatsu, the Japan Rolling Stock Company and

21. Details on these groups are to be found in Andrew Gordon, "Workers, Managers, and Bureaucrats in Japan: Labor Relations in Heavy Industry" (Ph.D. diss., Harvard University, 1981), pp. 185–86. In addition to Satiō's Machinists' Union, there were a Yūaikai local with thirty members, a small anarchist organization, and a study group led by Kamino Shinichi, who later founded the first ultraright "Japanist" (*nihonshugi*) union in the nation.

22. Author's interview with Saitō, June 3, 1979.

23. Komatsu, *Kigyō betsu kumiai*, pp. 189–94.

the Train Manufacturing Company. A fierce struggle took place at Japan Rolling Stock between 1920 and 1923 as workers loyal to the Sōdōmei fought with an independent, factory-based group calling itself the Japan Skilled Labor Association (Nihon rōgikai). The latter group triumphed; by 1922 it claimed 530 members out of about 600 employees.[24]

Some major Sōdōmei locals, while nominally inclusive industrial unions, were in fact single factory groups. This was the case with the Tokyo Skilled Rubber Workers' Union, centered on the Mitatsuchi Rubber plant, and the Takeuchi Safe Workers' Union at the Takeuchi factory. Workers at the Seikōsha Watch Factory created a succession of factory-based unions between 1919 and 1923.[25] Men at an area bicycle manufacturer formed the short-lived Kōtō Bicycle Workers' Union in 1921, while men at the municipal streetcar line's Honjo yard created their own moderate union, the Mutual Aid Association (Sōfukai). Finally, Watanabe Masanosuke and his associates in the Nankatsu Labor Association took the lead in organizing the Shinjin [New Man] Celluloid Workers' Union at a single Nankatsu celluloid factory·in 1923.

Workers organized explicitly for de facto factory-based unions throughout Tokyo. At the Shibaura Engineering Works on the other side of the city, for example, workers created the Shibaura Labor Union in 1921 after two years of bitter and embarrassing strife between a Yūaikai-Sōdōmei local and a company-sponsored union. Union bylaws limited membership to Shibaura workers, and half the force had joined by the end of November. Each workshop within the company functioned as a "local" chapter of the union. The union's founding manifesto reflected both self-awareness concerning the decision to create a factory union, and the ongoing concern of labor for dignity and respect, newly flavored in the postwar era with anticapitalist rhetoric:

> We are creators of all society's wealth, but we receive nothing as members of society. All the wealth we create is appropriated by capitalists. Our daughters spend the precious years of their youth in dark factories. We insist on our right to survive in dignity as civilized members of society. . . . While our union appears to be a vertical one, it is more than that. Although it is factory-based, reflecting a new trend, we will probably decide to affiliate in the future with some larger federation.[26]

24. Uno Shinjirō, *Kaisō: 70 nen* (Tokyo: Privately published, 1971), pp. 67–86, recalls the Japan Rolling Stock case. See also *Rōdō kumiai chōsa* (1923), OISR.
25. *Rōdō shūhō*, February 6, 1923, p. 3.
26. *Rōdō dōmei*, January 1922, p. 97. See also Gordon, "Workers, Managers, and Bureaucrats in Japan," pp. 164–69 on the Shibaura story.

In the postwar rush to organize, as in earlier years, the operative slogan and sentiment among Japanese workers was rarely "brothers in a trade," as it had been in the early days of unions in Western Europe.[27] Rather, in the words of the founding manifesto of the Machine Labor Union Federation, a loose grouping of factory unions at the Japan Rolling Stock Company, the Train Manufacturing Company, and four other Tokyo-area firms, "We will continue to progress, linking hands at the same factory, advancing on solid ground with strength, bravery, and courage." Or, as one sympathetic observer of the strife at the Train Manufacturing Company noted, "Laborers who work in a single factory are brothers."[28] Few of these groups were captive or "yellow unions." In several cases, factory unions originally formed as management tools turned on the company. The bylaws of some groups restricted membership to employees at one factory, but these unions often joined broader federations. Other groups, such as Kōrō at Ishikawajima and the Pure Laborers' Union, had no such restriction and did organize locals in other factories. Yet the crucial fact remains that even in "horizontal unions" such as the Pure Laborers' Union or the Sōdōmei, where a central headquarters exercised some control over local unions, the locals were factory-based groups, not trade or regional organizations.

The explanation for this inclination to seek solidarity in the factory community must be sought on two levels. From the ground-level perspective of the workers, factory unions were strategic choices: they promised to overcome several problems that divided workers at the point of production and obstructed united action. Problems included antagonism toward intellectuals, perceived as outsiders with suspect motives, as when the Machine Labor Union Federation spoke of building a "true and unspoiled union of genuine workers."[29] Factory unions also promised to resolve two other divisive tensions, between workers committed to the Sōdōmei and those supporting independent unions, and between supporters of Bolshevism and of anarchism. These twin divisions plagued workers at both the Train Manufacturing Company in Honjo and the Seikōsha Watch Factory, and the eventual solution in

27. This contrast is a relative one, not absolute. Victoria E. Bonnell describes the phenomenon of factory unions in prerevolutionary Russia; see her *Roots of Rebellion: Workers' Politics and Organizations in St. Petersburg and Moscow, 1900–1914* (Berkeley: University of California Press, 1983), pp. 145–48.
28. Federation quotation from Uno, *Kaisō*, p. 78; Train Manufacturing Company quotation from *Rōdō kumiai*, July 1923, p. 8.
29. *Rōdō shūdō*, May 31, 1922, p. 1.

both cases was creation of all-factory unions that merged two or more contending labor groups in each plant.[30]

From a broader perspective, the strategic wisdom of factory unions, and the dominance of a spirit of brotherhood in the factory, seems to reflect a more fundamental dynamic of capitalist development in Japan. Relatively late development meant the precocious emergence of highly capitalized, large enterprises at the cutting edge of the economy, indirectly nurtured, and on occasion directly managed, by the state. Compared to the experience of workers in Western Europe or even North America, a relatively small pool of skilled laborers with relatively shallow independent traditions of skill acquisition or organization emerged prior to, or independently of, the creation by monopoly capital and the state of these huge worksites. As heavy industries began sustained growth around the turn of the century, the organization and training of these skilled workers increasingly took place under the direct control of management in the large-scale sector.[31] Managers were loathe to lose relatively scarce skilled men, and they experimented with a wide array of policies to slow their mobility. Workers in such plants derived a fair degree of strength from this situation; quite naturally, both earlier labor disputes and many of the varied working-class initiatives of the post–World War I era centered on precisely these enterprises.

If late development gave such men the power to contest their bosses, it also focused their actions on the factory. The men in both the shipbuilding and the machine divisions at Ishikawajima had united effectively *within* their divisions prior to creating a factory union. If either group had had access to a citywide network of fellow tradesmen, it could have drawn on that outside support in contesting for higher pay or shorter hours; the need to form a shipyard-based union of machinists, shipbuilders, metalworkers, painters, carpenters, and more would not have been so acute or appeared so logical. But without vigorous trade traditions, the factory was the natural unit of organization and object of identification. Organizers groping for effective strategies willy-nilly came to recognize this.

In all likelihood additional labor organizing took place in Nankatsu;

30. On the Train Manufacturing Company, see *Rōdō shūhō*, February 27, 1923, p. 3, and *Rōdō kumiai*, July 1923, p. 8. On Seikōsha, see *Rōdō kumiai*, June 1923, p. 11.

31. See Ronald Dore, *British Factory, Japanese Factory: The Origins of National Diversity in Industrial Relations* (Berkeley: University of California Press, 1973), ch. 15, and Koike Kazuo, "Internal Labor Markets: Workers in Large Firms," in *Contemporary Industrial Relations in Japan*, ed. Shirai Taishiro (Madison, University of Wisconsin Press, 1983), pp. 59–60.

the devastation of the 1923 earthquake and the 1944–45 firebombings have made the area a poor repository of documentary evidence. Precise measurement of union membership is also impossible, but an estimate of 3,000 to 4,000 dues-paying union members in this area at any one time between 1920 and 1923 is conservative. Although not even one-tenth of the 50,000 workers in Honjo and Fukagawa wards and Minami Katsushika County, this was a significant core after less than a decade of organizing in a hostile environment. Building on workshop and factory units, workers organized a movement whose supporters increasingly considered themselves part of a class with interests opposed to those of owners and managers; their unions, committed to winning respect and changing society, were scattered throughout the industrial neighborhoods of major cities.

THE DISPUTE CULTURE
OF THE WORKING CLASS

In 1925 Murashima Yoriyuki, a journalist sympathetic to labor, wrote a book titled *Practical Knowledge of Labor Disputes.*[32] Drawing principally on examples from Osaka between 1921 and 1923, with occasional reference to cases from Tokyo, he codified the tactics employed by workers in disputes of these early postwar years. "Strike and it shall be given you," a play on the biblical injunction "Ask, and it shall be given you" (probably made familiar through the work of Christian social reformers), epitomized the militant spirit that fueled these actions, according to Murashima.[33]

Murashima captured the spirit behind the dramatic increase in labor disputes from 1919 through the early 1920s, a surge that in fact outpaced the building of unions and related organizations just described. Through his ethnographic account of worker culture, and by studying one major strike at the Ishikawajima shipyard, we can begin to reconstruct what I call the "dispute culture" of the post–World War I urban working class. My concern here is limited to the *political* culture of Japanese workers.[34] This is certainly just a portion of the totality of

32. Murashima Yoriyuki, *Rōdō sōgi no jissai chishiki* (Tokyo: Kagaku shisō fukyū kai, 1925).

33. "Sawage yo, saraba ataeraren" (literally, "Clamor, and it shall be given"). The biblical injunction in Japanese simply has *motome* instead of *sawage*. Murashima, *Rōdō sōgi*, p. 173.

34. I consider this a matter of culture rather than simply of ideology, insofar as it includes behavior as well as attitudes, both shaped by common experience as members of working-class communities.

worker culture, which includes patterns of family life and leisure activity, for example. By political culture I refer to the workers' shared understandings of society and polity and their place in it, as well as their common actions to change (or perhaps to accept) this system and their own status in it.

We shall see that attitudes and behavior with roots in the nonunion era were coalescing with the new unions. Workers at Ishikawajima and a host of other factories drew on a base of considerable community support; their repertoire of dispute tactics had gained rapidly in sophistication in just a few years and would continue to evolve.

The inquiry into the workers' dispute culture stretches across this and the following two chapters. We shall examine labor disputes to gain both a sense of how the Nankatsu workers conceived their relationship to employer, to society, and to the state, and a sense of their ambivalent opposition to the dominant social and political order. But first, my goal in the remainder of this chapter is to show how disputes were organized and how the dispute culture of the 1920s, consisting of knowledge of this form of action and the ability to carry it out, spread among workers concurrently with the building of a union movement.

MURASHIMA'S ETHNOGRAPHY OF LABOR DISPUTES

Some worker actions echoed the spirit of the urban crowd of 1905–18, now given specific, usually nonviolent, focus by organizations such as unions or strike groups. Thus, Murashima began his catalog with a look at the demonstration, effective both in building morale and gathering outside support. The police forbad more than double-file lines, more than five flags per march, and all songs or slogans considered inflammatory. To avoid these restrictions, Murashima noted, workers could disguise demonstrations as field days or visits to shrines, or use occasions such as the conveyance of supplies to strike headquarters or the receiving of delegations of supporters from other unions to justify impromptu demonstrations (see fig. 17). He noted, as well, the explosive potential in these actions, pointing to the 1922 example of Ōjima Steel in Nankatsu, which ended in the storming of the company, with much window-breaking and sixty-three arrests.[35] Variant forms of the demonstration included nighttime "visits" to executive homes. A worried wife, he claimed, could bring pressure on a stubborn manager as effectively as a union.

35. Murashima, Rōdō sōgi, pp. 122–46.

Murashima then described the speech-meeting, another action with preunion roots. In addition to building morale and support, it impressed the company with union power and raised money through admission fees. The choice of speaker was crucial and, in a comment reflecting the new political freedom granted women in 1922, he claimed that women were effective speakers no matter what they said; the novelty drew crowds and satisfied popular curiosity. The police were part of the theater of labor assembly, for expectations of some mild harassment added to the excitement and drew attendees. Unless a few speeches were halted, the crowd left unhappy. As the standards for intervention varied with the officer, speakers were advised indeed to prepare a full speech. Some unfortunates overly confident of drawing an order to "Halt!" were left stammering on the podium with nothing to say.[36]

The leaflet was a relatively recent addition to the dispute repertoire. Murashima described it as a form of popular literary culture. Leaflets were effective when addressed to a particular audience, such as the customers of a company, the company itself, the workers, or their families. He felt the distribution of leaflets condemning the Mizuno Sporting Goods Company to fans at a baseball game was particularly clever.[37]

Finally, Murashima cataloged the principal tactics of internal organization and control attempted by most unions. Most elusive was the control by central headquarters of decisions on when to strike. In these early years of union-led disputes, and later as well, decisions to strike were typically made at the local level.[38] After a local executive committee formulated a set of demands, an assembly of the entire local would usually vote on whether to strike and ratify the demands. Next came efforts to gain support from union headquarters and to organize various committees for accounting, research, publicity, demonstration control, executive visits, and more. Common tactics were picketing and ostracism of workers and families who betrayed a strike, the taking of "attendance" at strike headquarters each day, streets sales to raise funds, and job introductions for fired workers or for strikers during the duration of a dispute (see fig. 18).[39] Finally, in the wake of some major strikes, unions issued sets of picture postcards that both recorded the

---

36. Ibid., pp. 146–50.
37. Ibid., p. 150.
38. Ibid., pp. 178–81.
39. Ibid., pp., 178–237.

TABLE 6.2   LABOR DISPUTES IN THE
NANKATSU REGION, 1897–1923

	Minami Katsushika County	Honjo Ward	Fukagawa Ward	Total
1897–1913	5	12	7	24
1914	3	0	1	4
1915	0	0	0	0
1916	0	2	0	2
1917	1	3	2	6
1918	0	1	1	2
1919	12	20	5	37
1920	2	4	1	7
1921	6	1	2	9
1922	4	5	3	12
1923	2	6	2	10

SOURCE: Aoki Kōji, *Nihon rōdō undō shi nenpyō* (Tokyo: Shinseisha, 1968).

dispute for posterity and built a public store of movement memory (see fig. 21).[40]

DISPUTES IN NANKATSU

Disputes in Nankatsu were typical of those described by Murashima, and indeed furnished several of his choice examples. The absolute number of disputes in the Nankatsu region rose considerably from prewar and wartime levels, with a sharp peak in the most turbulent year, 1919. Although the numbers subsided after this, the annual totals were still more than double the levels of World War I (table 6.2).

Even during the war, most of the labor disputes in the area involved Yūaikai members, but the meaning of "involvement" shifted after the war (table 6.3). This shift is important evidence of the coalescence of union-organizing and nonunion dispute traditions that distinguished these years. In earlier actions, Suzuki Bunji mediated only after the dispute began, and strikers did not act in the name of the union. The year 1919, then, marked a turning point, with union locals actively taking

40. The 1921 Kobe shipyard strike was probably the first to be memorialized in this way.

TABLE 6.3   UNION INVOLVEMENT IN NANKATSU
REGION LABOR DISPUTES, 1918–23

	Nonunion Disputes		Union Disputes		Total
Pre-1913	24	(100)	0		24
1914–17	7	(58)	5	(42)	12
1918	1	(50)	1	(50)	2
1919	25	(68)	12	(32)	37
1920	3	(43)	4	(57)	7
1921	6	(67)	3	(33)	9
1922	9	(75)	3	(25)	12
1923	6	(60)	4	(40)	10
Total	50	(65)	27	(35)	77

SOURCE: Aoki Kōji, *Nihon rōdō undō shi nenpyō* (Tokyo: Shinseisha, 1968).
NOTE: Nankatsu region = Honjo and Fukagawa wards and Minami Katsushika County.
Figures in parentheses are precentages.

TABLE 6.4   UNION INVOLVEMENT IN NANKATSU
REGION LABOR DISPUTES, BY SECTOR, 1918–23

	Union		Nonunion		Total
Textiles	7	(78)	2	(22)	9
Machine and metal	14	(39)	22	(61)	36
Chemical	6	(67)	3	(33)	9
Other	1	(4)	22	(96)	23
Total	28	(36)	49	(64)	77

SOURCE: Aoki Kōji, *Nihon rōdō shi nenpyō* (Tokyo: Shinseisha, 1968).
NOTE: Nankatsu region = Honjo and Fukagawa wards and Minami Katsushika County.
Figures in parentheses are percentages.

the lead in forming strike committees, raising funds, and negotiating
with management from the outset. The union presence was spread un-
evenly through all industrial sectors (table 6.4). Unionized workers remained most active in disputes in the relatively mechanized, expanding,
capital-intensive industries: not only textiles, but machine and metal
manufacturing and chemical industries (rubber, glass). Just one of the
twenty-four disputes in all other sectors (such as food processing, transport, lumber, longshoremen, and day laborers) involved unions.

These events changed in three additional important respects: dis-

TABLE 6.5   PROPORTION OF THE NANKATSU REGION WORK FORCE
INVOLVED IN LABOR DISPUTES, 1897–1923

	Number of Disputes							
Year	0–25% Involved	26–50% Involved	51–75% Involved	76–99% Involved	100% Involved	Subtotal	Involvement Unclear	Total
1897–1917	6 (46)	4 (31)	1 (8)	1 (8)	1 (8)	13	23	36
1918	0	1 (50)	0	0	0	1	1	2
1919	7 (30)	3 (13)	1 (4)	3 (13)	9 (39)	23	14	37
1920	1 (25)	0	0	2 (50)	1 (25)	4	3	7
1921	0	0	1 (17)	0	5 (83)	6	3	9
1922	2 (17)	0	1 (8)	2 (17)	7 (58)	12	0	12
1923	2 (29)	0	1 (14)	2 (29)	2 (29)	7	3	10
Total, 1918–23	12 (23)	4 (8)	4 (8)	9 (17)	24 (45)	53	24	77

SOURCE: Aoki Kōji, *Nihon rōdō undō shi nempyō* (Tokyo: Shinseisha, 1968).
NOTE: Figures in parentheses are percentages of disputes involving the indicated proportion of the work force. Owing to rounding off, row totals are not always 100 percent. Nankatsu region = Honjo and Fukagawa wards and Minami Katsushika County.

TABLE 6.6   DURATION OF LABOR DISPUTES IN THE NANKATSU REGION, 1918–23

Year	Lasting 1 Day	Lasting 2–7 Days	Lasting 8–14 Days	Lasting 15–30 Days	Lasting 31 Days	Subtotal	Duration Unclear	Total
				Number of Disputes				
Pre-1918	23 (85)	3 (11)	0	1 (4)	0	27	9	36
1918	2 (100)	0	0	0	0	2	0	2
1919	19 (56)	10 (29)	4 (12)	1 (3)	0	34	3	37
1920	5 (71)	1 (14)	1 (14)	0	0	7	0	7
1921	5 (63)	1 (13)	0	1 (13)	1 (13)	8	1	9
1922	2 (17)	6 (50)	2 (17)	2 (17)	0	12	0	12
1923	2 (22)	3 (33)	2 (22)	1 (11)	1 (11)	9	1	10
Total, 1918–23	35 (49)	21 (29)	9 (13)	5 (7)	2 (3)	72	5	77

SOURCE: Aoki Kōji, *Nihon rōdō undō shi nenpyō* (Tokyo: Shinseisha, 1968).
NOTE: Figures in parentheses are percentages of disputes of the indicated duration. Owing to rounding off, row totals are not always 100 percent. Nankatsu region = Honjo and Fukagawa wards and Minami Katsushika County.

TABLE 6.7   DISPUTES IN THE NANKATSU REGION, BY ENTERPRISE SIZE, 1918–23

Year	Number of Disputes						
	5–29 Employees	30–99 Employees	100–499 Employees	500+ Employees	Subtotal	Size Unclear	Total
1914–1917	0	0	2 (18)	9 (82)	11	1	12
1918	0	0	0	1 (100)	1	1	2
1919	0	1 (3)	12 (41)	16 (55)	29	8	37
1920	0	0	1 (20)	4 (80)	5	2	7
1921	1 (12.5)	3 (37.5)	1 (12.5)	3 (37.5)	8	1	9
1922	5 (42)	2 (17)	1 (8)	4 (33)	12	0	12
1923	1 (13)	2 (25)	3 (38)	2 (25)	8	2	10
Total, 1918–23	7 (11)	8 (13)	18 (29)	30 (48)	63	14	77

SOURCE: Aoki Kōji, Nihon rōdō undō shi nenpyō (Tokyo: Shinseisha, 1968).
NOTE: Figures in parentheses are percentages of disputes of the indicated duration. Owing to rounding off, row totals are not always 100 percent. Nankatsu region = Honjo and Fukagawa wards and Minami Katsushika County.

putes involved a larger proportion of the work force than in the past, they were significantly longer, and by the early 1920s they were not confined solely to the largest workplaces (tables 6.5 through 6.7). In sum, disputes in postwar Nankatsu were far more numerous and intense than in the past, unions took a more active role, and while workers at large factories in the more mechanized, capital-intensive industries exhibited the greatest propensity to protest, we find labor activism beginning to spread to the increasingly numerous smaller places.

THE ISHIKAWAJIMA DISPUTE

The five-week strike at the Ishikawajima shipyard of October 8 through November 15, 1921, was the most intense and prolonged of the Nankatsu disputes of this era.[41] It came at the end of four months of unprecedented struggle in shipyards throughout Japan sparked by the strike of 27,000 workers at the Kawasaki and Mitsubishi shipyards in Kobe in July and August. It is a well-documented action, allowing us to view at close range the process of movement-building and the nature of the "dispute culture" of the 1920s.[42]

The strike began with a dispute between the company and the newly formed shipyard union, Kōrō, over the company's mutual aid society. The aid society can be seen as a local manifestation of the conservative program for imperial democracy in the workplace, the modernized paternalism promoted by major industrial managers: Ishikawajima management allowed workers to elect the aid society's officers, hoping to channel the workers' democratic spirit in a safe direction. The strategy backfired. Union candidates gained a majority of the offices in a September election, and they uncovered clear evidence of abuse: several thousand yen in profits from sales of bread to workers and 63,000 of the total reserves of 160,000 yen were missing, apparently "borrowed" by the company to cover other obligations.[43]

41. The main yard was on the island of Tsukishima, adjacent to Nankatsu, but not in it. But the company also ran a machine factory where the union enjoyed strong support, in Fukagawa ward in the Nankatsu region.

42. The primary source for the following account is the report compiled by the Kyū-kyōchōkai, *Ishikawajima zōsenjo sōgi, 1921,* held at the OISR. It is an extremely complete, rich description consisting of two separate reports compiled by Kyōchōkai staff members Machida and Kaya, as well as of union pamphlets and a complete set of the police reports prepared almost daily over the five weeks of the dispute and sent from the Tokyo Metropolitan Police Headquarters to the home minister and the governors of nearby prefectures.

43. Kyū-kyōchōkai, *Ishikawajima,* Kaya report. *Tetsuben* 2, no. 1 (January 1922): 3. Furuya Susumu, "Ishikawajima sōgi keika to hihan," in *Rōdō dōmei,* January 1922, p. 37.

The union leaders hoped to wait a few months before any strike so as to strengthen their organization, but sentiment among the mass of shipbuilders ruled this out. They were angry over a two-year hiatus in pay raises, which they felt violated a company rule specifying semiannual raises. A selective raise was finally granted to a small minority of supervisory foremen hostile to the union. This raise, combined with the mutual aid society abuse and the example of strikes elsewhere, made a confrontation inevitable. A steady stream of petitions entered union headquarters from the twenty-three or twenty-four workshops in the yard, each constituted as a union local, asking for action on issues ranging from wages to dirty toilets.[44]

In vain, union leaders sought to defer these demands and negotiate over the aid society question. When disputes began the same week at the Yokohama Dock, Asano Dock, and Uraga Dock companies, the Ishikawajima managers moved to head off any like action at their yard, but, ironically, in so doing, they precipitated the dispute. General Manager Kurita announced that a raise would be forthcoming; it would average 10 percent, but would depend on assessments of individual performance. The majority of union members opposed any such selective raise, and on October 7 Kōrō demanded a *uniform wage hike* of 10 percent, or 1.9 sen per hour. The factory director rejected this, and hinted he might also refuse any raise at all. A slowdown greeted this announcement, and until the lockout of October 14, the workers reported each day but did virtually no work.

At issue was far more than the amount of the raise. For labor at Ishikawajima, regularity of treatment was the sticking point; the stubborn insistence on a uniform raise was the issue that drew out the dispute for a full five weeks. The second central goal was increased security, in the face of a depressed economy and impending layoffs as well as the constant threat of illness or injury. A complex four-part demand called for improved allowances in cases of dismissal, voluntary separation, illness, and retirement. In an atmosphere of near riot, the union spent the first week consolidating the demands and organizing for an anticipated strike or lockout, all the while negotiating fruitlessly with the company.

The tumultuous scenes at union rallies held on company property just before the lockout are reminiscent of the rallies so common in

44. Kyū-kyōchōkai, *Ishikawajima*, Kaya report. *Tetsuben* 2, no. 1 (January 1922): 3–4. Interview with Saitō, June 17, 1979.

Tokyo since 1905. The mobilization by workshop is of a piece with earlier nonunion disputes in heavy industry. But the contrasts with both these forms of action are just as important. In the process of building a labor movement, that is, workers developed new abilities to act in concert by combining older experience of nonunion disputes and political crowd actions with the new union organizations.

Evidence of the learning process by which workers built the labor movement, and a clear contrast to earlier forms of action, is offered by several features of this dispute: both the "crowd" marching in demonstrations and its leadership consisted wholly of workers; all were joined in a formal organization; the mobilization was systematic, planned, and inclusive from the start; and the organization for the dispute was impressive. Each workshop elected representatives to a strike committee of 180 members prior to the slowdown. This group met again the next day to establish a great array of organizations: a marshal's squad, a communications section, a street sales squad, a supply section, a public relations section, an accounting section, and an external relations section to build ties to other organizations. Anticipating a lockout, the union set up sixty-five meeting places and arranged for communication by runners on bicycles between these sites and the union headquarters.[45]

Throughout the period of the lockout, from October 14 to November 5, demonstrations, meetings, and rallies, large and small, took place daily. Two great problems were police harassment and lack of access to a suitable large meeting place. The first day of the lockout was typical. Roughly 1,200 workers gathered by 8 A.M. at a vacant lot on Tsukishima to plan strategy. The police dispersed this group as an illegal open-air assembly. Workers regrouped at the Okumura Ironworks near the shipyard, but again the police dispersed them. They had no choice but to gather at the various scattered work-group meeting places in groups of 20 to 300. The police warned that these gatherings, too, were subject to dispersal if they appeared "inflammatory."[46]

Despite such difficulties, seven major demonstrations took place between October 16 and November 3. Each time the workers confronted massed policemen, and occasionally the incidents turned violent.[47] On

45. *Tetsuben* 2, no. 1 (January 1922): 5. Kyū-kyōchōkai, *Ishikawajima*, police report of October 11, 1921. Interview with Saitō, June 17, 1979.

46. *TAS*, evening, October 14, 1921, p. 2; *Tetsuben* 2, no. 1 (January 1922): p. 11; Kyū-kyōchōkai, *Ishikawajima*, police report, October 14, 1921.

47. See descriptions in *TAS* and Kyū-kyōchōkai, *Ishikawajima*, police reports on the days after the demonstrations of October 16, 18, 22, 24, 30, 31, and November 3.

October 18, for example, strike headquarters passed word of the demonstration, and by 10 A.M. nearly 1,000 workers had converged in small groups on a cemetery just across the Sumida River from Tsukishima. Sixty policemen ordered this group to disperse around 10:40, but the workers defiantly set off on a winding march through Mita and Shiba wards, ending in Shiba Park. They ignored another order to disperse and threw rocks at the police. The marchers finally headed back to Tsukishima on a circuitous route, clashing repeatedly with the police, who arrested twelve workers.[48]

The union also held major speech-meetings in rented halls on October 19 and 24 and November 4 to boost morale and report on negotiations with management. A morning rally on the 19th took place at the Tsukishima Movie Theater, observed by upwards of 300 policemen. The Tsukishima district police chief himself stood by the rostrum, but did not interrupt the speeches. The union announced that profits from street sales of daily necessities had reached 91 yen a day, and that the strike fund had accumulated 6,600 yen. The high point was a tearful presentation of 1.5 yen by five elementary school children.[49] An estimated 800 to 1,400 workers and sympathizers packed the Kanda Youth Hall in central Tokyo for the second "Strike Report Rally" on October 24. Laborers in work clothes and 200 people identified by the press as students or other supporters heard twenty-four speeches. The police observer this time did interrupt five of the speeches upon utterance of forbidden phrases such as "police brutality" and "social system." Police also arrested five members of the audience for disorderly behavior.[50]

A number of activities not found in nonunion disputes took place. Several hundred workers split into five-man groups, set up outdoor stalls or pushcarts, and sold toothbrushes, soap, and other such items, raising money for the strike fund and gaining local sympathy. The union also solicited contributions from neighbors and shopkeepers, as well as from workers at other factories in the area. The strike committee required each worker to report daily to his group's designated meeting place, and it kept "attendance" reports.[51] Union members visited those reporting ill, or reported to be destitute, and gave them financial aid.

48. TAS, evening edition, October 18, 1921, p. 2, and October 19, 1921, p. 5. Kyū-kyōchōkai, Ishikawajima, police report, October 18, 1921.

49. TAS, evening edition, October 19, 1921, p. 2.

50. TAS, October 25, 1921, p. 5; Kyū-kyōchōkai, Ishikawajima, police report of October 25, 1921.

51. The attendance and contribution records survive and are held at the OISR.

One committee sought temporary employment for workers at other local factories for the duration of the dispute. Another group "visited" the homes of major shareholders or company directors to encourage them to grant the workers' demands. Two of these visits became major confrontations, with 300 workers facing police cordons guarding the homes of the company president and the general manager. Another squad picketed the closed company gates daily.[52]

Reflecting the home minister's belief that company unions were acceptable, but horizontal association was dangerous, the police intervened swiftly to prevent other workers from expressing solidarity.[53] On October 15:

> Eighty workers at Tsukishima's Niigata Ironworks sympathetic to the Ishikawajima workers' plight loaded three wagons with a case of beer, five sacks of charcoal, twenty faggots of firewood, and eight sacks of rice. They set off for the strike headquarters at 6 P.M. waving one small banner reading "Justice and Humanity" [seigi jindō] and a large banner with an inflammatory slogan. Just as they were about to deliver the goods, 150 or more policemen, giving no reason, ordered them to retreat.[54]

A fight ensued and police arrested thirteen men, all workers at either Ishikawajima or the Niigata factory. The next day they arrested eleven members of the Japan Transport Workers' Union, who had visited strike headquarters, on suspicion of planning a sympathy strike.[55]

These varied tactics reflected the varied goals of the strike group: the network of scattered meeting places allowed organizers to avoid police harassment and keep tabs on union members; the outdoor demonstrations and marches, the indoor rallies, the peddling of daily necessities, the soliciting of outside contributions, and the delivery of strike aid in public processions all served the dual purposes of boosting morale and winning public support; finally, "home visits" to managers and owners sought to intimidate the opposition. Continuities with earlier forms of protest are clear, but the cohesive organizing and the diverse, creative activities reflect the presence of a union and distinguish this dispute from worker and urban crowd actions of the nonunion era.

52. *Tetsuben* 2, no. 1 (January 1922): 11–12; *TAS*, evening edition, October 17, 1921, p. 2; Kyū-kyōchōkai, *Ishikawajima*, police reports of October 22 and 29, 1921.
53. Sheldon Garon, *State and Labor in Modern Japan* (Berkeley: University of California Press, 1987), p. 51.
54. *TAS*, October 15, 1921, p. 5.
55. Ibid.; Kyū-kyōchōkai, *Ishikawajima*, police report of October 16, 1921.

The lockout lasted for five weeks. By early November the workers were exhausted, and the company was under pressure from the navy to complete an unfinished destroyer that was sitting in its docks.[56] On November 9 the company managed to sneak 60 strikebreakers into the main yard and resume limited operations.[57] Managers the next day predicted confidently that 2,000 of the 3,000 workers would be on the job by November 11. In fact, by the 14th only 400 had returned, despite visits by foremen to workers' homes and offers of double pay for the duration.

Both sides were ready to compromise. On November 15 the Tsukishima district police chief presided over a negotiating session that produced a settlement: a pay raise that would average 10 percent and range from 1.7 to 2.3 sen per hour; improved severance pay; special payments of 7,000 yen to 55 fired workers; loans of 10 yen to all workers needing them; no more strike-related firings; return of the missing funds to the mutual aid society.[58] Not surprisingly, considerable bitterness remained in the wake of the strike. Union members and strikebreakers practically came to blows on several occasions, and tensions growing out of this strike resurfaced in the following years.[59]

STRUCTURE OF WORKING-CLASS ACTION, 1921

The unity of sentiment, the perseverance, and the organizing skill of the Ishikawajima workers are impressive. Yet the union movement in Tokyo had a continuous tradition of just ten years, and it was only three years since even a portion of the workers had begun using a language of self-conscious class opposition. Not surprisingly, the detailed "Record of Contributions" maintained by the Ishikawajima union reveals a network of strong community support, but limited organized reach outside the local area.[60]

The contribution record lists 494 contributions totaling 12,878.48 yen. Several hands entered these on a daily basis, sometimes listing simply name, address, and amount, but on other occasions noting the

56. Kyū-kyōchōkai, *Ishikawajima*, police report of November 14, 1921.

57. *TAS*, evening editions, October 23, 1921, p. 2, November 9, 1921, p. 2, and November 10, 1921, p. 2; *Tetsuben* 2, no. 2 (February 1922): 6–7; Kyū-kyōchōkai, *Ishikawajima*, police reports of October 20 and 22, 1921.

58. *TAS*, November 20, 1921, pp. 4, 6; Furuya, "Ishikawajima sōgi," p. 47; *Tetsuben* 2, no. 2 (February 1922): 8–9.

59. On the aftermath of the strike, see Kyū-kyōchōkai, *Ishikawajima*, police report, November 18, 1921; *TAS*, evening edition, November 18, 1921, p. 2, and November 20, 1921, pp. 4, 6. *Tetsuben* 2, no. 2 (February 1922): 8.

60. Held at the OISR.

donor's occupation or recording a donation from an organization (see fig. 16). Individual residents of Tsukishima and surrounding wards of central Tokyo, of unspecified occupation, comprised the most numerous category; 241 donors, nearly half the total, contributed a total of 902.05 yen (see table 6.8). Most individuals gave 1 or 2 yen; many offered just a few sen. Other individual supporters or groups did identify their occupations; among these, local merchants, storekeepers, or their employees were numerous. Their 74 contributions averaged a sizable 10.98 yen each.[61]

These donors included an open-air vendor and an association of local vendors; two barbers, as well as the local barbers' trade association; six wholesale trading companies; nine restaurants; five shoestores; three tobacco shops; four firewood dealers; two hairdressers; three maids; two apprentice geisha; and eleven students. Ten well-known singers of traditional Japanese folk music (naniwabushi) together offered 100 yen. Of the 241 individual names, 30 were those of women. Many were surely the wives of workers; several were prostitutes.[62] The Ishikawajima strikers thus enjoyed the support of an urban community similar to that which had produced the political crowd actions of earlier years. While workers had organized their own groups, they built upon traditions of protest common to other lower- and lower-middle-class city-dwellers. No major tension between an urban petite bourgeoisie of shopkeepers, clerks, and artisans and a proletariat of factory labor in large firms is visible in 1921.

The Record of Contributions also suggests that an important limit to the organizational reach of the workers lay in the relatively informal links between the union at Ishikawajima and factory workers elsewhere in Tokyo. Wage laborers were of course the most numerous single

61. This list is silent on motives, of course. Could groups of strikers have roamed the streets and extorted funds? This did occur in rural uprisings of the nineteenth century, according to Sippel, "Bushū Outburst," pp. 294–95, and Roger Bowen, *Rebellion and Democracy in Meiji Japan: A Study of Commoners in the Popular Rights Movement* (Berkeley: University of California Press, 1980) pp. 58–62. Given the intense police surveillance of this dispute, and the extreme police hostility to all displays of outside support, such abuses were sure to have attracted police attention, yet no mention of coercion found its way into the thorough police reports on the strike. Also, it is unlikely the strike group would record ill-gotten funds, thereby offering evidence to a potential police investigator. Further, the chronologically recorded list reveals no geographic concentration, suggesting that contributors came to the strike headquarters. Finally, the great variety in amounts contributed, even from individuals or merchants in the same business, implies workers did not "suggest" a forced minimum contribution.

62. One donation of two yen is simply credited to "all the prostitutes" (shōgi ichidō) in the Sasaki district of Fukagawa. See fig. 16.

TABLE 6.8 CONTRIBUTIONS TO THE ISHIKAWAJIMA STRIKE FUND, 1921

Contributors	Number		Amount (yen)	Average Amount (yen)
Individuals (only name provided)[a]		241 (49)	902.05 (7)	3.74[b]
Workers, workers' organizations				
Ishikawajima workshops or work groups	66 (39)		8,096.67 (63)	122.68
Formal union, aid society, other workers' organizations	17 (10)		705.40 (5)	41.49
Informal groups, by factory or workshop[c]	70 (42)	168 (34)	2,278.87 (18)	32.56
Individual workers	15 (9)		39.84 (0)	2.66
Total workers	168 (100)		11,120.78 (86)	66.20
Merchants, storekeepers, clerks		74 (15)	813.15 (6)	10.99
Students		11 (2)	42.50 (0)	3.86
Total		494	12,878.48	26.07

SOURCE: *Kinsen shūnōbo* (Record of contributions), OISR.

NOTE: Figures in parentheses are percentages. Owing to rounding off, the totals may not be 100 percent.

[a] Approximately thirty, or 12 percent, of the individual contributors were women.

[b] The largest individual contribution was 200 yen.

[c] Of the seventy contributions coming from informal groups, thirty-six were from specifically named workshops or work groups; they contributed 1241.57 yen.

category among identifiable contributors. Individual workers, labor organizations (unions, friendly societies, aid societies, political groups), or groups of workers at a particular factory accounted for 168 of the identifiable contributions (66 percent). Of these, 66 Ishikawajima workshops or work groups contributed by far the greatest amount, a total of 8,096.17 yen, roughly three-fourths of the entire fund, but it is the other 102 worker contributions that are of greater interest.

Workers in the Greater Tokyo area, especially in the immediate vicinity of the shipyard, responded generously and in large numbers. Individuals listed as "workers" gave 15 of these donations. Of the remaining 87 contributions, only 17 came from formal organizations of workers. Fully 70 offerings came from informal groups listed simply as "worker supporters" from a particular factory or a workshop.[63] Support from the community of workers thus came only in small measure through organizations; the labor movement had far to go in channeling a sense of common interest in an organized direction.

Even the contributions from sites where unions were present sometimes came not in the name of the union, but in the name of "Worker Supporters at Ikegai Ironworks: 43.9 yen" or "Worker Supporters at the Tool Section, Shibaura Engineering Works: 62.9 yen." Over half the informal contributions (36 of 70) came from the "organic" constituent element of the working-class movement, the workshop or work group (*kumi*).[64] Thirteen work groups at Shibaura, eight at the Naval Shipyard in Yokosuka, seven at the Asano shipyard in Yokohama (all workplaces with unions), and a handful of others at smaller ironworks made their donations in such form.[65]

A second major limit to labor's organization in support of the strike was sectoral. Of the 70 "informal" worker contributions to the Ishikawajima strikers, 62 came from factories in heavy or chemical industries: engineering works, shipyards, ironworks, electric products manufacturers, or cement manufacturers. Of the remaining 8 donors, 6 cannot be identified with certainty. Only 2 contributions were from outside these sectors, one from a group of printers and another from construction workers. None were from textile workers.

---

63. The term was *shokkō yūshi*.

64. It is worth noting that the term for work group (*kumi*) is the same as the first character in the word for union (*kumiai*), which literally means a "collection of *kumi*."

65. This pattern is found in other documented cases. In the dispute at Adachi Engineering Works in 1921, twelve of twenty outside contributions came from "X work group at Y company" or simply "the employees of Z company," even when a union existed at that company. See list in *Rōdō*, March 1921.

The workers at Ishikawajima thus found widespread support in the local community and among factory workers in large heavy industrial plants throughout the area. The former support drew on traditions of lower-class urban protest, while the latter grew out of a feeling of common interest that had emerged among men in the workshops of heavy industrial firms prior to the creation of labor unions. The result by the early 1920s was an urban working-class political culture in which unions were increasingly common and in which dispute activities were widely understood, supported, and practiced among men in heavy industry. Yet in this "dispute culture" of Tokyo in the early 1920s, the workers' spirit of contention and desire for reform and advancement was only partially harnessed by the emerging networks of formal institutions such as unions, aid societies, cooperatives, and newspapers. In the aftermath of the devastating Tokyo earthquake of 1923, this spirit would spread widely among men in smaller factories and among women in a variety of workplaces, but the workers' movement would continue to struggle to sink secure institutional roots.

SEVEN

The Labor Offensive in Nankatsu, 1924–29

Between 1924 and 1929, organized workers in Tokyo achieved unprecedented breadth and depth of support. At the peak of labor strength in the late 1920s, roughly one-third of all factory workers in Nankatsu belonged to unions, and their dispute activity far exceeded that of the early postwar years. The labor movement moved beyond its centers of strength in large factories in heavy industry to win substantial support in medium-sized and smaller factories. Also, with the advent of universal male suffrage, new "proletarian" political parties contested for electoral support for the first time. Through this "labor offensive," the dispute culture had become a familiar part of working-class life throughout the city by the late 1920s.

PRELUDE:
EARTHQUAKE AND AFTERMATH

The Great Kantō Earthquake struck Tokyo and the surrounding prefectures on September 1, 1923, at 11:58 A.M., just as lunch fires were burning in thousands of charcoal and gas stoves around the city. Huge whirlwinds of fire swept the eastern wards of the "Low City" over the following two days, devastating the crowded industrial neighborhoods of the Nankatsu region. Estimates of the dead and missing range from 100,000 to 200,000, and tremors or fire destroyed 570,000 dwellings, roughly three-fourths of all those in the city.[1] (See fig. 13.)

---

1. See Edward Seidensticker, *Low City, High City, Tokyo from Edo to the Earth-*

Thousands of Japanese fell victim to fire, but an uncounted number of survivors in turn took their own victims, murdering several thousand Koreans and Chinese in Tokyo and neighboring prefectures.[2] Within hours of the earthquake, rumors began to spread: Koreans and socialists had started the fires; they had poisoned the wells; they were planning rebellion. Encouraged by the authorities, residents throughout the Kantō region organized nearly 3,000 vigilante groups, ostensibly to keep order in devastated neighborhoods and protect property from looters, as well as from rebellious Koreans or leftists. While some of these groups simply patrolled their neighborhoods in peace, and a few protected Koreans from vicious crowds, others turned violent. They typically forced passers-by to speak a few simple phrases and then murdered (and sometimes disemboweled) those believed to have Korean or Chinese accents.

The press, the police, and the military fueled the hysteria. On September 2, for example, the *Tōkyō nichi nichi* reported: "Koreans and socialists are planning a rebellious and treasonous plot. We urge the citizens to cooperate with the military and police to guard against the Koreans." Police and military troops themselves rounded up and murdered several hundred Koreans in at least two incidents in Ueno and Kameido.[3]

THE KAMEIDO INCIDENT

The earthquake also marked a turning point in the history of the nation's labor movement and in labor's relation to the state. In its aftermath, the union movement in Tokyo broadened its base of support with a surge of organizing in smaller workplaces and more diverse industries, and it enjoyed greater success than before in harnessing the energies of the dispute culture. A more tolerant policy in the bureaucracy and the

---

quake: How the Shogun's Ancient Capital Became a Great Modern City, 1867–1923 (New York: Knopf, 1983) pp. 3–7, for an English-language account. He notes that cooking fires were not the sole, or even necessarily the major, cause of the conflagrations. Chemicals and electrical wiring were also culprits. If so, this was less a natural disaster than one of Japan's early industrial disasters.

2. A low estimate, resulting from Yoshino Sakuzō's investigation, is 2,700. Official Korean sources calculate a higher figure of 6,400. The Japanese Ministry of Justice reported only 243 deaths, unquestionably far too low. Figures from Victoria Peattie, "The Korean Massacre of 1923" (seminar paper in Japanese history, Harvard University, 1984), Appendix A, drawn from Kan Toku San, *Kantō daishinsai to chōsenjin*, vol. 6 of *Gendai shi shiryō* (Tokyo: Misuzu shobō, 1963).

3. Peattie cites *Kantō daishinsai to chōsenjin*, part 1, for the newspaper reports, and Changsoo Lee and George De Vos, *Koreans in Japan: Ethnic Conflict and Accommodation* (Berkeley: University of California Press, 1981), p. 23, on the police atrocities.

Kenseikai/Minseitō Party eventually offered a kind of sanction to this activity. But in the immediate wake of the earthquake, these trends had not yet emerged; two brutal incidents reflected a still powerful legacy of official hostility to the young social movement.

In these two instances, the "forces of order" took advantage of the confusion to settle accounts with one dozen leaders of the labor, anarchist, and communist movements. In the first, the Amakasu incident, a military police officer (Amakasu) murdered the anarchist Ōsugi Sakae, the feminist Itō Noe, and Ōsugi's six-year-old nephew. The second, the Kameido incident, took place in Nankatsu.[4] The subsequent cover-up has obscured the full story of these events, but they appear not to have been impulsive, isolated, unfortunate acts by confused policemen in a time of chaos. They were both considered and fundamentally predictable in the sense that they reflected a widespread official view of social activists as outlaws beneath contempt who fomented disorder and subversion among the common people.

Relations were already tense between the police in the Kameido district (with jurisdiction over Minami Katsushika County) and both Hirasawa Keishichi and his Pure Laborers' Union, and Watanabe Masanosuke and the Nankatsu Labor Association. The dispute at the Ōjima Steel Company in 1922 had set Hirasawa's group against the police. In one violent confrontation 120 union members were arrested and 63 charged with rioting. At the time of the earthquake, 13 were still in jail. A group of lawyers led by Fuse Tatsuji, who also had negotiated for the Ishikawajima strikers, had formed the Liberal Lawyers' Association (*Jiyū hōsō dan*) in 1921 to defend the civil rights of social activists. In the summer of 1923 they were preparing a case against the Kameido police for illegal arrests and violation of human rights in the Ōjima dispute.[5]

---

4. The most complete account of the Kameido incident is to be found in the OISR's *Shiryō shitsu hō*, no. 138 (March 1968). It includes an introductory essay by Nimura Kazuo, "Kameido jiken shoron," and the transcripts of the 1922 investigation of the Liberal Lawyers' Association (*Jiyū hōsō dan*). Worthwhile memoirs of survivors, and biographical accounts of victims, include Okamoto Kōji, *Onna o nakasu na: Minami Kiichi arasoi no kiroku* (Tokyo: Mikasa shobō, 1971) and *Gama shōgun: Minami Kiichi* (Tokyo: Privately published, 1971), focusing on Minami Kiichi, his brother Yoshimura Kōji, and Watanabe Masanosuke. See also Tanaka Uta and Yamashiro Kikue, eds., *Tanno Setsu: kakumei undō ni ikiru* (Tokyo: Keisō shobō, 1969), pp. 9–39, on Watanabe and Tanno, and Matsumoto Kappei, *Nihon shakaishugi engeki shi* (Tokyo: Chikuma shobō, 1975), pp. 823–30, on Hirasawa Keishichi.

5. Nimura, "Kameido jiken shoron," pp. 12–13.

The several dozen members of the Nankatsu Labor Association had fought police on May Day and at other demonstrations. At the time of the earthquake they were supporting a dispute at the Hirose Bicycle Company, and the Special Higher Police officer assigned to the Kameido district was trying to settle it. Several members of the Nankatsu Association had joined the Communist Party or its youth organization. Watanabe himself had been jailed in June 1923 along with 20 other party members. At the time of the earthquake the party was essentially dissolved.

On September 1 and 2, Hirasawa, Watanabe, and their comrades, like most area residents, combed the rubble, searched for relatives or friends, and even joined the ubiquitous vigilante patrols. Hirasawa spent September 1 helping a friend save belongings from his collapsed house. On the 2nd he joined his friend in a fruitless day-long search for the friend's sister-in-law. That evening he joined a vigilante patrol in his own neighborhood. His activities on the 3rd were similar.[6]

The Kameido police began to take known social activists into custody on the evening of September 3, perhaps suspecting these men and women would spread disorder or foment revolution amid the confusion. Five patrolmen found Hirasawa at home, and he quietly went to jail. Police also arrested Nakatsuji Uhachi, a member of the Pure Laborers' Union, at a shrine in Kameido. That same night, around 10:00 P.M., officers of the Special Higher Police rounded up seven members of the Nankatsu Labor Association, who had been similarly occupied in patrols or salvage activity. Watanabe's companion, later wife, Tanno Setsu, hid on an upstairs balcony of the association headquarters behind sliding paper windows to avoid arrest (see fig. 12).[7] Army troops detained an eighth member of the association, Satō Kinji. The biographies of those detained convey the diverse trajectories of those who joined the social movement in Nankatsu (see Appendix B).

At this point the details become murky. Between late at night on September 3 and September 5, probably before dawn on the 4th, troops of the 13th Cavalry Regiment on emergency duty in Kameido shot and decapitated Hirasawa and nine others, probably in the jail yard. They apparently disposed of the bodies, together with those of Korean and Chinese massacre victims, along the banks of the Arakawa drainage

---

6. Matsumoto, *Nihon shakaishugi engeki shi*, pp. 823–24.
7. Tanaka and Yamashiro, eds., *Tanno Setsu*, pp. 20–21.

canal.[8] Police later claimed to have cremated the remains. In any case, they never produced them.[9]

The Kameido police told relatives who came to inquire after one or another of the arrested men on the night of the 3rd and subsequently that "We sent him home" or "We sent him to the main headquarters" (see fig. 14). Not until October 14 did they issue an official notice claiming that troops had shot the men because they were agitating among the 700 to 800 prisoners, mostly Koreans. Hirasawa was said to have joined Kawai Yoshitora in singing revolutionary songs, encouraging others to join, and berating the guards. That Hirasawa, criticized above all during his life for unwonted moderation and willingness to compromise, had been fomenting rebellion in the jail in tandem with his ideological and organizational foe strains credulity. Despite this, official explanations not surprisingly put the blame on the victims, or upon the outside troops on emergency duty, rather than the local police themselves. Although it appears that the cavalry troops indeed carried out the executions, only the Kameido police could have located and identified the victims for initial arrest and later picked them out from among the hundreds packed into the jail. Over the following year, the Liberal Lawyers' Association and union leaders worked to bring the facts to light and establish responsibility, with partial success. With no remains to bury, the survivors and many Tokyo unions held a memorial service in February 1924 (see fig. 15). The emotional event marked a regrouping and new departure for the union movement in the area.[10]

In a context of chaos, the murder of these ten was an unsurprising denouement to four years of confrontation in Nankatsu between police and social activists. A background of decades of mistrust between

8. Grisly proof of this resting place may be offered by a controversial photograph first made public only after World War II. The picture shows several naked dead bodies, with a severed mustachioed head lying next to one of them. The head resembles Hirasawa's and may well be his, but another interpretation claims this is a photo of Japanese atrocities in Nanking that circulated in China during the war. If the picture is of Hirasawa, it may have been taken and secretly preserved by a photographer employed by the police, or it might have been taken by a member of a vigilante group. For further discussion, see Matsumoto, *Nihon shakaishugi engeki shi*, p. 827; Nimura, "Kameido jiken shoron," pp. 15–16. For the picture itself, and the most recent discussion of the controversy, see the Japanese photo-journalism weekly, *Focus*, no. 147 (September 7, 1984), pp. 12–13, and no. 150 (September 28, 1984), pp. 56–57.

9. Matsumoto, *Engeki shi*, p. 826.

10. In 1970 a group of historians and activists was finally able to erect a memorial stone for Hirasawa and the other victims in the graveyard of the Jōshinji temple in Kameido.

police and the urbanites who made up the political crowd heightened this tension. But while police and prosecutors saw the leaders of the earlier crowd simply as cynical, irresponsible manipulators, they viewed these new labor leaders as subversives. The speakers at the strike rallies in 1921; Watanabe and his comrades in the Communist Party; the anarchist Ōsugi, with a twenty-year history of sparring with authorities; Itō with her precocious sexual politics; and even Hirasawa and his union, who spoke of direct action and led violent disputes, all skirted or crossed the edge of legitimate thought and action as defined by the keepers of order in early imperial Japan. The police and the soldiers in Kameido maintained a grim consistency in their extreme acts, offering an emphatic statement of the relationship between the political system and social activists. They simply turned an unexpected crisis into an opportunity to purge society of men and women defined as outlaws.[11]

THE LABOR MOVEMENT REVIVES

In Nankatsu the revival of labor in the winter of 1924 was as dramatic as the destruction of September. Led by Watanabe Masanosuke, just released from jail, the survivors of the Nankatsu Labor Association regrouped, dissolving the old association and merging with a small union of workers at a local bicycle factory to found the Eastern Tokyo Amalgamated Labor Union on February 22. Much of their emotional energy and initial funding came from an energetic, volatile man named Minami Kiichi, the older brother of a victim in the Kameido incident named Yoshimura Kōji.[12]

Minami had come to Tokyo before World War I and started a small factory manufacturing glycerine in Terashima. By the time of the earthquake he had become a community leader, employing seventy people and proud of his position as head of the local neighborhood association

11. A different perspective on these events asserts that the decisions to carry out the murders were made by individual police or military officers, with no convincing evidence of complicity among high officials of the Home Ministry. The Ōsugi murder (and by implication those in Kameido) is thus dismissed as an "insignificant accident . . . but a footnote to the period's history because [it makes] no statement about the political system or the government" (Thomas Stanley, *Ōsugi Sakae: Anarchist in Taishō Japan* [Cambridge, Mass.: Harvard University Council on East Asian Studies, 1982], pp. 160–61). This view strikes me as a shallow revision of a kind common among Western analyses of Japan that shrink from any structural critique and focus narrowly on individual agency and responsibility.

12. Kōji was one of eleven children born to the impoverished Minami family, who were farmers living outside Kanazawa. His name was changed when he was adopted by the Yoshimura family at the age of two.

(see fig. 11). He tolerated the activism of Kōji and another younger brother with mild disapproval.

Upon hearing a rumor of his brother's killing soon after the earthquake, Minami went to the station house and confronted the Kameido police chief. Because Minami's surname differed from Yoshimura's, the police chief apparently realized the brothers were related only at this point. In Minami's account, by turning pale, trembling, and failing to offer a coherent reply, the police chief confirmed the rumor. Minami exploded in anger and was nearly killed when he began fighting with another policeman at the station.[13] Five months later, at a public memorial service for the Kameido victims on February 17, Minami spoke on behalf of the survivors, declaring that his brother had not died in vain; before this, Minami declared, he "had known little of [social] ideas," but he now understood the violence of the "capitalist state" and its ill-treatment of workers.

His brother's murder transformed Minami. Through his efforts to establish responsibility for Kōji's death, he came to know several labor leaders. Impressed by their commitment, Minami resolved to avenge the killing by embracing Kōji's cause. Late in 1923 he liquidated his business, paid his former employees substantial severance settlements, and sent his wife and two children back to the country.[14] With the remaining funds in his pocket, Minami visited Watanabe Masanosuke, stated his desire to join the labor movement, and handed money to the astounded Watanabe for use in supporting movement activities. With an oft-stated philosophy of "leaving the ideas to Watanabe," Minami devoted his personal charisma and leadership talents to organizing labor disputes in left-wing unions throughout Japan over the following years.[15]

The Eastern Tokyo Amalgamated Union enjoyed fair success. In April it affiliated with the Sōdōmei, and by June a police report credited

13. See Okamoto, *Gama shōgun*, pp. 73–74, for a dramatic recounting. Minami's mother, already ill, took a bad turn on hearing the news, and she, too, died that winter—in Minami's view, another victim of the Kameido incident.

14. The reported severance pay of nearly 300 yen per person represented roughly six months' wages for an average worker.

15. The most detailed account of these events is found in Okamoto, *Gama shōgun*, pp. 59–90. Although portions of the work suggest the intervention of a dramatically minded biographer, all the major details, with the exception of the precise amount of Minami's donation (the figure of 100,000 yen may be exaggerated), are confirmed by other sources. A report on the funeral is found in *TAS*, February 18, 1924. Tanno Setsu tells a corroborating story from Watanabe's perspective in Tanaka and Yamashiro, eds., *Tanno Setsu*, pp. 41–43.

the union with 430 members in seven locals in the Nankatsu area, drawn from about thirty small factories employing a total of 2,600 men and women.[16]

THE LABOR OFFENSIVE

This union was just one of many created in the following years during the labor offensive in Nankatsu. Ironically, it was during the period of union growth after the earthquake that the Sōdōmei experienced two major ruptures. The first came in May 1925, when the noncommunist and anticommunist "realists" in the union expelled the Sōdōmei's left wing, which then formed the Japan Council of Labor Unions (Nihon rōdō kumiai hyōgikai, hereafter Hyōgikai). One locus of left-wing union strength within the Sōdōmei had been the Eastern Tokyo Amalgamated Union founded by Watanabe and Minami, and many of its leaders and locals shifted to the Hyōgikai.

The issue that divided the Sōdōmei was the new direction of "realistic socialism" adopted at its crucial 1924 annual meeting. The left objected to this new strategy of support for parliamentary political actions and accommodation with the institutions of capital and the state. The "realists" decided that a unity that embraced the revolutionary left would invite repression and prove more damaging than the disunity of a split.[17] Both Watanabe Masanosuke and the Ishikawajima shipyard organizer Saitō Tadatoshi were prominent among the leaders of the Hyōgikai federation formed by the ousted union leaders. It claimed 15,000 members nationally in 1925, including a strong contingent from the Communist Party.

A scant nineteen months later, in December 1926, a second major split occurred when twelve leaders of the noncommunist left wing that had remained in the Sōdōmei objected to the union's perceived rightward drift and were expelled. The dissidents were led by intellectuals Asō Hisashi and Katō Kanjū, but supporters and prominent future leaders in Nankatsu included workers such as Iwauchi Zensaku and Asanuma Inejirō.[18] They felt that the new Sōdōmei realism had hardened into a counterproductive, divisive anticommunism; further, the acceptance

16. A police report of June 16, 1924, contained in Kyū-kyōchōkai, *Kantō dōmei kai* (1924), held at OISR, describes the founding of the Eastern Tokyo Amalgamated Union.
17. For details on the split, see Stephen Large, *Organized Workers and Socialist Politics in Interwar Japan* (Cambridge: Cambridge University Press, 1981), pp. 62–67.
18. On Iwauchi and Asanuma, see chapter 8. Asanuma became chairman of the Japan Socialist Party in 1960.

of parliamentary politics and "sound unionism" had produced too much cooperation with government and capitalists and not enough principled opposition. When the passage of universal male suffrage set off a scramble in the Sōdōmei and Hyōgikai to form competing proletarian parties, Asō's group secretly planned to form a third party to mediate between proletarian forces of the "left" and "right" and bring labor unity to the political front. Despite the inclusive intent, this move brought further division. When news of the plan became public, the Sōdōmei expelled Asō and eleven others.[19] They founded the Japan Labor Union Alliance (Nihon rōdō kumiai dōmei, hereafter Kumiai dōmei) with about 17,000 members. The Sōdōmei retained about 30,000 supporters.

At this point three major streams traversed the national map of federated labor: the so-called right-wing Sōdōmei, the centrist Kumiai dōmei, and the Hyōgikai on the left. Just over one year later, on March 3, 1928, the Seiyūkai government ordered the mass arrest of over 1,000 suspected communists nationwide and simultaneously dissolved the Hyōgikai. A small corps of survivors went underground, maintaining a shadowy Communist Party structure and forming small cells of labor supporters in an uncountable number of factories. This three-way division of the labor movement persisted for about a decade, with the left stream underground, until the right and centrist groups reunited in 1936.

It would be logical to expect such divisive intramovement struggles to have damaged efforts to organize, but the numbers do not support such a view. It seems the competition between the several federations had a positive effect, as it stimulated intense efforts to enroll members and found new locals in places like Nankatsu. On the eve of the earthquake, when a united Sōdōmei was the only national federation, total union membership in Japan stood at approximately 125,000, with about 30,000 in the Sōdōmei. By 1927 the number of unionized workers had almost tripled, exceeding 300,000, a reported 6.5 percent of all wage laborers. The majority still belonged to independent unions or those in smaller federations, for the three major federations accounted for no more than 50,000 of the total. The diversity of activity and the heated local debates that accompanied each split reflected significant grass-roots vitality.

19. Large, *Organized Workers and Socialist Politics*, pp. 107–9.

UNIONS IN NANKATSU

This diversity also produced a dizzying array of unions in Nankatsu. On the occasion of a national split, the leaders of union locals would debate and vote, either in executive session or at a full union assembly, on whether to join the expelled dissidents or remain in the Sōdōmei. If the vote was close, the local itself might split in two, and invariably the several locals of any union in a given area differed in their decisions. By 1927, therefore, Nankatsu's unions included locals and industrial federations with right (Sōdōmei), left (Hyōgikai), and center (Kumiai dōmei) affiliations. Adding to the confusion, rump and dissident factions would fight over who retained rights to the existing union name.

Concurrent with such contention, a rush hour of the unions in prewar Nankatsu, and throughout the nation, began in 1924. The success of Minami Kiichi and Watanabe Masanosuke with their amalgamated union was duplicated throughout the area. Table 7.1 summarizes the range of union organizations and my best estimate of their strength in 1927, midway through the 1924–29 surge of organizing. The total membership exceeded 20,000, roughly one-third of the 63,000 wage laborers in the Nankatsu region. Membership figures broken down by ward and county are not available in each year for each union. Where possible, I have used data from 1927, but in a few cases the figures are from 1926 or 1928.

In the textile industry, women began to join labor unions in large numbers. The Kantō Textile Union in the Sōdōmei camp boasted 7,000 members as early as 1925, with locals in five major factories. The preponderance of these locals left the Sōdōmei with its second split of 1926, forming the Japan Textile Union in the centrist camp, which claimed 7,880 members in five factories by 1928. The Sōdōmei also retained a strong minority presence in several mills. Women at the huge Tōyō Muslin complex in Kameido (8,823 employees in 1926, 85 percent of them women, in three factories) were particularly vigorous supporters of both these unions. In 1925 roughly 100 employees in the Number 3 factory joined the Sōdōmei's Kantō Textile Union, and by early 1926 virtually all the workers in the three factories were union members. Their Jōtō local joined the Japan Textile Union in the centrist Kumiai dōmei camp after the December 1926 split, and this union led a successful drive for improved treatment several months later.

Numerous unions of the center, right, and left were active among

TABLE 7.1   PRINCIPAL UNIONS IN THE NANKATSU
REGION, 1912–29

	1912–18	1919–23	1924–29
	Yūaikai members in some fifty companies in metal, textiles, machine, rubber, glass, leather industries: eight locals	Tokyo Metalworkers' Union (several hundred)	Sōdōmei unions
		Pure Laborers' Union (ca. 300)	Metalworkers' Union (ca. 1,000)
		Japan Rōgikai Union (500)	Amalgamated (500)
		Rolling Stock Union (400)	Textiles (3,500)
		Takeuchi Safe Union	Shoe (460)
		Greater Japan Rubber Union	Hyōgikai unions
		Tokyo Rubber Union	Metalworkers' Union (500)
		Nankatsu Labor Association	Amalgamated (500)
		Textile Union (ca. 1,000)	Lumber (400)
		Lumber workers	Kumiai dōmei unions
			Metalworkers' Union (500)
			Communications (500)
			Amalgamated (700)
			Textiles (8,300)
			Free Laborer Fed. (1,100)
			Kōtō Free Labor Union (1,000)
Total union membership	ca. 1,000	ca. 3,000	ca. 20,000
Labor force	60,000 (1917)	70,000 (1919–20)	63,000 (1927)
Proportion in unions	1–2%	ca. 4%	32%

SOURCES: For the 1912–18 period, *Yūai shinpō* (1912–14) and *Rōdō oyobi sangyō* (1914–18). For other years, OISR and records of individual unions.
NOTE: Nankatsu region = Honjo and Fukagawa wards and Minami Katsushika County. Figures in parentheses indicate numbers of members.

metalworkers and machinists. The Tokyo Metalworkers' Union was probably the best-organized Sōdōmei industrial federation of the inter-war era. Before the earthquake it had founded a few short-lived locals in Honjo and Ōjima factories, and gradually, beginning in 1925 with a local founded at the Japan Casting Company, the Tokyo Metalworkers' Union established a presence in Nankatsu. By May 1928 twelve of the union's thirty-five locals were in Nankatsu. In addition, the Metal-workers' Union of the Hyōgikai and a similarly named group in the cen-trist Kumiai dōmei both won support in several factories, and a number of independent metalworkers' unions continued to maintain strength at the larger factories where they had established themselves soon after World War I.

Among the most active new unions were the catchall "amalgamated" federations, devised to encompass locals in a variety of industries, no one of which had enough strength to form a separate "industrial" federation. They centered principally upon diverse chemical industries (rubber, cellu-loid, pharmaceutical, fertilizer, explosives, cement, fabric dyeing), food processing, and even two hat manufacturers. Watanabe's Eastern Tokyo Amalgamated had joined the Sōdōmei in 1924. After the first Sōdōmei split, many locals followed him into the Hyōgikai, taking with them the union's name. Those remaining in the Sōdōmei regrouped as the Kantō Amalgamated, which grew to eight locals and 600 members in the area by mid 1926. With the second Sōdōmei split, in 1926, the leadership of the Kantō Amalgamated left the Sōdōmei and affiliated with the new Kumiai dōmei federation.[20]

These figures on union membership are necessarily imprecise, but even such an imperfect survey reveals a union presence that we must consider impressive. The earliest Nankatsu unions had been formed just over a decade earlier, and the first wave of organizing, after World War I, had enrolled perhaps 3,000 to 4,000 union members at its peak, pri-marily in the area's major factories. After the earthquake, union orga-nizers gradually broadened their focus to include a middle tier of fac-tories of about one to several hundred workers. The men and women at these sites, and in some even smaller workplaces, responded with alac-rity, and unions became a more widespread feature of the social land-scape than before. In addition, their members joined ever more frequent assertive disputes for a wide range of improved working conditions.

---

20. The records of the Kantō Amalgamated Union survive in abundance and are analyzed below.

DISPUTES IN NANKATSU

The link between disputes and union activities strengthened markedly after 1923. The two forms of action had been almost wholly separate before 1919. Between 1919 and 1923 they had begun to coalesce; unions led a substantial minority of disputes. During the labor offensive beginning in 1924 and 1925, union involvement in disputes jumped dramatically. Both national and Nankatsu data make this clear (table 7.2). In several other critical respects, as well, the disputes in 1924 and after differed markedly from those before. In simple quantity, the year 1924 saw a sharp increase from levels of the previous several years, and beginning in 1926, with the Sōdōmei-Hyōgikai rivalry in full swing, the number of disputes reached unprecedented levels (table 7.3).

The clear change in the quality of these actions is of greatest interest. Only one of the thirty disputes in Minami Katsushika County before 1924 had lasted for a month, and just one other had dragged on for over two weeks. Several long struggles such as that at Ishikawajima had shocked the elite in 1921 precisely because they were exceptional. The picture shifted suddenly after the earthquake, as practically one-third (58 of 177) of the Nankatsu disputes between 1924 and 1929 lasted two weeks or more (table 7.4). One in ten were month-long struggles. The capacity and determination of organized workers to press their demands had increased dramatically, and owners or managers likewise increased their resolve to resist the demands of organized labor.

The spread of disputes beyond the walls of the large factory was likewise a phenomenon of this era (table 7.5). The great majority of disputes before 1924 took place in factories of large (500 +) or medium (100–499) size. The locus of the labor movement in Nankatsu did not simply *switch* to small factories beginning in 1924. The success of managers in zaibatsu and state-run heavy industries in putting an end to labor disputes was not replicated in the large Nankatsu textile mills, or in the medium-sized machine and chemical plants, where the workers demanded reform or resisted pay cuts more frequently than ever. The noteworthy new development was the *spread* of disputes to smaller workplaces, together with their continued occurrence in medium and larger sites outside the zaibatsu and state-run sector. The center of gravity of the union movement shifted, and the majority of Nankatsu disputes (116 of 177) between 1924 and 1929 took place in factories of 100 or fewer workers.

Disputes thus became a commonplace part of factory life throughout the region. The most telling statistical representation of this new facet

TABLE 7.2   UNION INVOLVEMENT IN DISPUTES, MINAMI KATSUSHIKA COUNTY AND NATIONALLY

	No. of Disputes	No. of Disputes Involving Unions	% of Disputes Involving Unions
Minami Katsushika County, 1917–38			
1917–23	26	10	38
1924–29	189	113	60
1930–32	141	117	83
1933–38	152	110	72
All Japan, 1922–37			
1922–23	520	163	31
1924–29	2,477	1,545	62
1930–32	2,797	1,870	67
1933–38	3,001	1,288	43

SOURCES: Minami Katsushika County data through 1926 are from Aoki Kōji, *Nihon rōdō undō shi nenpyō* (Tokyo: Shinseisha, 1968); for 1927–38, from Kyū-kyōchōkai, *Rōdō sōgi*, Keishichō, *Rōdō sōgi junpō*, *Shakai undō ōrai*, and *Shakai undō tsūshin*. National data are from *Nihon rōdō undō shiryō* (Tokyo, 1959) 10:522.

TABLE 7.3   NUMBER OF DISPUTES IN MINAMI
KATSUSHIKA COUNTY AND TOKYO, 1897–1937

Year	Minami Katsushika County	Tokyo City
1897–1910	5	—
1911	0	—
1912	0	—
1913	0	—
1914	3	—
1915	0	—
1916	0	—
1917	1	—
1918	0	—
1919	11	—
1920	2	—
1921	6	—
1922	4	89
1923	2	106
1924	19	—
1925	11	193
1926	42	167
1927	52	163
1928	35	153
1929	29	392
1930	64	464
1931	40	564
1932	37	435
1933	42	322
1934	28	276
1935	22	248
1936	13	184
1937	39	396

SOURCES: Minami Katsushika County data through 1926 are from Aoki Kōji, *Nihon rōdō undō shi nenpyō* (Tokyo: Shinseisha, 1968); for 1927–38, from Kyū-kyōchōkai, *Rōdō sōgi*; Keishichō, *Rōdō sōgi junpō*, *Shakai undō ōrai*, and *Shakai undō tsūshin*. Tokyo data for 1921–23 and 1925–37 are from Keishichō, *Keishichō tōkei sho*; 1924 data are from Aoki, *Nihon rōdō undō shi nenpyō*.

TABLE 7.4   DURATION OF DISPUTES IN MINAMI KATSUSHIKA COUNTY, 1897–1938

Number of Disputes

Years	Lasting 1 day	Lasting 2–7 Days	Lasting 8–14 Days	Lasting 15–30 Days	Lasting 31+ Days	Subtotal	Unclear Duration	Total
1897–1916	5 (83)	0	0	1 (17)	0	6	2	8
1917–23	9 (38)	9 (38)	5 (21)	0	1 (4)	24	2	26
1924–29	5 (3)	78 (44)	36 (20)	40 (23)	18 (10)	177	11	188
1930–32	1 (1)	40 (32)	24 (19)	33 (26)	29 (23)	127	14	141
1933–38	9 (7)	64 (46)	29 (21)	22 (16)	14 (10)	138	15	153
Total	29	191	94	96	62	472	44	516

SOURCES: Data through 1926 are from Aoki Kōji, *Nihon rōdō undō shi nenpyō* (Tokyo: Shiseisha, 1968); for 1927–38, from Kyū-kyōchōkai, *Rōdō sōgi*; Keishichō, *Rōdō sōgi junpō*, *Shakai undō ōrai*, and *Shakai undō tsūshin*.
NOTE: Figures in parentheses are percentages. Owing to rounding off, the totals are not always 100 percent.

TABLE 7.5   DISPUTES IN MINAMI KATSUSHIKA COUNTY,
BY SCALE OF ENTERPRISE, 1897–1938

| | | Number of Disputes | | | | | |
Years	5–30 Workers	31–100 Workers	101–500 Workers	501+ Workers	Subtotal	No. of Workers Unclear	Total
1897–1916	1 (20)	0	1 (20)	3 (60)	5	3	8
1917–23	2 (8)	5 (19)	11 (42)	8 (31)	26	0	26
1924–29	46 (26)	70 (40)	32 (18)	29 (16)	177	11	188
1930–32	63 (45)	49 (35)	18 (13)	9 (7)	139	2	141
1933–38	63 (42)	47 (31)	25 (17)	15 (10)	150	3	153
Total	175	171	87	64	497	19	516

SOURCES: Data through 1926 are from Aoki Kōji, *Nihon rōdō undō shi nenpyō* (Tokyo: Shiseisha, 1968); for 1927–38, from Kyū-kyōchōkai, *Rōdō sōgi*; Keishichō, *Rōdō sōgi junpō, Shakai undō junpō, Shakai undō ōrai* and *Shakai undō tsūshin*.
NOTE: Figures in parentheses are percentages.

TABLE 7.6 ESTIMATED PROPORTION OF FACTORIES IN
ALL INDUSTRIES EXPERIENCING DISPUTES, MINAMI
KATSUSHIKA COUNTY, 1924–38

	No. of Employees				
	5–29	30–99	100–499	500+	Total
Total No. of Factories					
1924–29	879	131	35	12	1,057
1930–32	577	116	33	11	737
1933–38	1,307	213	49	15	1,584
No. of Factories with Disputes					
1924–29	32	48	18	11	109
1930–32	46	38	14	9	107
1933–38	48	44	17	8	117
% of Factories with Disputes					
1924–29	4	37	51	92	11
1930–32	8	33	42	82	15
1933–38	4	21	35	53	8

SOURCES: Dispute data through 1926 are from Aoki Kōji, *Nihon rōdō undō shi nenpyō* (Tokyo: Shinseisha, 1968); for 1927–38, from Kyū-kyōchōkai, *Rōdō sōgi*; Keishichō, *Rōdō sōgi junpō, Shakai undō ōrai,* and *Shakai undō tsūshin.* Number of factories for 1924–29 is from the *Tōkyō kōjō yōran* of 1928. The number for 1930–32 is from Tōkyō-fu, *Tōkyō-fu tōkei sho* (Tokyo, 1931). The number for 1933–38 is the mean of totals for 1933 and 1937 from Tōkyō-fu, *Tōkyō-fu tōkeisho.*
NOTES: Owing to fluctuations in the number of factories, especially smaller factories, the figure for "number of factories" across each span of several years is an approximation, and the resulting "proportion experiencing disputes" is an estimate. The figures from 1924–32 are relatively certain, for the total number of medium-sized and large factories changed little. Because the number of factories rose sharply from 1933 to 1938, I have taken the mean of the two available totals, from 1933 and 1937, as an approximation of the number of factories over this period.

of urban culture is presented in table 7.6, which shows the rough proportion of all factories of each size that experienced at least one dispute in three periods between 1924 and 1938. Over one-tenth of all Nankatsu factories of more than five employees experienced at least one dispute in the years from 1924 to 1929. The proportion of factories experiencing disputes in the "small" and "medium" categories of 30–99 and 100–499 employees reached 37 and 51 percent respectively. Only one of the twelve largest workplaces escaped labor unrest altogether. Furthermore, multiple disputes were common: a total of 188 incidents took place at the 121 factories that experienced disputes. Finally, the labor offensive was not restricted by industry or gender.[21] Women in each of the major textile mills launched at least one dispute in these years. Men in the machine industries, traditionally at the forefront of working-class actions, undertook disputes in all the largest factories and most of the medium and small ones. Large proportions of owners in the chemical, food-processing, and other industries also encountered organized labor protests for the first time.

Unfortunately, we have no count of factories broken down by comparable size categories from before 1924, so we cannot compare the frequency of disputes before and after the earthquake precisely, but between 1917 and 1923 disputes took place at only 18 of Nankatsu's 600 factories. The broad penetration of labor disputes to factories of each size and industry beginning in 1924, revealed by these data, was clearly unprecedented. By the late 1920s the owner of a small shop could no longer be sure that "his workers" were different from the rebellious mass in the huge shipyards or engineering plants. The working-class offensive of union-building and disputes had brought the labor problem home to the local industrial elite in Nankatsu.

THE STRUCTURE OF WORKING-CLASS ACTION, 1924–1929

The post-1924 disputes were noteworthy more for their spread to relatively smaller worksites than for entirely new tactics, but a few differences are apparent. A broadened range of workers had access to the sophisticated tactics already developed by men at places like Ishikawajima, thanks in part to the publication of "how-to" books written for workers, such as Murashima's guide, published in 1925. Workers used the communications media of the day, such as leaflets, newsletters, and posters, more extensively and with increased sophistication. Also, probably reflecting both the presence of radical intellectuals and increasingly educated workers, research and preparation of reports grew in importance; knowledge of conditions in other firms and industries aided in formulating demands and justifying them in both negotiating sessions and leaflets.[22] In this fashion, unions spread to numerous factories an awareness of the tactics and the gains made by workers at sites of earlier organizing.

21. I have omitted the unwieldy industry-specific data. They are published in Andrew Gordon, "Senzen Nankatsu chiiki ni okeru rōdō kumiai undō no tenkai," *Ōhara shakai mondai kenkyūjo zasshi*, no. 326 (January 1986): 12.

22. Murashima Yoriyuki, *Rōdō sōgi, no jissai chishihi* (Tokyo: Kagaku shisō fukyū kai, 1925), pp. 225–37.

TABLE 7.7   LONGEVITY OF NANKATSU REGION UNION LOCALS

| | No. of Locals | | | | |
Union	<1 Year in Existence	1–2 Years in Existence	3–4 Years in Existence	5+ Years in Existence	Total
Kanto Amalgamated Union, 1926–33	10	26	10	5	51
Tokyo Metalworkers' Union, 1925–38	2	4	6	21	33

SOURCES: "Kantō gōdō" file A-5 and "Sōdōmei Tekkō Kumiai" file, OISR.
NOTE: Nankatsu region = Honjo and Fukagawa wards and Minami Katsushika County.

Two aspects of the structure of worker action must be noted to conclude the analysis of the nuts and bolts of the making of the "dispute
culture" in this decade. The great majority of unions, even most of
those that were nominally trade or industrial federations, continued to
make the factory their basic building block. With few exceptions, each
local of a union such as the Amalgamated Union of the Kumiai dōmei
was drawn from workers at a single factory, with little concern for
trade distinctions within a workplace. In the few instances where workers from two or three factories joined in a single local, the small size of
each single factory group and their geographic proximity, not trade or
even industry, justified the merged form. Thus, the # 2 local of Kantō
Amalgamated in Nankatsu consisted of contingents from the Greater
Japan Fertilizer Company and a nearby dye factory. Organizing workers by factory remained the natural choice of unions, strong or weak,
moderate or radical.

The second noteworthy feature of the labor offensive was the fluidity
of union organizations, reflecting their symbiotic relationship with
labor disputes. Table 7.7 presents data on the longevity of the Nankatsu
locals of the Kantō Amalgamated and Metalworkers' unions. The ability of 21 of 33 locals to sustain themselves for five or more years is
testimony to the effective organization of the Sōdōmei's Metalworkers'
Union, as well as to the care the union took to choose struggles carefully and not draw the wrath of employers or government. Even so, the
failure of one-third of the locals within five years indicates the difficulty
of sustaining unions in the face of ongoing hostility from most owners.
More typical, it seems, was Kantō Amalgamated. Only 5 of 51 locals
survived five years. Over half (26 of 51) failed within two years.

A typical reason for the collapse of a local was the failure of a dispute action; owners would usually dismiss the union leaders in the wake of a failed dispute. Yet such hostility from owners was only part of the reason for the high failure rate. Both the ideology of union leaders and the somewhat different expectations of members favored dispute and struggle at the expense of institution-building. In actual practice, unions and disputes were inseparable components of the workers' movement. Of 37 new locals in the Kantō Amalgamated Union between 1926 and 1929, for example, 15 were founded during or just after a dispute, or engaged in one within six months of founding. Of 13 locals that folded in this span, 6 did so in the wake of a failed dispute action.

Similar patterns elsewhere in Japan led some contemporary unionists, as well as historians, to call prewar unions "dispute unions," entities that came into existence for the purpose of making particular demands and collapsed when the effort failed.[23] The label implies that workers lacked the commitment to unions or the understanding of them needed to sustain an organization over the long run.

The "dispute union" label is not wholly inappropriate in the case of Kantō Amalgamated in Nankatsu (or the well-documented Sōdōmei unions in Kawaguchi). But this negative connotation projects back the observer's opinion of what the unions ought to have done. Rather than view the dispute as one of several union tactics, to be used with great caution, many organizers at the time saw unions primarily as a means of carrying on disputes. For example, consider the text of a speech by Kikugawa Tadao, reflecting his philosophy from the mid 1920s through the 1930s. Kikugawa was a student radical turned labor activist who, beginning in 1926, played a leading role in the Education Section of the Kumiai dōmei. As the "first principle of union action," he listed "expansion and strengthening of the organization," but the process to achieve this was outlined in his notes as "organization → education → practice [i.e., dispute] → expanded, strengthened organization → toward new struggle."[24] In Kikugawa's conception, ongoing struggle and education built the organization, preparing the day for greater struggle and far-reaching social transformation.

23. For an example, see the Sōdōmei union monthly, *Rōdō*, September 1931, cited in Sumiya Mikio, ed., *Shōwa kyōkō: sono rekishiteki igi to zentai zō* (Tokyo: Yūhikaku, 1974), p. 267. For an interesting discussion of this issue, see Yamamoto Kazushige, "Daikyōkōki ni okeru rōdō sōgi to kumiai soshiki: Zenrō Kantō gōdō rōdō kumiai o sozai to shite," *Hokudai shigaku*, no. 26 (August 1986): 24–25.
24. Kikugawa Tadao's August 1932 speech "Labor Union Organization and Strategy" is in the "Zenrō: Tōkyō chiren" file, OISR.

We have seen that in the mid 1920s the union rank and file, as well as thousands of workers who only joined a union when a dispute began, were indeed ready and willing to initiate hundreds of labor disputes. Their energetic support of these disputes makes clear that Kikugawa's emphasis on struggle was shared widely, that factory workers were ready to put their jobs on the line to demand changes in workplace life. But the analysis of the working-class program in the next chapter will suggest that most of these workers did not share the long-range revolutionary goals of a man like Kikugawa, although they joined actions that he helped organize.

While unions did engage in a number of additional activities, many of these essentially complemented the orientation toward dispute. At the Kantō Amalgamated Union's headquarters, an active Research Section prepared lengthy, detailed surveys of the work force in area factories for the use of union organizers, and in 1927 and 1928 it examined the policies of local employers concerning health insurance, unemployment, and idle workers, as well as severance and retirement pay systems, to help union leaders formulate appropriate demands for reform.[25] The Education Section, created in late 1926, organized study sessions and "tea meetings" for the union locals. Discussion leaders ran over 100 gatherings in Nankatsu locals each year at least until 1931, with an average of thirty attendees per session. They discussed labor politics, the philosophy of labor unions, and current economic or political issues.[26] In addition, a citywide boom in worker education took place in 1924 and 1925, with eight "Labor Schools" founded in Tokyo. In 1927 fifty-four union members attended classes at three of these schools.[27] Union headquarters also organized a "Fighters' Club" of strong young men to counter strikebreakers and hired toughs and intimidate owners during disputes. Each local was required to send three members to the club.[28] While some of these research and education endeavors could encourage commitment to the union as a solvent institution able to support workers in times of need, many of these activities served primarily to nurture local activists and leaders, build political awareness among the rank and file, and prepare the way for future struggles.

25. "Kantō gōdō honbu" file, OISR.
26. Records are only available through 1931.
27. On Kantō Amalgamated education, see "Zenkoku rōdō Kantō gōdō kyōiku," file G-31, OISR. On labor schools, see Soda Tarō, Honpō rōdō gakkō gaikyō (Tokyo: Kyōchōkai, 1929), pp. 11–18.
28. "Kantō gōdō honbu" file, OISR, chart dated March 22, 1927.

The low priority assigned mutual aid activities is as striking as the vigorous research and leadership training. Some locals did offer aid to members, and a few created consumer cooperatives, but a "Local Report" distributed to the members of the # 2 local of Kantō Amalgamated in 1928 sheds light on the relative priority of disputes and institution-building. After describing in detail the two disputes involving this local then under way, the report cautioned: "However, disputes are not the only job of unions. At present we have consumer cooperatives organized in the Komatsugawa Sugar local, the Kawaguchi local, the Shinagawa local, and others, working for the benefit of members."[29] The need to remind members in this fashion is telling. Of seventeen locals in Nankatsu in 1928, only the Komatsugawa Sugar group had formed a cooperative. A Kumiai dōmei federation pamphlet several years later commented that "it is almost as if the union movement until now has been dominated by the concept that mass mutual aid or insurance were not labor movement tasks."[30]

The instability of these disputatious union locals, as well as the nature of their activities, suggests that the labor dispute, as much as the union, was the key working-class "institution" to proliferate in Nankatsu after 1923; a labor offensive centered on disputes was the culmination of the process of movement-building that began early in the century. The building of a durable institutional presence was extraordinarily difficult in factories whose owners saw unions as dangerous threats, even though state hostility to nonrevolutionary labor organizations abated after 1924. In addition, organization for narrowly focused wage demands was not the top priority of most union leaders, and reliance on the union as an ongoing institution of self-help and mutual support may not have been the primary goal of most of the rank and file. If we measure success or significance by the longevity of individual unions, their ability consistently to win pay increases, or the number of aid societies they created, the union movement even at its high-water mark had a limited impact.

Yet such a standard is too high, and it projects into the past norms and expectations not held by the workers or their leaders. However short-lived most locals were, the constant regrouping and founding of new locals implies that workers throughout the area wanted to improve their status and conditions at work and were willing to take risky ac-

29. Kumiai dōmei, Tokyo locals file, OISR, contains the April 1928 "local report" of Komatsugawa local # 2.
30. Kumiai dōmei, file E-3, OISR, 1935 pamphlet, p. 1.

tions to achieve this. Each union federation, with its local and regional headquarters, and its cadre of experienced organizers, represented a resource, increasingly familiar and accepted, to which working men and women could rally when a particular situation passed their point of tolerance. A few such clusters had been formed prior to 1923, notably those of Hirasawa, of the Sōdōmei, and of the Nankatsu Labor Association. By the late 1920s numerous centers of union expertise dotted the Nankatsu landscape, visible manifestations of a spreading working-class assertiveness and combative spirit.

POLITICAL ACTION

Outside the factory gates the political arena for workers had for decades been limited to the street, the assembly hall, and the park, where demonstrations, speech-meetings, and occasional riots took place. This changed with the passage of universal suffrage for men in May 1925. Unions of laborers and tenant farmers, as well as intellectuals active in the social movement, immediately undertook to create the groups that came to be known collectively as "the proletarian parties." Naturally enough, both political parties and campaigns drew on the experience accumulated through union-building and labor disputes, and these parties can be seen as an outgrowth of the dispute culture described above. For an activist in the Sōdōmei or Kantō Amalgamated, the drawing up of a platform, the planning of a series of speech-meetings, or the leafleting of a neighborhood were familiar tasks. Over the following decade the political party and the election campaign became as familiar a part of urban working-class life as labor unions and disputes (see fig. 27).

All three major union groupings took part in a flurry of meetings and negotiations in 1925 and 1926, intended to create a united party to represent wage laborers and tenant farmers. Ironically, the first major rupture of the Sōdōmei also took place in May 1925, the month the suffrage bill passed, and both ideological and personal antagonism ultimately rendered working-class political unity impossible for the next seven years. A bewildering series of tentative party foundings, ruptures, and renewed negotiations marked the first year of proletarian politics. Finally, by the end of 1926, after the Sōdōmei underwent its second split, the map of proletarian parties took shape. Although continued name-changing by the parties, usually involving only minor realignment of the key words used by each party ("Japan," "Labor," "Farmer," "Social") makes a clear recounting nearly impossible, three distinct political party groupings had emerged.

These streams ran parallel to those of the major union groupings. On the right, aligned with the Sōdōmei, was the Social Democratic Party, founded in December 1926. The centrist Kumiai dōmei union federation was founded simultaneously with a political party called the Japan Labor-Farmer Party (renamed the Japan Masses Party in 1928 and the National Masses Party in 1930). On the left, the Hyōgikai labor federation backed the short-lived Labor-Farmer Party. The Seiyūkai cabinet dissolved this group in its March 1928 purge, and for four years the Social Democrats and the Japan Labor-Farmer group were the two major working-class political organizations. In 1932 these two parties merged to form the Social Masses Party (SMP), which later became the most successful of the prewar proletarian parties.[31]

The first regular elections under the new law came in 1928. Between February 1928 and November 1929 four elections were contested in Minami Katsushika County and Honjo and Fukagawa wards in descending order from the national to local level. First came the National Diet election, followed in June 1928 by the Tokyo prefectural assembly election. March 1929 saw the first universal manhood suffrage election of the Tokyo City Council, and in November 1929, at the end of this era of the labor offensive, elections were held in Tokyo's ward, town, and village assemblies.

Victories for the divided, financially strapped proletarian parties were rare in these years, although their combined vote totals in areas of traditional union strength were substantial, offering promise for the day when a semblance of unity could be achieved. In the Diet election of February 1928, the proletarian camp ran 82 men nationwide and won just 8 (of 466) seats, with 4.7 percent of the total vote. Among the victors were Sōdōmei patriarchs Suzuki Bunji and Nishio Suehiro, both running in Osaka districts.

The Nankatsu region straddled two Lower House electoral districts. Honjo and Fukagawa wards constituted the relatively small Tokyo District 4. The industrial sections of Minami Katsushika County, together with the county's farming villages to the east of the Arakawa River, made up Tokyo District 6, the most populous electoral district in the nation. Under the system of multi-member districts used in both prewar and contemporary Japan, the top five vote-getters in District 6 and the top four in District 4 would win seats in the Diet.[32] Under this system, factional strife or poor assessments of party strength were disastrous. If

---

31. See Large, *Organized Workers and Socialist Politics*, pp. 101–18, for details.
32. Each voter casts only one vote.

a party with votes enough for one seat took a greedy chance and ran two men, both might fail. Similarly, if two or three candidates from different proletarian parties ran in a district, they might split the union vote and lose. This is precisely what happened to labor candidates in Nankatsu and throughout Japan, and it explains why the proportion of seats won in 1928 (1.5 percent) lagged so far behind the vote.[33]

In Honjo and Fukagawa (District 4) in 1928, the Minseitō and Seiyūkai each elected two men. The lowest winning candidate gained just 4,204 votes, establishing the cutoff line for victory in the district. Candidates of the Social Democrats and the left-wing Labor-Farmer Party together polled 6,426 votes, 11 percent of the total and enough to have elected a single labor M.P. By splitting those votes, they finished seventh and tenth in a field of sixteen.

The industrial neighborhoods of Minami Katsushika County confirmed their reputation as strongholds of the social movement, and the labor parties again learned the dangers of division. Three proletarian candidates together polled an impressive 25,065 votes, 15.5 percent of the total. But the Minseitō won three seats, the Seiyūkai two. The lowest winner polled 17,414 votes, so here again the proletarian camp had strength to elect at least one man. Matsutani Yojirō, the candidate supported by Kantō Amalgamated and other centrist union federations, came closest, with 12,438 votes (7.7 percent) and a sixth place finish. The irrepressible Minami Kiichi carried the banner for the left-wing camp as Labor-Farmer candidate. His 6,659 votes (eighth place, 4 percent) revealed some ongoing support for the Communist Party and Hyōgikai unions among Nankatsu workers. The Social Democrat candidate was close behind in ninth place with 5,938 votes.

The labor performance was similar in the prefectural assembly and city council elections that followed.[34] Competing proletarian candidates split their votes and failed in the Fukagawa, Honjo, and Minami Katsushika County districts of the Prefectural Assembly. In the city council voting, Asanuma Inejirō, future Diet member and president of the Japan Socialist Party in the 1950s, came closest to success, running in Fukagawa as a candidate of the centrist party. He polled 1,198 votes and finished ninth of nineteen, fewer than two hundred votes and two

33. Kenneth Colegrove, "Labor Parties in Japan," *American Political Science Review* 23 (May 1929): 337, cites an analysis in *Kaizō* claiming that the left could have doubled its Diet delegation through effective cooperation.

34. Results are from *TAS*. In most cases the press only reported vote totals for the winners and runner-up, so we cannot calculate voting percentages, only the order of finish.

places short of the lowest winner. Citywide, just three proletarian candidates won office.

At the most local level, the proletarian camp enjoyed scattered victories. Ward, town (*chō*), and village elections were contested in single at-large districts. In ward elections, the top forty candidates of seventy or eighty contestants won seats. With 20,000 to 30,000 votes divided by this huge field, a few hundred votes sufficed for the low-end winners, and one well-disciplined union local could deliver a winning bloc. Citywide results are not available from all parties, but we do know that the centrist Japan Labor-Farmer Party ran seven successful candidates in the 1929 town council races, including three from towns in Nankatsu. In addition, the textile union organizer Iwauchi Zensaku won a seat on the nearby Nippori town council, proving that his appeal extended beyond the still unenfranchised textile women.[35] A Social Democrat topped all seventy candidates in Fukagawa ward, although his lone presence among forty ward councillors was unlikely to change the local power structure. In Sumida township, the factory union at the Japan Rolling Stock factory union was large enough to field three successful candidates for town council, including their president.

Whether these showings are considered poor or impressive depends on the standard for comparison. The Japanese labor movement of the 1920s looks impotent compared to the British Labour Party, whose leader became prime minister of a coalition cabinet in 1924, and Japanese activists on occasion compared their political fortunes unfavorably and wistfully to those of the British.[36] But most urban working men in England had been voters since 1867, the year of the Meiji Restoration! Most rural working men had gained the vote in 1884. British unions were even more venerable. The comparison is unfair. On the other hand, in the United States workers historically have voted for the "established parties," in behavior perhaps comparable to that of the Japanese laborers who apparently supported the Minseitō in 1928. When a rare labor candidate, Henry George, polled just 28 percent of the vote in a field of only three in the New York mayoral election of 1886, the press hailed this as "extraordinary."[37] The Nankatsu vote totals are quite respectable by comparison.

35. Kantō gōdō headquarters file, OISR, 1919 annual meeting report.

36. See *Rōdō*, March 1928, "Seisen no go," cited in Yoshida Chiyo, "Suzuki Bunji to musan seitō undō," *Rōdō shi kenkyū*, no. 3 (February 1986): 33.

37. David Scobey, "Boycotting the Politics Factory: Labor Radicalism and the New York City Mayoral Election of 1886," *Radical History Review*, nos. 28–30 (1984): 286.

My object is, however, to explain labor's political performance and assess its significance, not label it a "success" or a "failure." Stephen Large offers one list of obstacles faced by labor in these years. Lack of public recognition hindered most candidates seeking to go beyond the union base. Voter suspicion of "socialism" likewise limited the attempt, especially of the Social Democrats, to seek votes among the new middle class of salaried men and the old middle class of shopkeepers. Lack of funds was a constant problem. Police disruption, harassment by other candidates, and pressure exerted by owners supporting bourgeois parties were also obstacles. Finally, the division of the proletarian camp prevented the winning of seats commensurate with vote totals.[38] The list is perhaps too formidable, the "failure" overdetermined. With all these problems, why were any victories gained?

Through repeated campaigns the labor forces in time overcame the visibility problem. Although funds were never sufficient for extensive vote-buying, the financial issue was not insuperable either. Indeed, so many candidates managed to scrape together the 2,000-yen deposit needed to file that excessive competition was probably the most acute of this catalog of obstacles. A more prohibitive deposit might have limited the proletarian field and improved the results! Clearly, the proletarian forces had strengths as well, in particular a union base of mobilizing expertise and a platform with some appeal. Neither factionalism, financial distress, nor repression of the Social Democrats and legal left was so daunting as to prevent thousands from casting votes for the proletarian candidates, and these parties, supported by the labor offensive and the dispute culture of the late 1920s, sunk roots that proved durable.

To thus describe the labor offensive of union-building, disputes, and electoral politics is a relatively straightforward task, although historians have not often recognized the extent to which disputes, in particular, became integral parts of the urban culture of Japan in the 1920s. To *explain* the timing and location of this offensive is more difficult. We must further examine the ideology of the dispute culture, as well as the broader political and economic contexts. Both the ascendance of a more liberal approach to labor in the bureaucracy and the Kenseikai/ Minseitō Party and changed attitudes among men and women in smaller workplaces fueled the labor offensive.

---

38. Large, *Organized Workers and Socialist Politics*, pp. 124–25.

EIGHT

Working-Class Political Culture under Imperial Democracy

Beginning in the early days of the Yūaikai, factory workers in Nankatsu had responded to their perceived low status, poor wages, insecure jobs, and degrading treatment in the workplace with a new and growing assertiveness. By the late 1920s they had devised a repertoire of collective actions—organizing unions, carrying out disputes, calling demonstrations, supporting candidates for national and local office—that together constituted their "dispute culture." To conclude the examination of this culture, we must reconstruct its ideological dimension: the Nankatsu workers' critique of the social and political order and their visions of the future. This analysis should clarify the links between the structure of imperial democratic rule and the labor movement and help explain the timing of the labor offensive.

THE AMBIVALENT CRITIQUE: IMAGES OF SELF AND SOCIETY

The Ishikawajima strikers of 1921 offer one window into the consciousness of Nankatsu's skilled male workers of the immediate postwar era. Clearly, by 1921 they trusted the power growing out of their unity more than the paternal benevolence of their employer. At the heart of their strike was a desire to win equality of treatment and respect from the enterprise, and to transform their workplace community. We have seen that they held together against a lockout, police harassment, company threats, and economic deprivation for six weeks not over the overall *amount* of a pay raise, for their initial demand was no different in total amount from the company's initial offer. The dispute resulted from their commitment to the principle of an equal raise for all, with no room for variation and judgment by foremen or the company.

A similar spirit seeking social respect and equality informed the union's program articulated in the September 1921 inaugural issue of its magazine, *Tetsuben* (The Iron Whip), which pledged to fight for a better life for "society and humankind" with moderate means based on the "strength of righteousness." Respect for the humanity of labor and the right to a secure livelihood, advances in skill and efficiency, and expanded rights for workers were the three basic union goals. The founding statement further called for the eight-hour day, increased unity among workers, and treatment as social equals (by management).[1]

The flip side of the Ishikawajima workers' self-perception was an acute, persistent sense of low status, and a resultant antagonism toward management. In the words of one official observer in 1923, "in the minds of workers the view prevails that a shipyard is a place that, even if it provides work, by no means does so with the workers' interests at heart."[2] As with thousands of others in the factories of Nankatsu, the Ishikawajima workers had been taught by managers how different they were from respectable folk. Low pay and long hours were only part of the "treatment" problem.[3] They entered work through separate gates, they ate separately, they used separate toilets, and on leaving work at day's end, to prevent theft of tools or materials, they were subjected to a body check. If the workers had been primarily Koreans or Chinese, we could explain this discrimination as treatment issuing from the intersection of race and class domination. If such treatment had been limited to the textile mills, it could be seen as a manifestation of unequal gender relations. And in fact, the treatment of both colonial labor and the textile workers was harsher than that of the shipbuilders.[4] But neither race nor gender differences were needed to reinforce an elaborate system of separate but unequal treatment; at the worksites of skilled Japanese

1. *Tetsuben* 1, no. 1 (September 3, 1921): 1–2. The final phrase read: "Shakaiteki byōdō naru taigū o ki su."

2. Masumoto Uhei, *Kokka no shōrai to kōjō kanri no hyōjun* (Tokyo: Waseda University Press, 1923), p. 47.

3. The term for treatment, *taigū*, carried with it the connotation of social or even moral judgment. See Thomas Smith, "The Right to Benevolence: Dignity and Workers, 1890–1920," *Comparative Studies in Society and History* 26, no. 4 (October 1984): 593–97.

4. On Korean labor, see Soon Wan Park, "The Emergence of a Factory Labor Force in Korea: A Case Study of the Onoda Cement Factory" (Ph.D. diss., Harvard University, 1985).

males in prewar Tokyo such inequalities flourished under a straightforward structure of economic class domination.

Yūaikai members in 1914 had complained consistently of this sort of
degrading treatment and social prejudice, but their laments were resigned more often than feisty, admitting some truth to notions of the
inferiority of the working man's character. In the surge of postwar
labor action, letters to the Ishikawajima union magazine that focused
on the issues of discrimination, petty abuse, and humiliation reveal that
workers continued to complain about their degradation and still viewed
poor treatment as an attack on their human worth, but a crucial change
in the sentiment of many laborers is obvious. They spoke with new
anger, and a new radical tone informed their grievances.

The inaugural issue of the Ishikawajima union magazine strikingly
links a broad structural critique of capitalist, corporate oppression with
rage at a new program of work discipline:

> The capitalist economic structure forces laborers into extreme poverty....
> Always borrowing the power of the authorities, capitalists oppress us....
> Our income is gradually decreasing; hasn't it fallen to about half that of last
> year, or less? And the company is meanwhile paying attention only to the
> picky details. To further humiliate us, they have made two badges, one to
> wear on the job, one to show as we are leaving. We work feverishly, sweat
> dripping from our brows, and because of the heat, we take our shirt off just
> for a moment, so that the badge isn't on. If the guard sees this, we're im-
> mediately penalized one day's pay for violating the rule on wearing the
> badge at all times.... The oppression of the company is astonishing.
> Wouldn't simply giving a warning to someone without a badge on be more
> humane?[5]

The first page of this issue proclaimed the resolve of "3,000 workers
in a corner of Tokyo" to unite and resist the cruelty and inhumanity of
a capitalist economic system plagued by chronic crisis and unemployment, and throughout the journal editors and rank-and-file contributors mixed persistent older calls for respect and social equality with a
new anticapitalist rhetoric. They identified both economic insecurity,
epitomized by unemployment, and the indignity of low social status, as
the essence of the "inhumanity of capitalism."[6]

An intensifying anger at degrading treatment such as the body check,
whether at company gates or in public parks, and a host of other every-

5. *Tetsuben* 1, no. 1 (September 3, 1921): 4–5.
6. Ibid.: 1–2.

day insults thus fueled the rapid growth of the Yūaikai from before World War I, the creation of strong and growing clusters of working-class institutions from 1919 on, and the proliferation of disputes during and after the war. Yet despite the rhetoric of publications and speeches, much of the activity of labor at the local level can be read as a call less to overthrow or replace existing economic or social structures than to transform them and gain access to them on dramatically improved terms.

Consider, for example, the drive carried out by the Tokyo Federation of the Sōdōmei in the winter of 1921 to raise funds to install a telephone at union headquarters. The practical rationale was clear: in order to fight the capitalists, workers needed their own network of communication.[7] At the same time, in a day when only a rare factory *owner* had a phone in his office or home, the telephone was also a symbol of status sending a message to the workers themselves and the rest of society: workers were people, too.[8] The handsomely printed postcards used to solicit contributions reinforced this message.

By the early 1920s unions had produced an extensive array of organizational paraphernalia: membership cards, badges and pins; flags and banners; admission cards for union lecture series (see fig. 25). These items were visible symbols of the separate collectivity of workers bent on asserting themselves and transforming the entire society, but insofar as they also involved workers for the first time in the social protocols of their status superiors, they simultaneously had the potential to encourage or meet aspirations to join the mainstream of existing society. The rhetoric of the inaugural issue of *The Iron Whip* reflected this dual orientation when it offered a *structural* critique of "crisis and unemployment." It blamed these ills on the society created by cruel, inhumane capitalists, but in the same paragraph it set forth goals of advancing in skill and efficiency and gaining social equality and respect for the humanity of labor. On the next page came the essay decrying the humiliation of work tags and fines, which implicitly called for better

7. The drive is documented in Kyū-kyōchōkai, "Tōkyō-fu ka no rōdō dantai" (1920), OISR.

8. Telephones were so rare in factory offices in the 1920s that the Factory Directory (*Kōjō yōran*) published by the city of Tokyo in 1925 and 1928 did not include a column for telephone numbers. In the 1933 edition (I could not locate directories for the intervening years) the directory did list telephone numbers as well as addresses, but even at this point, over a decade after the Sōdōmei campaign, the telephone was relatively unusual. Just 765 (22 percent) of roughly 3,400 factories in the textile, metal, and machine industries had telephones.

treatment within the existing system as much as a structural transformation.

Finally, by the early 1920s the leaders of Tokyo-area unions exchanged formal New Year visits, proudly announced to the membership in the union magazine. Major unions, prominent labor leaders, and progressive publishers all displayed New Year greetings in the January issues of typical labor publications. These practices naturally reinforced the morale of workers' organizations. They also allowed laborers to share practices of a previously separate middle- and upper-class culture.[9] One guide to life in Tokyo earlier in the twentieth century, aimed at middle-class readers, had contrasted the middle and upper classes' formal New Year visiting (one left one's calling card at the door) with the much more casual visiting of "labor society" and back alley slum dwellers.[10] To the extent that the new customs of visiting and greeting among labor union officials now partook of the formal flavor of middle-class, business world social protocols, workers were symbolically integrated into a mainstream culture.

Of course, goals such as eliminating fines and work tags or acquiring telephones, on the one hand, and socialist revolution, on the other, could be distinguished in strategic terms as short-term tactics and long-term objectives. Pursuit of the former did not automatically render the latter impossible. Yet in a society where the radical social movement was young, where mainstream ideologies to deny class difference or promote social harmony were promoted aggressively by educators and officials, the gap between these two levels of action could—and, I would argue, did—impede the spread of sentiment for radical change.

To note this tension between working-class ideals of social advancement and radical social transformation is not to call the labor movement flawed, distorted, or incomplete; it is certainly not meant to suggest a negative comparison to some supposedly purer "working-class" vision and movement found in the West. Japanese workers joining the postwar labor movement sought a society with attributes the reader can easily recognize as democratic. They demanded political rights to assemble without harassment and to participate in the political arena,

9. The Sōdōmei magazine *Rōdō* describes the official 1922 visits in the issue of February 1922, p. 10.

10. Ishikawa Tengai, *Tōkyōgaku* (1909), viewed their divergent modes of New Year socializing as evidence of workers' separate culture. See reference in Miriam Silverberg, "Living on the Urban Edge: Culture and Subculture in Taishō Japan" (paper presented at the annual meeting of the Association for Asian Studies, Chicago, March 21–23, 1986).

whether through suffrage or through direct action. They desired control over their lives at work, expressed in calls for predictable, nonarbitrary pay increases. They sought security in demands for better severance pay. And they sought dignity in the ubiquitous calls for "respect for the humanity of labor." Although these goals fall short of a recipe for revolution, it would require major change in the polity and the workplace to achieve them.

The fit between these goals and the language of class confrontation may have been uneasy; like a suit off the rack that did not quite fit, the radicalism of leaders influenced by the works of Marx or Lenin was a ready-made vision that could tap the energy of the rank and file of workers even if it did not accord fully with their aspirations. Much recent work on the history of labor, culture, and society in the West cautions us not to see this uneasy fit as proof that Japanese working-class culture was peculiarly resistant or ambivalent in the face of a socialist message.

The implications of this work on Europe and America are rather that workers, while degraded and threatened by the process of capitalist industrialization, were never so atomized, alienated, or proletarianized as to lose connections with the past (older forms of crowd behavior) or one another (family, community). Rather, they resisted the tendency of the new engines of accumulation of the industrial revolution to make them rootless, dependent, or helpless. Like the Japanese, they had their own visions of community, dignity, security, and advancement, which were not fully those either of the liberal philosophers of laissez-faire "market culture" or of the radical philosophers of a socialist solution.[11] If this was true of the workers of Paris, Caracas, or New York, it was also the case with laborers in Tokyo, who continued throughout the 1920s to seek dignity and security at work and in society.

11. For examples of such work on Europe and the Americas, see William H. Sewell, Jr., *Work and Revolution in France: The Language of Labor from the Old Regime to 1848* (Cambridge: Cambridge University Press, 1980), pp. 1–2; William M. Reddy, *The Rise of Market Culture: The Textile Trade and French Society, 1750–1900* (Cambridge: Cambridge University Press, 1984), pp. 1–18; Joan W. Scott, *The Glassworkers of Carmaux: French Craftsmen and Political Action in a Nineteenth-Century City* (Cambridge, Mass.: Harvard University Press, 1974), pp. 3–6; Charles Bergquist, *Labor in Latin America: Comparative Essays on Chile, Argentina, Venezuela, and Colombia* (Stanford: Stanford University Press, 1986), pp. 270–73. Also, Nimura Kazuo, "Ashio bōdō no shutaiteki jōken," part 4, *Kenkyū shiryō geppō*, no. 325 (December 1985): 25–26, argues a similar broad point forcefully for the Ashio copper miners in 1907.

THE SPREAD OF
THE WORKING-CLASS CRITIQUE

Until the earthquake, the leading advocates of this ambivalent, but forceful, critique of industrial capitalist society had been skilled male workers in the heavy and machine industries. The previous chapter has shown that a dispute culture then spread beyond their worksites to encompass many female textile workers, as well as men and women in Nankatsu's smaller factories. Yet it is by no means a simple or self-evident matter to explain the timing of this spread, which by the Great Depression made the working-class movement into a social force profoundly troubling to Japan's rulers.

Possible explanatory factors include change in the economic structure of areas such as Nankatsu, in the composition of the Nankatsu work force, and in the treatment offered by managers in the newly contentious workplaces, but I find these to be much less significant than change in the larger political environment, new policies of managers in huge enterprises elsewhere in the nation, and related change in the political or social consciousness of some of the same sort of workers who had been relatively acquiescent in previous years. After all, in Nankatsu as elsewhere, the basic features of the local economy had been established several years in advance of the earthquake and the labor offensive that began in 1924. Neither an immediate influx of workers, of new industries, or of major new employers by itself explains the dramatic gains for organized labor. Rather, workers themselves, stimulated in part by a new political context, changed their *perception* of relatively unchanged objective economic and social circumstances.

THE ECONOMY

Factory employment in all of Nankatsu increased only moderately in the mid 1920s before falling slightly in the depression, and the mix of industries in the area hardly changed. To be sure, the earthquake did change the economic geography of Nankatsu. By devastating the industrial base of Fukagawa and Honjo wards, it accelerated the westward shift of factories and worker residences to the less densely populated wards of Nankatsu County. Also, the ratio of small to large workplaces continued the increase that began during World War I. However, the pace of change was slow in the 1920s; the most dramatic changes in the extent and composition of industry in Nankatsu had already come before and during World War I (see graph 4.1 and table 4.2). These earlier changes provided the base in concentration and numbers for the spread of labor activity outside the largest factories, but they cannot explain its timing.

THE WORKERS

In similar fashion, we find no decisive changes in those characteristics of workers often associated with their proclivity toward activism, such as levels of education, urban living experience, or skill.[12] The workers at the forefront of the earlier postwar surge of the labor movement, primarily men in heavy industry, were not different in dramatic and predictable ways from workers in chemical, food-processing, or smaller machine factories, which only later experienced labor activism. Most important, no clear change occurred in the characteristics of the members of the latter group that could explain its new assertiveness.[13]

In several respects, the men in all these industries were similar. Taking the Ishikawajima shipbuilders to represent large, heavy industries, and Tokyo's rubber and bicycle factory workers to represent small workshops, we find levels of education were comparably high in 1924 and improved at a similar pace over time. In the fifteen Tokyo rubber factories surveyed in 1924, 88 percent of 2,025 male workers had completed at least a four-year elementary course, and 36 percent had completed six years of schooling. The corresponding figures for the Ishikawajima men were 91 and 42 percent.[14] Rubber and bicycle factory work forces were actually slightly more urban than those in the shipyard for the entire period.[15] Hours of work varied little, ranging between ten and eleven hours per day in all industries throughout the 1920s.

12. For Russia, for example, see Victoria E. Bonnell, *Roots of Rebellion: Workers' Politics and Organizations in St. Petersburg and Moscow, 1900–1914* (Berkeley: University of California Press, 1983), chs. 2, 5, and passim.

13. The analysis in the following several paragraphs is based on the government's triannual Field Survey of Labor Statistics (*Rōdō tōkei jitchi chōsa*), using data for shipbuilders at Ishikawajima and for rubber workers at a number of small factories in Tokyo as representative of the large-scale machine and small-scale chemical sectors. In this survey, all factories of a certain size (the cutoff differed by industry) were required to fill out a census-type form for each worker, listing characteristics such as gender, age, wage, birthplace, education, years of work experience, and more. The results were published both by local and national authorities. I have used the Tokyo City volume, *Tōkyō-shi oyobi kinkō ni okeru rōdō tōkei jitchi chōsa*, hereafter *TRTJC*. Although it does not identify individual enterprises by name, only one shipyard, with about 3,000 employees, is included in the Tokyo survey, and this can only be Ishikawajima.

14. *TRTJC*, 1924, pp. 126, 134; 1933, pp. 52, 61.

15. In 1924, 34 percent of rubber workers and 42 percent of bicycle makers were born in urban centers, in contrast to the 26 percent total of city-born shipbuilders. *TRTJC*, 1924, pp. 331–35, 367–71; 1933, pp. 37–47.

Skill can only be assessed indirectly, through data on work experience and age. At least four-fifths of the workers in all these industries
were adults over the age of twenty and were likely to have worked
several years since completing school. While the Ishikawajima workers
did have an edge in years of work experience, even the rubber or sugar
industries had significant nuclei of experienced adults.[16] The differences
are not dramatic; more important, they were not changing.

In one key aspect, the shipbuilders were quite distinct. Their income
was significantly higher. From 1924 to the depression, the average income for shipbuilders stood at roughly three yen per day, while for
rubber workers and others in the chemical industries, around two yen
per day was the average, and this gap remains if we hold age constant.[17]

Thus the shipbuilding workers were just slightly older, better educated, and more skilled than their counterparts in smaller rubber, bicycle, or sugar-processing plants from the 1920s through the early 1930s.
They had slightly less experience of urban life, and they were much
better paid. These data suggest we look elsewhere for explanations of
workers' behavior. Insofar as the latter men consistently received far
less pay, why had they been relatively quiet before the earthquake?
Conversely, to the extent that they differed little in other ways, how do
we explain their new interest in the labor movement beginning in the
mid 1920s, just when relative calm came to many larger workplaces?

Women in both large and small workplaces also joined labor actions
with unprecedented vigor between 1924 and the early 1930s. The difference between male and female labor in Nankatsu was profound. The
women were younger; in Nankatsu rubber factories, a typical example,
45 percent of the women and just 16 percent of the men were teenagers
in 1930.[18] The women thus had far less work experience,[19] and their
pay was consistently *under half* that of the men.[20] Neither did the
women benefit from the slight life-cycle wage curve enjoyed by the men:

16. I define "experienced" as six years or more in the industry. In rubber and sugar,
50 to 60 percent were experienced; in shipbuilding, 75 percent. *TRTJC*, 1924, pp. 220–
23; 1927, pp. 103–25; 1930, pp. 446–57.
    17. Daily income for shipbuilders aged 30–35 averaged 3.82 yen; for comparably
aged rubber workers, income averaged 2.62 yen. *TRTJC*, 1924, pp. 250–67; 1927,
pp. 256–311; 1930, pp. 490–501.
    18. *TRTJC*, 1930, pp. 490–501. Statistics concerning women in these three para-
graphs are drawn from the same sources as the data for men in the preceding four paragraphs unless otherwise noted.
    19. Only 25 to 30 percent of the women in rubber factories, but 50 percent of the
men, had six years' experience or more between 1924 and 1930.
    20. Male rubber workers had an average income of 2.15 yen in 1925, while women
averaged .95 yen.

women in their forties earned barely 10 percent more than those in their twenties; among men, the 40-year-olds earned 25 percent more than their juniors. Yet none of these distinctions were new. In themselves they cannot explain the new prominence of women in the labor movement.

The women of Nankatsu in the 1920s labored in two very different types of workplace. Indeed, two separate labor markets appear to have coexisted. The majority worked in the "segregated" textile industry, where about 80 percent of the work force was female. Other women worked in "integrated" chemical and food-processing industries with substantial proportions of both men and women. The great majority of textile women were temporary rural migrants; in 1924 over 90 percent of Tokyo's cotton-spinning workers had been born in rural areas.[21] In contrast, over half of the women in the chemical industry were of local origin. While few of the textile women were married, nearly half of those in the integrated sectors were.[22] Women in integrated industries were significantly older than the textile employees. Their workplaces were relatively small, and dormitories were rare, whereas most of the textile women worked in mills of 1,000 or more employees and lived in dormitories under strict supervision.[23] In sum, both physical and social barriers cut off the young women in the textile mills from the male-dominated unions and the surrounding community, but women in rubber, celluloid or food-processing plants were relatively settled members of the community. As the labor movement came to their worksites, they frequently joined unions and disputes with their male co-workers (see fig. 24).[24]

But this distinction, too, must not be overdrawn. Although the conditions of work appear to have been more conducive to labor action in the "integrated" industries than in textiles, women in both sectors eventually joined significant protests. The occasional pre–World War I dis-

21. *TRTJC*, 1924, pp. 336–39; 1933, pp. 36–37. I define "rural origins" as those listed in category *gunbu*.

22. *TRTJC*, 1924, pp. 2–49, 336–39; 1930, pp. 380–83; 1933, pp. 36–37. Around 10 percent of women in the textile industry were married.

23. The characteristics of the textile women seem comparable to those of the mill workers in Shanghai described by Emily Honig in *Sisters and Strangers: Women in the Shanghai Cotton Mills* (Stanford: Stanford University Press, 1986). The women at integrated sites seem more akin to those in a place like Lille as described in Patricia Hilden, *Women and Socialist Politics in France, 1880–1914: A Regional Study* (New York: Oxford University Press, 1986).

24. One would expect that male activists in Japan, as elsewhere, might respond with ambivalence or uninterest to protests by women workers, and this was probably often the case in Japan. Yet men and women did act jointly in numerous disputes of the late 1920s, and this dimension of the Nankatsu story requires further study.

putes involving textile girls in Nankatsu revealed their basic goals to be decent food and sufficient rest. Women in the 1920s made similar demands. Their youth, their lack of education, their limited experience living in the city, and their physical segregation in the dorms did impede sustained, effective action, but these characteristics were not insuperable obstacles. The 1922 political reforms and Minseitō support for gradual extension of suffrage created a favorable context for those feminists already active. In the late 1920s some of these women began to join forces with factory laborers in a manner that the Meiji-era feminists had not, and the joining of nonworker activists with profoundly unhappy young textile workers proved effective.[25] The textile girls tended to seek respect for themselves within their inherited social world rather than to challenge the fundamental subordination of women to men, but even this goal implied dramatic change and met stubborn resistance.

In one final respect, a significant change did come to the women in Nankatsu. Their levels of education rose substantially in the 1920s. The number of women in rubber factories who had completed the basic four-year elementary education rose sharply, from 64 percent in 1924 to 94 percent by 1933.[26] Increased schooling probably imparted skills useful to the labor movement by allowing workers to assess their situation critically.

In sum, while the objective characteristics of women workers and of male workers in smaller factories changed relatively little in the 1920s, new perceptions took root among them of the broader political order and of the contrast between their situation and that of labor in the privileged heavy industrial sector. As this happened, both men in small factories and women in the textile and chemical industries joined labor activities previously limited to men at large heavy industrial workplaces. More important than changes in a worker's skill, urban experience, age, or pay was a changed understanding of his or her relationship to an employer and the broader society.

THE EMPLOYERS

Just as the relatively unchanging social characteristics of the employees in large and small workplaces cannot explain the spread of activism

---

25. See Sharon Seivers, *Flowers in Salt* (Stanford: Stanford University Press, 1983), pp. 85–86, on the lack of contact between Meiji feminists and workers.

26. *TRTJC*, 1924, p. 134; 1933, pp. 60–61. A similar increase can be observed for textiles. *TRTJC*, 1933, pp. 61–63.

from one group to the other, neither can the unchanging contrast between the work environments of small and large factories explain the spread of the labor movement. Features of smaller factories can be invoked to account for both passivity and activism on the part of the employees, and these features of small workplaces appear unchanging. Descriptions from the 1920s, 1930s, and 1940s are remarkably similar.

A more personal connection to the owner or boss, fewer rules, less hierarchy, and more independence for the adult workers were all reported to be characteristic of the small factory in the 1920s and 1930s. Such features may account for the lack of labor unrest before 1924, but not the spread of protest later. Sources proclaiming the beauty of personalism in such workplaces, also known for long hours and low pay, must be regarded with suspicion, but the homey picture of the smaller workplace was not fabricated of whole cloth.

In the nation's very smallest manufacturing and commercial endeavors, those employing 10 people or fewer, the employees often were indeed family, or treated as such. One Tokyo survey in 1935 revealed that 73 percent of 23,163 men and women in factories with fewer than 10 employees were either family members (32 percent) or apprentices (41 percent). Fully three-fourths of even the unrelated employees lived with the owner. Ninety-three percent of these Tokyo workers had been hired on the recommendation of relatives or acquaintances.[27] Not surprisingly, such tiny sites had seen no labor organizing in the era before 1923 and would see little thereafter. The "small" workplaces that did experience polarization and noteworthy labor organizing after 1924 were distinct from such tiny family businesses. A few disputes did occur in factories with under 30 workers, but almost none are found in places with fewer than 10. Most of the sites of the new activism of this era were in ranges I define as small (30 to 99 employees) and medium (100 to 499 employees).

Even in such small- to medium-sized workplaces, in Nankatsu and elsewhere, owners appear to have been relatively close to the community and their employees, and oppressive hierarchy is not prominent. In workplaces of 30 to 50 people (in a 1937 Osaka survey) 17 percent of

27. Unfortunately, the only relevant available data are from the 1930s, but there is no reason to think matters had changed dramatically since the 1920s. See Tōkyō shiyakusho, *Tōkyō-shi shokōgyō chōsa* (1935), pp. 65, 98, 107. Nishinarita Yutaka, "Manshū jihen ki no rōshi kankei," *Hitotsubashi daigaku kenkyū nenpō: keizaigaku kenkyū*, no. 26 (January 1985): 261 has similar data for Osaka. Of 22,379 men and women in machine shops with under ten employees, 69 percent were either family or apprentices.

10,001 employees were either family or apprentice labor.[28] A 1935
study of such factories found that most recruiting was done through
relatives or acquaintances of the workers.[29] At the small end of this
small-to-medium range, the owner was usually the boss on the shop
floor and was likely to be quite familiar with the backgrounds and personal affairs of the workers.[30] Even in a factory of several hundred
workers, the hierarchy was not extensive; between owners and workers
might stand a "factory director" (*kōjō chō*) and several trusted foremen. The owner would find it possible to know at least the names of
most workers.

Some medium-sized places were subsidiaries of larger corporations,
with absentee ownership and professional management; the Royal Celluloid Company in Kameido, for example, home to a bitter series of
disputes in the late 1920s, was part of the Mitsui zaibatsu. But other
firms with several hundred employees, such as the Mitatsuchi Rubber
Company and the Aoki Dye Company, were owned by men who lived
in the ward. Aoki was particularly active in local politics and community affairs.[31] Virtually all owners of factories employing fewer than 100
workers were local residents, living adjacent to or nearby the factory.
Like Aoki, many won election to the ward, village, or county assembly,
and maintained ties to the Minseitō or Seiyūkai Party.[32]

Factory life was relatively informal. The independent, freewheeling
spirit of the Edo artisan was commonly noted to be flourishing still in
smaller factories.[33] Workers typically spoke of the owner as the *oyaji*,
loosely translatable as "the old man," or "the boss," whereas those in

28. Nishinarita, "Manshū jihen ki," p. 261.
29. Murayama Shigetoshi, "Chūshō kōgyō no rōdō jijō," *Shakai seisaku jihō* no. 175
(April 1935): 371. Murayama never clearly defines the exact size of the "small to
medium" group to which he continually refers. We may infer his range to be 10 to 500
employees, for at one point he notes that he is "excluding small household enterprises" (p.
374) and elsewhere he used 500 employees as a line separating large from medium firms
(p. 396). In this publication, intended for an audience of policymakers and academics,
Murayama and his editors were either careless or assumed these distinctions would be
obvious to readers.
30. See John Pelzel, "Factory Life in Japan and China Today," in *Japan: A Comparative View*, ed. Albert Craig (Princeton: Princeton University Press, 1979), for a sensitive
picture of similar factories in Kawaguchi in the late 1940s.
31. Sally Hastings, "The Government, the Citizen, and the Creation of a New Sense
of Community: Social Welfare, Local Organizations, and Dissent in Tokyo, 1905–1937"
(Ph.D. diss., University of Chicago, 1980), pp. 152–53.
32. Honjo and Fukagawa both had ward assemblies. Minami Katsushika County had
a county assembly, and each town or village within it (Kameido, Azuma, etc.) had an
assembly. All were elected bodies.
33. Murayama, "Chūshō kōgyō," p. 373. *Kawaguchi-shi shi: kindai shiryō hen*
(1982), 2:635, 653–62. The cliché for this spirit was *shokunin kishitsu*.

big companies spoke of "the president."[34] Labor mobility was reported to be high, although reliable statistics on this are not available.[35] Skilled adult men entertained the hope, certainly faint, but by no means ridiculous, of starting their own factories with a small stake from relatives, friends, or a trusting employer.[36] In fact, a survey of 1,073 Tokyo factories of under 30 employees carried out in 1937 found that 20 percent of the owners had previously been wage laborers (shokkō).[37]

Hours were long, but irregular. The Japanese equivalent of Blue Monday was still reported common in small factories at least into the 1930s. The term was urazuke, literally "back-up" or "reinforce," meaning to reinforce an official day off with an unofficial carousing holiday.[38] The complex and unpopular premium pay systems found in the large companies, often accompanied by time and motion studies, were rare. Pay was typically a day wage, simple piecework, or a combination of the two.[39]

Thus, the informal, personal management of the smaller workplace of the 1920s and 1930s could make a person feel part of a social world that included the owner as a sympathetic leader or role model rather than an exploiter. The workplace could offer the satisfactions of community belonging and hope of eventual independence, rather than foster alienation and protest. On the other hand, one could make a strong case that smaller factories should have been hotbeds of resistance all along. Pay was low relative to major zaibatsu firms. As failures were frequent, jobs were not secure. Owners in smaller firms hardly ever offered bonuses, even for attendance; overtime pay was rare; regular pay raises were unusual, and standards never explicit when pay did increase; formal programs of severance or retirement pay were also exceptional.[40] Factory councils or programs of company-sponsored education were even rarer.

The negative features of work in smaller factories had not been sufficient to cause widespread protest before 1923; the satisfying features

34. Author's interview with Komatsu Shōtarō, March 5, 1985.
35. Murayama, "Chūshō kōgyō," p. 372.
36. See Pelzel, "Factory Life," pp. 389–93.
37. Tōkyō shiyakusho, gakumu-bu, Chūshō kōjō no keiei jijō to totei no rōdō jijō chōsa, 1939, p. 11.
38. Murayama, "Chūshō kōgyō," p. 375. Kyōchōkai, ed., Kawaguchi imonogyō jitchi chōsa, 1933, pp. 135–38. Tōkyō tekkō kumiai, Kawaguchi-shi-bu, ed., Jūnen shi, 1934, pp. 85–87, 95–96.
39. Murayama, "Chūshō kōgyō," p. 376.
40. Murayama, "Chūshō kōgyō," pp. 387–92. The few such programs he mentions in this 1935 report probably came as a result of labor actions of the 1920s.

did not prevent protest thereafter. There is no evidence of major change in the 1920s on either the positive or negative side. The most important causes of the labor offensive of the mid-to-late 1920s originated outside the world of the small factory. New management paternalism in large factories stimulated a new sensitivity, among many of the men and women just described, to the disjunction between their treatment and the apparent respect and benefits offered men in the privileged large-scale sector, and the social policies of the imperial democrats in power in the 1920s promoted a new belief in the legitimacy of unions and disputes as a means of narrowing this gap.

THE PROGRAM FOR BETTER TREATMENT

The key to explaining the labor offensive that began in 1924 thus lies in the workers' subjective understanding of changed managerial and state policy; in the era of imperial democracy, workers changed both their perception of the broader political world and their view of desirable standards in both large and small workplaces. By the mid 1920s, a new sort of paternalism had been implemented in many large factories. It *appeared* to be offering more respect in the form of councils or greater benefits.[41] Owners of small plants could not compete with their capital-rich large competitors. They had no direct access to foreign models of "progressive" labor management. Even if they knew of the few "labor management consultants" available for hire, few could afford their services or could subscribe to their newsletters.[42] They lacked the funds, and probably the inclination, to offer the accoutrements of the revised paternalism adopted by some large companies after World War I.

After the earthquake, the dispute culture spread to smaller places, and working men and women began to demand precisely those standards assumed to prevail in large factories, to criticize their owners as stingy and arbitrary, and to demand policies to reduce the insecurity of their existence. They placed less value on the personal touch of an owner, and showed more concern with low pay and insecurity, when

---

41. See Andrew Gordon, *The Evolution of Labor in Japan: Heavy Industry, 1853–1955* (Cambridge, Mass.: Harvard University Council on East Asian Studies, 1985), chs. 4–6, on appearance and reality at large firms. For our purposes here, the important point is that some changes were made in large firms and that the perception of difference was prevalent.

42. Examples include Uno Riemon, active in Osaka, and Araki Tōchirō, active in the Tokyo area. On Uno, see Hazama Hiroshi, "Japanese Labor Relations and Uno Riemon," *Journal of Japanese Studies* 5, no. 1 (Winter 1979). On Araki, see Andrew Gordon, "Araki Tōichirō and the Shaping of Labor Management," in *Japanese Management in Historical Perspective*, ed. Tsunehiko Yui (Tokyo: University of Tokyo Press, 1989).

their views of places such as the Koishikawa arsenal or the Mitsubishi shipyard, once seen as impersonal and regimented, began to change. When this happened, the Nankatsu workers in small- and medium-sized places were not so close to the "old man," either physically or emotionally, as to be unable to distance themselves from him, join unions, or organize disputes.

As the social movement thus gained force, the labor critique remained ambivalent. The earlier radical message of the Sōdōmei may not have accorded fully with labor aspirations, but neither had managerial statements of paternal solicitude. Would the new Sōdōmei realism of 1924 triumph, confirming to the social bureaucrats and the Kenseikai the wisdom of tolerating "sound unions"? Put differently, would the growing numbers of disputatious workers indeed fulfill the expectations of liberal imperial democrats and consent to their own incorporation into the existing economic and political system or would they build their own entrenched oppositional culture? Ironically, while the working-class vision possessed an accommodating core, both imperial democrats in power and their elite opponents were troubled to see workers articulate it boldly.

Discerning the goals of the men and women who organized the unions and engaged in disputes is difficult because expectations imposed upon the rank and file by professional organizers at the time, and upon the movement as a whole by later generations of historians, obscure our vision. The centrality of dispute actions in many unions derived in part from a continuing commitment on the radical left to challenge the premises of imperial democracy. However, the structures of working-class action and the nature of its program for "better treatment" reveal that the union rank and file and the leaders diverged considerably in their reasons for emphasizing disputes.

A leader such as Kikugawa Tadao envisioned a process by which struggle-oriented unions would produce an expanding, ever stronger mass of battle-hardened laborers, who would lead a drive for revolutionary change. While workers in all sorts of unions certainly launched unprecedented numbers of disputes through the 1920s, the rank and file did not fully share the transformative vision of union leaders. The record of union meetings and disputes in Nankatsu suggests that most workers rather sought immediately to remedy intolerable circumstances and to attain respect and security over the long run. They were inclined to use disputes to push the company to offer aid, severance pay, and insurance, rather than to build unions into alternative institutions capable of providing these benefits. This strategy did not simply derive from their lack of resources; it reflected their conception of a proper social and political order. The implicit labor program, that is, interwove older themes of respect as a human being with a new popular conception of the political rights of a member of the nation (*kokumin*) under imperial democracy.

The year 1924 marked a turning point in the formulation of labor demands, much as it had in the quantity and quality of disputes, and in the ascendance of a more liberal version of imperial democracy in the government. These three changes, as well as the emergence of a revised paternalism in big business several years earlier, were surely related; the newly disputatious workers in Nankatsu in the mid-to-late 1920s responded to a changed political environment by drawing on the language of the democratic movements of the previous decade and formulating their own program for dignity and "improved treatment."

Table 8.1 reveals the sudden rise to prominence of this demand for "improved treatment" (*taigū kaizen*), raised by all sorts of Nankatsu unions, including Kantō Amalgamated. Beginning in 1924, "improved treatment" became the most common "offensive" demand of labor in Nankatsu, and its prominence increased into the 1930s. This phrase joined the old concerns for status, security, and the respect due a member of the nation (*kokumin*) with newer concerns for legal protection and the rights of workers.

For 200 workers in a Sōdōmei Metalworkers' Union local at the Tokyo Zinc Company in 1925, "improved treatment" meant fair, open calculation of contract pay, regular bonuses, semiannual raises, a severance pay program, shorter hours, and an annual Recreation Day. Pay levels in themselves were not the core issue. In 1928 over 100 men and 40 women in another Metalworkers' local, at the Greater Japan Bicycle Company, raised similar demands in a bitter three-month dispute: reform of the incentive pay system, public commitments on severance and retirement pay, improved dining facilities, and distribution of accumulated funds in a company aid society.[43]

These demands were typical elements of a platform that transcended the Sōdōmei. In 1928 the annual meeting of a Kantō Amalgamated local at a wood-preservative plant discussed its goals for the coming

43. Kyū-kyōchōkai, *Rōdō sōgi: kagaku kōgyō*, 6 (1925) for November 11, 1925, police report on the Tokyo Zinc dispute. Kyū-kyōchōkai, *Rōdō sōgi: kikai, kigu, kinzoku*, 2 (1928) for police reports of May 8 and 30, 1928, on the Greater Japan Bicycle dispute. Both held at OISR.

TABLE 8.1 DISPUTES IN MINAMI KATSUSHIKA COUNTY,
BY PRIMARY DEMAND, 1897–1938

Demand	1897–1916	1917–23	1924–29	1930–32	1933–38	Total
Offensive						
Improved treatment	1 (13)	1 (4)	16 (14)	31 (22)	41 (27)	90
Wage increase	1 (13)	10 (40)	12 (10)	2 (1)	7 (5)	32
Firing of superior	0	1 (4)	2 (2)	0	3 (2)	6
Other	2 (25)	3 (12)	10 (9)	4 (3)	3 (2)	22
Total offensive	4	15	40	37	54	150
Defensive						
Oppose dismissal	1 (13)	5 (20)	27 (24)	34 (24)	42 (27)	109
Oppose pay cut	0	1 (4)	15 (13)	27 (20)	19 (13)	62
Pay upon factory closing	0	0	15 (13)	28 (20)	17 (11)	60
Other	3 (38)	4 (16)	18 (16)	14 (10)	21 (24)	60
Total defensive	4	10	75	103	99	291
Total demands	8	25	115	140	153	441
Unclear demands	0	1	73	1	0	75
Grand total	8	26	188	141	153	516

SOURCES: Data through 1926 are from Aoki Kōji, *Nihon rōdō undō shi nenpyō* (Tokyo: Shinseisha, 1968); for 1927–38, from Kyū-kyōchōkai, *Rōdō sōgi*; Keishichō, *Rōdō sōgi junpō*, *Shakai undō ōrai*, and *Shakai undō tsūshin*.
NOTE: Figures in parentheses are percentages. Owing to rounding off, the column totals are not always 100 percent.

year: force the company to offer reformed retirement pay, mourning leave, benefits for drafted workers, semiannual bonuses, and recreation facilities for employees. Other locals adopted similar platforms, each with a variation or two on the basic theme of improved treatment befitting a human being, an employee, and a member of the nation. Workers in the Suna Sugar local in 1928 resolved to seek improved, company-supplied box lunches as well as a public commitment on severance and retirement pay levels; in August 1929 they included opening of company recreation facilities to workers in their agenda for the coming year. "Fairness" was the watchword not only in calls for improved treatment when speaking of bonuses, regular raises, or contract pay; to workers at the Honjo # 1 local in 1930, foul box lunches were unfair too.[44]

The workers in Kantō Amalgamated were clearly contentious and willing to dispute. But their program for workplace reform, centered as it was on severance and retirement pay, regular raises and bonuses, fair output pay, and diverse company benefits and services seems a far cry from the conception of Kikugawa Tadao in the Education Section of the national headquarters. If successful, were not these workers more likely to bask in the glory of social recognition than to demand a continued social transformation? They were seeking treatment perceived as the norm in the leading firms in the zaibatsu sector, which would constitute admission to mainstream society (*ippan shakai*) and even promised access to the beckoning new urban consumer culture of the 1920s. This labor platform drew on themes earlier articulated in Yūaikai speeches and writings and in the speeches and slogans of the imperial democracy movement. It focused on winning for workers the status and security due a human being, a member of the nation, and an employee.

The sudden rise to prominence of this demand for "improved treatment" in the mid 1920s reveals this platform to be more than a traditional plea for a paternal gift. In a new era understood by many workers to be a time of expanded democratic practice, the rights of labor under the law were critical components of "improved treatment." Such rights were well assimilated among activists at the local level; they do not appear to have been a conceit of intellectuals and headquarters leaders that the workers themselves failed to understand. In numerous disputes

44. The term was *fukōhei*. The "Kantō gōdō shibu" file, no. E-24, OISR, includes reports on all these annual meetings. See "Kantō gōdō honbu" file, E-21, OISR, for other examples.

workers demanded that owners respect the standards spelled out in the new factory law, that they offer health insurance programs in accord with the insurance law. Local voices also reflect an awareness of rights. A leaflet distributed "To the townspeople" by Tokyo Zinc Company workers during their 1925 dispute claimed:

> The company ignores social evolution and offers this shoddy treatment of a bygone era. We can no longer stand this violation of the human character [*jinkaku*] of those of us who are workers. This is an era in which the government has recognized labor unions. It is an era when the strike is our unquestioned right.[45]

This complex, fascinating statement reveals the diverse intellectual roots of the consciousness that characterized the dispute culture of the 1920s. The term for *jinkaku* (character, personal dignity, autonomous moral development) entered Japan early in the twentieth century as a Christian concept, and it was first associated with a middle-class notion of the autonomous individual as the source of value. Workers in the Yūaikai era began to use the term in their demands that managers respect their personal worth, but as Hirasawa Keishichi's rhetoric suggested, they did not typically link this to a claim that the working class needed an *independent* social identity. In this 1925 leaflet, however, the Zinc Company workers see the achievement of human character, or *jinkaku*, as something to be gained through the exercise of new rights, as workers in a new social era, to strike and to organize unions.[46]

Workers in a local of Kantō Amalgamated at the Tokyo Hat Company in Honjo, on strike in June 1929, explained their actions in similar fashion: "We have realized that no solution is possible through negotiations or moderation in the face of the company's repression. The only solution is through a battle with the company using the right to strike that we have been granted."[47]

The passive construction in the original Japanese rendering of this final phrase hides the identity of the grantor of the right to strike. Possibly a leafleteer of Christian spirit felt it to be a God-given right. Perhaps he simply meant it was a natural right, without concern for the grantor. Very likely, however, he referred to government policy. Just three years

---

45. See Kyū-kyōchōkai, *Rōdō sōgi* 6 (1925), OISR, for leaflet of November 15, attached to police report of November 17, 1925. Three thousand copies were reportedly distributed.

46. Smith, "The Right to Benevolence," pp. 606–7.

47. The phrase "right to strike that we have been granted" was *ataerareta higyōken.* "Kantō gōdō" file, E-36, OISR, leaflet titled *Tōkyō bōshi kōjō sōgi ni kan shite.*

earlier, the passage of the Labor Disputes Conciliation Bill, and repeal of Article 17 of the Public Order Police Law, had sent an important, if implicit, message to workers: the labor dispute was now the legal object of conciliation, not repression; in the eyes of the state, it was a legitimate form of behavior. The press had called these reforms, together with the proposed union law, "universal suffrage for industry."[48] The comment of a union leader in the Kawaguchi local of the Kantō Metalworkers' Union is equally telling. He and his fellow unionists had understood the 1926 legislation to constitute in his words a "bill of rights for workers."[49]

Thus, a concept of rights was clearly present in the labor platform of the mid 1920s and after, but these were not simply the rights of labor. Some organizers retained the ambivalence expressed earlier in Hirasawa's call to act as humans and members of the nation, not as workers. One dissenter in a union of transport workers affiliated with Kantō Amalgamated wrote, "I proposed changing the name of the union from Japan Transport Workers' Union to Japan Transport Employees' Union because the term 'worker' was a problem. With 'worker' the clerical staff at the station would not join the union."[50] Presumably these reluctant unionists were willing to seek their rights as "employees" but not their rights as "workers."

Finally, consider the rhetoric of workers on strike at the Greater Tokyo Bicycle Company in the spring of 1928. The company president, Okazaki Kujirō, was a Minseitō Diet representative, elected from his home district in Kanagawa Prefecture, neighboring Tokyo. The Minseitō had, of course, for several years been calling for a labor union bill, so the workers had an easy target to blast in their leaflet; they claimed Okazaki had "betrayed his promise as a public official" and "trampled upon the right of workers to organize and to maintain a decent living." The leaflet thus called upon all residents to support the strikers, not only because it was a "life or death matter for 260 employees," but for "the sake of the progress of state, society and the prosperity of all the people."[51] In this closing flourish, which neatly vaults from a limited focus on the rights of the workers to a national concern with all the people, the Sōdōmei workers echoed the idiom of imperial democracy:

48. Garon, *State and Labor*, p. 126, cites the *TAS* in 1925 and 1926.
49. Interview with Kurasaki Daikichi, August 28, 1983.
50. "Kantō gōdō honbu, 1929" file, OISR, undated report.
51. Kyū-kyōchōkai, *Rōdō sōgi, 1928*, OISR, includes this leaflet attached to a police report of May 30, 1928.

the progress of "state and society" (*kokka shakai*), a term that blurred the line between a state (*kokka*) implicitly centered on the emperor and a society (*shakai*) centered on the people, clinched the argument in favor of labor's cause. The formulation in this leaflet presents a concept of rights as those of labor, of employees, and of members of a great nation.

The women in Nankatsu textile mills produced their own version of this program for rights and better treatment. On May 27, 1927, the 5,000 employees in the Textile Union at the Number 1 and Number 2 factories of the Tōyō Muslin complex in Kameido submitted demands that the company:

1. Revoke the transfer of three workers [these were union leaders] at the Number 2 factory.

2. Make public the severance allowance.

3. Allow dormitory women freedom to come and go from the dorm.

4. Consider drafted workers [who had hitherto been dismissed] to be on leave.

5. Convert temporary employees to regular status.

6. Revive the rent allowance.

7. Pay a night shift allowance [a maximum of ten sen per night].[52]

The third demand was the key one; the Tōyō Muslin women were allowed out of the dormitory only to go to work and for an occasional company-sponsored outing. The following day, management, fearing a strike, agreed to allow the dormitory girls their freedom and also consented to the other demands.[53]

This and similar issues of basic human freedoms were not instantly resolved. Following this victory, a controversy over mismanagement of union funds in 1928, combined with pressure from the company, led to the reconstitution of the union as an independent, but much weakened, Tōyō Muslin Employees' Union. On July 1, 1929, the long-delayed prohibition on night labor (between 11 P.M. and 5 A.M.) for women and children finally took effect, and the union feared that either layoffs or wage cuts and speedups would follow as the company sought to com-

52. Suzuki Yūko, *Jokō to rōdō sōgi: 1930 Tōyō mosu sōgi* (Tokyo: Renga shobō, 1989), p. 28.
53. See Watanabe Etsuji, and Suzuki Yūko, eds., *Tatakai ni ikite: Senzen fujin rōdō e no shōgen* (Tokyo: Domesu shuppan, 1980), p. 174, on change in dormitory conditions.

pensate for the lost operating time. Between February and September of 1929, twenty disputes took place nationwide in large cotton mills alone, as workers and managers jockeyed to protect themselves or their profits. At Tōyō Muslin, the employees' union, its membership diminished to a mere 200 (150 women), submitted a ten-point petition to the company in mid June. In addition to a guarantee that no wage cuts would accompany the night-work prohibition, the union won promises to "handle the present system of freedom to leave the dormitory with greater kindness," to improve dormitory food, set up a dormitory lounge, and "consider" several other similar steps.[54] Even in a situation where the threat to jobs and wages was great, the textile women continually and with some success returned to these unresolved basic issues. For the women who worked in the Nankatsu mills, winning better food and the freedom to leave the dorm was part of a struggle, which reached a peak in the late 1920s, to live "human" lives, to win respect for themselves and their contributions to their families or to their nation.

Sata Ineko, a well-known writer of "proletarian fiction," has left us one evocation of the sense of isolation from the mainstream culture felt by these women and their discontent at insulting treatment. "From the Caramel Factory" is a short story set in an unnamed Tokyo neighborhood, very likely Kameido, in the late 1920s. The heroine, Hiroko, reluctantly takes a job at a candy factory at the urging of her alcoholic father. As she works she gazes out of the window at billboard ads for soap and sake mounted on the roofs of houses across the river. She notes that the ads reflect sunlight all day long, while her work room receives only shade: "The sunlight [shining on the ads] seemed happy." She and her co-workers complain that "we can't even afford to buy New Year's gifts." On their once-daily break, the workers are allowed outside in pairs to buy snacks; in Hiroko's eyes, the poorly clothed factory girls appear somehow deformed walking along the main street. And at the end of the day, the employees line up at the gate for a body check. Waiting in a sharp, cold wind, each woman has her kimono sleeve pocket, breast pocket, and lunch box inspected for stolen candies, and Hiroko and her friends complain bitterly about the inspector's arrogance.[55]

Iwauchi Zensaku, a shrewd organizer in the Japan Textile Union

54. Suzuki, *Jokō to rōdō sōgi*, pp. 32–33.

55. *Sata Ineko shū*, vol. 25 of *Gendai Nihon no bungaku* (Tokyo: Gakujutsu kenkyūsho, 1971), pp. 255–56.

who played a major role in building the local at Tōyō Muslin, was one man who recognized the depth and basic nature of these grievances and turned complaints to concerted action. The son of a middling farmer in Niigata, he came to Tokyo in 1917, aged twenty-eight, and began to work in a celluloid factory in Kameido. Here he came under the influence of Watanabe Masanosuke, joining his New Man Celluloid Union and then the Yūaikai. In the early 1920s he threw himself into a variety of movement causes centered in the poor neighborhood of Nippori, just to the north of Nankatsu. He was a leader of the Nippori Yūaikai, then of the Sōdōmei, was active in organizing tenant farmers in the outlying suburbs, and engaged in charity work as well. By the mid 1920s he had decided to devote his primary energy to labor union organizing, first in the Kantō Amalgamated locals in Nippori and then, beginning in 1926, in the Japan Textile Union locals in the Nankatsu mills.[56]

As he recalled his efforts decades later, he had realized the need to speak to the young female workers in their own language. He would begin with a humorous story of, for example, the Zen priest Ikkyū. The monk was famous for his reverence for women, who were the "storehouse of the [Buddhist] law." Why? Because, after all, a woman gave birth to Shakyamuni. He then might pose the simple question, "If you work so damn hard, why are you poor?" His goal was to build pride among the young women and promote a critical spirit, but "you had to start with interesting or amusing things. Talk of 'labor unions' and 'class struggle' went nowhere."[57]

Even this man committed to a socialist future worked in the idiom of imperial democracy. His most effective piece of movement literature, he claimed, was a pamphlet titled "For the Woman Worker," a play on Lenin's "For the Poor Farmer." He recalls it sold 10,000 copies at ten sen each. Its message, he claimed, was simple: "Spun silk and cotton were the nation's two greatest exports. The working girls who produced that huge quantity, earned money through exports, and made Japan a wealthy nation were themselves great. I wanted to show them in simple language how much the female workers were doing for the nation."[58]

Iwauchi also confessed that he probably had been wrong to encourage relatively few of the women themselves to become union officials

56. Watanabe and Suzuki, eds., *Tatakai*, p. 164.
57. Ibid., pp. 180–83.
58. Ibid., p. 182.

and leaders. It would be tempting to dismiss as the condescending reminiscence of an old man his portrayal of the textile girls as naive and apolitical souls who attended meetings more for his anecdotes than anything else.[59] Yet the recollections of women involved in a parallel effort at organizing and educating the textile girls are remarkably similar. Tatewaki Sadayo was one of these, the independent-minded daughter of a small landowner who came on her own to study in Tokyo in 1920, supporting herself as a waitress. In 1925 she married a student radical in the Tokyo University "New Man Society" and herself obtained a radical education, beginning with a borrowed copy of *The Communist Manifesto*. In the late 1920s she became one of a handful of female leaders in the Japan Textile Union, editing the popular union magazine, its dimensions chosen to fit in the pockets of the spinning girls, and its articles also tailored for this audience. In August 1929 she and several other female organizers, most of the others actually mill workers, founded a Women's Labor Academy in Kameido, offering classes in "proletarian economics," the women's movement, and politics, as well as sewing, cooking, and flower arranging. Despite her own acute political awareness, in a touching comment on the consciousness of the mill workers she readily admitted that the chance to learn to sew and to cook was the school's great attraction: "They all said they just wanted to do what human beings do."[60]

The Japan Textile Union local at Tōyō Muslin declined after the scandal over union finances in 1928, but both it and the textile union in the Sōdōmei sustained active locals in several other Nankatsu mills. In the process of negotiations over food, wages, and dorm life in 1929, the union regained prestige and membership at Tōyō Muslin. Its program clearly reflected deeply felt sentiments among the textile women. By early 1930 it had enrolled over half the 6,868 employees in preparation for what would prove to be the most tumultuous year of labor conflict in Nankatsu history.

THE POLITICAL PROGRAM

In addition to analyzing labor union programs, dispute demands, and rhetoric, we must scrutinize the platforms and appeals of the proletarian political parties. Did these groups fashion a program and an alternative vision attractive to their intended constituency?

59. Ibid., p. 171.
60. "Tonikaku, ningen no suru koto o yaritai tte, minna iu n desu" (ibid., p. 206).

In strange contrast to the tedious succession of bitter ruptures and personal recriminations between the several proletarian parties, their platforms and the tone of their speeches differed remarkably little. Few other than true adepts could unerringly match speeches, platforms, and parties. One platform sought a "political and economic regime with the working class as its foundation"; another called for "the complete emancipation, political, economic, and social, of the proletarian class." One sought "rational reform" of "the capitalist system of production and distribution," which was "injurious to the people's interests"; another wanted "to reform by legislative means the present unfair conditions regarding land, production, and distribution of wealth."[61] All opposed the "established [i.e., bourgeois] parties" that catered solely to the "privileged classes."

In addition, in the 1920s all the proletarian parties opposed Japanese imperialism and expansionism, criticizing the aggressive "send-in-the troops" China policy of the Seiyūkai, and supporting the Chinese people against the Japanese military in speeches and slogans. The center and left supported the Chinese communists, while the Sōdōmei / Social Democrats supported Chiang Kai-shek. The political voices of the working class persisted with this decisive break with the foreign policy of imperial democracy right through the 1920s, until the fall of 1931. Even the "go-slow imperialist" of the Minseitō, Foreign Minister Shidehara, without question had a very different perspective on China than any of these labor parties, as he consistently defended what he called Japan's "visible and invisible rights and interests" there.[62]

Of course, none of the legal labor parties unequivocally called for the overthrow of the emperor. They would not have remained legal had they done so. Although anti-imperialist and antimilitarist rhetoric was prevalent, condemnation of this nationalist symbol was not possible. In such a context, the depth of popular support for this anti-imperialist stance is difficult to measure. Workers' rhetoric could be ambiguous, as with the Nankatsu bicycle workers on strike in 1928 who had called on local residents to support them for the sake of the "state and society."

In the debates that did take place among party theoreticians, the cen-

---

61. The former quotation in each pair is from the Social Democratic platform on the "right"; the latter is from the Labor-Farmer platform on the "left." Stephen Large, *Organized Workers and Socialist Politics in Interwar Japan* (Cambridge: Cambridge University Press, 1981), p. 115.

62. Akira Iriye, *After Imperialism: The Search for a New Order in the Far East, 1921–1931* (Cambridge, Mass.: Harvard University Press, 1965), p. 111.

ter and left criticized the Social Democrats, rejected "realistic social-ism" and accommodation, and saw capitalism, imperialism, and the emperor as interdependent parts of a system they opposed fundamentally. But for readers of the relatively simple slogans, platforms, or speeches through which party positions were actually conveyed to the majority of voters, this difference was obscure. When it came across, anti-imperialism seems to have won few votes for proletarian party candidates who criticized the dream of glory for the nation too harshly when blasting China policy. Nankatsu workers apparently supported the Minseitō, which was responsible for implementing "universal suf-frage for industry" and gave moderate support to the empire, with some generosity at the polls. While the Minseitō and Seiyūkai split four seats in Honjo-Fukagawa (District 4) in 1928, the Minseitō men placed first and second. The party won 51 percent of all votes in the district, com-fortably above its national total of 43 percent. In Nankatsu (District 6) the Minseitō took three of five seats, again exceeding its national share of the vote. For such a victory in this district, the Minseito must have had substantial working-class support.

The evidence for labor attitutes toward empire and imperialism is ultimately ambiguous. The proletarian camp went on to make consider-able political gains in the mid-to-late 1930s, persisting in its domestic critique of capitalism and its call for social reform, but returning to the themes of empire and emperor with extraordinary alacrity and verve. This makes the twelve-year interlude (1919–31) of working-class anti-imperialism seem to us now a fainter and more fragile vision than it may have been.[63] While the liberal Minseitō program apparently appealed to some workers, the proletarian parties' call to reform or transform capitalism and restrain or reject empire also won significant support from workers in Nankatsu.

CONCLUSION

The men and women who labored in Nankatsu factories produced a dispute culture of the working class through a decade of union-building, strikes, and political action. Children played "make-believe demonstration" in the Nankatsu streets in the late 1920s and sang their

---

63. For examples of antimilitary spirit among the Tokyo populace, see Matsuo Takayoshi, "The Development of Democracy in Japan—Taishō Democracy: Its Flower-ing and Breakdown," *Developing Economies*, December 1966, p. 630.

own abbreviated versions of the Internationale (see fig. 26).[64] A young man just arrived from working in a mine or on a farm was as likely to attend union speech-meetings as movies for entertainment; a casual visit to a dispute rally in 1924 was indeed the first exposure to the labor movement of one future leader of Kantō Amalgamated.[65]

A core of men and women developed self-awareness as leaders and organizers of a working class with a mission to remake society or simply to make it livable for workers. By the middle of the decade, at least a handful of men shared this attitude in any one of the dozens of union locals in the smaller and medium-sized factories. Usually the union officers, they were the ones who attended regional or national conferences, studied books on the theory and practice of the social movement, and engaged in heated debates over the merits of left, centrist, and right positions on the numerous occasions of party and union splits and mergers.[66] These were the people who wrote the leaflets, who spoke of the rights to strike, to organize unions, to live a decent life. They were the ones who sought to reform or transform what they defined as the capitalist system. In each textile mill, too, a core of spirited women had educated themselves on labor issues, and they encouraged others to support the union or a dispute. Despite their relatively small numbers, they managed to terrify and outrage owners and galvanize many of their fellow workers in moments of contention.

Other men and women gravitated to the causes of this core only in times of need, their commitment ebbing and flowing. They heard the language of class mobilization and confrontation in speeches, or read it in leaflets, but they reinterpreted the message. They conceived the desirable future as a world of justice and respect for themselves not only as workers with the right to strike, who were protected by a factory or health insurance law; they identified themselves also as employees entitled to bonuses and an annual field day, as Japanese who deserved respect for their contribution to national industry, as women who deserved a chance to learn cooking and sewing, and as human beings who deserved a "normal" life.

This dispute culture thus existed in a complex relationship both to a

64. Watanabe and Suzuki, eds., *Tatakai*, p. 144. They played *demo-gokko* and sang "Kikeban, yo rō yo," improvised from "Kike bankoku no rōdōsha" (Hark, workers of the world).
65. Author's interview with Komatsu Shōtarō, March 5, 1985.
66. Ibid.

political order dominated by the bureaucracy and the imperial democratic parties and to a mainstream urban culture dominated by a new
salaried middle class whose members valued education, upward mobility, and even consumption for its own sake. The relatively liberal programs of the bureaucracy and the Minseitō after 1924 had helped stimulate the labor offensive of these years, but these programs also had the
potential to coopt the labor movement. The emerging middle-class culture of the urban salaried employee likewise had the potential to define
the character of the "human" life to which workers aspired, and the
spread of a reformed paternalism to workers in large enterprises surely
provoked workers elsewhere to demand similar treatment. Some of the
ideas generated by the social movement genuinely threatened the order
the ruling imperial democrats sought to protect. This was true of the
sharp critique of imperialism, and it was especially true of the independence spoken of by some female leaders and the attack on the emperor
system by the communists. But other ideas, such as the calls for "better
treatment," even if they implied recognition of the rights of labor, could
be met within the context of imperial democracy. The ongoing response
of the state to the spreading movement of disputes and unions, the economic context, and the international environment would do much to
determine how workers would build on their gains of the 1920s. The
fate of the labor offensive was far from clear in 1929.

The possibilities were several. If the economy had picked up in the
late 1920s, workers might well have generated a movement too strong
to repress or ignore by the early 1930s. If the government, with or without such pressure, had passed a union bill, the effect might have been
comparable to that of the Wagner Act of 1937 in the United States. In
the years after American unions first gained legal protection, unions
increased their membership from just 13 percent of the nonagricultural
work force (1935) to 29 percent (1939).[67] The Japanese unions had
enrolled 7.9 percent on the eve of the final push for a union bill in
1931.[68] If the bill had succeeded, it might have generated comparable
enthusiasm for unions, and a surge of union-building would have resulted. Of course, the bill failed. Even if unions had been granted legal
protection in 1931, they surely would have rallied round the flag in the
foreign policy crisis of 1931–32. A liberal Japanese polity incorporat-

---

67. U.S. Bureau of the Census, *Historical Statistics of the United States, Colonial
Times to 1970* (Washington, D.C.: GPO, 1975), part 1, p. 178.
    68. *NRUS*, 10:424.

ing an independent labor movement could have marched into the swamp of an Asian land war as readily as did the anti-union, antidemocratic regime that actually prevailed in the 1930s or the American system that engaged in such a war in the 1960s.

In sum, while the working-class ideology of this era was ambivalent, the 1920s saw more than a short, superficial fling with a democratic fad. The idioms and ideas of empire, emperor, *and* democracy reached deep into Japanese society. Variously interpreted, of course, they nonetheless touched many and moved them to act. The future of the workers' movement remained contingent on the international environment and on domestic economic and political developments. In the twenty-five years since the Hibiya anti-treaty riot, the changes in working-class society and in the larger political order had been dramatic and profound. It required a crisis of unprecedented dimensions in the economy at home and the empire abroad to bring turmoil to the workers' movement and transform the political order of imperial democracy.

PART THREE

The Collapse
of Imperial Democracy

NINE

The Depression and the Workers' Movement

In just three years, the multiple shocks of the depression, military expansion, assassination, and intense social conflict foreclosed Japan's liberal and democratic options. An imperial democratic structure and ideology of rule that had tolerated and even sanctioned independent labor or farmer organization gradually crumbled. In its wake emerged a system and ideology of rule with greatest contemporary kinship to the fascist systems of Germany and Italy. Between 1936 and 1940, independent political parties, business associations, producer cooperatives, labor unions, and tenant unions were replaced by a series of state-controlled mass bodies intended to mobilize the nation for its "holy war" with China and bring harmony and order at home.

The fascist *regimes* of these three nations had more in common than the *movements* that produced them. European fascist models inspired the men who erected Japan's "New Order," and the regime shared with the two European cases the objective of funneling the energies of a glorified national body (whether the *Volk* or the Yamato race) into a quest for military hegemony, autarchic economic empire, and an antidemocratic, hierarchic new political and economic order at home. The regimes also shared (the Japanese and Italian in particular) an inability ultimately to dissolve or fully control all existing plural bases of political and economic power. While numerous observers have noted correctly that a fascist party as such never came to power in Japan, the context that produced these regimes shared important general characteristics: economic crisis, intense polarization of left and right, labor-management conflict, catalytic right-wing terror, a perception among intellectuals and the political elite that established gender roles were breaking down and that a cultural malaise gripped the nation, and a widely shared sense that Anglo-American power blocked the nation's legitimate international aspirations to empire.

The focus of the remainder of this book shifts considerably as we seek to understand the collapse of the imperial democratic system. The relative weight of the attention we give to the workers of Nankatsu and their organizations, disputes, and electoral participation will decrease while we investigate in greater depth the language and the programs of Japan's bureaucratic and military rulers and business leaders.

This shift reflects, first, a change in the quality and nature of documentary sources available from the 1930s. The union movement peaked in proportional terms in 1931; it reached a numerical peak in 1936. Disputes declined sharply in number between 1930 and 1936, and the brief surge of 1936–37 centered on nonunion factories in relatively newer industrial areas. Unions in Nankatsu were greatly weakened by factional strife. These factors combined to produce a relatively impoverished store of documentation of labor actions, for Nankatsu in particular.[1]

Second, this shift reflects the somewhat different concerns of this final portion of the book. In previous chapters we have examined riots, labor disputes, and union-organizing in order to understand the emergence of workers and other city-dwellers as political actors in Tokyo in the early twentieth century. The primary goal has been to understand the dispute culture that workers created between the turn of the century and the 1920s. A related goal has been to understand the interaction between this evolving workers' movement and the changing configuration of elite rule. The priority given these two goals is reversed in the final chapters, in part because of the documentary problem, but also because I believe the relationship between labor and social problems and the "big story" of the ascendance of the military and fascism in the 1930s has been insufficiently studied and its significance underappreciated.

The existence of such a "relationship," for example between the re-

1. The shelf space at the OISR taken up by all union documents for 1932–40 is about one-twentieth that of the previous eight-year period. There is virtually no documentation of the Sanpō labor front in Nankatsu.

pudiation of party rule in 1932 and the social turmoil of the previous three years, is difficult to prove. No radical push from below, either of the left or the right, directly ousted the parties; Admiral Saitō did not proclaim that the nation was turning to military rulers because radical unions were too powerful. Yet a range of evidence examined below, from diaries and memoirs to newspaper and magazine articles, suggests that a relationship did exist. We shall see, first, that the newly ascendant military men and bureaucrats, among many others, truly feared that domestic social order might collapse during and after the depression, and, second, that this fear informed, and at times propelled, a wide range of new domestic and foreign policies.

The depression generated a crisis of multiple dimensions. Objective statistical indicators, imperfectly gathered and subject to various inter-pretations, are often as confusing as they are revealing, but it appears that unemployment rose sharply in the cities (see figure 8), that bank-ruptcies and closings among retail traders and factory owners reached unprecedented levels, that nominal agricultural income plummeted, and that real farm income probably fell as well. The precise statistical, eco-nomic impact of the depression, however, is not our concern in this chapter.[2] Rather, I seek to analyze, first, the social response to the de-pression of men and women of Nankatsu, and, second, the perception of political crisis and social chaos among a wide variety of actors, from the nation's leading military figures to bureaucrats, zaibatsu business leaders, small factory owners in Nankatsu, and right-wing union leaders.

The simple conclusion is that during the relatively brief years of de-pression, social conflict in working-class districts such as Nankatsu in-tensified dramatically. Although workers and farmers did not mount a

---

2. For discussion of the economic background to the depression, see Hugh Patrick, "The Economic Muddle of the 1920s," in *Dilemmas of Growth in Prewar Japan*, ed. James Morley (Princeton: Princeton University Press, 1971), pp. 252–59. On unemploy-ment, see Andrew Gordon, "The Right to Work in Japan: Labor and the State in the Depression," *Social Research* 54, no. 2 (Summer 1987). On agriculture, see Nakamura Masanori, "Daikyōkō to nōson mondai," in *Iwanami kōza: Nihon rekishi 19* (Tokyo: Iwanami shoten, 1976), p. 138; Nishida Yoshiaki, "Shōwa kyōki ni okeru nōmin undō to tokushitsu," in *Fuashizumu ki no kokka to shakai, 1: Shōwa kyōkō*, ed. Tokyo daigaku shakai kagaku kenkyū jo (Tokyo: University of Tokyo Press, 1979), pp. 319–25; Richard Smethurst, *Agricultural Development and Tenancy Disputes in Japan* (Princeton: Princeton University Press, 1986), p. 330. On retail traders and manufacturers in the cities, see Eguchi Keiichi, *Toshi shoburujoa no kenkyū* (Tokyo: Miraisha, 1976), p. 387, and Tōkyō shiyakusho, ed., *Tōkyō kōjō yōran* (Tokyo: Tōkyō shiyakusho, 1933), pp. 2–3.

genuinely revolutionary threat, their actions were sufficient to provoke a widespread vision among a variety of elite groups, both local and national, of a society and an economy on the verge of ruin, and of a political leadership too corrupt and too weak to deal with the crisis.

NANKATSU IN TURMOIL

The social conflict experienced by residents and workers in Nankatsu during the depression of 1930 to 1932 was unprecedented. Union membership declined slightly, but unions remained a formidable presence. Disputes became more numerous than ever. Managers and owners grew increasingly hostile toward both unionized workers and the state. They also became increasingly fearful, and began to speak incessantly of impending social catastrophe, echoing the rhetoric of radical unions and right-wing groups.

In 1931 the national rate of unionization reached its prewar peak of 7.9 percent. In Nankatsu most of the smaller unions gained membership between 1929 and 1931, while the large textile unions suffered major defeats and lost members. Precise calculation is impossible, but it appears that by 1931 the overall Nankatsu union membership fell to about 16,000, still a significant 25 percent of the work force.

The continued turbulent experience of Kantō Amalgamated was typical. In 1930 twenty-two of its locals collapsed citywide, but union fortunes then revived (table 9.1). By April 1931 membership in Nankatsu stood at an all-time high of about 1,500, organized in twenty-two locals at about thirty-five factories.[3]

As such unions struggled to survive, the incidence of labor unrest in Nankatsu rose sharply in 1930 to a prewar high of sixty-four disputes. The disputes of these three years were longer than ever; half of them lasted two weeks or more, and more than one-fifth continued for over a month. These were overwhelmingly union actions; between 1930 and 1932 unions led 83 percent of these actions, the greatest proportion in Nankatsu disputes for the prewar era (see tables 7.2–7.6 and 8.1).

The workers were desperate and defensive. Their actions were thus prolonged and bitter, but usually failed. Disputes considered "worker victories" by third-party observers over this span fell to 7 percent, down from an average success rate of 22 percent over the previous five years; labor "defeats" reached a prewar high of 34 percent. In addition, most

3. *NRN,* 1929–31; Zenkoku rōdō, "Kumiai chōsa hyō" file, OISR.

TABLE 9.1   KANTŌ AMALGAMATED UNION LOCALS,
TOKYO, 1928–31

	Newly Founded Locals	Failed Locals	Total at Year End
1928	16	12	31
1929	18	10	36
1930	18	22	30
1931	32	6	53

SOURCE: "Kantō gōdō" file, A-5, OISR.

of the remaining so-called compromise settlements were simply defeats, slightly softened. In nearly two-thirds (64 percent) of all disputes, workers sought to save jobs, prevent pay cuts, improve severance pay in cases of dismissal, or simply force payment of back wages when a factory suddenly closed. A "compromise" settlement in such a case usually meant improving severance pay, but accepting dismissal, or tempering, but not preventing, a pay cut. Such incidents constituted the typical "depression dispute," comparable to the era's anti-eviction disputes on the land (table 9.2).

This crescendo of labor protest polarized labor and capital throughout the Nankatsu region. The largest employers in the area continued to face serious organized resistance from workers unwilling to accept dismissal, pay cuts, or speedups. At the same time, union-led protest continued to spread among medium and smaller scale worksites. Although the proportion was low, the greatest absolute number of disputes took place in the smallest factories, those employing under thirty people, while of the 160 factories with thirty or more employees, fully 38 percent (61) experienced disputes. Table 9.2 documents the extraordinary penetration of labor disputes in the neighborhoods of Nankatsu. For the first time, even a small local owner faced the likelihood of serious labor unrest at his own factory and the certainty that even if he escaped challenge, several of his fellow local industrialists would face this threat. Throughout the major cities of Japan, where disputes occurred in numbers comparable to those in Nankatsu, a local business elite that saw itself much as the small landlord class in the countryside did, as a pillar of social order and the nation, felt the greatest sense of crisis and embattlement.

TABLE 9.2   THE DEPRESSION DISPUTE PATTERN IN
NANKATSU FACTORIES, 1930–32

Disputes in Nankatsu, by Primary Demand

Offensive		
Improved treatment	31	(22)
Wage increase	2	(1)
Other	4	(3)
Total offensive	37	(26)
Defensive		
To oppose dismissal	34	(24)
To oppose pay cut	27	(20)
For back pay	28	(20)
Other	14	(10)
Total defensive	103	(74)
Total disputes	140[a]	

Disputes in Nankatsu, by Result

All demands gained	2	(7)
Compromise	17	(59)
All demands denied	10	(34)
Subtotal	29	(100)
Result unclear	112	
Total disputes	141	

Disputes in Minami Katsushika County

No. of Employees	No. of Factories, 1931	No. of Factories with Disputes, 1930–32	% of Factories with Disputes
5–29	577	46	8
30–99	116	38	33
100–499	33	14	42
500+	11	9	82
Total	737	107	15

SOURCES: Data on disputes from Kyū-kyōchōkai, *Rōdō sōgi*; Keishichō, *Rōdō sōgi junpō*, *Shakai undō ōrai*, and *Shakai undō tsūshin*; data on number of factories from Tōkyō-fu, *Tōkyō-fu tōkei sho* (Tokyo, 1931).
NOTE: Figures in parentheses are percentages.
[a] One case unclear.

GENERAL STRIKES AND TERROR IN THE FACTORY

The height of unrest in Nankatsu came in the fall of 1930. The timing was critical. The Hamaguchi cabinet was preparing its most serious push yet for a labor union bill for the coming winter session of the Diet; industrial groups, orchestrated by the Japan Industrial Club, were lobbying furiously against it. The dispute culture of industrial Nankatsu generated a shocking series of events, in close proximity to the Diet, that exerted an influence well beyond the local sites of dispute.

A total of sixty-four labor disputes took place in Minami Katsushika County during 1930. The centrist Kumiai dōmei federation played the leading role in twenty-seven of these incidents, including one of the longest and certainly the most noticed, the struggle at the Tōyō Muslin factory in Kameido. Fourteen of the Nankatsu disputes overlapped with the Tōyō Muslin strike, and twenty-six occurred during this time in Honjo and Fukagawa wards. At the height of the Tōyō Muslin strike, some union activists on the left wing of the movement even began to promote the idea of a regional general strike.

Tōyō Muslin produced both cotton thread and cloth. In 1930 it employed roughly 6,000 women and men in four factories in Kameido. In the 1920s the export market for spun cotton declined owing to new competition from Japanese-owned producers in China, and labor costs rose with the 1927 abolition of night work for women. Even before the depression, the cotton-spinning industry felt pressure to rationalize production with more efficient spinning equipment and automated looms, and a surge of investment in 1928–30 in both the spinning and weaving industries substantially raised output per worker. With the depression, companies sought further savings in labor costs to pay for these investments. They dismissed workers, reduced wages, and raised operating speed.[4] Workers at virtually every major textile producer responded by striking. Between April and October of 1930 unionized women and men at four of the "Big Five" in the cotton-spinning industry led nationally publicized disputes against pay cuts, plant closings and firings; they typically stopped work at several plants in each company.[5]

The confrontation at Tōyō Muslin drew even greater attention for at least two reasons. The dispute took place in the center of Tokyo with

---

4. Suzuki Yūko, *Jokō to rōdō sōgi: Nihon josei rōdō undō shi ron* (Tokyo: Renga shobō shinsha, 1989), pp. 11–15; Nishinarita Yutaka, "Rōdō ryoku hensei to rōshi kankei," in *1920 nendai no Nihon shihonshugi*, ed. 1920 nendai shi kenkyūkai (Tokyo: University of Tokyo Press, 1983), pp. 174–76.

5. Kanebo, Fujibō, Greater Japan Textiles, Osaka Textile, Tōyōbō.

the labor union bill about to be considered; and the young women who marched in the streets and literally fought police and company guards shocked both management and the public. These combative textile girls were neither the pitiful victims portrayed in muckraking exposés nor the satisfied brides-to-be of company public relations campaigns.[6]

According to Suzuki Yūko's thorough history of the dispute, two factors accounted for its fierceness.[7] The company had not earned a profit since 1928 and was desperate to cut wages and reduce personnel. In the frank words of the company president, it was determined to "root out" the union, which obstructed these plans.[8] The female workers, whose parents on the farm needed their incomes more than ever, were equally determined not to give up their jobs and return home; at one rally during the strike, an impassioned speaker shouted, "Even if we go back to the country, our parents and our brothers do not have enough to eat. Knowing this, how can we possibly go back?"[9]

The dispute began in late September 1930 when the company announced the imminent closing of the spinning division at its Number 3 factory and the firing of 500 of the 2,350 employees. (Tōyō Muslin had closed the smaller Number 2 factory in Kameido in February 1930, dismissing 157 workers and transferring 600 at reduced pay to the remaining plants.) The union sought to commute the September dismissals into three-month layoffs with "idle pay." When this proposal was rejected, the strike began. All workers at the Number 3 factory and many from the other three Tōyō Muslin factories in Kameido joined the action. For about two weeks the strike group's unity held, but management launched a fierce counterattack. It fired 137 additional workers, recruited miners to serve as company guards, and called for parents to take the strikers home from the dormitory to the countryside for the duration. By the end of October, about 60 percent of the strikers had abandoned the strike group: 890 returned home, 390 quit their jobs, and 179 returned to work. The settlement reached on November 11 was a total defeat for the workers. No dismissals were revoked, the company remained free to fire additional "rule-breakers" as it "rebuilt," and the union was in disarray (see figs. 21, 22, and 23).[10]

6. Hosoi Wakizō, *Jokō aishi* (1925; reprint, Tokyo: Iwanami shoten, 1982) was the premier muckraking account of the day. See also Suzuki, *Jokō to rōdō sōgi*, p. 10.

7. Suzuki, *Jokō to rōdō sōgi*, pp. 11–15 and passim.

8. Speech of Umemura Kenkichi, October 25, 1930, delivered at the Japan Industrial Club. A transcript held in the closed Japan Industrial Club archive was kindly shared with me in 1985 by Ueda Hirofumi.

9. Suzuki, *Jokō to rōdō sōgi*, pp. 16–17, cites *TAS*, September 22, 1930.

10. See Suzuki, *Jokō to rōdō sōgi*, pp. 47–89, for a complete account of the strike.

In this broad outline, the dispute was typical of dozens of textile strikes in 1930. The additional event that made the Tōyō Muslin workers famous was the riotous demonstration on October 24 joined by hundreds of young female workers. A support group led by the prominent left-wing socialist Katō Kanjū organized the demonstration as part of its effort to build a regional general strike out of the widespread unrest in Nankatsu factories. Representatives from 115 factories in the area had attended a "Factory Representatives' Council" on October 7 and resolved to support all area strikes in hopes of bringing on a general strike. At a second meeting on the 21st, they resolved to rally in support of the Tōyō Muslin strikers on the night of the 24th. The women themselves were not supposed to join, but an undetermined number, probably several hundred, did. When authorities extinguished the street lighting, the demonstrators marched through darkened streets toward the Tōyō Muslin factory singing the Internationale and shouting slogans. They threw stones, smashed streetcar windows, and fought police, who arrested 197 demonstrators, including 4 of the women. Over 20 workers were injured. The event was subsequently dubbed simply "the street war."[11]

The intensity of the Tōyō Muslin strike was echoed immediately in Nankatsu and around the nation in dozens of incidents. We may briefly note three.

Just as the Muslin strike ended, Nankatsu resident Daiwa Shintarō decided to confront a Kantō Amalgamated local that had enrolled 37 of the 270 employees at his rubber factory. He fired 2 union members and housed his nonunion workers in the factory for the duration of a bitter two-month strike. Violence instigated by the strike group or the company guards resulted in broken windows, injuries, and arrests on at least four occasions, but the company had announced the firing of the remaining strikers and was operating comfortably with its nonunion majority. The union's best hope was to draw the local police in as mediators likely to force a compromise on Daiwa to bring peace to the neighborhood.

The union succeeded in late January 1931. A nonstriking worker picked up Daiwa's daughter at her prefectural girls' high school in a company car. The vice-chairman of the strike group, hiding nearby, jumped on the running board of the car and tossed a light bulb filled with sulfuric acid through the window. The driver sustained serious

11. *Shigai sen*. Ibid., pp. 89–99, gives detailed account of the "street war."

injuries. Company guards immediately retaliated by severely beating a dozen picketing strikers (see fig. 20). The next day police presided over a negotiated settlement in which Daiwa actually rehired 18 of the 33 strikers and gave the injured workers 1,250 yen each![12]

More famous and theatrical was the concurrent escapade of the "chimney man."[13] When a small group of workers at the huge Fuji Cotton Spinning Company in Kawasaki (between Yokohama and Tokyo) went on strike in November 1930, one of their number scaled the factory's smokestack and announced that he would not descend until the strike was settled. The genius of this tactic was that the emperor was scheduled to pass directly beneath the "chimney man" in his luxurious imperial railroad car a few days later. Just as no buildings close to the imperial palace offer a downward view of it today, no one, and certainly no union radical, could be allowed to look down upon a passing imperial procession from such heights. The police mediated during several frenzied days of negotiation, covered in detail by the press. Several hours before the emperor's passage, the chimney man descended.[14]

Workers typically resorted to such tactics, not always quite so gruesome as at Daiwa or as spectacular as at Fuji, in order to break stalemates where a company was determined to dismiss large numbers, to destroy a union, or to cease operations.[15] In a series of strikes at several factories of the Royal Celluloid Company in Nankatsu, workers employed the full repertoire of tactics familiar from disputes of the 1920s to mobilize the community and pressure the company, and they added a few new wrinkles. Female union members sold tickets door to door for a production by a "Proletarian Theater Troupe"; eight workers declared a hunger strike and "sat in" at the famous Asakusa Kannon temple; female employees divided into three squads to visit the homes of executives and press their demands, and a group of strikers invaded company headquarters en masse to demand satisfaction. They later taunted the police and management with the public claim that they had

12. Kyū-kyōchōkai, *Rōdō sōgi*, 4 (1930), police reports of October 27, 1930 to January 24, 1931; "Kantō gōdō" file, G-26, OISR, documents on "Daiwa sōgi"; Nihon kōgyō kurabu chōsakai, ed., *Saikin ni okeru rōdō sōgi no jirei*, vol. 3 (May 1931), pp. 27–46.

13. *Entotsu otoko*. After this incident, several imitators carried out the same stunt in other disputes.

14. Tanabe Satoshi, "Ani yori mitaru entotsu otoko," *Chūō kōron*, January 1931, pp. 227–28.

15. Miwa Yasushi, "1930 nendai ni okeru rōdō seisaku to Sōdōmei," *Rekishi hyōron*, no. 380 (December 1981): 37.

merely "dropped in" to visit after a shopping trip to the Mitsukoshi department store downtown. Window-breaking and fighting between company guards, workers, and police were also part of the dispute.[16]

The new assertiveness of the women workers, especially in the Royal Celluloid dispute, must be read in part as a calculated, double-barreled attack on social norms of both class and gender subservience, likely to shock the general public, the management, and the police, and force a favorable settlement. The tactic usually worked in the short run. Unless they had evidence of Communist Party involvement, the police rarely pressed serious charges against arrested workers, and by splitting the difference between a minimal management offer of severance pay and a huge labor demand, they helped workers gain a cushion of several months' pay in typical disputes over dismissal.[17]

OFFICIAL REACTION

For the Home Ministry, the violence in many of these disputes was new and disturbing. In the first nine months of 1930, and again in 1931, the ministry recorded "criminal incidents" in 12 percent of all labor disputes, and a Police Bureau report on labor described new "terror" tactics and worried that arrests in connection with disputes were on the rise.[18] In Nankatsu, workers were arrested in at least 11 percent of all disputes between 1929 and 1932, compared to just 3 percent in the previous two years.[19] Yet the Home Ministry continued its policy of close surveillance but noninterference in most disputes, despite increasing violence; its Police Bureau's report of early 1932 reiterated a hands-off approach to disputes judged "economic" and a parallel determination to "control" political incidents involving "communist agitators."[20]

This relatively unchanged response was probably an appropriate means to achieve the basic goal of the police, and of the Home Ministry as a whole. The ministry sought to maintain social peace and the existing social order, and the demands raised in labor disputes do not offer evidence that a broad-based movement for radical change was building. Workers resisted dismissals and pay cuts in their defensive actions, and

16. For details of this dispute, see Gordon, "Right to Work," pp. 257–62.
17. Ibid., pp. 260–61.
18. Home Ministry, Police Bureau, Security Section, "Rōdō undō narabi rōdō sōgi no jōkyō kore ga torishimari taisaku" (February 1932). Riku-kaigun monjo, reel 205, item 1434.
19. Data from the survey of Nankatsu disputes are given in chapter 7, tables 7.4–7.6.
20. Home Ministry, Police Bureau, "Rōdō undō narabi rōdō sōgi" (February 1932). Riku-kaigun monjo, reel 205, item 1434.

continued to call for "improved treatment" in most of their offensive disputes. Any such dispute, of course, was an implicit challenge to managerial authority, but the social bureaucrats and the local police did not discern in these incidents the same challenge to the existing hierarchy that managers did. The rhetoric of the labor union leaders was one of struggle, even of apocalypse, but the underlying goal of the rank and file appears still to have been security and respect within the existing social and economic system. To the managers, however, the depression disputes were volatile and scary. Violence was more common than ever. They read slogans such as the one used by the Daiwa Rubber strike group: "Only through struggle will we build organization."[21] They were aware that representatives of 115 factories had discussed a general strike in Nankatsu, even if they could not execute it. Their response to such disputes, as much as the events themselves, eventually led the Home Ministry bureaucrats to rethink their support for liberal solutions to social problems.

THE CRISIS OF IMPERIAL DEMOCRACY

The well-known social critic Ōya Sōichi offered a perceptive picture of Japanese society and culture in crisis at the end of 1930, evoking the specter of the women at Tōyō Muslin taking to the streets:

> The supervisor at X printer, largest in the Orient, claims he is always running out of two characters, no matter how many pieces he casts. These are the characters for "woman" and for "class" [onna and kai]. Demand for the former, especially, recently has risen suddenly, and if he stocks 10,000 pieces he runs out before he knows it. . . . Doesn't the fact of rising demand for these two characters give realistic color to the social face of 1930? . . . The bedroom has moved into the foyer, into the living room, and finally into the streets.[22]

Images of gender anarchy and class war were not always juxtaposed so strikingly, but a sense of crisis and imminent social chaos was palpable in Japanese political discourse during the depression. Intensified conflict in places like Nankatsu fueled this fear, and as early as 1929 an essayist in the magazine Kaizō had offered this picture of a polarized urban landscape in Nankatsu:

> As one walks the streets [of Kameido] one finds the following such posters plastered to every available telephone pole or wall: "Demand a 30 percent

21. "Kantō gōdō" file, G-26, OISR, "Strike Group Report of January 23, 1931."
22. Ōya Sōichi, "1930 nen no kao," Chūō kōron, December 1930, pp. 303–4.

rent reduction! Unfair Rents! Refuse to Pay! National Renters' Federation," or "Absolute opposition to closing Tōyō Muslin! Don't let the capitalists feuding take food from the workers! Don't destroy the retail traders' living!"[23]

A police report of August 1, 1931, on the Royal Celluloid Kameido dispute echoed this description with a comment that management and the union were engaged in a "battle of leaflets" (*bira gassen*).[24] The metaphor is appropriate. With tremendous energy and effort, both sides in the depression disputes printed and distributed leaflets and posters explaining their position to townspeople, to workers at neighboring factories, to the families of striking workers, and, in the case of women workers living in dormitories, to parents back on the farm.[25]

MANAGEMENT VISIONS OF SOCIAL COLLAPSE

The tone and substance of management rhetoric changed in the depression, and events in Nankatsu were partly responsible. The Japan Industrial Club had coincidentally scheduled a meeting to discuss labor-capital relations and the union bill for the day after the "street war" in Nankatsu. The featured speakers were the president of Tōyō Muslin and managers or owners of three smaller firms. In the audience were Home Minister Adachi, Social Bureau Chief Yoshida, and Police Bureau Chief Ōtsuka, the three ranking officials in the ministry.[26]

Zen Keinosuke, former manager at Yahata Steel and, as executive director of the club, a leading voice of business interests, set the tone in his introductory remarks, noting that "yesterday's incident" at Tōyō Muslin was on everyone's mind. Recent labor disputes, mainly in small and medium-sized factories, had become more intense, so the club had surveyed seventy disputes in depth. These were not properly economic actions, Zen had discovered, but politically inspired acts; the organizers had created regional networks and were promoting a general strike. Workers increasingly used violence against the families of owners and staff, and toward a company's customers and bankers.[27]

Tōyō Muslin's president, Umemura Kenkichi, echoed Zen, express-

23. Nakamoto Takako, "Kameido zakkei," *Kaizō*, April 1929, p. 94.
24. Kyū-kyōchōkai, *Rōdō sōgi* (1931), vol. 150D, police report of August 1, 1931.
25. See Suzuki, *Jokō to rōdō sōgi*, pp. 20–26, for good examples of company leaflets.
26. Nihon kōgyō kurabu, "Rōdō sōgi jikkyō chōsa sokkiroku" (October 25, 1930). This transcript is held in the archives of the Japan Industrial Club. The composition of the audience is described in *25 nen shi*, ed. Nihon kōgyō kurabu (Tokyo: Nihon kōgyō kurabu, 1943), p. 723.
27. Transcript cited in n. 26 above, pp. 9–14.

ing his horror at the acts of his employees and the response of the state: the strikers had used violence against his staff and company property, yet until he had threatened to hire his own toughs, the police had remained aloof. He demanded that the police act more firmly to protect company assets. The union had a revolutionary agenda and had provoked the street fight, he claimed, and "we shudder as we observe this situation." His women employees had been transformed. In addition to joining the riot, "several hundred" had trampled guards who sought to remove the belongings of fired women from the dorms. He was "aghast." He wanted the police to take a tougher stance against illegal union acts, and he warned that the passage of a union bill would have the worst possible consequences, for it would sanction such organizations and give workers a new sense of "rights."[28]

The speeches of that evening articulated three central themes in a new business perspective on social order and the appropriate roles of corporate management, unions, and the state. In dozens of additional speeches, resolutions, and magazine articles, business leaders such as Zen and Fujiwara Ginjirō of the Mitsui zaibatsu and representatives of hundreds of industrial and employer federations repeated this new chorus.

First, unions had changed. Rather than promoting labor rights and welfare, they supported strikes for the sake of creating chaos, challenging managerial authority, and furthering revolutionary goals.[29] In union platforms and strikes workers embraced "class-struggle socialism," the idea that the working and capitalist classes could not coexist.[30] Business leaders in 1930 and 1931 thus echoed, with fear, of course, rather than hope, the claim of contemporary Marxist critics that so long as the capitalist political order in Japan maintained its current course, it faced a "dead end" or a "third-stage" crisis.[31]

Second, the class that served as "the mainstay" of social order and national strength was crumbling in the face of depression, disputes, and foolish liberal policies. This class was composed of the owners of smaller and medium-sized commercial and manufacturing establishments.

28. Umemura speech is in ibid., pp. 22–40. The quotations in this paragraph are from pp. 22, 26, 27, 40.

29. For Fujiwara Ginjirō's statement to this effect, see "Rōdō kumiai hō seifu an ni hantai su," *Chūō kōron*, August 1930, pp. 111–12.

30. Nihon kōgyō kurabu, *Wa ga kuni kokujō ni tekisezaru rōdō kumiai hō*, October 1930, pp. 8–12. Fujiwara, "Rōdō kumiai hō," p. 112.

31. For such a claim from the left, see Inomata Tatsuo, "Nihon ni okeru dai 3 ki kyōkō no tokushitsu," *Chūō kōron*, January 1931, pp. 104–6.

Beginning in the late 1920s, and reaching a crescendo during the depression, came an outpouring of virtually identical lamentations of apocalypse. They combined and repeated a handful of key words endlessly: "weak small and medium-sized factories"; "lawless disputes"; "virulent labor-capital conflict"; "mainstays [*chūken*] of the nation"; "foundation of the state"; "pillars of society." Typical was a resolution of twenty-eight Keihin-area industrial associations of June 1930 claiming that "as small-to-medium sized industrialists are feeling the most pressure from unions . . . this law will endanger the existence of the small and medium industrial producers who constitute the mainstay class in society."[32]

The key word *chūken*, translated here as "mainstay," begins with the character for "middle." Those who used the expression saw the small business class as an intermediary stratum between the managers of the zaibatsu firms and the mass of wage workers. The conception of these advocates, in the words of the president of an Osaka paint company talking to a group from the House of Peers in July 1930, was of a middle group of loyal subjects and taxpayers, the "mainstay of the nation," who needed state protection, not harassment, and whose health would avert a disaster that could "destroy the nation": polarization into a few giant firms and a mass of antagonistic workers.[33]

Third, managers had lost confidence in their ability to handle the labor problem unaided by the state. Umemura of Tōyō Muslin, for example, was furious at the police for not coming to his immediate rescue, and his response was typical of the new managerial perspective in large and small enterprises. Factory owners clearly took even the matter of leafleting and postering quite seriously. Confronted with a dispute by some of his machinists, the owner of the Watanabe Engineering Works in Honjo, who employed ninety-seven men in 1930, complained to the police of their general failure to harass the strikers and their specific refusal to intervene in the leaflet battle.

32. *25 nen shi*, ed. Nihon kōgyō kurabu, 721–22. A partial survey of business statements concerning disputes and the union bill turned up similar statements too numerous to cite fully. The *25 nen shi* of the Japan Industrial Club quotes a number of these. See also Nihon kōgyō kurabu, *Rōdō kumiai hōan ni kansuru jitsugyō dantai no ikken*, May 1930, and Eguchi, *Toshi shoburujoa*, pp. 437–41, for many examples.

33. Kobatake Gennosuke, president of the Japan Paint Company, spoke to the Kōsei Club, an organization of members of the House of Peers, in Osaka on July 12, 1930. Kobatake Gennosuke, "Rōdō kumiai hōan o chūshō kōgyō no tachiba kara mite," *Kōgyō*, no. 49 (August 1930): 8–9. See also Awaya Kentarō, "Fuashyoka to minshū ishiki," *Nihon fuashizumu no keisei: taikei Nihon gendai shi* (Tokyo: Nihon hyōronsha, 1978), 1:259.

I told him, "Why don't you arrest the ones who put posters on the telephone poles?" The policeman replied, "In the old days we could control these disputes because we had the Public Order Police Law, but now the do-gooder Dietmen, like the one you chose, have abolished it, and there's not a thing we can do."[34]

In earlier debates over state social policy and social unrest, dating back to opposition to the factory law before 1911, the business elite had consistently rejected state involvement. What they had called "beautiful customs" of paternal care and devotion would suffice to maintain peace and order in the workplace.[35] In the multitude of business statements on the union bill and the depression-era disputes, the phrase "beautiful customs" is noteworthy for its absence. Owners of smaller firms explicitly noted that while large companies had resources possibly to revive this spirit of labor-management cooperation, they did not. The union bill, which did not restrict unions to economic actions, would destroy their already weakened control of politicized workers.[36]

This reaction to state social policy went beyond ferocious attacks on the union bill to call instead for a "Law to Control Labor Disputes." Versions put forward by business groups called on government to prohibit sympathy strikes and outlaw participation of minors or public employees in strikes. Business wanted the government to prohibit demonstrations, third-party involvement in strikes or even the all-encompassing "obstruction of an enterprise." This last phrase essentially would have declared strikes illegal. The demand for this alternative law was a major focus of the campaign against the union bill.[37]

Although no Dietmen actually introduced such legislation, the very call for government involvement in the legal regulation of labor relations marked a shift in the stance of the organized business community toward the state. For three decades business interests had been insisting there was no need for a factory law or a health insurance law. They had mounted a sustained and ultimately successful campaign to repeal the business tax.[38] The Tokyo Federation of Business Associations had sup-

34. Nihon kōgyō kurabu, "Rōdō mondai kondan kiroku: Kōtō hōmen" (August 7, 1930). Unpublished transcript in the archives of the Japan Industrial Club.
35. Andrew Gordon, *The Evolution of Labor Relations in Japan: Heavy Industry, 1853–1955* (Cambridge, Mass.: Harvard University Council on East Asian Studies, 1985), pp. 64–69.
36. Kobatake, "Rōdō kumiai hōan," p. 12.
37. Miwa Ryōichi, "Rōdō kumiai hō seitei mondai no rekishiteki ichi," in *Ryō daisenkanki no Nihon shihonshugi*, ed. Andō Yoshio (Tokyo: University of Tokyo Press, 1979), pp. 266–71; one business group's draft of such a bill is summarized on p. 268.
38. Eguchi, *Toshi shoburujoa*, chs. 1–3, for a definitive account.

ported a union bill in 1925, and the group's overall stance in the 1920s was to tell the government to leave business alone, rather than to protect or regulate it.[39]

The depression crisis did not, however, lead business groups to surrender autonomy on all fronts at once. Resistance to tax increases and the nationalization of strategic industries remained vociferous until the late 1930s, but the crisis clearly generated a new uncertainty among small businessmen. They now wanted the state to ensure access to capital, to protect small retail shops from department stores, and to protect manufacturers from radical labor.[40] A fundamental shift in the stance of business vis-à-vis the state in economic and social issues had begun.

Parallel and concurrently, key elements in the bureaucracy were changing their stance toward business. In particular, the social and economic upheaval of the depression stirred the "economic bureaucrats" who would play such a major role in structuring and mobilizing the economy under the wartime regime to advocate a more activist state role.[41] In 1930, Yoshino Shinji, one of the most important of the economic bureaucrats, issued a call "to offer order and control to small and medium industry through activation of state authority."[42] His reasoning is critical: not only did the small and medium-sized sector account for half of Japan's export earnings; in addition, it constituted the middle class that stabilized society by mediating between capital and labor, and it prevented social conflict "as in Europe" by offering the outlet of social mobility to workers, who often became small owners.[43] Thus, in Yoshino's vision, the policy of economic rationalization was to serve a social goal as well.[44]

The new business conception of the labor problem came as part of an unprecedented half-year campaign against the Minseitō's labor union bill of 1931. Should we therefore discount it as inflated political rhetoric? I think not. Consider the business community's very different response to Home Ministry draft legislation of just three years earlier,

39. Tōkyō jitsugyō rengōkai, 70 nen shi (Tokyo: Tōkyō jitsugyō rengō kai, 1975), pp. 136–39.

40. See ibid., pp. 120–22, on the call for a government bank for small business; Eguchi, Toshi shoburujoa, pp. 448–64, on department stores.

41. See Chalmers Johnson, MITI and the Japanese Miracle: The Growth of Industrial Policy (Stanford: Stanford University Press, 1982), chs. 3 and 4 on Yoshino Shinji and the economic bureaucrats.

42. Yoshino Shinji, Wa ga kuni no gōrika (Tokyo: Nihon hyōronsha, 1930), p. 203.

43. Ibid., pp. 149, 200–201.

44. Ibid., p. 265.

which in fact had been more favorable to labor. Then the rhetoric of those opposed was restrained, and a significant minority opinion among organized business groups had favored legal recognition of unions. For most of the 1920s, opponents of the union law had rejected it, not in principle, but rather because the time for this step had not yet arrived. By contrast, in 1930 and 1931 a more typical claim was that recognition of unions would lead to revolutionary working-class action.[45] The explanation for the change lies in the new atmosphere of fear that gripped owners and managers trying to stave off bankruptcy and cope with labor militance even among women and men in small companies.

This crisis of confidence on the part of the urban business class extended well beyond discussion of labor legislation. It also manifested itself as a loss of confidence in the established political parties, and even in some cases in the parliamentary structure as a whole. The radical activist Asō Hisashi commented in 1931 that the urban business class had turned against the bourgeois parties owing to the economic crisis. In fact, several new political parties of small urban tradesmen and manufacturers enjoyed brief electoral success in Tokyo, Yokohama, and Osaka.[46]

These groups lambasted the ruling Minseitō as well as the Seiyūkai as "running dogs of big capital" who had failed their constitutional duty to represent the masses.[47] The provocatively titled Imperial Middle Class Federated Alliance claimed "the established parties have betrayed us, becoming the political servants [goyōtō] of the capitalist cliques and trampling the middle class of commercial, industrial, and agricultural producers."[48] The "masses" here referred to a heretofore silent middle class that "supported the state financially and defended the country resolutely," only to bear the brunt of the depression and a surge of "extreme labor disputes."[49] These groups called for a "revolution in economic thought" in which new state policy and support would ensure the "prosperity of the mainstay class" of taxpayers, producers,

45. See Nishinarita Yutaka, "Ryōdaisenkanki rōdō kumiai hōan no shiteki kōsatsu," *Hitotsubashi kenkyū nenpō: keizaigaku kenkyū*, no. 28 (April 1987): 79–93, on the restrained spirit of the 1925 opposition. For the tone of 1930 opposition, see Nihon kōgyō kurabu, *Wa ga kuni kokujō ni tekisezaru rōdō kumiai hō*, October 1930, p. 12.
46. Asō Hisashi, "Chūshō shōkō tō no hassei to sono shōrai," *Shakai seisaku jihō*, June 1931, p. 237.
47. Eguchi, *Toshi shoburujoa*, p. 430.
48. Ibid., pp. 431–32.
49. Ibid., pp. 418–19.

and exporters. This class in turn would save Japan from "a bloody war of labor and capital."[50]

These parties collapsed in the wake of the Manchurian Incident and economic recovery. Even so, they helped dissolve imperial democracy as a structure of rule. Although they called for constitutional government that represented the will of the masses (now interpreted as the middle class against the rich *and* the poor) and reconciled this will with the imperial will, they denied that the bourgeois parties were fit to play this role. They turned a vociferous, activist portion of the bourgeois party constituency against the parties at a turning point in the history of parliamentary rule.

RIGHT-WING MOBILIZATION AND RHETORIC

In the earliest days of the movement for imperial democracy, around the turn of the century, some activists had eschewed calls for democracy entirely and promoted a political vision centered solely on the fortunes of emperor and empire. One of the most famous was Uchida Ryōhei, founder of the Black River Society, who pushed consistently for four decades for expansion on the mainland and reform at home to bolster patriarchy and the glory of imperial rule. He attacked both the weakness of the oligarchs and the democratic ideas of party leaders and liberals. But probably the most influential right-wing thinker was Kita Ikki. In 1919 he articulated his basic stance in *A Plan for the Reorganization of Japan*, written independently of, but concurrently with, the earliest European fascist thinking, and bearing striking resemblance to it.[51] Kita rejected class struggle at home, but transposed it abroad; Japan was an "international proletarian with the right to go to war and seize their [Anglo-American] monopolies in the name of justice."[52] At home, he sought a revolution to be realized by a vanguard of young military officers and civilians, who would seize power, suspend the constitution, and remake the political structure to unite the emperor and the people. These leaders would also reorder the economy, honoring private prop-

50. Ibid., pp. 438–39.
51. For summaries of Kita's thought, see George M. Wilson, *Radical Nationalist in Japan: Kita Ikki, 1883–1937* (Cambridge, Mass.: Harvard University Press, 1969), ch. 4; Itō Takashi, *Taishō ki kakushin ha no seiritsu* (Tokyo: Hanawa shobō, 1978), pp. 196–226; Kobayashi Hideo, *Shōwa fuashisuto no gunzō* (Tokyo: Azekura shobō, 1984), pp. 32–69.
52. Wilson, *Radical Nationalist*, p. 82. For one survey of comparable European fascist ideas, Anthony J. Joes, *Fascism in the Contemporary World: Ideology, Evolution, Resurgence* (Boulder, Colo.: Westview Press, 1978), esp. p. 53 on Corradini's notion of Italy as a "proletarian nation" and the impact of this idea on Mussolini.

erty but redistributing wealth and managing growth through a set of "production ministries." Kita would have returned land to tenant farmers and shared profit with factory workers, but he insisted that women remain "mothers and wives of the people [*kokumin*]."

In the 1920s dozens of organizations sprang up devoted to some measure of Kita's program of emperor-centered, antiparty reform at home and to expansion abroad, and opposed as well to the class-based ideology of the labor and tenant movements.[53] Throughout the decade, these groups generated a sustained rhetorical attack on imperial democracy. Most Japanese historians see them as progenitors of Japanese fascism. They drew considerable support from the military, in some cases from top brass such as Army Ministers Araki Sadao (Nogi Society) and Ugaki Kazunari (Kokuhonsha), or Admiral, later Prime Minister, Saitō Makoto (Kokuhonsha), in other cases from clandestine groups of young officers and civilians.

During the depression, numerous right radicals leaped from talk to action. In a shocking series of attacks in 1930 and 1932 they assassinated several venerable superintendants of the imperial democratic order: Minseitō Prime Minister Hamaguchi Osachi (November 1930), former Finance Minister Inoue Junnosuke (February 1932), Mitsui zaibatsu chief Dan Takuma (March 1932), and Seiyūkai Prime Minister Inukai Tsuyoshi (May 1932). In addition, in March and October 1931, young military officers miscarried plots for coups d'état that had at least tacit approval from top officers. They justified their acts with a radical critique of the parties and the capitalist elite, seen as standing between the wills of emperor and people. In this, they echoed party leaders of 1905 through World War I who had criticized the Meiji oligarchs and bureaucracy for the same sin. They offered no consensus on what new groups should now speak for emperor and people; some pinned their hopes on the military, others on the agricultural mainstay class of owner-farmers, others on the urban mainstays in trade and industry. Yet their actions played a significant role in dooming the imperial democratic system of the 1920s.

Western scholars who reject the "fascist" label for these groups stress their failure to build an organized mass base.[54] Japan's radical national-

---

53. For a catalog of those in existence as of 1932, see *NRN* (1932), pp. 800–815. Annual editions of *NRN* detail these "antisocialist" movements throughout the 1920s and 1930s.
54. Gregory J. Kasza, "Fascism from Below? A Comparative Perspective on the Japanese Right, 1931–1936," *Journal of Contemporary History*, no. 19 (1984): 618–20.

ists created study groups, academies, and associations with members nationwide, but no fascist party ever won even modest electoral support. This argument is true, as far as it goes, but it does not fully appreciate the dynamics of the collapse of imperial democracy.

Although its electoral impact was small, a significant right-wing grass-roots movement that repudiated the democratic parliamentary structures of the 1920s did arise among working people. By the early 1930s thousands of workers had joined so-called "Japanist" or "national socialist" unions that echoed the ideas of young officers and fractious civilian rightists. The majority of organized workers still supported existing social democratic or revolutionary unions, but like the splinter parties of the petit bourgeois business class, whose ideas were similar, these "anti-union unions" exerted a key impact during the watershed era of the late 1920s and early 1930s.[55] They destroyed revolutionary or social democratic labor unions at a number of key workplaces. Between 1931 and 1935 several prominent mainstream union leaders themselves converted to "Japanist" or "national socialist" programs, throwing their organizations into disarray. This debilitated the union movement at the critical juncture when the government was rethinking its liberal labor policy, when economic recovery offered workers renewed bargaining power, and when support for parliament, party rule, and liberal democratic solutions to national problems was weakening throughout society. The Japanist unions, in particular, received support from managers desperate to retake control of their work forces, and they also attracted the social bureaucrats groping for a new social policy after the decisive defeat of the union bill in 1931.

The Ishikawajima shipyard was home to the first stirring of the Japanist union movement. By the mid 1920s its militant Kōrō union was one of the strongest unions on the left wing of the labor movement, but in 1924 a skilled machinist and foreman, Kamino Shinichi, led a portentous challenge to Kōrō that quickly drew attention and support from both Ishikawajima's managers and the state. After an early flirtation with socialism, Kamino (in his retelling) had become an ardent nationalist in 1920 upon viewing firsthand the discrimination of the white colonialists against the Chinese in Shanghai. His ideological and political trajectory toward "Japanism," as he came to call it, began with

---

55. For a contemporary government recognition of this impact, see Home Ministry, Police Bureau, Security Section, "Rōdō undō narabi rōdō sōgi no jōkyō oyobi kore ga torishimari taisaku." Riku-kaigun monjo, reel 205, item 1434.

a concern to carve out a place for the Japanese empire, as Kita's international proletarian, in competition with the Anglo-American powers. He hoped to improve the lives of workers by identifying their fortunes with those of empire and emperor.[56]

In 1924 Kamino founded the sixth factory-based unit of a national organization called the Nogi Society, established in 1915 with strong military backing, and hitherto active mainly in the countryside.[57] The group took its name from the renowned General Nogi, who observed feudal custom by committing suicide in 1912 to follow his lord, the Meiji emperor, in death. The society preached the need for a Nogi-esque spirit among common Japanese of loyalty to the emperor and national polity (kokutai). In the factory this was to be a nonunion spirit appropriate to "men of industry." Araki Sadao, later army minister, was among the prominent military men who spoke to meetings of the Ishikawajima group. By mid 1926 the society had drawn a significant minority of support away from Kōrō, but Kamino felt he needed a more powerful counterforce to root out socialism among the workers. He founded the Jikyōkai labor union with company support in late 1926, with Nogi adherents at its core. Three hundred Kōrō members stormed the Jikyōkai founding ceremony in one of several violent clashes between the two groups. With strong company support, it took less than a year for the Jikyōkai to claim 1,500 members, far more than the shrinking Kōrō group.

In the late 1920s similar clashes took place at scattered factories between communist or social democratic unions and such anti-union groups calling on workers to abandon class struggle for a greater national struggle. The Jikyōkai did not limit membership to Ishikawajima workers, and when it accepted the dismissal of 550 employees at Ishikawajima in 1930, it set up a "job exchange" through which dismissed members were sent to replace workers fired in nearby strikes. With this tactic, the Jikyōkai founded locals in a number of factories in the Nankatsu area.[58]

One such factory was a major Nankatsu machine-maker, Sumidagawa Ironworks, which employed about 450 men in the late 1920s and

56. See Gordon, *Evolution of the Relations*, pp. 225–30, for details on Ishikawajima case.

57. Other early factory units were at Japan Steel in Muroran, Hokkaidō (four units founded in 1921), and the Tokyo Arsenal (one unit, 1923, in the precision machine shop). See *Nogi kō no jigyō genkyō*, October 1924, pp. 8–13.

58. Kakeya Saihei, "Rōdō undō ni okeru fuashizumu no tanshoteki keisei," *Ritsumeikan bungaku*, no. 277 (July 1968): 597–98.

was a stronghold of the Sōdōmei Metalworkers' Union. In 1928, after several bitter disputes, the company sponsored a new union to challenge the Sōdōmei union. By about 1930 this group had joined forces with Kamino and had ousted the Sōdōmei from the factory.[59] Likewise, just to the north of Nankatsu at Tokyo Kentetsu, a manufacturer of sheet metal with 700 employees, a fierce eight-month dispute over dismissals in 1931 offered an opening to the Jikyōkai. A group of workers unhappy with the Kantō Metalworkers' Union's confrontational tactics gained Jikyōkai assistance in reaching a separate peace with management. The company closed down, changed its name, and reopened in early 1932 with just 240 workers, members of a new "Japanist union" devoted to the nation and the welfare of labor. By the spring of 1932, the union had repeated this tactic at a neighboring engineering factory as well.[60]

By the early 1930s these labor organizations constituted one small, but growing, network of local rightist activity in Tokyo. Fervently anticommunist, they rejected the purportedly destructive spirit of class struggle. The heart of Kamino's message was a call to replace disputes and polarization with a spirit of sacrifice, national loyalty, and what he called "fusion." Japanese workers, he asserted, "must work for the sake of the nation and abandon concepts of labor and capital."[61] He distinguished "labor-capital fusion" (yūgō) from the ideology of "cooperation" (kyōchō). The cooperative vision of factory council supporters in business, union bill advocates in the government, and moderates in the labor movement, he said, assumed "a prior conflict that may reemerge at any time. Fusion asserts a fundamental unity of purpose. Workers, technicians, and capitalists are of one mind and spirit, fused in an inseparable solidarity."[62]

The "Japanist" vision thus affirmed the legitimacy of capitalist enterprise, so long as capital, with labor, focused on national glory. These "unions" were part of what some have labeled "the spiritual right," which attacked party corruption, labor selfishness, democracy, and materialism run wild. Their critical vision of the status quo called for a

59. See Aoki Kōji, Nihon rōdō undō shi nenpyō (Tokyo: Shinseisha, 1968), pp. 616, 678, 701, and 734, on 1925–26 disputes, and Shakai undō ōrai, March 1933, p. 89, and March 1934, pp. 70–71, on the new union.
60. Shakai undō ōrai, July 1931, pp. 67–68, February 1932, p. 40, December 1932, pp. 45–47; Rōdō jidai, January 15, 1932, p. 3, November 20, 1932, p. 4.
61. Rōdō jidai, July 15, 1930, pp. 6–8.
62. Kamino Shinichi, Nihonshugi rōdō undō no shinzui (Tokyo: Ajia kyōkai shuppanbu, 1933), p. 131.

radical recreation of community using traditional symbols as rallying points, but it nonetheless accepted existing institutions such as the private corporation. It attracted and was shaped not only by civilian rightists, such as Yasuoka Masahiro (see below), but by leading figures in the military, the civil bureaucracy, and business.

Several key bureaucrats in the Home Ministry, charged with handling the "social problems" of the interwar era, were intrigued by these groups well before the defeat of the union bill in 1931. The meeting place for bureaucrats, civilian rightists, and Kamino's organization was the Golden Pheasant Academy, a right-wing training center and incipient political force founded by Yasuoka Masahiro in 1927. Three men who dominated the Home Ministry in the 1930s, Matsumoto Gaku, Gotō Fumio, and Yoshida Shigeru, served as advisors to the school. Machida Tatsujirō of the Kyōchōkai was also an advisor. The academy applauded Kamino Shinichi's endeavors at Ishikawajima and encouraged him to organize similar unions elsewhere. For such men, the Japanist unions provided an enticing alternative to the ministry's program of social liberalism. They offered ideas and mass organizations that defended the social and economic order of imperial Japan while replacing liberal, democratic political forms with an emperor-centered focus on hierarchy, sacrifice, and the fusion of diverse functional interests.[63]

Another network of rightist groups stressed nativism, patriarchy, empire, and emperor in similar fashion, but it differed in its more radical anticapitalism. In Nankatsu, right-wing political activists founded several local units of a group launched in 1929, called the Radical Patriotic Labor Federation.[64] It published a newspaper whose title can loosely be translated as "The People Aroused" (Kōmin shinbun). Details on membership are sketchy, but between 1929 and 1931 the federation held a number of rallies in Nankatsu, founded a "national socialist" printers' union in Tokyo, and played a role in several labor disputes in Nankatsu.[65] In January 1932 this group, with nineteen other organizations on the right, joined the recently founded Greater Japan Production Party (Dai Nihon seisantō), led by the still-active

63. Odabe Yūji, "Nihon fuashizumu no keisei to shinkanryō," in Nihon fuashizumu: kokka to shakai, ed. Nihon gendaishi kenkyū kai (Tokyo: Ōtsuki shoten, 1981), pp. 85–87.

64. Tsukui Tatsuo, Watakushi no Shōwa shi (Tokyo: Sōgensha, 1958), pp. 52–55.

65. Kōmin shinbun, August 1, 1931, p. 4, October 1, 1931, p. 2, December 5, 1931, p. 2; Tsukui, Shōwa shi, p. 52.

Uchida Ryōhei, patriarch of right-wing activists. Supporters of the Production Party generally sought more extensive domestic reform than the Japanists. Part of what historians term the "control" or "reform" element of the Japanese right wing, they supported bureaucratic control of the economy both to solve social problems and to focus industrial enterprise on national, primarily military, goals.[66]

This stance differed from that of the Japanists, but the two camps agreed on fundamental themes. All right-wing groups abhorred class struggle, were fiercely anticommunist, attacked the parties as corrupt, and castigated either "bad capitalists" or capitalism itself for exploiting the people. They rejected liberalism and democracy as the ideologies of a decadent, materialist West. Their solution to the dead end of the depression, social conflict, and international tension was to eliminate all intermediate groups standing between the emperor and the "national masses" and build a new order premised on "unity of emperor and subject."[67]

Left unresolved by the panicky lobbying of small businessmen and the fierce critiques of these rightists was the political heart of the matter: if not the bourgeois parties, and certainly not the proletarian parties and unions, what institutions would carry out the unified will of emperor and subject? Both bureaucrats and military men, unhappy with their relative eclipse by the parties in the 1920s, had ideas about possible answers.

THE END OF IMPERIAL DEMOCRATIC RULE

The turmoil in Nankatsu was part of a generalized crisis in which the elite superintendents of the political order such as Prince Saionji presided over, and the party leaders themselves accepted, the gradual transformation of imperial democracy into a Japanese species of fascist rule.

The crisis had a major international component. A rising tide of nationalism in China promoted a sense of embattlement throughout the army, while the contentious process and disappointing outcome of naval arms negotiations with the United States and Britain soured

66. Production party platform in *Kokkashugi dantai*, ed. Zenkoku sangyō dantai rengō (Tokyo: Zenkoku sangyō dantai rengō, 1932), pp. 37–44.
67. This language, reflecting the core right-wing platform, is from yet another group, the Patriotic Labor Party, founded on February 11, 1930, in Tokyo. Zensanren, *Kokkashugi*, p. 28.

many in the navy on the prospects for big power cooperation. The Kwangtung Army took matters into its own hands with the Manchurian Incident of September 1931. The Minseitō cabinet was unable to restrain the army, and by March 1932 Japan had occupied Manchuria and created the puppet state of Manchukuo. The takeover of Manchuria was arguably Japan's most significant step toward military rule at home and world war abroad; many Japanese historians understandably date the "Fifteen Years' War" from September 1931.

The key point is that the domestic crisis described in this chapter unfolded parallel to the international crisis. One was not a cause of the other; rather, each made the other more acute. In the minds of elite bureaucrats, military leaders, major capitalists and small owners, as well as right-wing activists and labor unionists, the problems in Manchuria and at home were linked inextricably, as were the solutions. We must view the overall crisis in holistic fashion, as contemporaries such as the key army leader Suzuki Teiichi, recalled it: "One cannot distinguish domestic and foreign policies. The two evolve influencing each other. Without attention to the external [problem], the internal [society] will not cohere. If you ignore the external, you may think you can unify domestically, but you cannot."[68] International and domestic crisis combined, not merely to lead to a shift in the balance of elites, but to produce a basic change in the way Japan was ruled, and in how that rule was conceived.[69]

On the surface the Diet session of the winter of 1931 was the high tide of prewar liberalism. The ruling Minseitō Party, with significant bureaucratic support, proposed an unprecedented legislative package: a bill to recognize labor unions, a tenant bill to define a set of economic and political rights for tenant farmers, a bill of rights for women that permitted them to vote in local elections and hold local office.[70] If approved, these measures would dramatically have extended the legiti-

68. Nihon kindai shiryō kenkyū kai, ed., "Suzuki Teiichi shi danwa sokkiroku," 1971, p. 325. Mimeograph interview transcript held at Tokyo University Library.

69. Gregory J. Kasza, *The State and Mass Media in Japan, 1918–1945* (Berkeley: University of California Press, 1988), p. 167.

70. On labor, see Sheldon Garon, *The State and Labor in Modern Japan* (Berkeley: University of California Press, 1987), ch. 5. On tenants, see Miyazaki Takasugi, "Taisho demokurashii ki no nōson to seitō (3)" in *Kokka gakkai zasshi* 93, nos. 11–12 (November–December 1980): 111–16. On female suffrage, see Sharon H. Nolte, "Women's Rights and Society's Needs: Japan's 1931 Suffrage Bill," *Comparative Studies in Society and History* 24, no. 4 (October 1986): 690–714.

mate social base of imperial democracy. Businessmen, in particular, carried out an extraordinarily energetic nationwide campaign to defeat the union bill, and while the Lower House in fact passed all three bills despite this pressure, the House of Peers rejected them all.[71] The prewar Diet never again considered granting these rights to women, tenant farmers, or unions.

The surface appearance of near victory for a liberal democratic program is deceiving. The labor bill of 1931 was already a major retreat from more liberal versions of the 1920s; the suffrage bill offered such limited gains that most women's groups opposed it. Minseitō Home Minister Adachi still insisted in 1930 that only a union law could resolve social problems, but by year's end, in the wake of the Tōyō Muslin and other upheavals, the Hamaguchi cabinet decided to weaken the bill given the "current situation" of depression, disputes, and business opposition.[72]

The year 1931 was thus a watershed in both domestic and foreign policy. The domestic shift came first. Although it would be five years before a coherent new rationale and program to solve the ongoing "labor problem" produced the program for a Nazi-style patriotic labor front, the turn to a new policy informed by "Japanist" social thought began in the spring of 1931, five months before the Manchurian Incident. Within the Home Ministry, the social bureaucrats shifted their position on the means to the end of social order and harmony immediately after the union bill was defeated. Matsumoto Gaku, a bureaucrat with experience mainly in the police and local government, succeeded Yoshida Shigeru as Social Bureau chief. As he later recalled those days:

> Above all, the industrial world had assembled that great a collection of big shots and crushed [the bill], and so for the officials to chase after them asking, "How about this?" "Or this?" would be poor policy. We had to cool the fever down. I couldn't think of resubmitting Yoshida's bill with a few small changes. I decided to move away from the whole idea of legislation and, as [a solution to] the more fundamental problem, promote what we called a "movement for industrial peace." That is, *the idea of fusion of labor and capital rather than mutual cooperation.*[73]

71. Garon, *State and Labor*, pp. 177–84. Nishinarita, "Ryōdaisenkanki no rōdō kumiai hōan," pp. 118–28.
72. Nishinarita, "Ryōdaisenkanki no rōdō kumiai hōan," pp. 106, 109, 123.
73. Naiseishi kenkyūkai, ed., "Matsumoto Gaku shi danwa sokki roku, 1963" 2:69. Emphasis added. Mimeograph interview transcript held at Tokyo University Library.

By the spring of 1932 the ministry had gone public with a new "plan for industrial peace" and dismissed the union bill as "too theoretical and unbalanced."[74]

A few weeks later, on May 15, 1932, an act of right-wing terror ended the era of rule by imperial democrats. A group of young naval officers assassinated Inukai Tsuyoshi, the 76-year-old prime minister and Seiyūkai Party president. The conspirators had hoped their acts would lead to imposition of martial law and policies of "national renovation," but simultaneous attacks on the Mitsubishi Bank, the Seiyūkai headquarters, the home minister's residence, and six power-generating stations caused little damage, and these grand ambitions were foiled. Even so, the impact of their actions was profound. Although the Seiyūkai retained its Diet majority after the assassination, the military refused to allow it to form a new cabinet. On May 26, Admiral Saitō Makoto took office as prime minister of a national unity cabinet that included only five party men among its fifteen members. General Araki Sadao was retained as army minister.

Key military men explicitly connected the repudiation of party rule with the crisis of the past several years. Suzuki Teiichi was a leader of a group of officers who had been meeting regularly for several years to promote related programs of expansion in Manchuria and reform at home. A confidant of Araki's, Suzuki viewed the top civilian politicians, especially the surviving oligarch, Prince Saionji, as opponents of reform, essentially dedicated to preserving the status quo.[75] In tense negotiations between the army and Prince Saionji over the choice of a new prime minister and cabinet, Suzuki represented the military. In daily contacts over a ten-day period, Suzuki repeated his basic position: "The army will not recognize a political party cabinet." On the day after Inukai's assassination, Suzuki told Saionji's personal secretary that the next cabinet should not be a party cabinet, for "the fundamental causes [of such radical acts] are political, economic, and other social problems, and a thorough renovation is needed [to solve these problems]."[76] Suzuki's views prevailed.

---

74. *Miyako shinbun*, April 11, 1932, and *Yomiuri shinbun*, April 28, 1932, both in Kyū-kyōchōkai collection of press clippings, volume on "Social Policy, 1932–1936," Ohara Institute.

75. Itō Takashi and Sasaki Takashi, "Shōwa 8–9 nen no gunbu to 'Suzuki Teiichi nikki,'" *Shigaku zasshi* 86, no. 10 (October 1977): 83–100, on Suzuki's views and actions in this era. Suzuki survived the war. He died in 1989, aged 101.

76. "Suzuki Teiichi nikki: Shōwa 8 nen," *Shigaku zasshi* 87, no. 1 (January 1978): 93.

In the following years, Suzuki continued to advocate forceful new policies at home and abroad to eliminate "social unrest" and bolster "national defense," and a similar set of new solutions attracted others at the pinnacle of power. Even a relative moderate such as General Ugaki Kazunari echoed Suzuki's basic sense of crisis. To be sure, he criticized Araki Sadao for not resigning his post as army minister after the Inukai assassination, castigated the cowardly Seiyūkai for not insisting that its new president form the next cabinet, and wrote that although "there is a need to restrain the domination of capital, the means to this end are not the power of the sword." Yet he followed Suzuki in June 1932 by claiming that a crisis at home and abroad had been "gradually building for three years," and in his diary he repeatedly called for "renovated" foreign policy and a new political party.[77]

Ugaki's fascinating diary brings into clear focus the sense of a linkage of international and domestic crisis among the elite during the depression. Ugaki, who served as army minister in both the Seiyūkai cabinet of 1927–29 and the Minseitō cabinets of 1929–31, was arguably the army's most influential "moderate" between 1927 and 1937. Both Minseitō leaders and senior statesmen such as Saionji looked to him as a potential prime minister in the 1930s. However, radical young officers also saw Ugaki as *their* ally, and in March 1931, just as the Diet was passing judgment on the Minseitō social program, they launched an abortive coup attempt on his behalf.[78]

In 1930 and 1931 Ugaki remained committed to the defense of capital, the glory of emperor and empire, and the power of the state, but he clearly was shaken by the mounting social unrest. He consciously or unconsciously drew on the ideas of men such as Kita Ikki as he rethought his support of party rule as the means to these ends. In a formulation virtually identical to Kamino Shinichi's call to fuse the energies of labor, capital, and technicians, Ugaki continually invoked his mission to defend the nation and its social order by "preserving capital, labor, and technology."[79]

77. Ugaki Kazunari, *Ugaki Kazunari nikki* (Tokyo: Misuzu shobō, 1968), 2:848–50 entry of May 27, 1932, criticizes Araki and the Seiyūkai; 2:863–64 entry of September 7, 1932, eschews the power of the sword. For policy prescriptions of June 15 and August 21, 1932, see 2:854, 860, and passim.

78. The incident was kept from the public at the time. It seems Ugaki sent confused signals to the officers and then repudiated their plan at the last moment, but the extent of his involvement is still unclear. See Ben Ami Shillony, *Revolt in Japan: The Young Officers and the February 26, 1936 Incident* (Princeton: Princeton University Press, 1973), pp. 26–27.

79. *Ugaki Kazunari nikki* 1:749, January 6, 1930, and passim.

At the start of 1930 Ugaki lamented the power of "scoundrels who abuse and hide behind the beautiful name of freedom to poison the state and harm the social order," but his entries over the following year reveal a sophisticated appreciation of systemic crisis.[80] Ugaki did not simply pin the blame on a few radical "scoundrels" of the right or left, who might be exorcized. Much like those radicals, he blamed Japan's disorder and weakness on a capitalist system and a parliamentary democracy run amok, and his critique of capitalism was harsh. In August 1930 he observed:

> If the present situation continues, the middle class of farmers, traders, and manufacturers will collapse and be absorbed by capitalists, and the nation [*kokumin*] will be divided into small groups of rich and a proletarian mass. . . . Children of the emperor are equal and should share happiness. It is not good to leave the current favoritism of capitalists as is.[81]

As labor unrest intensified toward the end of 1930, Ugaki's concern focused squarely on labor. He lamented the self-interest that led to strikes, and he rejected the idea of a union bill as a solution. Ugaki traced the labor problem back to Japan's position "as a late-developing industrial nation" that absolutely required "cooperation and unity of labor and capital" to catch and surpass "the advanced nations." He called confrontation between the two sides "suicidal" and praised "Tokyo [*sic*] Muslin workers" who reportedly "have said they will accept wage cuts, but not if the money saved simply goes to fill bankers' pockets as the company repays loan interest. 'First, bankers and capitalists must cooperate and reduce debt interest; then we'll accept pay cuts.'"[82] He maintained that "the union law should not be introduced in these times, but the party is bound by public promises and goes ahead with it. This [inability to change with the times] is disgraceful."[83]

Ugaki is considered by historians to have been a relatively moderate voice in the military; the officers planning the 1936 coup placed him on their hit list for apparently backing down in March 1931, and in 1937 the army vetoed Saionji's plan to make him prime minister.[84] That his

---

80. Ibid. 1:747, January 2, 1930.
81. Ibid. 1:766, August 21, 1930.
82. Ibid. 2:782, December 15, 1930. Tokyo Muslin was another factory in Nankatsu, a separate company from Tōyō Muslin. Ugaki may be correct in his reference, although there was no major public protest at Tokyo Muslin at this time, and the Tōyō Muslin dispute had just ended.
83. Ibid. 2:783, December 21, 1930.
84. James B. Crowley, *Japan's Quest for Autonomy: National Security and Foreign Policy, 1930–1938* (Princeton: Princeton University Press, 1966), pp. 314–16.

program to restore balance between labor, capital, and technology, and order to society, involved radical departures from the status quo is thus all the more significant. Even this "moderate" wanted to restructure both economy and polity and embark on a newly expansive foreign policy.

To overcome "unrest and depression" Ugaki called for "control and fundamental reform of basic industrial organizations (agriculture, industry, commerce, transport, finance) for the future development of our imperial nation."[85] He was likewise intrigued by alternatives to party rule, as he reflected that "a dictator does not necessarily ignore the popular will. But he must make great efforts to understand the populace. The government is not the possession of the Seiyūkai or Minseitō; when a great crisis faces the imperial nation, we must not be restricted by a pattern of two-party opposition. Especially, in the face of various external problems, we must be united."[86]

Turning to international problems, Ugaki asserted that Japan would not rely on "defense limited to our territory" to "solve the population problem and ensure foodstuffs and outlets or markets for our products."[87] In one critical, dense passage, he explained how economic, social, and foreign problems were entwined:

> Industrial rationalization will only increase unemployment and lead to social tragedy unless accompanied by expanded markets as outlets for our goods. These markets will be won in economic competition over price and quality. But if foreign relations atrophy, the competition will be restricted. We greatly need renovation of foreign policy and rationalization of industry.[88]

That is, the rationalization programs promoted by the economic bureaucrats were supposed to make industry more productive, and in a friendly world, the more competitive output of these rationalized plants would win new foreign customers. Yet the real trading system of autumn 1930 did not strike Ugaki as open, and without expanded markets, "rationalized" industries would have to lay people off, causing intense labor conflict. Ugaki thus concluded that without a renovated— read, more aggressive—foreign policy to accompany industrial rationalization, the nation faced "social tragedy" at home.

Likewise, political reform was inextricable from the social and for-

85. *Ugaki Kazunari nikki* 1:760, July 16, 1930.
86. Ibid. 1:767, August 26, 1930.
87. Ibid. 1:758, June 10, 1930.
88. Ibid. 1:778, November 1, 1930.

eign problems, for "two-party politics can be a meaningful way to generate good policy for a wealthy, advanced nation. But a weak, poorly endowed late developer needs to seek the welfare of the people not only at home but in development abroad. This requires national unity, and two-party conflict is not welcome. A structure of one nation—one party is possible, or a great union of multiple parties."[89] Ugaki thus presented a powerful indictment of the imperial democratic structure and ideology of rule. If necessary, he would abandon democracy to preserve the empire and social order and would restructure the economy in basic ways.

Though few among Japan's rulers have left records as explicit and detailed as Ugaki or Suzuki Teiichi, the concerns of these men were informed by, and echoed in, public discourse among intellectuals and radicals of the left and right. One contributor to *Chūō kōron*, a respected forum of intellectual and elite opinion, writing just days before the Manchurian Incident, felt that the military could potentially represent the popular will and redirect concern with domestic problems abroad. Another referred to the "domestic and foreign impasse" and called for "a new political force with a critical awareness of the needs of the Japanese race." A voice for the Japanist labor unions called for a leader to inspire the masses and rebuild the relationship between emperor and people.[90] In April 1931 Ōyama Ikuo predicted an imperialist war and blasted parliament and the parties; in June he predicted "social fascism" would come when both rulers and social democratic parties turned to imperialism in the face of domestic tension.[91] And the organ of the Radical Patriotic Labor Union Federation, just before the outbreak of war in Manchuria, wanted to "use the intensified Manchurian problem as the motor for domestic reform."[92]

The crises of 1930 and 1931 at home and abroad destroyed both elite consensus and popular support for imperial democracy. By 1931 the contradictions of Japan's pursuit of empire, capitalism, and democracy through the 1920s had issued in depression, international confrontation, and intense social conflict; this in turn had rendered the

89. Ibid. 1:795–96, June 12, 1931.
90. *Chūō kōron*, October 1931, pp. 110, 132, 139.
91. Ōyama Ikuo, "Dai 59 gikai no sōkessan," *Chūō kōron*, April 1931, p. 138, and "Nihon fuashizumu e no tenbō: fuashiyoteki keikō to sono shōrai," *Chūō kōron*, June 1931, p. 123.
92. *Kōmin shinbun*, August 1, 1931, p. 1.

Minseitō vision of international unity through cooperative diplomacy and social cohesion through broadened popular rights politically untenable. A wide array of military, bureaucratic, and even some party leaders, as well as intellectuals and right-wing activists, reached similar conclusions, whether disapproving or applauding: the abandonment of democratic political rule was needed to preserve empire and social order. When the military repudiated party cabinets in 1932, it thus reflected a belief broadly held in society and among the elite that the ruling system of imperial democracy had failed; politics as usual were out of the question. As Suzuki Teiichi and Army Minister Araki Sadao agreed on the day of Inukai's assassination in 1932, Japan badly needed leaders who would implement new policies.[93]

The subsequent transformation of imperial democracy was complex; the road from Manchuria to Pearl Harbor, from Inukai to Tōjō, was twisted. Nonetheless, the Saitō cabinet marked a turning point abroad and at home: encroachment on, then invasion of, China proper; rule by military men and civilian bureaucrats; censorship and repression, first of leftists, then of liberals; corporatist restructuring of the place of labor; and mobilization of the economy for war.

93. Entry of May 15, 1932, in "Suzuki Teiichi nikki," *Shigaku zasshi*, January 1978, p. 93.

TEN

The Social Movement Transformed, 1932–35

The polarization of working-class neighborhoods such as Nankatsu was a major internal element in the depression-era crisis that brought down imperial democracy, but over the next few years, the labor movement foundered. Proletarian candidates fared worse at the polls between 1932 and 1935 than they had in the first universal manhood suffrage elections of the late 1920s. Union membership did not keep pace with the expanding work force after 1932, and disputes declined in number and intensity. Union leaders in the Sōdōmei renounced disputes and embraced a program of "industrial cooperation." Unions of all stripes stopped criticizing imperialism and began supporting Japan's mission in Asia.

Documentary sources for unions and disputes are relatively scarce, although we can detect this critical shift in labor union policy and rhetoric. Election results are easy to obtain; far more difficult is judging which elements in a party's program actually drew support in some cases, but drove it away in many others. In this chapter, I use the limited available evidence to analyze factors that damaged the fortunes and transformed the platforms of both unions and proletarian parties. As the single greatest factor was indeed the new political environment generated by the Manchurian invasion and the Inukai assassination, we must pay special attention to ways in which bureaucrats and the military promoted nationalism and the anti-union "Japanist" movement to resolve continuing social tensions.

UNIONS, DISPUTES,
AND PROLETARIAN POLITICS

While most of the industrial world was mired in depression in the early 1930s, Japanese industrial production, exports, and employment first recovered and then surged. Industrial output rose 82 percent from 1931 to 1934, and in 1937 one brilliant young economist, Arisawa Hiromi, in fact anticipated the cliché of the 1960s when he labeled this recovery a "Japanese miracle."[1] The older industrial neighborhoods of Honjo and Fukagawa became even more densely packed, as factory labor expanded 43 percent, from 28,000 men and women in 1932 to 40,000 in 1937. In Minami Katsushika County, with more room to grow, factory employment nearly doubled in these six years, from 30,000 to 58,000.[2] By the mid 1930s numerous employers were complaining of labor shortages.

In other circumstances, this quick recovery might have favored organized labor, allowing unions to press demands for better pay and "improved treatment." In fact, while the number of union members nationwide rose slightly through 1936, industry as a whole grew much faster and the organized proportion declined. In the case of the Nankatsu region precise local statistics cannot be compiled, but the general trends are clear; union membership fell in both absolute and relative terms. It appears to have fluctuated between 10,000 and 15,000 members in the various locals of the Sōdōmei, Kumiai dōmei, and other federations, roughly 15 percent of a factory work force that approached 100,000 by 1937. While still above the national average, the unionized proportion of Nankatsu workers had fallen from its peak of the late 1920s and the depression.

Dispute activity paralleled the retreat of the unions. Across Tokyo, disputes peaked in 1931 and declined sharply by 1934. In Nankatsu County, workers initiated an average of forty-seven disputes annually between 1930 and 1932, and just twenty-five on average in 1934 and 1935 (table 7.3). Although unions in Nankatsu still carried out a strong 72 percent of all actions, they led fewer disputes than before (table 7.2). Disputes were significantly shorter than during the depression; just one-fourth lasted over two weeks, compared to one-half between 1930 and

1. Arisawa Hiromi, *Nihon kōgyō tōsei ron* (Tokyo: Yūhikaku, 1937), p. 4, cited in Chalmers Johnson, *MITI and the Japanese Miracle: The Growth of Industrial Policy* (Stanford: Stanford University Press, 1982), p. 6.
2. Tōkyō-fu, ed., *Tōkyō-fu tōkei sho* (Tokyo, 1937), p. 164.

1932 (see table 7.4). And disputes affected a smaller proportion of all factories in the area (see table 7.6).

Both during and after the depression, proletarian parties also fared poorly at the polls. In the second and third national elections under universal manhood suffrage in 1930 and 1932, and in local elections of the early 1930s, the still-divided proletarian parties struggled, and in some cases they lost ground. The Diet's proletarian contingent fell from eight seats in 1928 to five in 1930 and 1932, and vote totals declined as well. In local elections across the nation in 1931, the proletarian camp elected just twelve men to prefectural assemblies, compared to twenty-eight in 1927.[3] The "delegation" of worker representatives in the Tokyo prefectural assembly stood at one man in both 1928 and 1932 elections, and the proletarian group on the Tokyo City Council fell from six in the 1929 voting to just two in 1933.

One bright spot for the labor parties was the election of Matsutani Yojirō of the Japan Masses Party to the Diet from Nankatsu (District 6) in 1930. Born in Kanazawa, but educated in Tokyo, Matsutani became a lawyer in 1914, and as a member of the Liberal Lawyers' Association in the 1920s he played an active role in various liberal and left-wing social movements. He ran a close sixth in the five-man Nankatsu district in the Diet election of 1928. In 1930 he conducted a spirited campaign, speaking at ninety-one rallies to an average of 735 attendees in the short official campaign period, and his 25,000 votes made him the fifth (and last) man elected. The centrist unions provided the heart of his labor support, as thirty-one locals joined in a variety of campaign activities, but his fifty-man election committee also included leaders of independent unions in the area.[4] The party had begun to consolidate a base (*jiban*) of electoral support grounded in non-party organizations, mainly unions. The base proved more durable than the candidate, and it was inherited by new parties created in subsequent mergers.

In 1932, his party twice renamed (now the National Labor-Farmer Masses Party), Matsutani managed to win reelection. Before the election he suddenly converted to support the military takeover of Manchuria, although this does not seem to have helped him, for his own vote total declined from 1930, as did the combined total of all proletarian candidates in the district. Proletarian party candidates fared poorly

3. Sekiguchi Yasushi, "Fukenkai senkyō no kekka," *Toshi mondai* 21, no. 5. (November 1935): 1215–43.
4. Details of Matsutani campaign and organization in "Nihon taishūtō: 1930" file, OISR.

all around Tokyo, and a postelection report of the Labor-Farmer Masses Party blamed this on "organizational chaos." In the four-man Honjo-Fukagawa District 4, Asanuma Inejirō placed a weak ninth of eleven candidates.[5]

Over the following three years, the proletarian forces continued to struggle at the polls, but did achieve significant new unity, if only occasional victories. In July 1932 the Social Masses Party (SMP) was founded through a merger of the two major proletarian parties of the center and right. This new party remained intact for the next eight years. For the first time since the 1925 suffrage reform, the proletarian movement was in a position to make significant electoral gains.[6]

In Tokyo the SMP consolidated its two inherited organizations into thirty-one party locals by 1933, with five of these in Nankatsu, Honjo, and Fukagawa. Tensions between the two sides to the merger continued for several years, and some locals were clearly more active than others, but most survived until 1940.[7] At first, electoral results were spotty. In contests for ward assemblies in 1932 and 1933, ten of twenty party candidates won seats, but in the 1933 city council race, the party elected just two of twelve candidates to the 144-seat assembly.

Nankatsu was the one area where the party made some gains in these years; eight of the party's ten ward assemblymen were from wards in Nankatsu, and the two city councilmen were Abe Shigeo in Honjo and Asanuma Inejirō in Fukagawa.[8] These victories foreshadowed a platform and a pattern of organization that would soon enjoy fair success in cities nationwide. The platform in local contests focused on ending corruption in government and protecting workers and small business-men with lower utility costs, taxes, and rent. The new organizational strategy sought to broaden the party base to small traders and white-collar workers, and to this end the party created a variety of "citizen" (*shimin*) support groups. A party report from 1934 listed eight such groups, with 2,500 members in Tokyo, formally allied to the party, and twelve "supporting" groups that had founded an "Association for the Rebirth of Small and Medium Traders and Manufacturers."[9]

5. On the Asanuma campaign, see "Rōdaitō 7: Senkyō ippan 2" file, OISR.
6. Masujima Hiroshi, Takahashi Hikohiro, and Ōno Setsuko, *Musan seitō no kenkyū* (Tokyo: Hōsei University Press, 1969), pp. 440–52, for general discussion of SMP fortunes of 1932–35.
7. Party annual reports (*hōkoku sho*), 1932–40, OISR.
8. The ward representatives numbered two in Jōtō, one in Minami Katsushika, three in Honjo, and two in Fukagawa.
9. Shakai taishū tō, *1934 nendo tōsō hōkokusho*, p. 71, OISR.

Asanuma was a pioneer who created this new type of coalition and won the first electoral victory of his long political career in 1933. In his campaign for the Fukagawa City Council, he won endorsements from at least ninety-four groups: fourteen labor unions, a "renters' mutual aid society," and a "Kōtō mutual aid society"; forty-nine informal groups of workers from individual factories, and twenty-two groups called "ward committees" or "neighborhood supporters."[10] Through such extensive mobilization, which drew from the union core but moved beyond it, Asanuma topped all candidates in the district with 37,000 votes.

One could, then, call the glass half full. Union activity was less than it had been at its peak in the late 1920s and the depression, but it remained at least as extensive and intense as in the early 1920s. The same was true of disputes, which had only declined relative to a major surge in the years just past. Organized and contentious factory labor remained a visible feature of Nankatsu's social landscape between 1932 and 1935, and it would increase its activity in 1936 and 1937. Those workers who did launch disputes fared better than they had previously; one-third of all disputes were classified by the government as worker victories. The proletarian parties were laying a base for substantial gains won between 1935 and 1937.

But this type of anticipatory focus is ultimately misleading. From 1932 to 1935 the left was on the defensive and lost much ground. The Social Masses Party's consolidation had not yet born fruit, and the labor movement failed to build upon the energies and anger expressed in previous years. While a historian has a harder time in explaining that which fails to happen than in accounting for what does occur—a surge of disputes leaves a better documentary trail than a quiet period—the labor movement's failure to thrive under positive economic conditions can be explained by a forbidding new political context. This brought to the surface organizational and intellectual tensions that had existed in the movement since its origins early in the century.

CHANGED POLITICAL CONTEXT

As the economy expanded and factories scrambled to hire new workers, large numbers of inexperienced single young men and women were hired at Nankatsu factories.[11] Would movement activists be able to

10. See campaign ad in *Shakai shinbun*, June 3, 1933, p. 4.

11. Data on age, years of experience, and marital status for workers in Nankatsu rubber, textile, metal, and shipbuilding industries in 1930, 1932, 1933, 1937 are found in *TRTJC* (1930, 1933) and *Tōkyō-fu tōkei sho* (Tokyo, 1932, 1937).

mobilize the new recruits? In Nankatsu the greatest influx of workers came in precisely those industries (metal, machine) with the richest labor movement tradition, and the economic expansion should have supported union organizers. But, in sharp contrast to the economically similar period during World War I, when a sharp growth in employment was accompanied by unprecedented labor activity, they fared poorly.

The retreat of labor and the left had basically political causes. The crisis of imperial democracy led various ruling groups to three critical initiatives: the army decided to take Manchuria, the Home Ministry retreated from its relatively liberal social policy of the 1920s, and both military and bureaucrats promoted, from above, those right-wing forces already emerging at the grass roots. Together these new departures, which gained force gradually between 1932 and 1935, put the working-class movement on the defensive and helped transform it.

THE MANCHURIAN FACTOR

For over a decade until the eve of the Manchurian Incident, virtually all proletarian parties and unions condemned imperialism. Some warned that the ruling class would embark on an "imperialist war" as a cynical strategy to survive the depression.[12] The popular reception of this message changed dramatically in the months after the invasion. Asanuma Inejirō's Diet campaign newsletter in 1932 reported that his Minseitō opponent typically spoke of Asanuma's party as "a group of traitors. ... And there are two or three in this hall." A plant (according to the newsletter) would then stir up the crowd by shouting, "Tell us where!" Even Asanuma's social democratic opponent consistently denounced him as a "traitor" [literally, non-*kokumin*] who cared nothing for the 130,000 lives and two billion yen sacrificed in Manchuria.[13] The attacks apparently worked. Asanuma finished ninth of eleven candidates. In an internal report assessing the poor showing of proletarian forces in 1932, one activist in Nankatsu offered a typical postmortem: war fever hurt badly, and the Labor-Farmer Masses Party had gained almost no support outside its few areas of organized strength.[14]

The police and the army were extremely sensitive to all criticism of

---

12. For example, the December 1930 platform of Zenkoku rōnō taishū tō, in "Zen taishū dai 2 kai gian," Kyū-kyōchōkai, *Zenkoku rōnō taishū tō*, vol. 19C, OISR.

13. "Senkyo Nyūsu," February 7 and 19, 1932, Kyū-kyōchōkai, *Zenkoku rōnō taishū tō*, vol. 19C, OISR.

14. Komatsubara Kōtarō, "Sōsenkyo sen hōkokusho," February 20, 1932, in *Rōdaitō*, vol. 20: Tokyo (2), documents of the Rōnō taishū tō, OISR.

the military and Japan's Manchurian policy. In 1931 police halted over
5 percent of *all* speeches at political rallies in Tokyo, the second highest
rate of suppression ever recorded, before or since.[15] The statistics do
not break this down by month or give reasons, but increased sensitivity
to even muted attacks on foreign policy was certainly important. The
army carried out its own investigations of 262 antiwar incidents between September 1931 and the election in February 1932. Most were
just cases of antiwar postering and leafleting.[16] The Manchurian offensive thus led to intensified surveillance and repression and brought on a
new mood of popular nationalism, changes that together isolated and
pressured the labor and proletarian party movements.

THE JAPANIST OFFENSIVE

The Manchurian Incident offered a major boost to the scattered
"Japanist" labor unions that had emerged between 1926 and the depression. From 1932 to 1935, in at least fifteen Tokyo factories, newly
formed Japanist groups destroyed and replaced mainstream unions,
usually those of the Sōdōmei. Five of these companies were in Nankatsu, including the Sumidagawa Ironworks described above. In each case
the process was similar. At Tokyo Wire Rope in 1932 (100 employees),
Japan Casting in 1933 (over 200 employees), and Nasu Aluminum in
1934 (250 employees), groups of workers joined to oppose what they
called the uncooperative, unpatriotic radicalism of the existing Sōdōmei
union. They criticized the Sōdōmei as selfish, greedy, and dominated by
bosses who made promises but delivered nothing. The Japanists promised to work together with patriotic owners to raise production for the
sake of the nation, overcome a selfish spirit of class struggle, and yet
gradually improve working conditions. In each case the Sōdōmei resisted, and the two groups fought with bricks or metal rods. The companies and Japanist groups condemned "communist" union radicals
and agreed to work together. Eventually the Sōdōmei workers switched
sides, quit, or were fired, and the new unions triumphed.[17]

Similar confrontations took place in centers of union strength

15. Keishichō, *Keishichō tōkei sho* (1931), p. 117. Volumes from 1922–37 offer
comparable data. The highest rate came in 1927, the peak time of Hyōgikai action.
16. "Manshū jiken to shakai undō," Rikugunshō, *Chōsa gahō*, no. 30 (February
1932), in *Shiryō: Nihon gendai shi shiryō* (Tokyo: Ōtsuki shoten, 1983), 8:174.
17. On Tokyo Wire Rope, see *Rōdō jidai*, September 20, 1932, p. 2; *Shakai undō
ōrai*, December 1932, pp. 51–53. On Japan Casting, see *Shakai undō ōrai*, September
1933, pp. 43–47, November 1933, pp. 62–66; *Nihon sangyō rōdō*, July 1934, p. 2. On
Nasu Aluminum, see *Nihon sangyō rōdō*, October 1934, p. 6.

nationwide. Japanist unions attacked Marxism, class struggle, materialism, and weak foreign policy toward the West, the Chinese, and the Soviet Union; they put themselves forward as the true foundation of national strength, and they won support among metalcasters in Kawaguchi, transport workers in Osaka, Kobe, Yokohama, and Nagoya, dock workers and shipbuilders in Yokohama, and steelworkers in Kyūshū.[18] The Tokyo-area groups closest to Kamino Shinichi and the Jikyōkai, including those in Nankatsu, formed a Japan Industrial Labor Club with fourteen member unions and 12,000 members in 1933, and comparable efforts took place elsewhere to federate scattered rightist unions. In early 1933 Japanist forces organized a National Defense Fund Labor Association that drew support from thousands of workers not part of the movement. At factories throughout the nation in the winter of 1933, an estimated 80,000 union workers and 20,000 nonunion employees agreed to work on a Sunday or holiday and donate that day's wages to the army's National Defense Fund Drive.[19]

While the anger, fear, and nationalism of workers who joined these groups appear to have been genuine, and the street-fighting that invariably accompanied their formation was probably not instigated by the authorities, in virtually all cases, including the earliest beginnings at Ishikawajima in 1926, highly placed men aided the Japanist movement. Some Japanist leaders such as Kamino Shinichi did emerge from within the factory, but elite promotion was an inseparable part of their story. A diverse array of bureaucrats, civilian rightists, military men, and businessmen offered both open and clandestine support to the Japanist right. This support was not yet official government policy, for between 1932 and 1935 the ministry publicly promoted a program of "industrial peace" that recognized a role for mainstream unions, but behind the scenes two divergent schools of thought struggled to control social policy.[20]

A Home Ministry old guard resisted the Japanist wave and continued

18. *NRN* (1936), pp. 459–71, lists all Japanist unions as of 1935.

19. The army began this campaign soon after the Manchurian Incident to raise money for fighter planes from the general public. By September 1932 it had purchased fifty airplanes with contributions of six million yen primarily from individuals. See Awaya Kentarō, "Fuashoka to minshū ishiki," in *Taikei Nihon gendai shi (1): Nihon fuashizumu no keisei* (Tokyo: Nihon Hyōronsha, 1978), pp. 275–77.

20. Nishinarita Yutaka, "Manshū jihenki no rōshi kankei," in *Hitotsubashi daigaku kenkyū nenpō: keizai gaku kenkyū*, no. 26 (January 1985): 284–87, 309–11, elaborates on this clash. See also Sheldon Garon, *The State and Labor in Modern Japan* (Berkeley: University of California Press, 1987), pp. 198–208.

to encourage, or at least tolerate, moderate unions as a source of social stability. A Social Bureau veteran, Kitaoka Juitsu, together with the chief labor mediator for the Tokyo police, Ōtsubo Yasuo, represented this position in a spirited debate published in late 1933 in the chief journal of the Japanist movement. Both men exuded confidence and calm: if a military crisis arose, labor and capital would join forces out of patriotic spirit. Kitaoka doubted in any case that war was imminent and found the presence of 2,300 communists in Japan (the number arrested in a recent crackdown on the underground communist union Zenkyō) no cause for alarm. Kitaoka did comment that selfish capitalists impeded effective social policy, and Ōtsubo wanted greater police power to force mediation, but both men wanted to limit state involvement. They believed existing procedures allowed organized labor and capital to iron out most conflicts on their own.[21]

Until 1935 Home Ministry practice tended to reflect the spirit of these remarks. The ministry pressured managers in smaller, legally exempted factories to "regularize" labor relations by respecting the Factory Law. It promoted mutual restraint and cooperation between unions and management, encouraging both sides to create more factory councils and sign collective bargaining contracts. It placed labor representatives on advisory councils (*shingikai*) to the ministry on unemployment policy and health insurance.[22] And it found an important segment of the labor movement, centered on the Sōdōmei, eager to cooperate.[23]

The position of the Japanist faction differed sharply. Suzuki Teiichi spoke for this group, and for the army, in his capacity as military press attaché in the 1933 debate with Kitaoka and Ōtsubo. He criticized zaibatsu capital for its amoral pursuit of profit: the zaibatsu even sold cement to the Soviet Union over military objections! He feared an "unthinkable" outcome if the working class maintained a spirit of selfish gain, class struggle, and pacifism in time of national emergency. To prevent this, he called for two initiatives, one representing the right wing's "spiritual" impulse, the other its "control" inclination. Both of these were gradually carried out. On one hand, he felt organs of education and the media should use moral suasion to ensure social order and popular loyalty to the state. At the same time, he wanted the state to

21. *Shakai undō ōrai*, November 1933, pp. 10–11; April 1933, pp. 39–40.

22. Andrew Gordon, "Business and Bureaucrats on Labor," in *Managing Industrial Enterprise: Cases from Japan's Prewar Experience*, ed. William D. Wray, (Cambridge, Mass.: Harvard University Council on East Asian Studies, 1989), pp. 66, 69.

23. Garon, *State and Labor*, pp. 198–200. Hayashi Hiroshi, "Nihon fuashizumu ki ni okeru naimushō no rōdō seisaku," *Hisutoria*, no. 102 (March 1984): 3.

allocate labor to industry in rational fashion through a mobilization law.[24]

Suzuki's public stance reflected the ongoing concern with "domestic unrest" of Prime Minister Saitō and his cabinet, a concern bordering on obsession. Suzuki's diary from 1933 to 1934 notes numerous lengthy discussions on the subject with Army Minister Araki, as well as with the ministers of finance, foreign affairs, and agriculture, and also reports on the deliberations at several cabinet meetings. It records a consistent military chorus at such meetings, echoed by reform-oriented bureaucrats in the Home Ministry such as Gotō Fumio: "domestic unrest" was a great problem, impeding national defense; the "only solution was the benevolence of the emperor, which would evoke the loyalty of the people."[25] In February 1934 Suzuki conveyed to Saionji the military conviction that party rule remained out of the question, and in a meeting with Kido Kōichi and Konoe Fumimaro he argued that "without fundamental political reform, rumors abound and social unrest increases; we must have a great leader." He told a colleague the next day that Japan needed a cabinet close to the hearts of the people.[26]

A sense of entwined domestic and international crisis thus propelled Suzuki and the segment of the bureaucratic and military elite that would eventually triumph to advocate economic and political reform at home and expansion abroad. Suzuki repeatedly told his associates that "a great war would fundamentally strengthen the people and their nationalism."[27] These men believed that radical policies to nationalize industries, control private property, and thereby eliminate popular discontent were essential to the national defense. To complete the circle, they felt that reforms by the army in Manchuria would stimulate needed domestic reforms to reduce the tremendous gap between rich and poor. This in turn would help build a "total war system."[28] At the cabinet level, they saw the labor problem as one of several related manifestations of continued, intolerable levels of what they time and again called "domestic unrest."

While Suzuki articulated this military position in occasional inter-

24. *Shakai undō ōrai*, November 1933, pp. 10–12, 13, 16.

25. Itō Takashi, "Suzuki Teiichi nikki," *Shigaku zasshi* 87, no. 1 (January 1978), entry of September 28, 1933, pp. 69–70. Identical sentiments from October 4 cabinet meeting, p. 73, November 7 meeting with the foreign minister, p. 82, and November 22 meeting with the agriculture minister, p. 84.

26. Itō Takashi, "Suzuki nikki," *Shigaku zasshi* 87, no. 4 (April 1978): 65.

27. Itō Takashi, "Suzuki nikki," *Shigaku zasshi* 87, no. 1 (January 1978): 78.

28. Nihon kindai shiryō kenkyū kai, ed., *Suzuki Teiichi shi danwa sokkiroku*, 1971, pp. 28, 339–40.

views, in his diary, and in private councils of state, a group within the Home Ministry, led by former Social Bureau Chief Matsumoto Gaku, orchestrated a grass-roots program of official and private support for the Japanist forces. As Social Bureau chief just after the defeat of the union bill, Matsumoto had decided Japan needed a policy of "labor-capital fusion based on Eastern concepts."[29] In early 1932 he had participated in founding Yasuoka Masahiro's National Mainstay Society. Under Saitō's national unity cabinet, Matsumoto became Police Bureau chief, one of the three top posts in the ministry.

His appointment, together with several others, including the choice of Gotō Fumio to run the Agriculture Ministry, signaled the emergence of the so-called new bureaucrats to positions of power. The timing of their appointments in the wake of the Manchurian takeover and coincident with the end of party cabinets, in the aftermath of the union bill failure, reveals a link between the crisis of imperial democracy in the depression, and new departures in domestic politics and social as well as foreign policy. These men were linked in their personal associations via Yasuoka's Golden Pheasant, then National Mainstay, Society; ideologically they shared a distaste for party rule and a commitment to preserving social order, international prestige, and the imperial system through state-led programs of ideological guidance and popular mobilization.[30]

Police Bureau Chief Matsumoto's concerns included, but went beyond, labor. He actively suppressed communists, and during his term arrests under the Peace Preservation Law reached a prewar peak. In February 1933 he founded a shadowy organization called the Japan Culture Federation to promote throughout society a new spirit of "Japanism": loyalty to the state, antimaterialism, anti-Westernism, and anti-Marxism. Secret funding of 250,000 yen annually from 1933 to 1937 came almost exclusively from the Mitsui, Mitsubishi, and Sumitomo zaibatsu. The federation founded and funded twenty-three "cultural organizations," whose memberships ranged from doctors and educators to youth leaders and workers, but its role as the guiding force behind these disparate groups was hidden.[31]

---

29. Naiseishi kenkyū kai, ed., *Matsumoto Gaku shi danwa sokkiroku*, 1963, vol. 2, p. 70.

30. On Matsumoto, see Otabe Yūji, "Nihon fuashizumu to shinkanryō: Matsumoto Gaku to Nihon bunka renmei," in *Nihon fuashizumu (1): Kokka to shakai*, ed. Nihon gendai shi kenkyū kai (Tokyo: Ōtsuki shoten, 1981), pp. 85–91.

31. Ibid., pp. 92–96 on funding; p. 101 on secrecy of its activities.

One offspring of the Japan Culture Federation, the Japan Labor Alliance, was conceived to promote the Japanist forces among workers. With the death of the Japanist labor movement's charismatic founder, Kamino Shinichi, in September 1933, the alliance was well placed to play this role. With an annual budget of 20,000 yen, the alliance acted as a self-styled "General Headquarters" to "solve social problems by promoting a Japanese spirit," maintaining intimate ties with bureaucrats and military men, identifying and recruiting converts from the left through lectures and study groups, and placing these cadres back in the factory to spread the Japanist message.[32] Records survive only from September 1933 through February 1934, but they offer a detailed snapshot of alliance activities.

Over these six months, the group arranged eight to twelve "factory visits" monthly. Several of the alliance regulars, including representatives from the Kyōchōkai, the Home Ministry, the right-wing press, and Japanist unions, would spend an afternoon or evening at a factory, offering a pep talk to a Japanist union or seeking to recruit a wavering group. All the Japanist groups in Nankatsu hosted at least one visit.[33] Most visits were to member unions of the Japan Industrial Labor Club, which the alliance apparently used as a front. While the alliance's own internal records make its role as sponsor clear, the published reports of these events at the time did not mention the alliance; they suggested that the unions themselves or the Japanist publication *Shakai undō ōrai* had arranged the visits.[34] Alliance leaders also met management lobbyists in Zensanren to assuage management fears of this horizontal movement. The alliance argued that its drive for labor-capital fusion and Japanist unions was needed in a time of crisis; it would bolster, not threaten, private business.[35]

The Japan Labor Alliance also campaigned for a Japan Labor Day. The issue recalls the symbolic battles waged by imperial democratic activists in the 1910s over the February 11 Founding Day. The Japanists had from the outset condemned May Day as an anti-Japanese symbol of all that was wrong with the mainstream labor movement. Kamino had long wanted to launch a counter-holiday, and he first held a

---

32. "Nihon rōdō rengō kiroku," *Shiryō: Nihon gendai shi* (Tokyo: Ōtsuki shoten, 1984), 9: 104.
33. Ibid., pp. 105–18.
34. *Shakai undō ōrai*, February 1934, pp. 68–74, March 1934, pp. 69–73, December 1934, pp. 69–71.
35. "Nihon rōdō rengō kiroku," pp. 116–17.

"Patriotic Labor Day" on April 29, 1933 (the Shōwa emperor's birthday). In January 1934, after Kamino's death, the alliance leadership settled on April 3 (the memorial day of the mythical first emperor, Jinmu), as the occasion for the first Japan Labor Day.[36] Japanist and allied groups were able to mobilize 3,000 to 10,000 adherents to celebrate this new occasion in a handful of major cities in 1934, 1935, and 1937. During this same period, nationwide attendance at May Day rallies dropped from a peak of 40,000 in 1932 to about 20,000 in 1935. The Home Ministry banned both celebrations in 1936 in the wake of the February coup attempt. It permitted only the Japan Labor Day in 1937, and in subsequent years forbad both demonstrations.[37]

By 1935 the Japan Industrial Labor Club had expanded to claim 20,000 members and had joined in a new national superfederation, the United Discussion Group of Patriotic Labor Unions, also actively promoted by the government. At the outset this umbrella group embraced fifteen federations with roughly seventy individual unions and 65,000 members in all. By the time of its first annual convention in 1935, the group boasted 80,000 members, an impressive one-fifth of all organized labor in Japan.[38]

This outward unity concealed stagnation within. The objectives of the member federations were diverse. Some sought radical action and were willing to use strikes; others relied on discussion to fuse the interests of labor and capital. Some advocated political action; others opposed all electoral politics. The platitudes in the group's platform (expand the organization, encourage industry to grow, solve international problems, promote unemployment policy) reflected the absence of a common ground upon which to build a detailed program. Beginning in 1935, articles began to appear in the Japanist press that criticized the movement's "dead end"; they complained that the movement had neither clear goals and theories nor broad popular support.[39] In Nankatsu, no new Japanist union locals were founded after 1934.

As the paltry numbers of Japan Labor Day celebrants and the concurrent decline in May Day participation suggest, the significance of the

---

36. Ibid., pp. 113–14. Awaya, "Fuashoka to minshū ishiki," p. 277.
37. *NRN*, 1936, p. 299; 1937, p. 174; 1938, p. 182; 1939, p. 151.
38. *NRN*, 1937, pp. 218–36, 264–72.
39. *Shakai undō ōrai*, August 1935, pp. 72–75, November 1935, pp. 73–77, December 1935, pp. 21–31. Miwa Yasushi, "1935 nen ni okeru Nihonshugi rōdō undō no hatten," *Nihon shi kenkyū*, no. 189 (May 1978).

right-wing union movement lay not in broad popular appeal but in its chilling and divisive impact on the mainstream of the labor movement. The Japanist movement stalled in its drive to "fuse" diverse social groups through broad popular mobilization on behalf of the emperor and the empire. Yet the Japanists and their high-powered secret backers in the bureaucracy and military exerted a critical impact in an indirect sense. Together with the politics of assassination, military expansion, and domestic repression, and the shift to non-party cabinets dominated by the military and the "new bureaucrats," they created a political context that brought to the surface latent contradictions in the ideology of the labor and proletarian party movements.

TRANSFORMATION OF THE SOCIAL MOVEMENT

In December 1931 a leaflet distributed by the Fukagawa local of the Labor-Farmer Masses Party announced a grand farewell party to send off two drafted members to serve in the "Second Imperialist War." The leaflet suggested the draftees would carry the party's struggle into the military itself: "We feel the great significance of sending two comrades from our camp into the midst of their military forces."[40] This hope proved vain. Support for empire, reaching back to the earliest days of the movement for imperial democracy, was too deeply embedded in Japan's modern tradition of popular protest to allow this or any other party of the left to sustain the stark opposition here so clearly expressed between "our" proletarian forces and "their" military.

THE PROLETARIAN PARTIES

Instead, proletarian parties first splintered when early converts repudiated anti-imperialism and class struggle and formed new parties. Those remaining then gradually shifted their position in similar fashion.

As early as 1927, Akamatsu Katsumarō of the social democratic wing of the proletarian movement had made contact with young dissident officers of the Cherry Blossom Society. Both he and the centrist leader Asō Hisashi had been involved in the abortive coup of March 1931, when they hoped to use labor unrest to spark a coup to bring radical military reformers to power.[41]

Then, just weeks after the Manchurian Incident, Akamatsu led a fac-

---

40. December 27, 1931, leaflet, "Nyūei sōbetsukai annaijo," in *Rōdaitō (19): Tōkyō (1),* documents of the Rōnō Taishū tō, OISR.
41. Masujima et al., *Musan seitō,* p. 14.

tion of seven leaders in his party on a tour of observation to Manchuria. Upon its return the group announced its apparently sudden, and certainly dramatic, choice of a "changed path to social democracy."[42] They proclaimed their respect for the "essence of the nation" (*kokutai*). They denounced the "empty" doctrine of Marxist and international working-class solidarity. They condemned class struggle within Japan. They proclaimed the state a neutral managerial entity, not an inevitable tool of bourgeois class rule.[43] They maintained that capitalism in Japan faced a dead end, and they embraced the military program to occupy Manchuria as the way to break the systemic impasse.[44] When the party's executive committee narrowly refused to adopt this as an official position, Akamatsu's group split off to form the Japan National Socialist Party.[45]

The centrist Labor-Farmer Masses Party split in similar fashion, with Nankatsu's only proletarian Diet representative, Matsutani Yojirō, at the center of the storm. With a delegation from the Diet in October 1931, he too made a trip to Manchuria. A "Top Secret" military police report quoted Matsutani, upon his return, as still "opposed to imperialist invasions that send workers to die to profit capitalists." But he had changed his view of the Manchurian action. It was "based on the imperial nation's right to self-defense, and was not a war of capitalist invasion." He went on to make the internal link crystal clear:

> We've lost two hundred thousand soldiers and spent two billion yen on military operations. We've further invested two billion yen with no policy except to profit the Chinese workers [employed in Manchuria]. Our existing political leaders have erred in failing to seek relief of domestic unemployment in Manchuria.[46]

Matsutani did not leave the party immediately, and he managed to win reelection to the Diet in February 1932 while calling for the government to send two million unemployed as emigrants to Manchuria.[47] In August of 1932, however, he was ejected from the newly formed Social Masses Party, and he subsequently led a succession of national socialist

---

42. Military police directive, "Shakai minshūtō hakenin no kōdō ni kansuru ken hōkoku," November 17, 1931, in *Shiryō: Nihon gendai shi* 8:127.

43. Masujima et al., *Musan seitō*, pp. 18–19.

44. "Manmō mondai ni kansuru shirei," November 22, 1931, in *Musan seitō shi shiryō*, ed. Suzuki Mōsaburō, p. 269.

45. Masujima et al., *Musan seitō*, p. 19.

46. Military police directive, "Rōnō taishū to daigishi Matsutani Yojirō no dōsei ni kan suru ken hōkoku," November 2, 1931, in *Shiryō: Nihon gendai shi* 8:102.

47. Army Ministry, "Manshū jihen to shakai undō," February 1932, in ibid., p. 179.

parties. As Diet candidate from Nankatsu for the Laboring Japan Party in 1936, he finished a poor tenth in an eleven-man field. He had won 19,000 votes as a new convert to the cause of social reform through empire in 1932; in 1936 he polled just 7,500 votes.[48]

Matsutani Yojirō's declining fortunes coincided with his rising nationalism, but this does not mean that Nankatsu's working-class voters turned against Japanese hegemony in Asia between 1932 and 1936. Rather, those who remained in the Social Masses Party also shifted gradually, but inexorably, in Matsutani's direction. Well before 1936 they, too, supported empire, while retaining their commitment to social and economic reform. By working with the bureaucratic and military rulers, the party hoped to serve as popular guarantor of a fundamental, top-down reform of capitalism on behalf of a "national defense state." In moving to this position, the party was able to undercut the national socialists, retain its working-class support, and move beyond it to become a potentially important political force by 1937.

The first major successes came in elections between 1935 and 1937, but a quiet, threefold transformation of the proletarian party mainstream had begun around the time of the founding of the Social Masses Party in 1932. First, between 1931 and 1933 the Social Masses Party (SMP) redefined the foreign problem from one of imperialism to one of capitalism; rather than "absolutely opposing an imperialist invasion" of Manchuria, as it did in 1931, the party opposed "capitalist domination" of Manchuria in 1932. By 1934 Asō Hisashi wrote of an alliance, consecrated by the emperor, "who embodied the spiritual faith of the race," between the proletarian forces and the "anticapitalist," "reformist" military.[49] These groups would develop Manchuria in the interests of the Manchurians, not the Japanese zaibatsu or the feudal Chinese.[50]

Second, the party abandoned the rhetoric of class struggle and returned to that of the united citizenry (shimin) or the "nation's people" (kokumin). In place of a "struggle of workers and farmers" the new party platform in 1933 called for a "broad struggle encompassing the general citizenry, the small and medium traders and manufacturers."[51]

---

48. Matsutani died in a traffic accident in 1937.
49. Masujima et al., *Musan seitō*, pp. 28, 30. The 1931 platform was that of the Labor-Farmer Masses Party, which merged with the Social Democrats to form the SMP.
50. *Shōwa 8 nendo gian*, p. 18, in "Shakai taishū tō taikai kiroku" file, OISR.
51. Masujima et al., *Musan seitō*, pp. 448–49, citing 1933 Home Ministry, *Shakai undō no jōkyō*.

In a third, related, shift, class liberation was transmogrified into racial liberation; in December 1932 the first party convention agreed that "the construction of socialism in Japan is needed to ensure self-preservation and the international right of the Japanese people to exist."[52] By 1933 the party had unequivocally repudiated what it called a "selfish class interest which set class against race and ignored the permanence of the *kokumin*."[53]

While some party locals criticized and resisted this shift, most adapted with ease.[54] This was the case even in local elections such as the 1932 contest for the Jōtō ward assembly, where the party won broad support by calling for lower utility costs, rent control, unemployment relief, low cost loans for tradesmen and manufacturers, and reform of corrupt city government. The leaflet of successful SMP candidate Gotō Chōnosuke, a foreman at Nankatsu's Sakurada Machine Manufacturing Company, linked these local economic and political reforms to the party's new spirit of popular nationalism by featuring an endorsement by Asō Hisashi and Abe Isō. They described Gotō as "a man to save the nation in this time of great national distress."[55]

A remarkable flyer produced in 1934 on the other side of Tokyo by the party's powerful Setagaya local more blatantly joined the new SMP concern for foreign policy and national defense with the cause of anti-capitalist domestic reform. The army had designated September 1 as Air Defense Drill Day. "However huge the military budget, how can we have national defense without secure livelihoods for the proletarian masses?" the Setagaya party newsletter asked. "We are absolutely opposed to wars of invasion to protect capitalist profits, but we will rise with arms in hand for a people's [*kokumin*] war of national defense," it proclaimed. In preparation for the defense drill, the party distributed leaflets calling for "Air Defense of the National Capital by the Hands of the Masses!! True National Defense with Secure Lives for the Laboring, Farming People."[56]

The Social Masses Party thus dealt with the new political context after 1932 by riding the tiger. It embraced the idea of a national defense

---

52. Ibid., p. 442.

53. *Shōwa 8 nendo gian*, p. 17, in "Shakai taishū tō taikai kiroku" file, OISR.

54. The Nakano local remained a staunch opponent of the new party line. Perhaps the political independence and support for socialist politics of Nakano residents even into the 1980s was rooted in this era.

55. Campaign leaflet in *Shadaitō (14): Tōkyō-fu ren (7)*, OISR.

56. "Setagaya shibu nyūsu, No. 5" and attached leaflet in *Shadaitō (12): Tōkyō-fu ren (5)*, OISR.

state, hoping to increase its popular appeal and gain powerful allies on behalf of its domestic program. In the event, its considerable success at the polls was matched by its eventual failure to sustain a voice in national policy.[57]

THE UNIONS

The union story in the early 1930s mirrored that of the proletarian parties. First, splinter groups of national socialists or Japanists deserted the Sōdōmei, the independent Sōrengō, and the Kumiai dōmei camps. In May 1932 a leading figure in the Kantō Amalgamated Union, shipbuilder and machinist Mochizuki Genji, led a sizable minority of the Nankatsu locals into a new Japan Labor Alliance (Nihon rōdō dōmei) allied to Akamatsu's National Socialist Party. This defection and the bitter recriminations that ensued in Kumiai dōmei locals throughout the city permanently crippled this union.

Second, the increasingly defensive and isolated mainstream union federations, the Sōdōmei and the Kumiai dōmei, followed the lead of their affiliated political parties in gradually transforming their organizations, action, and ideology. In September 1932 the two federations finally patched over their differences of the past five years and reunited.[58] Although each federation retained its independent identity within the umbrella group, this newly formed Congress of Japanese Labor Unions (Nihon rōdō kumiai kaigi), covering nearly two-thirds of the nation's union members, changed its rhetoric and its workplace behavior in a fashion similar to that of the newly united Social Masses Party. As early as December 1931, the Sōdōmei journal called for "comprehensive national economic planning. . . . Unions are less organizations to demand fair distribution of profits than important organs for control of industry." The same issue of the union magazine described the conflict in Manchuria as a "struggle for survival of the race."[59]

The Congress attacked "unproductive, asocial, non-national" capitalism and called for state economic controls to reform capitalism and improve workers' welfare.[60] The Congress, like the SMP, was riding the

57. Garon, *State and Labor*, p. 198, shows that the government did implement a few social welfare measures supported by the SMP in 1936–38.

58. Ibid., p. 193.

59. Yamada Takeo, "Dai kyōkō ki no rōdō kumiai undō," *Rekishi hyōron*, no. 380 (December 1981): 61; Miwa Yasushi, "1930 nendai ni okeru rōdō seisaku to sōdōmei," ibid., p. 40.

60. Nishinarita, "Manshū jihen ki," p. 296; Garon, *State and Labor*, p. 194.

tiger; in Nishinarita Yutaka's persuasive depiction, it sought to borrow
the power of the state to compensate for its own weakness and achieve
parity with capital.[61] The Sōdōmei, for its part, took practical steps to
realize this vision of parity and participation. It disavowed strikes in
1932 in a spirit of "industrial cooperation" and sought collective contracts or factory councils as instruments to achieve its goals. Its cooperative program echoed calls of Home Ministry bureaucrats for a movement for industrial peace, and in fact, unionized workers concluded
contracts in thirty-seven factories in 1931 and 1932, compared to just
twenty-eight contracts nationwide between 1918 and 1930, while from
1932 to 1936 the number of factory councils in Japan rose by two-
thirds, from 173 to 274. Although the contracts, all but one in relatively
small workplaces, covered just 10,000 or so factory workers (plus
about 110,000 seamen), a tiny portion even of the organized work
force, the councils by 1936 represented 500,000 workers, a larger
number than the 420,000 union members that year.[62] Finally, the Sōdōmei even proposed amending the Labor Disputes Conciliation Law of
1926 to enhance state power to arbitrate.[63]

Information on the actual workings of councils and contracts is
scarce, but workers appear to have promised much in the way of "cooperation" and to have received little in the way of new security or improved conditions in return. The language of most contracts was similar; as at the Chiyoda Shoe Factory in Nankatsu, they typically began
with an article recognizing the union's right to bargain collectively and
guaranteeing a closed shop, but followed this with a second article
promising that in discussion of work conditions both union and company would take heed of the condition of the economy, the industry,
and the company.[64] By 1933 most Sōdōmei union contracts had introduced a new element of patriotism by promising "industrial service to
the nation."[65] Despite clear reluctance to bargain aggressively, a union
that simply concluded such a contract or participated in a council may

61. Nishinarita, "Manshū jihen ki," p. 296.
62. On contracts, see Naimushō, shakai-kyoku, *Honpō ni okeru rōdō kyōyaku no
gaikyō* (Tokyo: Naimushō shakai-kyoku, 1933), p. 23. On councils, see Naimushō,
shakai-kyoku, rōdō-bu, *Wa ga kuni ni okeru rōdō iinkai no gaikyō* (Tokyo: Naimushō
shakai-kyoku, rōdō-bu, 1937), pp. 5, 8–10. There is considerable overlap in the totals of
workers in unions and in councils.
63. Garon, *State and Labor*, p. 113 n. 151, cites Saitō Kenichi, "Jiji kaisetsu," *Rōdō*,
no. 279 (October 1934): 13.
64. Naimushō, *Honpō ni okeru rōdō kyōyaku*, pp. 39–42.
65. The term was *sangyō hōkoku*. Yamada, "Dai kyōkō ki no rōdō kumiai undō,"
p. 61.

well have satisfied workers, especially those in smaller places, that they were respected employees as well as participants in an important national endeavor.

While the spirit in the national federations was noncombative, a number of disputes did take place in the Nankatsu region between 1932 and 1935. Whether led by the right or left wings of the mainstream unions, they revealed a dramatically changed grass-roots conception, or at least presentation, of labor's place in the nation: capitalists were still the enemies, but the military was no longer criticized as spearheading imperialism; the bureaucracy was no longer presented as a repressive enemy; the state was rather a potential ally, ensuring respect and just rewards for working people.

Consider the bitter dispute at the Lion Soap Company in Honjo in July 1932, which set the company against a portion of its 101 employees, who were mostly women. The irrepressible Minami Kiichi, representing a loose local federation of left-wing unions, successfully negotiated for the union, gaining improved wages and working conditions. When the company sought the understanding, and perhaps strikebreaking support, of the local Neighborhood Association and Military Reservist Association, the union reacted with a flyer that typified this new conception. Addressed to "fair-minded citizens" but aimed at the reservists, the flyer asked them not to support the capitalists, for the state's role was not to protect the profit of capitalists but to protect the productive proletariat. After all, the flyer claimed, a number of Lion Soap employees were themselves reservists, and "the union struggles with determination for the honor of the reservists and the honor of the *kokumin*."[66]

A small group of strikers at the Hi no de Rubber factory in nearby Terashima offered a similar appeal to the local reservists and youth groups during a dispute the next winter. Imploring the "reservists, youth groups and citizens" not to be misled by cries of "time of state emergency" (*kokka hijōji*) to view the workers as selfish, the leaflet claimed:

All the world calls for "national unity," "building an industrial nation" and "labor-capital cooperation," and we also joined in the Defense Fund Drive. We do this entirely for the fortune of the Japanese people [*kokumin*] as a whole. However, there are those who fatten their own purses while manipu-

---

66. The flyer is included in the police report of June 28, 1932, concerning the Lion Soap dispute, in Kyū-kyōchōkai shiryō, *Kagaku kōgyō sōgi: 1932*, OISR.

lating our fervent "patriotism." Selfishly, not for the country and not for the people, this tiny group only thinks of its personal gain—these are the capitalists!. . . They tell us to work cheaply, but not one company obeys the factory law.[67]

These workers had appropriated the language of "national emergency." By placing the word *patriotism* in quotes, they still distance themselves from uncritical hypernationalism, but the authors of this leaflet have also moved far from typical union ideas of the 1920s. They have certainly accepted the idea that as *kokumin* they have an obligation to serve a state now controlled by the bureaucracy and the military, insofar as the state in turn furthers the welfare of workers as *kokumin*. But Nankatsu workers continued to blast capitalists, in the words of a 1934 leaflet from striking rubber workers at the Ichikawa Rubber factory, also in Terashima, as "enemies of the *kokumin*" whose selfish acts "violated social morality," or (according to a different group of machinists in Terashima in 1935) as "traitors who pursued personal gain" while hypocritically invoking a sense of "state emergency."[68]

TOWARD A SOCIAL POLICY CONSENSUS

The rulers of the 1930s were extremely sensitive to the broad political context shaping the newly cooperative behavior of most unions. They quickly recognized connections between foreign policy, domestic politics, the retreat of the social movement and a new social peace. General Ugaki confided in his diary in December 1931 that the major objectives of his tenure as army minister had been achieved through the Manchurian offensive: the unity of the military and the people and the "popularization" (*kokuminka*) of national defense.[69] In 1932 the Justice Ministry's *Monthly Thought Bulletin* stressed that in a time of intense social ferment, the surge of support for foreign expansion after the Manchurian Incident was a "divine wind."[70] And a May 1932 paper of the Army Ministry titled "Judgment of the New Situation in the Far East" could not have been clearer on this connection:

---

67. February 16, 1933, leaflet, from "Hi no de sogi," Kyū-kyōchōkai, *Kagaku kōgyō sōgi shiryō: 1933*, OISR. *Hi no de* means "rising sun."

68. August 22, 1934, leaflet of Ichikawa strikers and May 3, 1935, leaflet of Sakai Electric Generator Company workers, collected in "Kōtō chihō: shokumiai," File V6, OISR.

69. Ugaki Kazunari, *Ugaki Kazunari nikki* (Tokyo: Misuzu shobō, 1968), 2:817, entry of November 13, 1931; 2:822, entry of December 30, 1931.

70. Yasuda Hiroshi, "Manshū jihenka ni okeru gunbu," *Nihonshi kenkyū*, no. 238 (June 1982): 42, quotes *Shisō geppō*, no. 29, p. 78.

Since the Manchurian Incident, confrontational attitudes between social classes with differing economic interests appear to have gradually subsided. . . . [The incident] seems to have bred a spirit of solidarity. . . . However, this surge in unified racial sentiment has mainly developed with a focus on external problems, and there is no evidence yet of adjustment or reform in the domestic economic relations that are the basic causes of social class division.[71]

Closer to the Nankatsu scene, the police mediator Ōtsubo Yasuo remarked in December 1933 that a popular sense of national emergency (the so-called *hijōji*) had been of tremendous importance in promoting industrial peace. Ōtsubo echoed the army's 1932 judgment, however, for he saw no guarantee that this peace would continue. He wanted to act swiftly to create a system of industrial relations to forestall future conflict. In 1933 he maintained his ministry's traditional commitment to factory councils and labor-capital bargaining, but his reasoning was new and noteworthy. He explicitly rejected a "European" view that labor disputes were unavoidable. Councils and contracts would nurture a spirit of accord and cooperation; labor and management would work together like "two wheels of a cart, two wings of a bird."[72] His imagery was organic; his vision of a social order in which conflict was inherently unnatural and destructive had diverged sharply from that of his ministry just two years earlier and converged toward that of the "Japanist" unions.

By 1935 a more complete convergence of elite opinion took place. The Home Ministry bureaucrats abandoned even Ōtsubo's commitment to collective contracts as the means to social peace. Preventive early intervention by the police in labor and land disputes increased sharply in 1935.[73] The Home Ministry came officially to deny the validity of an independent organized labor interest and to promote in its place "fusion of labor and capital in service to state goals of industrial development." Over the following several years the ministry and the military both began to promote labor-management discussion groups in place of factory councils or unions.[74]

The early 1930s witnessed the logical unfolding of a circular vision of Japan's dilemma held by the nation's most influential social and eco-

71. Yasuda, "Manshū jihenka," p. 53.
72. *Shakai undō ōrai*, December 1933, p. 15.
73. Hayashi, "Nihon fuashizumu ki ni okeru naimushō," p. 7.
74. Nishinarita, "Manshū jihen ki," pp. 288–289. Miwa, "1930 nendai ni okeru rōdō seisaku," pp. 41–43.

nomic bureaucrats and by military leaders as diverse as Araki Sadao, Suzuki Teiichi, and Ugaki Kazunari. The social polarization of the depression had been dangerous, and Japan's international position had been threatened. To resolve this crisis, achievement of order at home was as important as aggressive action abroad. To succeed on both fronts required new rulers to repudiate the 1920s system of imperial democracy, party rule, cooperation with the West, restraint in China, and relatively liberal social policies. In the wake of the Manchurian Incident, a seemingly promising resolution of the foreign policy crisis appeared for a time to be solving the multifaceted domestic crisis as well. But the circle was actually a spiral; each new step abroad intensified the perceived need for unity, order, and control at home. Yet, as both the police mediator Ōtsubo and the 1932 army report recognized, despite Japanist unions and programs of industrial cooperation, fundamental class divisions remained.

By 1936 labor protest was on the rise again, the Social Masses Party was gaining dramatically, and even the social bureaucrats wanted more active state policy to mobilize popular energy and restore social harmony. The great irony, seemingly lost on rulers obsessed with order and control, is that the organized social movement had been so transformed as to rule out any fundamental challenge to capitalism, the emperor, the empire, or the military.

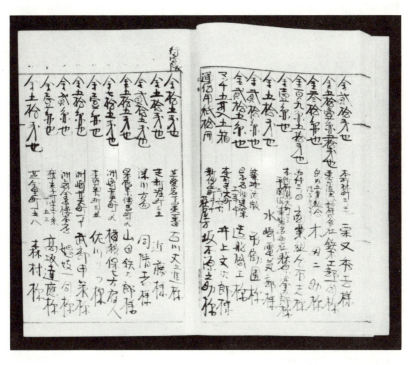

16. Ledger of contributions to support the Ishikawajima shipyard strikers in 1921.

17. A "demonstration" in the form of a procession to supply food to the Ōjima Steel Company strike group in 1930.

18. "Street sales battalion" during the October 1930 strike at Daiwa Rubber Company.

19. Speech-meeting to support the strikers at the Ōjima Steel Company in 1930, with policeman sitting on stage.

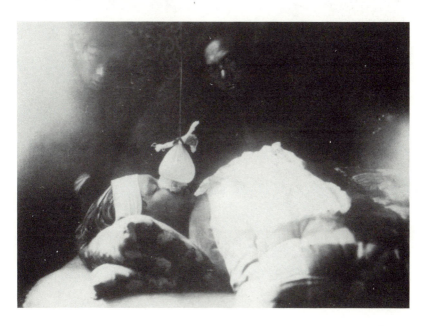

20. Injured workers beaten during the Daiwa Rubber Company strike.

21. Postcard issued to commemorate the 1930 Tōyō Muslin strike.

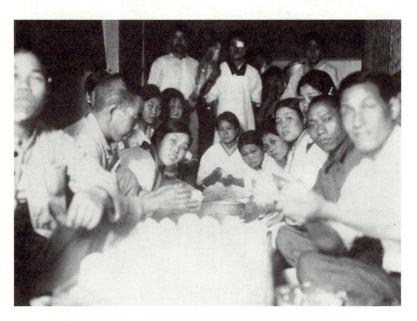

22. Union members prepare food for strikers at Tōyō Muslin in 1930.

23. Activists in the Women's Alliance (Fujin dōmei) supporting the Tōyō Muslin strikers in 1930.

24. Men and women in the strike group at the Tsuge Rubber Company in 1930.

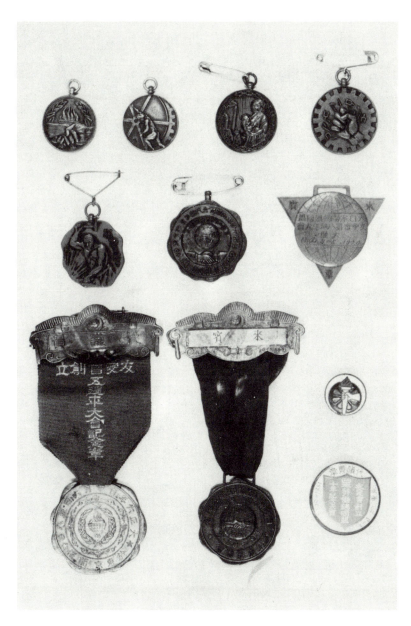

25. Badges and pins of unions in the 1910s and 1920s.

26. Demonstration by the children of Ōjima Steel Company strikers in 1930.

Elections under Universal Suffrage

27. "Candidates Night" speech-meeting in an early universal suffrage election in Tokyo (1928 or 1930).

28. Tokyo candidates of the Social Masses Party celebrate Lower House election victory in 1937 (Asanuma Inejirō is first from right).

ELEVEN

Imperial Fascism, 1935–40

REVIVAL OF THE SOCIAL MOVEMENT

After several years in which unions grew slowly and job actions decreased, the labor movement revived in the mid 1930s. Unions began to expand once more in the major urban centers of the Keihin and Kansai regions in 1935; in Tokyo the number of organized workers rose 25 percent from a 1934 low to a peak of 81,500 in 1936, and after three years of decline even the national proportion of organized workers increased ever so slightly from 1934 to 1935.[1] For a time labor disputes lagged, and unions played a diminished role in them, but in the first six months of 1937 disputes soared in number throughout Japan. The count of workers joining strikes or slowdowns jumped from 31,000 in 1936 to 124,000 the next year, exceeding even the 1930 peak of 81,000. Four-fifths of these actions, involving 89 percent of the strikers, took place between January and June; had it not been for the extraordinary dampening effect of the war in China, which began in July and led workers to restrain demands in cooperation with the "holy war," the year 1937 would have been by far the time of greatest labor protest in Japan's history.[2] The number of participants per strike increased substantially in 1937, and these strikes were far more assertive than the defensive actions of the depression; over two-thirds of the 1937 strikes were classified by the government as "assertive," compared to well

1. *NRUS* 10:424.
2. Ibid., pp. 440–41, 520–21.

under one-fourth in 1930 and 1931.[3] The economic pressures of inflation and a tight labor market had begun to overcome the restrictive
political environment of "national emergency."

Nankatsu reflected most of the national trends, although the long
tradition of labor organizing meant that unions continued to play a
greater role here than elsewhere. The thirty-nine disputes reported in
1937 represented a sharp increase over the previous three years. The
workers' posture was significantly more assertive, as in half the disputes
of 1936 and 1937 they demanded better treatment or higher pay, compared to just one-fourth during the depression. The results improved as
well, as workers won their demands in one-third of their actions in
1936–37, up from just 7 percent during the depression.

The lag between union growth, which came in 1935–36 centered on
the older industrial centers, and the disputes, which came in 1937 centered on newer, outlying districts, was important. Unions were not at
the forefront of most strikes in 1937; they joined only 38 percent of all
disputes that year, down sharply from the peak national rate of about
70 percent during the depression.[4] Also, the proportion of all strikes
taking place in the major urban centers, where unions were strongest,
fell from depression levels of 50 percent to under one-third by 1937.[5]
This shift in location of disputes away from areas of union growth
reflected the change in Japan's industrial structure that accompanied
the economic growth and military production of the 1930s. New centers of small manufacturing enterprise grew in provincial cities and the
outlying districts of major urban centers, relying primarily on subcon-
tracts from large military producers.[6]

The ruling bureaucrats and military men found this pattern disturbing. Social unrest was on the rise, with larger, more assertive, more
successful labor actions. In addition, the unrest was taking place not
only in traditional centers of the social movement such as Nankatsu; it
was spreading to new locations, and it was affecting military industries.
The increasingly moderate unions, which old-line social bureaucrats
had hoped would contain social problems, were not in charge; their
leaders appeared out of touch with a frustrated rank and file of workers. In the late spring of 1937, a contributor to *Chūō kōron* warned that

---

3. Nishinarita Yutaka, "Manshū jihen ki no rōshi kankei," in *Hitotsubashi daigaku
kenkyū nenpō: keizaigaku kenkyū*, no. 26 (January 1985): 276.
4. *NRUS* 10:522–23.
5. Nishinarita, "Manshū," p. 276.
6. Ibid., pp. 257–61.

the pace of labor unrest was far ahead of the most turbulent year of the depression. Disputes were more intense, more politicized, and not often led by unions. The unrest, he concluded, was an inevitable product of the war economy; management paternalism was wholly insufficient in the face of it. Unstated, but clearly implied was the call for a new state policy.[7]

Of equal moment were the dramatic concurrent gains of the "proletarian parties," in particular the Social Masses Party (SMP). In both local and national contests between 1935 and 1937, they surprised observers and even themselves. They won new support throughout the nation, but their most significant strength was in the major urban industrial centers.

The first new proletarian successes came in the nationwide elections for prefectural assemblies (excluding Tokyo and Kanagawa) in October 1935. Proletarian parties tripled their seats and vote totals, from twelve seats in 1931 to thirty-six in 1935, with the SMP winning twenty-four of these. This was still a tiny 2 percent of all seats and 3 percent of 6.7 million votes, but most observers found it the most significant development of the election.[8]

In Tokyo three local elections in close succession furthered this trend (table 11.1). In June 1936 the proletarian parties placed twenty-two men on the prefectural assembly, eighteen from the SMP. With one-fifth of the seats, they held a "casting vote" since neither major party had a majority. Five months later, elections for ward assembly were held in twenty outlying wards recently annexed to the city proper, including new wards in what had been Minami Katsushika County. The SMP made inroads into these bastions of "local notable" power, winning forty-four seats overall and establishing blocs of 10 percent (three or four out of thirty-five or forty seats) in a number of working-class wards. In the industrial sections of Nankatsu, newly designated as Jōtō and Mukōjima wards, the party won eight seats.[9] In city council elections in March 1937, proletarian parties suddenly captured 16 percent of the 160 seats, again a potentially decisive bloc, as both of the major

7. Inada Tetsuo, "Rōdō sōgi no boppatsu," *Chūō kōron*, June 1937, pp. 339, 341, 346.

8. Analysis of this election in Sekiguchi Yasushi, "Fuken kai senkyo no kekka," *Toshi mondai* 21, no. 5 (November 1935): 1215–31. SMP documents claim thirty-eight proletarian seats.

9. *Shōwa 11 nendo tōsō hōkokusho*, pp. 66–67, "Shakai taishū tō taikai kiroku" file, OISR.

TABLE 11.1   TOKYO ELECTION RESULTS, 1936–37

	Prefectural Assembly, June 1936	Ward Assemblies, November 1936	City Council, March 1937
Proletarian parties			
seats	22	44	26
vote %	16	—	15
Minseitō			
seats	49	—	64
vote %	47	—	36
Seiyūkai			
seats	34	—	52
vote %	40	—	33
Other			
seats	4	—	18
vote %	10	—	16

SOURCES: Prefectural election data from *Toshi mondai*, July 1936, p. 111. Ward election data from *Shōwa 11 nendo tōsō hōkokusho*, pp. 66–67, in "Shakai taishūtō taikai kiroku" file, OISR. City council election data from *Toshi mondai*, April 1937, pp. 599–607.
NOTE: The Social Masses Party accounted for 18 of the 22 proletarian seats in the prefectural assembly, all 44 ward assembly seats, and 22 of 26 city council seats. The SMP had held just one prefectural assembly seat and 2 city council seats prior to these elections.

parties stood well short of a majority. This advance was part of a national trend for the SMP, which also gained substantially in Kyoto, Kobe, Osaka, Yahata, and Yokohama.[10]

But the most striking advance for the SMP came in Japan's major cities in the two Diet elections of February 1936 and April 1937. The party won eighteen seats in 1936 with 5 percent of the total vote; in the nation's largest cities, Tokyo, Osaka, Yokohama, Kobe, and Fukuoka, the SMP garnered from 13 to 17 percent of the vote and thirteen of its seats.[11] In Tokyo's District 5, a mixed industrial and middle-class residential area on the west side of the city, Asō Hisashi of the SMP and Katō Kanjū, standard bearer of the left-wing Proletarian Party, ran

10. Maeda Tamon, "Tōkyō-shi kai senkyo to kakushin seiryoku no shinshutsu," *Toshi mondai* 24, no. 4 (April 1937): 599–607; *Shōwa 12 nendo tōsō hōkokusho*, pp. 39–45, "Shakai taishū tō taikai kiroku" file, OISR.
11. "Shisō dantai kaku ha no shūgiin giin senkyo kekka ni kansuru chōsa," *Shisō geppō*, no. 26 (August 1936): 55.

second and first, each polling over 50,000 votes for a combined 40 percent of the district's votes. In the two Nankatsu districts, Asanuma Inejirō and Suzuki Bunji were elected with ease. Asanuma's 13,000 votes (17 percent in a sixteen-man field) topped the ticket in Honjo and Fukagawa (District 4); Suzuki's 38,000 placed him second in Minami Katsushika County with 14 percent. Of course, this still left 439 seats and 93 percent of the vote in the hands of the Minseitō and Seiyūkai, a fact duly stressed in the Justice Ministry's *Monthly Thought Bulletin*; nonetheless, this report called the SMP gains a noteworthy phenomenon, and a sign of the "emergence and development of the so-called renovationist forces which no one, including the party itself, anticipated."[12]

If the 1936 results were surprising, those of 1937 astonished most observers. The SMP doubled its delegation, returning thirty-seven men to the Diet, and in three urban districts it elected two candidates. It polled 930,000 votes, 9 percent of the total. When combined with the facts that neither major party won more than 40 percent of the seats or votes and that unprecedented numbers (around 40 percent of eligible voters in most urban districts) did not bother to vote, the results signaled popular discontent with both of the bourgeois parties, the increased irrelevance of the Diet, and significant support for the SMP program.[13]

In Tokyo the SMP elected eight men, at least one in each of the city's districts, and Katō Kanjū was again the sole victor from his Proletarian Party (see figure 28). SMP and Proletarian Party candidates took 28 percent of the city's votes, and their nine Tokyo seats gave them a Diet contingent just below the eleven Minseitō M.P.'s and ahead of the eight from the Seiyūkai. Table 11.2 reveals the party's impressive support throughout the city. It took no less than 16 percent in any district and placed its candidate first in five of seven contests. By the end of 1937, the Tokyo locals of the SMP boasted ninety-nine elected representatives: eight in the Diet, fifteen in the prefectural assembly, twenty-two on the city council, and fifty-four in the ward assemblies.[14]

The SMP's "great leap" of 1936–37, as it was dubbed in the press,

12. "Shisō dantai," *Shisō geppō*, no. 26 (August 1936): 54, for this quotation; pp. 69–83 for complete results.

13. Official observers were extremely concerned with the apathy indicated by low turnout. See data in Keishichō, "Shūgiin giin senkyo tōhyō kekka hyō," April 30, 1937, in Rikugun-kaigun monjo, microfilm reel 207, item 1455. Also, Sakisaka Itsurō, "Chishiki kaikyū to seiji," *Chūō kōron*, June 1936, pp. 142–48.

14. *Shōwa 12 nendo tōsō hōkokusho*, pp. 96–100, "Shakai taishūtō taikai kiroku" file, OISR.

TABLE 11.2   PROLETARIAN PARTY RESULTS IN TOKYO
IN THE APRIL 1937 DIET ELECTION (* = ELECTED)

District	Candidate	Party	No. of Votes	%	Place
1 (5 seats)	*Kōnō Mitsu	SMP	14,798	22	1 of 10
2 (5 seats)	*Abe Isō	SMP	19,251	27	1 of 7
3 (4 seats)	*Asanuma Inejirō	SMP	12,590	19	2 of 10
4 (4 seats)	*Abe Shigeo	SMP	12,096	16	1 of 11
5 (5 seats)	*Asō Hisashi	SMP	34,143	15	1 of 11
	*Katō Kanjū	JPP	32,914	15	2 of 11
	*Miwa Jusō	SMP	27,847	12	4 of 11
6 (5 seats)	*Suzuki Bunji	SMP	37,949	16	1 of 9
	Suzuki Mōsaburō	JPP	20,181	9	7 of 9
7 (3 seats)	*Nakamura Kōichi	SMP	14,133	20	2 of 6
Total			225,902	28	

SOURCE: Keishichō, "Shūgiin giin kōhosha betsu tokuhyō shirabe," May 1, 1937. Riku-kaigun monjo, microfilm reel 207, item 1455.
NOTE: SMP = Social Masses Party; JPP = Japan Proletarian Party (Nihon musan tō). The two parties jointly took nine of the thirty-one Diet seats at stake in Tokyo, and nine of their ten candidates were elected.

came less than a decade after the first election in which Japan's male workers and landless farmers could vote. In comparative perspective, this was a relatively short gestation period for a working-class party. Not only was this a significant development in its own time. In addition, the core of SMP support and organization remained alive, though in hibernation, during the years of war and the party's dissolution between 1940 and 1945. Within a decade of this first "leap," a "new" Socialist Party seemed to emerge in sudden fashion to contend seriously for power in the first postwar elections.[15] In fact, it built its strength on the considerable foundation in place by the late 1930s.

THE PARTY AND UNION PROGRAMS

The resurgence of the labor movement and advance of the proletarian parties influenced the political trajectory of 1930s Japan. First, thousands of workers, including many nonunion employees, demanded

15. In 1947 the Socialists won 31 percent of 466 seats and 26 percent of 27 million votes.

with renewed vigor that their workplaces honor "mainstream" standards of security and respect. Ironically, given the moderation of this stance and the fact that union leaders looked to the state, in particular the Home Ministry, as a potential ally in this quest, this increased unrest convinced the social bureaucrats and other rulers, whose threshold for disorder was extraordinarily low, that the social foundation of industrial production remained dangerously unstable in a time of national emergency.

Second, after several years of stagnation, the SMP built a stable organization, and the urban constituency of the early proletarian parties expanded dramatically. In the 1920s these parties of the left had opposed the bourgeois parties, the capitalist system, and imperialism, but the resurgent SMP only won broad support when it sharply modified this radical program; in essence, it returned to the spirit of the early movement for imperial democracy, but with a striking new appreciation of the place of the bureaucracy and military. The SMP success made clear the ongoing appeal of the imperial democratic movement's vision of respect for the popular will and popular welfare, but it revealed the malleability of that vision as well, as the party recast the bourgeois parties and capitalists, rather than the bureaucrats or military, as the forces opposing the popular will.

WORKER OBJECTIVES: JOINING THE GENERAL SOCIETY

In the few well-documented Nankatsu labor disputes of early 1937, the area's metal and chemical workers, both men and women, reiterated their intense concern for what the labor offensive of the 1920s had called "better treatment." By far the greatest proportion of the offensive demands of the entire span from 1933 to 1938 sought "better treatment" (see table 8.1). By 1937 the two primary concrete manifestations of better treatment were severance pay and equal treatment of "temporary" workers. The former was now legally and the second informally sanctioned by the state. This sanction is evident not simply in passage of the Law for Retirement and Severance Pay in 1937, but also in the fact that beginning in 1934, confidential police reports on labor disputes added a new category: in addition to size of work force, each report noted the extent of formal retirement or severance pay and other welfare programs.[16] Home Ministry officials in 1936 also began quietly

---

16. Reports held in the Kyū-kyōchōkai collection, OISR.

to pressure employers to extend these benefits to temporary workers or convert them to regular status.[17]

Rank-and-file workers were aware of this official posture and sought to use it. In a dispute at the Greater Japan Oils and Fats Corporation, a Nankatsu factory owned by the huge Kao Soap Company, which employed 450 regular women and men and 69 temporary workers, the latter joined the Kantō Amalgamated Union and demanded the status of regular workers. They asserted that their temporary status was a company ploy to avoid obeying the law (presumably the law requiring severance pay). After a week of negotiations, but no strike, the company agreed to grant the temporaries "regular" work.[18]

The full program for "better treatment" was articulated in a dispute at a Nankatsu metal factory in the winter of 1937. A handful of the 330 male workers at Tōyō Steel had sought out the Sōdōmei as their discontent mounted and had then enrolled 70 members within several weeks. They demanded and won semiannual pay raises with guaranteed minima, conversion of temporary workers to regular status, "consideration" of a severance pay system, 60 percent "idle pay" in slow times, reform of the unit price system, and a more consistent "unified" labor-management structure, as well as a 30 percent average raise.[19] This incident, too, was settled through negotiations, and although the police did not mediate formally, the detailed police account of daily negotiations makes it clear that they were talking to both sides. The police combined concern that negotiations remain calm and nonpolitical with some respect for the union position.

These Nankatsu workers, and the Sōdōmei local office that helped them draw up their demands, were explicitly seeking to improve their treatment to what they called, in one negotiating document, "levels of the general society."[20] They seem to have remained suspicious of, and willing to confront, employers and owners, who in their view were dedicated to accumulating wealth by exploiting their labor, yet the rank and file no longer viewed the bureaucracy or even the military with

17. Andrew Gordon, *The Evolution of Labor Relations in Japan: Heavy Industry, 1853–1955* (Cambridge, Mass.: Harvard University Council on East Asian Studies, 1985), pp. 259–60.

18. Police report of April 19, 1937, in Kyū-kyōchōkai, *Rōdō sōgi: Shōwa 12 nen*, OISR.

19. Police reports of February 12 and 18, 1937, in *Rōdō sōgi: Shōwa 12 nen*, OISR.

20. "*Ippan shakai nami.*" Police report of February 18, 1937, in *Rōdō sōgi: Shōwa 12 nen*, OISR.

comparable suspicion. In a rare survey of the attitudes of 162 male metalworkers at a comparably sized factory in Osaka in 1935, 77 percent asserted that capitalism was either "a belief in getting rich" (30 percent), "poison to society" (25 percent), or "exploitation of workers" (22 percent), even though by a two-to-one margin they denied socialism was an "ally of the working class" or a system to create a "society without exploitation." Eighty percent thought the established parties were "useless."[21] The report's authors, writing in a Home Ministry publication, were anxious to discern evidence of antagonism toward the bureaucracy or the military, yet they found no such sentiments. In their conclusions they took comfort in the "virtual disappearance of revolutionary ideas from among today's workers. . . . They seem to have awakened to the true mission of the state."[22]

In this time of increased censorship and repression, the respondents to this survey may have decided to hide feelings of unhappiness with the bureaucracy, yet they were free enough with criticism of capitalism and with a sprinkling of sarcastic responses to some questions. We can never be certain what these workers "truly" believed, but declined to say. What is significant is that behavior and expressed ideas pointed in the same direction: continued hostility toward the economic system and acceptance of the new military-bureaucratic regime.

WINNING ELECTORAL SUPPORT: ORGANIZATION AND PROGRAMS

In these same years the Social Masses Party built a durable local network of organizations. This achievement explains much of the party's success. Prior to the Diet election of 1937, the Tokyo University newspaper commented that "if a socially trusted [proletarian party] candidate stands, he is certain to win even if he plunges into [an entirely new district], and where a strong organized party base has developed, even an unknown has a strong chance of victory."[23] Asanuma Inejirō, first elected to the Diet from Honjo (District 4) in 1936, was one of three Diet candidates who confirmed this judgment.[24] In 1937 he announced

21. Umehara Sōichirō, "Ōsaka bō kinzoku kōjō ni okeru shokkō shisō mondai," *Sangyō fukuri* 10, no. 9 (September 1935): 82–99. Published by the Home Ministry Social Bureau.

22. This last expression was *kokka honrai no michi*. Ibid., p. 97.

23. Kuratsuji Heiji, "Tōkyō shikai giin senkyo no kekka," *Toshi mondai* 24, no. 4 (April 1937): 714.

24. Two others who gave over secure bases (*jiban*) and won election in new districts were Kamei Kanichirō in Fukuoka and Kawakami Jōtarō in Kobe. See Asō Hisashi speech, Keishichō jōhō-ka, "Shūgiin giin sōsenkyo ni okeru genron ni yoru undō jōkyō," April 20, 1937, in *Shiryō: Nihon gendai shi* (Tokyo: Ōtsuki shoten 1984), 9:190.

his candidacy in Tokyo's District 3, which had never returned an SMP representative. He began his typical stump speech by declaring, "I've given District 4, where election is guaranteed, over to Abe Shigeo, and I am standing in the virgin territory of District 3."[25] The strategy worked; both he and Abe were elected. Their victories signaled a new level of maturity for the party and its organization.

Organization alone cannot explain the sudden surge from three to thirty-seven seats across two elections in just fourteen months. After the 1936 election, the Tokyo police credited the party's victory to a program that appealed to "intellectuals, and middle and lower classes," and for an observer on the left, its success likewise derived from both organization and an attractive platform.[26] More than the established parties, the SMP relied on direct mass appeals through speeches and rallies to win support; the party drew on traditions of popular mobilization reaching back to the early twentieth century. In all but two of the seven Tokyo districts in the 1937 campaign, the SMP and Proletarian Party candidates attracted larger audiences than those of the bourgeois parties. The total of 14,300 attendees at Asanuma's twenty-nine public speeches was double that of any opponent, Suzuki Bunji reached the largest total audience in the Nankatsu race, and SMP rallies dwarfed those of opponents in Districts 1 and 5 as well.[27]

The program articulated at these events was in significant measure a return to the broadly gauged rhetoric of economic justice and respect for the popular will at home that had distinguished the popular movement for imperial democracy of 1905 to 1918, as well as a subtle version of that era's appeal for empire abroad. Party representatives won their votes by calling for "a prosperous populace to perfect national defense," "domestic reform first," and a "people's foreign policy."[28] Abandoning all talk of a class-based social movement, not to mention of a class revolution, the party claimed to represent the political will of the entire *kokumin*.

25. Ibid., p. 187.
26. Keishichō, "Senkyo undō jōkyō," February 1936, *Shiryō: Nihon gendai shi*, 9:150; Morito Tatsuo, "Musan seitō no yakushin," *Chūō kōron*, April 1936, pp. 16–19.
27. Keishichō, "Shūgiin giin senkyo enzetsukai jōkyō hyō," April 20, 1937, in *Shiryō: Nihon gendai shi* 9:196–204.
28. For the 1936 Diet election, see "Shisō dantai kaku ha no shūgiin giin sōsenkyo taisaku ni kansuru chōsa," *Shisō geppō*, no. 23 (May 1936): 169–76. For 1937, see "Musan seitō oyobi aikoku dantai no sōsenkyo taisaku ni kansuru chōsa," *Shisō geppō*, no. 36 (June 1937): 25–28.

In its successful campaigns of 1935–37, the SMP above all stressed domestic social and economic reforms. In local "daily struggles" waged by the party between campaigns in Tokyo, it lobbied for rent controls, lower utility prices, reform of the municipal streetcar system, and honest city government.[29] In national campaigns the party called for a vast array of government programs aimed not only at workers and tenant farmers, but also at small tradesmen, manufacturers, and owner-farmers. Thus, in addition to seeking a union bill and protective legislation for labor, a minimum wage, and a tenant farmer bill, the party proposed "fundamental tax reform to eliminate taxes on the masses," health insurance, an old-age pension, and state financing for tradesmen, small manufacturers, and farmers.[30] The Tokyo police felt this platform, more specific and moderate than those of earlier elections, was a key factor in Asanuma's victory in 1936. The police attributed his election to "middle class voters who abandoned the existing parties" as well as his "passionate speeches and a program that addressed [the concerns of] the people's lives." They offered a similar analysis of Suzuki Bunji's success.[31]

The SMP gave foreign policy relatively less prominence in speeches and campaign literature from 1935 to 1937 as it followed a tortured trajectory from the pacifist anti-imperialism of its predecessor parties before 1932 to a fervent embrace of the China War upon its outbreak in July 1937. Asanuma's 1936 leaflets relegated foreign policy to a small corner of the page. His position, and that of the party, was hard to follow as well as hard to find. He called for an "independent ethnic state" in Manchuria, opposed Anglo-American domination of China proper (but did not advocate Chinese sovereignty or independence in its place), and called for "a new international solidarity with the oppressed masses of Asia."[32] The party in this ambiguous presentation implicitly accepted Japanese hegemony in an independent "Asia for the Asians" without fully repudiating its earlier internationalism.

The heart of the SMP stand on foreign policy, and the portion that clearly and for the first time echoed the spirit of the imperial democrats of the early twentieth century was the formulation in 1936 and 1937 of its "broad definition" of national defense. The opposed "narrow defini-

29. *Shōwa 11 nen tōsō hōkoku sho*, pp. 97–98, "Shakai taishū tō taikai kiroku" file, OISR.
30. "Shisō dantai," *Shisō geppō*, no. 23 (May 1936): 171–73.
31. The phrase was "Minshū no seikatsu ni soku shitaru seisaku." Keishichō, "Sen-kyō undō jōkyō," February 1936, in *Shiryō: Nihon gendai shi* 9:152, 155.
32. Special number of *Shakai shinbun*, January 1936, p. 2, OISR.

tion," according to the party platform, was one serving the interests of the military and finance capital. In the broad definition, protection of the popular (*kokumin*) livelihood came first, and "a prosperous people [will] fulfill the national defense." Only with the domestic reforms sought by the party could Japan pursue an effective foreign policy and long-term defense of the nation.[33]

The foreign and domestic components of the SMP program thus reinforced each other. In addition, the party drew on the ideology of imperial democracy by asserting that only the Social Masses Party could honestly and effectively represent the popular will. Shortly after the 1936 election for Tokyo's prefectural assembly, the party's large new delegation made symbolic claim to a position as uncorrupted representatives of the people by righteously boycotting the lavish traditional banquet, complete with geisha, given for assemblymen by the governor and police chief.[34]

In the 1936 and 1937 campaigns, both bourgeois parties, but particularly the Minseitō, also drew on time-honored political themes. Each party claimed to best serve the people's needs and represent the popular will in the Diet. The "unconstitutional" behavior of the Hayashi cabinet in suddenly dissolving the Diet came in for special attack by candidates from all three parties. In addition, the Minseitō in both 1936 and 1937 expressed concerns for the welfare of the people and their "economic security" similar to those of the SMP and proposed some specific programs, such as health insurance.[35] These similarities prompted Abe Isō, standing for the SMP in Tokyo in 1937, to complain that whereas his party had been talking of a "secure popular livelihood" since 1928, the established parties and even the government had suddenly joined the bandwagon. Likewise, Suzuki Bunji began his standard election speech in Nankatsu by attacking the secret machinations of the two major parties, blaming them "as much as the government" for the sudden dissolution, and concluding that "in this time of emergency only the Social Masses Party can truly represent the people's interests."[36]

One key difference between the SMP and bourgeois parties in these

---

33. "Shisō dantai," *Shisō geppō*, no. 23 (May 1936): 170; "Musan seitō," *Shisō geppō*, no. 36 (June 1937): 25, 29.

34. *Shakai shinbun*, July 10, 1926, p. 2, OISR.

35. See election speeches in Keischichō, "Shūgiin giin sōsenkyo," April 20, 1937, in *Shiryō: Nihon gendai shi* 9:182–95. Also, Naimushō, jōhō-ka, "Senkyo ni kansuru tsūtatsu," has a lengthy draft of a standard Minseitō election speech from 1936. In Riku-kaigun monjo, reel 205, item 1451.

36. Keishichō, "Shūgiin giin sōsenkyo," April 20, 1937, in *Shiryō: Nihon gendai shi* 9:186, 192.

years was that to achieve their common end of popular representation the former proposed specific political reform, while the latter usually issued general, time-tested calls for constitutional party government. The SMP called for a "national people's economic council" as well as a reformed House of Peers composed of occupational representatives; the Minseitō simply called for a return to "constitutional government that respects public opinion."[37]

The great irony was that so long as the bureaucracy and military were allowed to run the government, these proposals were simply campaign rhetoric. The voters recognized this by staying away from the polls in record numbers. On occasion the SMP acknowledged that powerful interests opposed its program, as when its 1937 platform claimed that not only the parties, but also the military and bureaucracy, were "forces to preserve the status quo," unable to deal with the current crisis.[38] Occasionally, too, individual candidates recognized the futility of electoral politics in their speeches, with the Japan Proletarian Party far more forthright than the SMP in criticizing "government dictatorship."[39] But on the whole, while the SMP consistently attacked capitalists for betraying the nation and selfishly exploiting the people, and continued to blast the "corrupt" established parties for failing to uphold constitutional government and represent the people's interests, it seldom criticized directly the military or even the bureaucracy.

A growing portion of the Tokyo electorate by 1937 appears to have become either too apathetic or too disillusioned to vote; these voters probably had little use for the tepid critique offered by the SMP or that presented by the major parties. Thus, an extraordinary survey of the political graffiti scrawled on 7,866 invalid ballots in the 1937 Diet election in Tokyo reveals that of a sample of 132 ballots with graffiti listed as typical by the police investigator, the largest number (28) lamented the uselessness of voting given the poor quality of the candidates or the weakness of the Diet.[40]

Such evidence does not tell us with certainty what the nonvoters thought, and we cannot be sure that voters who chose the SMP were

37. For SMP, see "Shisō dantai," *Shisō geppō*, no. 23 (May 1936): 171. For Minseitō, see undated "Enzetsu sōkō" from the 1936 election, in Riku-kaigun monjo, reel 205, item 1451.

38. "Musan seitō," *Shisō geppō*, no. 36 (June 1937): 29.

39. See Katō Kanjū's speech in Keishichō, "Sōsenkyo," April 20, 1937, in *Shiryō: Nihon gendai shi* 9:190.

40. "Shūgiin giin senkyo mukō tōhyō naiyō shirabe," May 7, 1937, in *Shiryō: Nihon gendai shi* 9: 214–18.

pleased with the party's very muted critique of military-bureaucratic rule. Many might have voted for the SMP to protest the weakness of the "established parties." At the same time, there is little evidence that a more direct challenge to the government would have fared better. Only 4 of the 132 defaced ballots contained antimilitary messages. The SMP was walking a tightrope. It made strategic compromises with state power, and the evidence does allow us to conclude that it offered an electorally effective claim to represent the interests of the lower- and middle-class "masses" or *kokumin*. The party echoed themes of the imperial democratic ideology in a way that earlier proletarian parties had not, and it won significant new support.

THE REGIME OF IMPERIAL FASCISM

The ideology of the movement for imperial democracy prior to 1918 had been at its core an attack on all selfish authoritarian interests standing between the people (*kokumin*) and the emperor. It sought a polity in which government actions would follow the will of both the ultimate ruler and the ruled. In the early era of popular agitation and the rise to power of the bourgeois parties, the imperial democrats had rendered the oligarchy, the bureaucracy, and even the leaders of the military as self-interested, arrogant, unresponsive opponents standing between emperor and people. Many imperial democracts had seen the parties as their allies, with a legitimate mission to represent and implement the popular will in the government, but at times and places, even in the era of imperial democracy as a movement, activists depicted the parties as selfish interests that betrayed the popular and imperial wills. The movement thus never unambiguously affirmed parliamentary institutions as the mechanism to create and defend an imperial democratic polity.

For most of the era that followed, from 1918 to 1932, the parties in fact played the dual role of a ruling elite group and the elected representatives of an expanding portion of the populace. Yet the hard-nosed, pragmatic party leaders were fearful of the popular energies that had helped them take power. This fear grew acute when articulate, organized elements of "the people" went beyond the imperial democratic ideology to challenge capitalism, empire, parliamentary politics, and in rare cases, the imperial institution itself. Because of this fear, the bourgeois parties did not cultivate broad intellectual and popular legitimacy in their dual roles as rulers and representatives.

Given this fragility of imperial democracy as a ruling system, and the serious popular and international challenge to it, the depression crisis sufficed to force the parties out of power. In their place, career bureaucrats, admirals, and generals came to run the government in uneasy cooperation with the bourgeois parties, as they had done before 1918. The parties, in retreat, mounted occasional calls for a return to "constitutional" government, with the Minseitō a bit more vociferous. A newly unified labor and proletarian political movement weathered several difficult years to emerge, on the eve of full-scale war, with unprecedented, although still minority, support for its claim to represent the interests of the nation.

In some surface respects, then, the political landscape by the mid 1930s was similar to that before 1918, when the movement for imperial democracy had challenged the rule of the emperor's oligarchic military and bureaucracy. But there were two crucial differences that make the image of a historical pendulum swing misleading. First, the only potential leaders of a renewed movement for imperial democracy were the bourgeois parties and the SMP, but the former only weakly, the latter almost never, criticized bureaucratic-military rule as a betrayal of the emperor and the people, as the imperial democrats had before 1918. Such a critique would have completed a full swing back to the configuration of the imperial democratic movement, but the established parties preferred to protect their local bases of power and as many of their Diet prerogatives as possible by compromising with the trends of the times, and the SMP found it ideologically simpler and politically safer to focus its criticism on capitalism and the bourgeois parties. Its leaders generally viewed the state not as an opponent of the people but as a potential ally. They dreamed of representing the people and collaborating with bureaucrats and military men who loyally served the emperor.

Second, by the mid 1930s the bureaucratic-military state refused to countenance any direct criticism of itself or "political" (that is, opposition) invocation of the emperor. Moreover, it also played an unprecedented political role in its own right, seeking to mobilize popular support for its goals. This was not the aloof bureaucratic state of the Meiji era, wisely serving the emperor on behalf of itself and the stupid commoners. It was an activist state ruled by bureaucrats and military men intent on maintaining social order, promoting industrial development, and expanding a hegemonic position in Asia. In the face of a surge of labor unrest, a mild challenge from the SMP, the resilience and feistiness of the "parties out of power," and growing mass political apathy, these rulers sought to secure their position in two ways: first, by suppressing all opposition and rooting out leftist and, by 1935, even liberal ideas; and second, by "unifying the wills" of people, officials, and sovereign and mobilizing the populace *in organized fashion* to serve self-proclaimed "national" goals under the aegis of the state. This was the most important feature that distinguished the regime of imperial fascism of 1937 to 1945 from that of the imperial bureaucracy before 1918.

My concern for the rest of this chapter will be to describe some of the ways in which the new regime pursued this goal of mobilization. Of necessity, this will take us some distance from the workers of Nankatsu into the national story of political, economic, and social mobilization, but the link between these two stories is important. The ongoing labor unrest in Nankatsu and new centers of industry around the nation, and the electoral appeal of calls for imperial democratic rule, provide the domestic context that helps explain the urgent pursuit of these mobilization programs.

MONOPOLIZING THE IMPERIAL WILL; MOBILIZING THE POPULAR WILL

One initial difference between the eras before and after party rule was that the state now forcibly possessed the imperial symbol. Before 1918 imperial democrats and bureaucrats had clashed over possession of Founding Day, February 11. Under the rule of the imperial democratic parties, February 11 had for a time been considered "Constitution Commemoration Day." By 1937 the struggle was over. The labor movement, of course, had long since abandoned Founding Day for its own celebration on May Day. Now May Day, too, was banned by the Home Ministry, as was the right-wing Japan Labor Day. Founding Day itself was stripped of its earlier opposition dimension of celebrating suffrage, democracy, and constitutional government. It became a tightly policed, nonpartisan, state-run public celebration of emperor and empire.[41]

By 1937 the state's determination to suppress any remotely "political" (that is, unofficial) use of the emperor was truly remarkable. One of the unsuccessful Diet candidates standing in Honjo-Fukagawa in 1937 printed 100,000 copies of a speech by "the God of constitutional government, Ozaki Yukio," in which the four characters in the compound for the emperor, *Ten-nō-hei-ka*, were scrambled to read *Ten-hei-nō-ka*.

41. For the spirit of these celebrations, see *TAS*, February 12, 1937, p. 1, and February 12, 1938, p. 1.

Not only did the Tokyo police take the trouble to investigate the matter, concluding the misprint "was simply carelessness," but their "Top Secret" report on this matter went all the way to the home minister's desk.[42] In a similar spirit, the Police Bureau chief's extremely detailed instructions of April 1937 to prefectural and metropolitan officers enjoined "extreme caution" to "prevent any appearance of the use of the imperial throne in political battles." Of most interest, while the crowds at rallies of the early imperial democratic movement commonly linked emperor and populace in shouts such as "Long Live the Emperor! Long Live the Citizens of Tokyo!" the Police Bureau chief warned local authorities that "although it is permitted to shout 'Long Live the Emperor!' and 'Long Live the Greater Japanese Empire!' shouts such as 'Long Live such-and-such Party!' will excite [popular] spirits, and moderators [of political rallies] should be warned in advance [not to use such words]."[43]

These new rules to keep the emperor out of electoral politics suggest a second difference between the regime of imperial fascism and the eras of imperial democracy both as movement and regime: the extraordinary new intensity with which the government policed elections to shape a political climate supporting its own initiatives. Beginning in 1935, the Home Ministry under Gotō Fumio promoted a nationwide Election Purification Movement to eliminate both official corruption, such as favoring of a party's candidate by partisan bureaucrats, and party corruption, such as vote-buying. The movement was to combine a public relations education campaign for "election purification" with closer police monitoring of elections.[44] In Gotō's words, as the movement began in 1935, "under constitutional government the people bear an important responsibility to assist imperial rule, strengthen the foundations of the nation, and plan for the nation's prosperity with the vote they cast."[45] But by 1937 a new motive for "purifying" elections can be detected, as the movement reflected and furthered the state's trajectory from the monitoring to the shaping of mass politics. The more specific, activist state goal in running "pure" elections was to ensure the unity of the wills of the people and state officials.

42. Top secret item 231. Police Chief Yokoyama Sukenari to Home Minister Kawarada Kakichi, April 22, 1937. Riku-kaigun monjo, reel 207, item 1455.

43. Police Bureau directive # 17. Home Ministry Police Bureau chief to each prefectural police chief, April 9, 1937. Riku-kaigun monjo, reel 207, item 1455.

44. Susan Beth Weiner, "Bureaucracy and Politics in the 1930s: The Career of Gotō Fumio" (Ph.D. diss., Harvard University, 1984), pp. 133–48.

45. Ibid., p. 144.

The surviving records of police intervention in the Tokyo contests are remarkably detailed. They make clear that the police discriminated with care when they issued warnings to speakers or halted speeches; they were repressing not a particular party but a particular set of ideas. Just two unusually oppositional SMP candidates (out of eight) accounted for twenty-two of the thirty-one warnings issued to that party's speakers. Warnings to the Minseitō and Seiyūkai candidates were similarly concentrated on a small number of the feistier speakers. Because the SMP tended to ally itself with the state, it made fewest offending statements. Police halted only one SMP speech in the entire city throughout the campaign, while they stopped eight speeches of the Japan Proletarian Party and eight of the two bourgeois parties combined.[46]

The catalog of offending statements that drew warnings or, upon repetition, would bring a speech to a halt, reveals the police seeking to prevent any public utterance that set the people in opposition to either the military or the bureaucracy. The vast majority of forbidden phrases were of three related sorts: either they criticized "fascism" ("fascist sentiment in the military rejects Diet politics" [warning!]), they criticized the "dictatorship of the military and bureaucracy" (warning!), or they so much as mentioned a "gap between the military and the people." Even speeches lamenting such a gap were offensive to the police: "those screaming 'people-military gap' are traitors" (warning!). Such a statement, one may imagine, intended to blame the government for the problem.

Asanuma's careful campaign had received just a single warning by April 20. It came when a speaker claimed "the present cabinet has no party members. It is a dictatorship of the military and bureaucracy that does not consider the people's livelihood." Katō Kanjū of the Japan Proletarian Party, on the other hand, was the second most interrupted candidate in Tokyo. Police warned speakers at his rallies on seventeen occasions not to refer to "separation of military and people."[47]

On the popular side, one can read in this forbidden litany of campaign criticism an implicit call for imperial democracy. Those speakers, of whatever party, who bore the brunt of repression were precisely those most clearly suggesting a vision of a constitutional polity in which

---

46. Data compiled from Keishichō, "Shūgiin giin sōsenkyo enzetsukai jōkyō hyō," April 20, 1937, in *Shiryō: Nihon gendai shi* 9: 196–213.
47. Examples compiled from ibid. Asanuma quotation, p. 198. Katō, pp. 201–2.

popular representatives, in one or another political party, would defend the interests of the people and, thereby, the empire, bringing unity to the wishes of ruled and the unmentionable ruler. The "dictators" in the military and bureaucracy were selfish interests that ignored the people, distorted the constitutional polity, and thus, ironically, produced the very "gap" between ruler and ruled and between military and people that they deplored.

By carefully policing the boundaries of legitimate discourse, the state revealed its own political vision. Within the military and bureaucracy, a decision was being made to promote the unity of officials and people in a new way. The state would place itself in the role of political mobilizer, not mediator, of diverse groups in society; it would not undertake to "represent" the imperial and popular wills, as the parties sought, but to mobilize and to direct the will of the people in service to an emperor whose will the state defined.

This brings us to the third difference between the regimes of fascism and democracy, the concern of the rest of this chapter. Beginning in the mid 1930s, and gathering decisive momentum from 1937, the state fostered a broad spectrum of new organizations to create this mobilized polity. These new programs absorbed the strong imperial and emperor-centered dimension of popular thought and action, effectively denying the possibility of opposition based on this dimension. The state then repressed or coopted any remaining grass-roots impulse to participate, and shaped a regime with new mass organizations embracing (among other elements) labor, businesses small and large, and the political parties. Although the fascist movement from below never left the ground unaided, leaders such as Prince Konoe and Home Minister Suetsugu (December 1937–January 1939) made dramatic, and at times perhaps decisive, use of civilian right-wing groups as they pressured the parties and, however imperfectly, consolidated this regime.[48]

THE LABOR NEW ORDER

As with most elements of the regime, the "New Order for Labor" evolved in fits and starts. It took six years for the social bureaucrats to move from the liberal system of tolerance for unions as a means of achieving social order to the fascist program of the Industrial Patriotic

48. For an example, see Gordon M. Berger, *Parties Out of Power in Japan, 1931–1941* (Princeton: Princeton University Press, 1977), pp. 141–44.

Association (hereafter Sanpō).[49] A major turning point came in late 1936 when the army, fearing an "anti-fascist front" of unions and proletarian parties in military plants, forced 8,000 arsenal workers to withdraw from the huge Sōdōmei union of government employees.[50] The Home Ministry had not at this point wholly rejected unions, but it had retreated greatly from its earlier vision of their positive role. After the February coup in 1936, while the ministry reluctantly recognized unionism as necessary in some cases to ensure the "improvement of workers' status and respect for their character (*jinkaku*)," it announced that "it would be inappropriate to legally sanction unionism as the leading spirit of a social movement."[51]

As the Home Ministry and the military gradually retreated from commitment to, or even tolerance for, unions, key bureaucrats were formulating a sharply different strategy for labor-management peace and stepped-up production. The ministry's Social Bureau and the powerful Cabinet Research Bureau considered a variety of plans in 1936 and 1937, all focused on using "discussion councils" composed of worker and manager representatives to prevent labor conflict. Councils were to be created in workplaces throughout the nation. In most plans, and in the actual wartime system, the councils were to replace labor unions, and they were to be linked to the state through regional councils and a tripartite national organization dominated by officials.

The advocates of such plans, led by Minami Iwao, a labor manager turned bureaucrat, consciously drew on German Nazi or Italian Fascist models. The Nazi model was the most attractive, although when it publicly promoted the plans, the government often downplayed or ignored this foreign inspiration. In particular, bureaucrats drew on the 1934 Nazi Law for the Organization of National Labor, which had created advisory "Councils of Trust" in all German factories of twenty or more employees. The common ideological and organizational core to the German and Japanese labor systems is clear: both programs sought a classless national community, both replaced unions with universal plant

49. Sheldon Garon has analyzed the transformation of the state's labor policy (*State and Labor in Modern Japan* [Berkeley: University of California Press, 1987], pp. 198–218), and my own previous work has looked at Sanpō in large workplaces (Gordon, *Evolution of Labor Relations*, pp. 258–63, 299–326). Details on the promotion of Sanpō in the smaller factories of Nankatsu are not available. Here we shall briefly consider the significance of the wartime labor order.

50. Garon, *State and Labor*, pp. 208–9.

51. Hayashi, "Rōdō seisaku," p. 20.

advisory councils, and both waxed eloquent over the organic harmony and unity of an industrial "shop community" based on mythic village, folk, or family models.[52] The Sanpō ideology explicitly repudiated laissez-faire liberalism and class-struggle ideas; it affirmed a literally "corporate" view of the enterprise as a functional community where each member, equal before the emperor, had a vocation (*shokubun*), and where labor and capital fused together into a "single body" (*ittai*).[53]

The Sanpō program, while drawn up within the Home and Welfare Ministries, and discussed among Kyōchōkai members and business leaders, was conceived in a broader context of tremendous enthusiasm, among important intellectuals and many of the nation's most powerful rulers, for an all-encompassing New Order in Japan that drew on Fascist or Nazi models. The enthusiasm grew not simply because the Germans had gained new international power, but also because these Japanese considered the Germans, Italians, and themselves to be facing similar dilemmas. Consider, for example, the views of Admiral Godō Takuo, formerly head of the Kure Naval Arsenal. He was later appointed a peer, and he held two portfolios in the Hayashi cabinet (February–June 1937) as minister of commerce and of railroads. Like Minami Iwao he had become an exuberant advocate of Nazi programs after a trip to Germany, and just as the Sanpō program was being implemented he published his "lessons for Japan" in a 1938 book, *Germany on the Rise*. In it, he extolled the Nazi Labor Organization in which racial spirit overcame class conflict and service to the state substituted for destructive class consciousness. He argued for close ties with Germany, since the two nations shared an anticommunist mission. He felt Japan's mission to "stabilize" Asia would outlast the China War, and thus called for long-term mobilization of the people, who must repay their debt to the state. He concluded that Japan needed a labor service program on the German model, centered on an "absolutist Japanese spirit."[54]

In this context of enthusiasm for a new labor program inside and outside the ministry, the surge of disputes of early 1937, coupled with the economic pressure of the expanded war, catalyzed the bureaucratic decision to launch the Sanpō regime. In the army, by the spring of 1937

52. Garon, *State and Labor*, pp. 211–14.
53. Nishinarita Yutaka, "Nihon fuashizumu to rōshi kankei," *Hitotsubashi kenkyū nenpō: shakaigaku kenkyū*, no. 25 (July 1987): 159–60, cites official writings of 1938.
54. Godō Takuo, *Nobiyuku Doitsu* (Tokyo: Nihon hyōronsha, 1938), pp. 84–86, 94–100.

even General Ugaki, by now on the moderate fringe in the military, agreed that the spread of labor disputes required state attention, for the current expansion "did not have truly healthy [social and economic] roots."[55] The powerful advisor to the throne, Kido Kōichi, who formally presided over the implementation of the Sanpō program as both education and welfare minister in Konoe's first cabinet (June 1937–January 1939) and as home minister under Hiranuma (January–August 1939), was deeply troubled by increased social unrest in 1937 and again in 1938, when he wrote that persistent inflation and a "sharp increase" in nonunion disputes were once more creating a "confused" social context vulnerable to communist agitation.[56] Thus, the designers of the Sanpō system were propelled by their ongoing reading of social contention and breakdown.

In April 1938 a special committee of the Kyōchōkai, composed of leading social bureaucrats, top businessmen, and one Sōdōmei representative, recommended a compromise version of the Sanpō system. In August the government created the semiofficial Industrial Patriotic Federation to promote councils throughout Japan. The next April, during Kido's tenure as home minister, the Home and Welfare Ministries took full control of Sanpō, placing the workplace units under prefectural federations reporting to the prefectural governors.

Throughout this process, industrialists naturally feared losing autonomy to a state-run organization that reached into every workplace in the nation via mandatory councils, and the social bureaucrats agreed to allow managers to appoint worker representatives and promised that councils would not impose decisions on a company.[57] SMP and labor leaders, of course, also feared their groups would be overrun. In September 1938 a key bureaucrat assured the SMP's Miwa Jusō that Sanpō would not be used against unions, even as he said in the very next sentence that he personally saw the Sanpō principle as one of "absolutist labor-capital fusion." This remarkable "assurance" left no doubt that autonomous unions were indeed intolerable. SMP support for statist solutions is clear; the party agreed to back the Sanpō movement.[58]

55. Ugaki Kazunari, *Ugaki Kazunari nikki* (Tokyo: Misuzu shobō, 1968), 2:1145, entry of May 12, 1937.

56. For 1937, see Kyokutō kokusai gunji saiban kenkyū kai, ed. *Kido nikki*, 1947, pp. 52, 56. For 1938, see Kido nikki kenkyū kai, ed., *Kido Kōichi kankei bunsho* (Tokyo: University of Tokyo Press, 1966), pp. 396–98.

57. Garon, *State and Labor*, pp. 217–18.

58. *1938 shakai taishūtō katsudō hōkokusho*, p. 96. In "Shakai taishū tō taikai kiroku" file, OISR.

As in Italy and Germany the industrialists unsurprisingly fared far better than labor under the Sanpō regime.[59] Many large companies joined the federation by simply renaming existing factory councils as Sanpō units, while some major enterprises took the opportunity to reshape their councils and intensify control of the workplace. Owners of smaller factories, few of which had preexisting factory councils, were reluctant to join the federation. In the vast majority of cases it appears that the local police intervened to force these factories to form Sanpō units, but few of them seem to have been very active.[60] By the end of 1939, 19,000 enterprise-level units had been formed, covering 3 million employees, and by 1941 some 85,000 units enrolled 4.8 million.[61] In July 1940 the Konoe cabinet inaugurated its multifaceted New Order, and despite the assurances given the SMP two years earlier, the government forced Japan's 500 remaining unions (360,000 members) to dissolve "voluntarily." Not until 1942 did the National Federation of Industrial Organizations follow a similar course and reconstitute itself as a subdivision of Sanpō.[62]

The decision for Sanpō concluded the search for an alternative to a liberal social policy that began in 1931 when an earlier surge of disputes had galvanized industrial opposition and doomed the union bill. This was no random shopping spree for models in some "Western Policy Boutique" where British fashions of the 1920s had given way capriciously to German fashions of the 1930s. The trajectory from an imperial democratic to an imperial fascist system of labor control reflected both a process of social learning that crossed national boundaries and the working out in diverse nations of comparable dynamics of social conflict, economic stagnation, and frustrated international ambition. The fact that Japan's New Labor Order in the late 1930s could be persuasively presented as nativist, despite decisive outside influence, reveals the complex of common internal experience, international connections, and nationalistic fervor that contributed to the rise of fascist systems.

59. On Italy, see Roland Sarti, *Fascism and the Industrial Leadership in Italy, 1919–1940: A Study in the Expansion of Private Power under Fascism* (Berkeley: University of California Press, 1971).
60. See Nishinarita, "Nihon fuashizumu," pp. 151–56, on formation of factory units in large and small enterprises.
61. *NRUS* 10:438–39.
62. Andrew Gordon, "Bureaucrats and Business on Labor," in William Wray, ed., *Managing Industrial Enterprise: Cases from Japan's Prewar Experience* (Cambridge, Mass.: Harvard University Council on East Asian Studies, 1989), p. 83.

THE ECONOMIC NEW ORDER

Prince Konoe Fumimaro returned as prime minister in July 1940 with the enthusiastic support of bureaucrats, military men, politicians, and intellectuals anxious to create a New Order that would remake the relationship between state and society. The Labor New Order, which was to dissolve organized labor into the Sanpō structure, constituted one major facet of this radical agenda for change. At the same time, a group of reform-oriented "economic bureaucrats" and military men centered on the Ministry of Commerce and the Cabinet Planning Board, together with intellectuals in Prince Konoe's brain trust, the Shōwa Research Association, were the driving force behind a parallel Economic New Order. Through it, Konoe and his allies strove to restructure the economy to ensure that industry fulfilled "public" goals of the state, not private goals of capital.[63]

The bureaucrats and intellectuals who created the Economic New Order and prepared the climate of ideas in support of economic controls, were moved by many of the same concerns, especially with the social disorder of the depression, as were the social bureaucrats who created the Labor New Order. In addition, together with military men such as Suzuki Teiichi, they saw an important part of the solution to lie in access to an economic empire. Both these concerns continued prominent in the thought of Yoshino Shinji, introduced in chapter 9, who with Kishi Shinsuke and Shiina Etsusaburō was a principal architect of the economic controls of the late 1930s.

Yoshino elaborated his position in a 1935 book on *Japan's Industrial Policy*, in which he echoed and refined points he had been making since at least 1930. Although rationalization and control of big business was an important concern for the economic bureaucrats, Yoshino particularly emphasized the need to control and restructure the vast sector of small and medium manufacturers. His reasoning was simple: the small manufacturers were the foundation of industrial power and social order. They brought order by preventing society from bifurcating into "fundamentally opposed" classes of capitalist and worker; so long as small manufacturing thrived, the nation's workers could reasonably aspire to own their own tiny factories. These factories served as "the foundation of our nation's industry" because of their international role;

63. Chalmers Johnson, *MITI and the Japanese Miracle: The Growth of Industrial Policy* (Stanford: Stanford University Press, 1982), pp. 150–54.

he claimed they were responsible for over half the nation's export earnings in the recovery of 1933.[64] To ensure that small businesses continued to play these roles, Yoshino called for a national system to inspect their products to ensure quality. Most important, he wanted a compulsory structure of state-guided "industrial unions" to increase their productivity.[65]

The salience of the "labor problem" to the state's drive for economic controls is also made clear in the work of the economist Arisawa Hiromi. In 1937 he wrote an influential book arguing for state control of industry, and after the war he emerged as Japan's leading academic expert on economic policy. In his 1937 book, Arisawa made essentially the same points as Yoshino in unusually clear and persuasive academic language. Small-scale manufacturers were far less productive than larger plants, but they were superior in their ability to absorb excess population, for as output rose, so did the labor demand in these labor-intensive factories.[66] Arisawa agreed that smaller factories played a significant role in the export economy, but he qualified Yoshino slightly. For Arisawa, the heart of the matter was that smaller factories absorbed excess population but subjected the workers to inferior conditions: the "problem of small industry . . . is essentially a labor problem, a social problem."[67]

To solve the problem, Arisawa called for stronger controls. Existing cartels, created under the 1930 Important Industry Control Law, were too weak. Membership must be compulsory in a given sector, and the cartels needed more power over members.[68] He agreed with Yoshino, and indeed quoted him approvingly, in calling for mandatory "industrial unions" to restructure the small-scale sector. These unions were to regulate prices and output of members, provide credit, inspect products, and supply technology. The result would be a "state solution" to the social and labor problems of the smaller factories, which if unresolved would continue to harm the national economy.[69] In the conclusion to this powerful treatise, Arisawa insisted that the capitalist's demand for "self-control" was misplaced. Invoking Marx's belief that the social function of capital would be separated over time from the private own-

---

64. Yoshino Shinji, *Nihon kōgyō seisaku* (Tokyo: Nihon hyōronsha, 1935) pp. 127–28, 131.
65. Ibid., pp. 136, 163–69.
66. Arisawa Hiromi, *Nihon kōgyō tōsei ron* (Tokyo: Yūhikaku, 1937), p. 12.
67. Ibid., pp. 42–49, 66.
68. Ibid., p. 159.
69. Ibid., p. 178.

ership of it, Arisawa maintained that "step by step we must progress toward state capitalism."[70]

Despite differences in emphasis, both Arisawa and Yoshino looked back on the era of imperial democracy and concluded that the only resolution to the crises of depression and social conflict lay in a state-controlled, yet capitalist, economy. Both men sought a similar structure of controls centered on mandatory industrial unions and central state planning.

Advocates of economic controls and restructuring won a critical victory with the passage of the National Mobilization Law in 1938, which gave vast power to the state to deploy human and material resources "in times of emergency" through bureaucratic acts that would not require Diet approval. As with the Sanpō labor order, economic controls were implemented gradually, with two major periods of intensified control coming under the Konoe cabinets of June 1937 to January 1939 and July 1940 to October 1941. Also, as in the case of the Sanpō regime, big business managed to protect itself, retaining significant "self-control" over the structure of cartels and "control associations" erected in 1941. Smaller businesses, too, managed to retain some autonomy for several years after the Economic New Order was proclaimed, but in early 1943, with the Law for Commercial and Industrial Unions, the government created a uniform national system of industrial unions with mandatory membership. Once this law took effect, thousands of small manufacturers were forced to pool resources and dissolve themselves as independent firms, often shifting to military production as the state mobilized the entire economy for the continuing war.

THE POLITICAL NEW ORDER

The Political New Order meant different things to different people. As early as 1931, Ugaki Kazunari had envisioned leading a united new mass party to break the social and international impasse of the depression, but the bourgeois party leaders, not surprisingly, had balked.[71] In 1937 advocates of a new mass party coalesced around Prince Konoe in the first major drive to transform the political order. Konoe was a reluctant radical, however, and after much waffling, he shrank from leading a new party during his first cabinet.[72] It was not until two years later, at

---

70. Ibid., p. 212.
71. *Ugaki Kazunari nikki* 1:795–96, June 12, 1931, and 2:800, June 18, 1931; Berger, *Parties*, p. 45.
72. Berger, *Parties*, ch. 4.

the outset of his second term as prime minister, that Konoe inaugurated the political regime of imperial fascism, proclaiming the Political New Order in July 1940 and creating the Imperial Rule Assistance Association (IRAA).[73]

In contrast to the supporters of the new system of labor control, the advocates of the Political New Order were not primarily concerned with eliminating potential resistance on the part of the working class, whether defined as wage laborers or as their putative political representatives in the SMP. After the China War began, the SMP leaders quickly made their final peace with the state. In fact, they became fervent supporters of the "sacred war" and the "emperor's warriors," and vociferous advocates of fundamental political and economic reform "standing on a totalitarian principle."[74] The party's revised wartime platform of 1937 completed its transformation from a group representing the masses to one seeking, with the state, to mobilize and reshape them, as it called for "constructing a new culture, neither communist nor capitalist, befitting Japan's history and ethnicity."[75] Some members in the party's old social democratic wing refused to make this transition. They broke with the party in 1940 when the SMP sided with the military to oust a rare antiwar, antimilitary M.P., Saitō Tadao of the Minseitō. As the SMP never subsequently participated in a Diet election, we cannot fully gauge the popular appeal of its transformation, but in occasional special elections in 1939 it fared poorly.[76]

Supporters of the New Order were principally concerned to deal with the obstreperous bourgeois parties, which were still strong enough in the wartime Diet session of 1937–38 to force the government to modify its plans. They interpreted low voter turnout as apathy or resistance, a result of the poisoning of the masses by individualism or socialism, which rendered them insufficiently committed to the state. A Political New Order was conceived to halt such poisoning and turn apathy to enthusiastic support.[77]

The years from 1937 to 1940 witnessed a complicated series of strug-

---

73. Ibid., p. 304, for a diagram of the IRAA structure.

74. *1937 zenkoku taikai kaigi an*, p. 1, and *1939 shakai taishū tō katsudō hōkokusho*, p. 1, both in "Shakai taishū tō taikai kiroku" file, OISR. See also Suzuki Mōsaburō, ed., *Musan seitō shi shiryō* (Tokyo: Kashiwa shobō, 1965), p. 300.

75. *1937 zenkoku taikai kaigi an*, p. 9, OISR.

76. *1939 shakai taishūtō katsudō hōkokusho*, pp. 109–12, 132–33, OISR.

77. See Berger, *Parties*, pp. 137–38 on Seventy-third Diet; pp. 231–37 on passivity of populace. *Ugaki Kazunari nikki* 2:1144, May 3, 1937, on the significance of low voter turnout.

gles between advocates and opponents of the New Order. On one side, placing their hopes in Prince Konoe, stood those, mainly in the military, the bureaucracy, the SMP, and the civilian right, who supported a relatively pure fascist regime; in Gordon Berger's term, they sought a "political" version of the New Order.[78] Radicals in the army and Cabinet Planning Board wanted basic economic reforms as well as a "powerful organ of mass mobilization necessary to channel the economic and spiritual energies of the citizenry toward the implementation of a new system of state."[79] This would have required Konoe or some other leader to head a mass campaign against the established parties, and in 1937 Konoe's home minister, Admiral Suetsugu, seemed to be paving the way for Konoe to move in this direction. Suetsugu encouraged civilian right-wing groups to demand eradication of "the root of evil—[political party] opposition within the country." Such groups wanted to amalgamate all parties into a single organization, "uniting Japan on the principle of emperor-centered politics."[80] But Konoe hesitated, then demurred.

Against this, for a time, stood most of those in the bourgeois parties and their supporters, particularly the zaibatsu business leadership. In the event, they agreed to accept Sanpō, to go along with the massive system of economic controls, and to dissolve the parties. In all cases they made strategic compromises and succeeded in preserving many prerogatives *within* the new structure. In the case of the Political New Order, they gradually switched from opposing the state's threatening programs for "political" mobilization in 1937–38 to accepting the compromise of what Berger calls "public mobilization" in 1940. The parties, or their individual members after dissolution, would continue to mediate between their constituents and government, mobilizing "public" unity and support for the state.[81] In this settlement, party men represented the survival of a limited pluralism within the new regime, comparable to the plural bases of political power that persisted throughout Mussolini's reign in Italy. Yet at some point compromise on form fundamentally alters function or substance. Insofar as the parties' "compromise" meant that they abandoned their role as *representatives of popular interests* for that of *transmitters of state interests to the people*, we must recognize that despite the significant fact of their survival,

78. Berger, *Parties*, pp. 182–84.
79. Ibid., p. 133.
80. Ibid., p. 142.
81. Ibid., pp. 182–84, 197–98, 208–18.

the parties had completed their transformation from institutions of imperial democracy to elements in a regime of imperial fascism.[82]

The Labor New Order, the Economic New Order, the IRAA, and the Political New Order were thus responses of the "imperial bureaucrats"—nobles, generals, and civil bureaucrats who had ruled alone through the Meiji era and accepted the rule of the parties in the 1920s—to a perceived crisis of imperial democracy. Throughout the 1930s, but particularly in 1930–31 and 1937–40, they could not tolerate the inherent unruliness of imperial democracy in a time of international challenge to Japan's aggressive military policy. Their response in the more socially turbulent depression crisis was to repudiate the Minseitō social program and then to replace rule by parties with rule by the military and bureaucracy. Their solution at the end of the decade was to mobilize the masses directly to support their rule on behalf of the emperor, bringing all societal "interests" into harmonious union under one institutional roof.

As the new regime took shape, significant, though limited, "pluralism" remained. The IRAA, the Economic New Order, and Sanpō failed to give the state total and effective control over capitalists or workers; neither the IRAA nor Sanpō proved to be dynamic instruments of mobilization. Even so, effectiveness should not be the standard by which to judge the undeniable *existence* of a new structure of rule. Between 1937 and 1940, the Diet became a peripheral institution. However passively, the people were instead linked to the state and the emperor through a vast and expanding network of functional organs imposed upon them by the state: youth groups, women's groups, village and neighborhood associations, Sanpō workplace associations, and agricultural and industrial producers' unions. All the independent organizations of workers, tenant farmers, businessmen, and politicians, so painstakingly and haltingly created over the previous thirty years, were dissolved or destroyed.

82. Ibid., p. 210.

Conclusion

A principal objective of this book has been to place social contention, broadly conceived, and the working-class movement specifically, at the center of twentieth-century political history. By the 1920s workers who called for social respect and belonging, for equity, or for the radical transformation of society, secured a small portion of their demands in changed treatment at work and broader political participation. Their actions, together with those of poor farmers and others not treated here, also provoked an intense search among bureaucratic, party, and military elites for effective means to protect their interests in the existing social order. This search helped guide the trajectory from imperial bureaucracy, the system and ideology of rule ascendant by the late nineteenth century, to imperial democracy, first a movement that challenged the imperial bureaucrats and then a system and ideology of rule in its own right after World War I, to the imperial fascism consolidated as a ruling system by 1940.

In addition to social conflict, it is certain that a sense of foreign threat, a drive for empire fueled by strategic and economic interests, and a variety of Japanese readings of trends to be emulated in the advanced Western states also shaped the nation's twentieth-century trajectory. The key word is *also*. In the minds and the programs of rulers and activists from 1905 through 1940, the domestic context of contention and disorder brought by the rise of capital and the industrial revolution was linked with the international context of Japanese empire and frustrated ambitions. The domestic context shaped their decisions, which in turn influenced the thought and action of people out of power. Western historians, as outsiders, must make special efforts not to drop the internal dimension from our picture of the whole, or place it in the margins, implicitly falling back on a tired paradigm of "Western challenge and Japanese response" to depict modern Japanese history.[1] In this book I have attempted to contribute to a fuller picture by focusing on the internal context.

Across the decades described here, popular ideas and actions were transformed three times. First, beginning even in the late decades of the Tokugawa era but accelerating sharply in the Meiji years of "nation-building," Japanese commoners shifted from relatively uninvolved bystanders in the affairs of the nation to active participants who aggressively expressed their "will" and, in the case of the propertied, educated classes, organized to secure their interests. Second, after World War I, a significant minority of urban laborers and rural tenant farmers seceded from this movement for imperial democracy, creating a dispute culture through which they offered an ambivalent critique of existing structures of economy, society, and polity. In some cases they called for economic gains and social respect—in terms derived from imperial democratic programs—and in other cases they demanded a radical socialist restructuring. Finally, after the Manchurian Incident, the leaders of the labor and proletarian party movements reformulated their critique, deciding to ride the tiger of bureaucratic-military rule and imperialist expansion, while justifying their stand with ideas drawn from the earlier movement for imperial democracy. They drew significant electoral support, unprecedented for a proletarian party. Yet much of the populace—a plurality in urban electoral districts—grew disillusioned and apathetic, turning away from conventional forms of political engagement.

Across these same decades, the structure of rule and the justification for it was likewise transformed three times, through a dialectic of chal-

---

1. I am thinking here of treatments such as William Beasely's interpretation in *The Meiji Restoration* (Stanford: Stanford University Press, 1972), which plays down the domestic background in favor of stressing the impact of Perry's "opening" of Japan. Such a perspective is found in many textbook treatments of modern Japanese history, such as John W. Hall, *Japan from Prehistory to Modern Times* (New York: Delacorte Press, 1970), pp. 245–47, and John K. Fairbank, Edwin O. Reischauer, and Albert M. Craig, *East Asia: Tradition and Transformation*, rev. ed. (Boston: Houghton Mifflin, 1989), pp. 490–91. For a discussion of problems with such a "challenge-response" paradigm in the case of Chinese history, with relevance for Japan as well, see Paul A. Cohen, *Discovering History in China: American Historical Writing on the Recent Chinese Past* (New York: Columbia University Press, 1984), ch. 1.

lenge from and response to popular forces. A ruling system of imperial bureaucracy gave way to an imperial democracy, in turn supplanted by Japan's imperial species of fascism. Certainly important continuities linked these three eras. The adjective *imperial* highlights the continuous centrality of the emperor and the aspiration for empire in all three ideologies and systems of rule. Second, contending elite groups were not liquidated and did not drop from sight when they lost power, so that under each of the three systems of rule, these elites continued to play a role. In the years of imperial democratic rule, the House of Peers, the Privy Council, the bureaucracy, and the military housed factions that, although in eclipse, were opposed to the new parliamentary order; in the fascist era, plural centers of power survived and cooperated with the military and bureaucratic rulers. Thus, these systems of rule were neither "purely" democratic nor "purely" fascist, if ever such have existed. Yet despite these continuities, a shifting constellation of ruling groups did indeed adopt three distinct and conflicting programs and ideologies of rule.

Few Western scholars of Japan use the term *fascism* to describe wartime Japan. Many recognize "fascist" elements scattered here and there, whether in parties, programs, or structures of mobilization, but as a summary concept referring to a dominant ideology, regime, or system of rule, the word *fascism* is not often used. Indeed, in 1979 two prominent American scholars declared the term a "failure" in the *Journal of Asian Studies*, provoking almost no published dissent.[2] This is particularly striking when contrasted to the widespread use of the term by a strong, until recently overwhelming, majority of Japanese historians.[3] They use the term in part out of a belief that Japan's modern historical experience ought to be seen in comparative terms. In a similar spirit, I have spoken of fascism in these last chapters in hopes of reopening the issue of its conceptual relevance to Japan. It strikes me as a concept that has been too easily dismissed, which, if developed systematically and applied

---

2. Peter Duus and Daniel Okimoto, "Fascism and the History of Prewar Japan: The Failure of a Concept," *Journal of Asian Studies* 39, no. 1 (November 1979): 65–76. Two exceptions, both in the *Bulletin of Concerned Asian Scholars* 14, no. 2 (April–June 1982): 2–33, are Herbert P. Bix, "Rethinking 'Emperor-System Fascism': Ruptures and Continuities in Modern Japanese History," and Gavan McCormack, "Nineteen-Thirties Japan: Fascism?" McCormack is more equivocal than Bix, but he clearly sees potential for a concept of Japanese fascism similar to that introduced here.

3. As McCormack notes, this perception gap "is an astonishing fact, worthy of close attention from the sociologist of knowledge" ("Ninteen-Thirties Japan: Fascism?" p. 29).

more broadly than has been possible in these final chapters, offers one comparative approach to understanding the dissolution of imperial democracy.

Such an approach would begin by noting that two basic problems mark the stance of the Western critics who reject the fascist concept for Japan: an implicit Eurocentrism and an explicit nominalism. These critics typically generate a shopping list of characteristics of a "fascist" movement, regime, program, or ideology based on one or two European cases, most often Germany. Finding a significant number of items on the list absent or quite different in the Japanese case (no equivalent to the Fuehrer, no takeover by a fascist party, no burning of the Reichstag, and so on) they conclude that fascism is a misleading category for comparative analysis.[4]

The logical problem with such a strategy is that it will always be possible, if one so desires, to disqualify a non-European case, or indeed to disqualify any case that is neither Germany nor Italy.[5] There is no standard apart from the scholar's intuition for identifying the threshold where "incidental differences" add up to "essential" ones.[6] Some even conclude that the threshold is reached in contrasting Italy and Germany, and solve the problem by calling the former Fascist, the latter Nazi.[7] Such radical nominalism leads down a conceptual cul-de-sac where communication among scholars in diverse, yet related, fields of modern history ultimately becomes impossible, and where students are presented with a multitude of separate national historical experiences with no connecting threads.

My inclination is to avoid the nominalist and Eurocentric snares by coming at the problem from the opposite direction and starting with a search for similarities that might create an analytic common ground among these three national experiences. If we can identify these, then

4. Those who prefer not to use the term *fascism* for the Japanese case are certainly correct to note that it has been used sloppily as an epithet for "bad" in popular political discourse, and scholars have forged no consensus on its definition, but this does not mean we should abandon the term, although some would take this position, any more than we should abandon *democracy* as an analytic category because it is often tossed around carelessly. On this point, see Paul M. Hayes, *Fascism* (New York: Macmillan Free Press, 1973), pp. 9–10; Ernest Nolte, *Three Faces of Fascism*, (New York: Holt, Rinehart and Winston, 1966), pp. 6, 16; and Yamaguchi Yasushi, *Fuashizumu* (Tokyo: Yūhikaku, 1979), pp. 14–15.

5. The problem exists in the case of a concept such as feudalism, as well.

6. Duus and Okimoto, "Fascism," p. 66.

7. Stanley Payne, *Fascism: Comparison and Definition* (Madison: University of Wisconsin Press, 1980), pp. 195–96, offers a critique of this position.

the remaining differences, while certain to be numerous, important, and deserving of close study, become *qualifications* that reveal key variants of a shared historical process or formation, not *disqualifications* that prevent our use of common concepts of analysis.

In the cases of Germany, Italy, and Japan, we first find critical similarities in the trajectory of national experience from the late nineteenth through the mid twentieth centuries. These three societies were relatively late in developing capitalist economies and the apparatus of the modern nation-state, and equally important, many in all three societies considered this lateness a source of critical problems. Leaders in each nation harbored both imperial aspirations and fears that the British or the Americans would preempt or deny these. In each nation traditions of bourgeois democracy struggled to sink roots in a hostile environment and enjoyed brief periods of uneasy ascendance. In each nation social class conflicts intensified during and after World War I and intersected with frustrated international ambition to generate the perception of an international and domestic crisis among elites, intellectuals, radicals of left and right, and the populace at large. At some point in the interwar era, critical elements in each nation responded by repudiating parliamentary rule and turning to shrill nationalism, anticommunism, and antidemocratic, yet capitalist, programs to restructure the economy and polity and mobilize for total war.[8] In sum, the elites in these three relatively late developing interwar capitalist societies were rocked by economic crisis and by domestic upheaval unprecedented by the standards of each society; they also felt that aspirations to empire, which could help relieve the domestic problems, were blocked by the Anglo-American powers.[9]

This is an impressive realm of shared historical experience, and one analytic advantage to considering the Italian, German, and Japanese cases as variant species of fascism is that the term focuses our attention on this common historical process unfolding in different nations over the same broad timespan. The fascist concept also brings into sharper focus two further elements shared by these interwar societies: common ideas that justified the new regimes, and the common programs they adopted.

8. To gain one perspective on the common historical process described here, read the outline of Italian history from unification through Mussolini's rule offered by R. A. Webster, *Industrial Imperialism in Italy, 1908–1915* (Berkeley: University of California Press, 1975), p. 3. If one changes the relevant proper nouns and dates, the page reads like a description of Japan's history from 1890 to 1932.

9. Yamaguchi, *Fuashizumu*, pp. 6–8.

Considering ideology first, even scholars such as Peter Duus and Daniel Okimoto, who believe fascism has "failed" as a concept, agree that fascist ideas were influential in Japan in the 1930s. They describe a "new political theory" of what we might call mobilized collectivism, in which the state manipulated neotraditional values to solve modern social problems. They see parallels in the attack on "economic man" by the European fascists and the concerns both of intellectuals in the Shōwa Research Association and of Kita Ikki, a thinker who "wanted a 'revolution from above' to forestall the possibility of 'revolution from below.'"[10] Their description has much in common with the generalized fascist ideology considered by Yamaguchi Yasushi to characterize all three cases. In his view, fascist ideas addressed a crisis in the cohesion and control of nation and society (*kokumin shakai*) with a vision of ultranationalism and a radical, but authoritarian, remaking of the existing system of rule. This was a two-sided ideology that rejected the conservative status quo as well as Marxist or socialist solutions. The result was, on the one hand, an affirmation of war, expansion, and a recreated, glorified national racial community and, on the other hand, a negative attack involving at least five "anti's": it was anti-Marx, anti-liberal, anticapitalist, anti-internationalist, and against the status quo.[11]

Second, one can identify key elements in a common fascist program. S. J. Woolf seeks to do this, and he concludes that fascist economic programs on the one hand "differed notably from those of the capitalist countries in the 1930s," while on the other hand "fundamental differences" in the system of production and control of labor distinguished these fascist cases from the other major new political and economic system to emerge in the interwar era, that of the Soviet Union.[12] The similarity between programs to mobilize labor in Japan and Germany has been discussed in chapter 11. Although a full comparative analysis is impossible here, I believe one finds broad common ground among Japan, Italy, and Germany in their sweeping programs of economic reform, economic and social mobilization, and mass political control and mobilization.

One also finds a comparable disjunction between intent and outcome. This last point is critical. Many critics of the "fascist" label for Japan contend that, in contrast to cases of fascism in Europe, decisive

---

10. Duus and Okimoto, "Fascism," pp. 68–69.
11. Yamaguchi, *Fuashizumu*, pp. 24–25.
12. S. J. Woolf, "Did a Fascist Economic System Exist?" in *The Nature of Fascism*, ed. S. J. Woolf (London: Weidenfeld & Nicolson, 1968), p. 142.

and distinctive continuities linked the 1930s to earlier eras, and that a distinctive degree of limited pluralism survived both in politics and economic structure.[13] Such critiques are problematic on three counts. First, a case can be made for some important continuities between fascism and prior systems in Europe. Second, the "administrative revolution" that *was* imposed in Japan between 1937 and 1940 indeed led to crucial discontinuities.[14] As Gavan McCormack suggests, to dismiss fascism as inapplicable to Japan "because there was no radical disjuncture between pre-fascist and fascist Japan" is to misread how dramatically key relations between state and society, including those analyzed in this book, changed in the 1930s.[15]

Most important, such critiques err in comparing limited Japanese *outcomes* to sweeping German or Italian *intentions*. Even for Germany outcomes fell short of fascist intentions. The German army has been described by Paul Hayes as a "bastion [of the right] which only finally capitulated to Nazism in the aftermath of July, 1944." He also concludes that "fascist [economic] policy only gradually ate away the resistance of conservative forces, thus introducing change, albeit hardly radical change."[16] The outcome of fascist programs in Italy clearly involved continuities and the survival of limited pluralism, as industrialists, military leaders, the church, the police, the judiciary, and the monarchy retained some autonomy throughout the war; these elements cooperated with a fascist system but were not dissolved into it.[17] The survival of limited pluralism in the relationship of Japan's business and political party elites to the "administrative revolutionaries" who dominated the bureaucracy and the military seems particularly comparable to the Italian case.

Despite clear differences in the role of a fascist party and the movement from below, then, we can find similarities in the historical contexts to the rise of fascist systems in Italy, Germany, and Japan, the ascendant

13. Duus and Okimoto, "Fascism," p. 70; Ben-Ami Shillony, *Politics and Culture in Wartime Japan* (Oxford: Oxford University Press, 1981), pp. 172–77; Gordon Berger, *Parties Out of Power in Japan, 1931–1941* (Princeton: Princeton University Press, 1977), p. 344.

14. Gregory Kasza's *The State and the Mass Media in Japan, 1918–1945* (Berkeley: University of California Press, 1988) is an important account of one aspect of this revolution.

15. McCormack, "Nineteen-Thirties Japan: Fascism?" p. 31.

16. Hayes, *Fascism*, pp. 158–59, 132. See also the distinction between attempts and outcomes in Payne, *Fascism*, p. 95.

17. Sarti, *Industrial Leadership*, pp. 82, 101, 132; Anthony J. Joes, *Fascism in the Contemporary World: Ideology, Evolution, Resurgence* (Boulder, Colo.: Westview Press, 1978), p. 73; Payne, *Fascism*, pp. 74–75.

ideas that justified the new order in each society, and the programs that resulted. These constitute an "essential" minimum commonality that allows us to escape a conceptual dead end giving decisive weight to the contrasts between Italian Fascism, German Nazism, and Japanese militarism. Historians can explore the significance of variations among these and other cases after recognizing the significant parallels among these intertwined cases of late-developing empires in the interwar era.[18]

One scholar who has done an excellent job of defining fascism with such a strategy and using the concept in a comparative analysis of Italy, Germany, and Japan is Yamaguchi Yasushi.[19] His 1979 book *Fascism* distinguishes fascist ideologies (*shisō*), movements (*undō*), and ruling systems (*taisei*), a term that encompasses both regime and program. He begins with movements and, of course, recognizes the differences between the two processes by which fascist systems have emerged. In Germany and Italy fascist party movements took power and created single-party regimes; in Japan radical reformers in the bureaucratic and military elites took political control, stimulated by the violent outbursts "from below" of the civilian and military right.[20] Maruyama Masao has called this process "fascism from above," and Gregory Kasza has recently described it as an "administrative revolution."[21]

Maruyama's classic argument, echoed by Yamaguchi, remains suggestive. He recognizes the importance of "the unprecedented advance of the labor movement" in Japan in the late 1920s and the "crisis in ¬ural tenancy disputes," and he asserts that Marxism had a broad impact on Japanese society, beyond the "lecture platforms and journals" of the intellectuals.[22] He then contends that the popular social movements of

18. This is similar to suggesting that the industrial revolution be defined, not with primary reference to the British case, but after consideration of the several national cases of industrial revolution in the nineteenth century, including Japan. It is also similar in spirit to Duus and Okimoto's proposal (p. 72) that "we abandon the ethnocentric biases inherent in attempts to find [European-style] fascism in Japan and search instead for alternative paradigms that might fit both [i.e., Japan and Europe—they collapse Germany and Italy into one] cases." I differ in arguing that we use a more globally defined interwar fascism as this "alternative," for I feel the "corporatist" paradigm they suggest instead raises most of the same problems they find troubling in the case of fascism.

19. Yamaguchi, *Fuashizumu*, pp. 1–38.

20. Ibid., pp. 32–34.

21. Maruyama Masao, "The Ideology and Dynamics of Japanese Fascism," in *Thought and Behaviour in Modern Japanese Politics*, ed. Ivan Morris (New York: Oxford University Press, 1969), p. 65; Kasza, *State and Mass Media*, p. 296.

22. Maruyama, "Ideology and Dynamics," p. 65.

the left, of workers or farmers, in Japan, when contrasted to the tremendous force of the German communists and socialists or the Italian socialists, were relatively weak. This *relative* difference explains the variance between Japan's "fascism from above" and European "fascism from below": "the power of the mass-movement in Germany and even Italy...is the reason that popular bases had to be preserved to some extent in the fascist organization."[23] Another way of putting this is to echo a point made in the introduction to this book: Japanese elites historically have had a comparatively low threshold for social crisis.[24] This phenomenon deserves further study; it gives the trajectory traced here a particularly "Japanese" quality, but should not rule out comparative analysis.

In a similar spirit to Maruyama, but with greater emphasis on the impact of movements from below, the goals of parts 2 and 3 of this book have been, first, to show that by the late 1920s the working-class movement became an important social force and, second, to demonstrate that this movement constituted a key part of a challenge that shook the ruling imperial democrats, the bureaucracy, and the military. The social crisis was most intense from 1930 to 1932, the time of the critical first turn down the road to a new system of rule. In a context that included acts of terror by right-wing civilians and low-ranking officers, bureaucratic and military elites began to create what Maruyama calls fascism from above. By 1937 these new rulers had gone so far down this road that a relatively milder surge of social unrest, followed by the decision for war in China, sufficed to catalyze decisive steps toward imperial fascism at home.

EPILOGUE

The experience of imperial democracy bequeathed legacies to postwar Japan among both elites and the general populace. The rule of the Liberal Democratic Party and its early postwar predecessors grew from the bourgeois democratic roots sunk by the Seiyūkai and the Minseitō and from the experience of "constitutional" party government between 1918 and 1932. The division among party leaders and bureaucrats in the prewar era over how much democracy Japan needed, for whom, and to what effect was carried over into the postwar policy debates of

23. Ibid., p. 76.
24. See Introduction, pp. 9–10.

conservative party rulers.[25] Managers in the early postwar era disagreed sharply among themselves on their approach to powerful newly legalized unions, and their debates and strategies grew directly out of divisions among leading capitalists reaching back to the 1920s. Zen Keinosuke, the executive director of the Japan Industrial Club who coordinated the offensive against the union bill in 1930, reemerged in the occupation era as a preeminent business leader still bitterly opposed to and fearful of labor unions. On the other hand, the "reform capitalists" of the Keizai dōyūkai business federation accepted unions as partners in capitalist economic development in a spirit that echoed and extended the positions of a significant minority of business groups of the 1920s.[26]

At the popular level, the social movement of the interwar decades reemerged in the late 1940s as a force now able to contend seriously for power. In electoral politics, in union organizing, in patterns of dispute activity, and in central objectives of organized workers, the prewar experience shaped postwar developments. This claim reads like a truism, but overemphasis on the undeniably important impact of the American occupation can easily obscure these continuities. The Japan Socialist Party, in particular, built on the electoral base secured by the Social Masses Party in the 1930s, and strongholds of SMP strength before the war, such as Nankatsu, became centers of socialist support through the 1970s.

This continuity was brought home dramatically to me in 1985 when I was in Japan conducting research for this book. I spent a day—it happened to be the day before a Tokyo metropolitan assembly election—interviewing veteran union organizers of the 1920s and 1930s, all men in their seventies and eighties. That evening one of them led several of us to the election eve rally for a socialist candidate running in the Nankatsu area, where he was recognized and greeted by the younger party workers. It was an ill-attended event, and the next day the four wards that today encompass the territory of prewar Nankatsu failed to return any socialists for the first time since the prefectural

25. On continuities among bureaucrats dealing with labor issues, see Sheldon Garon, "The Imperial Bureaucracy and Labor Policy in Postwar Japan," *Journal of Asian Studies* 43, no. 3 (May 1984): 441–55.

26. As director of the Economic Stabilization Board under Yoshida, Zen consistently sought to undercut the new labor unions, pushing SCAP, without success, to ban strikes in 1946. See Theodore Cohen, *Remaking Japan: The American Occupation as New Deal* (New York: Macmillan Free Press, 1987), pp. 262, 271–72. On Keizai dōyūkai, see p. 203.

assembly election of 1932, a sign that the 1980s represented a new era of conservative ascendance and decline of the traditional left.[27]

The dispute culture of the 1920s also resurfaced, alive and vigorous, in the early days of the occupation, to puzzle even the most informed Western observers. The chief of the Labor Divison in the American occupation staff, Theodore Cohen, has described a labor dispute of the 1946 October offensive:

> The Tōshiba workers set up a strike headquarters of 700 men and women divided into twelve departments, from finances and liaison to public relations and publications. They sent emissaries to all the neighboring factories and unions to collect strike funds. They reported every few days to GHQ. To keep up morale they arranged marches, joint meetings with other unions, picnics, theatricals, arts and crafts instruction, flower arrangement classes, and lectures. They published reams of reports, comparative wage studies, special bulletins, a regular strike newspaper, schedules of events, and financial statements.[28]

Cohen prefaced this description by noting that "the unions surprisingly displayed a degree of maturity and organizational sophistication comparable with much older unions in America."[29]

Despite his familiarity with the formal history of Japan's prewar unions, Cohen was surprised by this event because he did not see that these well-organized disputes had roots reaching back to prewar working-class actions. Yet the similarity between the behavior of the Tōshiba workers in 1946 and that of the Ishikawajima workers in 1921 or the men and women at Royal Celluloid in 1930 is clear. The postwar workers inherited and recreated the prewar dispute culture described in this book; Cohen's description, minus the reference to GHQ, could be inserted into Murashima Yoriyuki's 1925 account with no dissonance.[30]

The adjective *imperial* points to the final legacies from the era of

27. The date was July 6, 1985. Interviewees included Shimagami Zengorō, the Nankatsu socialist leader of the prewar and early postwar eras. For election results, see *Asahi shinbun*, July 9, 1985, pp. 1, 4. The four wards are Kōtō, Sumida, Katsushika, and Edogawa. The socialist resurgence of 1989, I would argue, was built on a very different social base than that which supported the Social Masses Party before the war and the earlier postwar socialists.

28. Cohen, *Remaking Japan*, p. 270.

29. Ibid.

30. See chapter 6. In a similar fashion, John Pelzel's fieldwork and description of labor disputes in Kawaguchi in the late 1940s evokes the atmosphere in that town of twenty years earlier, although Pelzel, unlike Cohen, was aware of the historical roots of the Kawaguchi workers' behavior. See John C. Pelzel, "Social Stratification in Japanese Urban Economic Life" (Ph.D. diss., Harvard University, 1950).

imperial democracy: the ambivalence of so many Japanese over their
nation's role in the world and the suppressed, but seemingly widespread, anxiety over the future place of the emperor and the imperial
line. The devastation of defeat, of fire bombing, and the atomic bomb
certainly eliminated support for formal empire, extensive military
power, and an aggressive international posture from the mainstream of
political debate and policy for at least forty-five years. Yet consider
the extraordinary force of the national consensus reached by the 1960s,
which supported not simply economic growth and prosperity, but
Japan's breathtaking climb up the ladder of GNP rankings—at considerable personal sacrifice and social cost—and by the mid 1980s supported the notion of at least a co-hegemonic economic position with the
United States. Can we not conclude that in the history of postwar
Japan, popular aspirations to imperial democracy were narrowed and
transposed to the realm of economic power and prosperity?

Appendix A

Public Assemblies in Tokyo, 1883–1938

A. I   FIVE-YEAR TOTALS AND ANNUAL AVERAGES, 1883–1919

	Total Assemblies	Annual Average
1883–84	170	85
1885–89	187	37
1890–94	2,340	468
1895–99	556	111
1900–1904	1,015	203
1905–9	781	156
1910–14	1,218	243
1915–19	2,344	469
Totals	8,611	233

SOURCES: Figures from before 1890 are for "political assemblies" listed in Keishichō, *Keishichō jimu nenpyō*, 1888, 1890; 1890–99 figures are for "political assemblies" listed in the annual Keishichō, *Keishichō tōkei sho*; figures from 1900 on are for "assemblies requiring permit" from *Keishichō tōkei sho*. The appellation changed with adoption of new regulations for public assembly in 1900, but the categories appear to be identical.

A. 2 ASSEMBLIES (SHŪKAI) IN TOKYO, 1900–1938
(* DENOTES NATIONAL ELECTION YEAR)

Year	Assemblies Requiring Permit		Not Requiring Permit	
	Indoor	*Outdoor*	*Indoor*	*Outdoor*
1900	64	—	46	7
1901	113	3	626	—
1902*	172	16	597	—
1903*	292	9	900	67
1904*	261	85	1,843	15
1905	119	114	2,716	61
1906	118	7	387	31
1907	84	3	892	157
1908*	241	2	845	94
1909	92	1	541	97
1910	108	5	461	42
1911	193	10	542	4
1912*	325	1	337	13
1913	173	—	445	—
1914	396	17	511	—
1915*	876	1	765	—
1916	178	—	524	—
1917	817	—	511	—
1918	210	—	584	—
1919	261	1	802	—
1920*	807	24	1,167	2
1921	511	38	2,326	3
1922	1,070	39	3,149	1
1923	138	9	726	—
1924*	—	—	—	—
1925	1,502	7	4,014	8
1926	3,249	16	2,965	2
1927	2,241	19	3,152	4
1928*	11,507	21	1,537	1
1929	8,243	13	4,685	3
1930	9,482	3	1,741	1
1931	4,012	10	2,397	4
1932*	14,540	8	3,210	—
1933	8,853	21	4,407	18
1934	4,562	12	5,318	16
1935	5,842	11	5,731	7
1936*	20,725	6	6,451	7
1937*	17,863	22	10,568	22
1938	3,139	20	11,063	23

SOURCE: Annual volumes of Keishichō, *Keishichō tōkei sho*.
NOTE: No data were available for 1924.

Appendix B

Victims of the Kameido Incident,
September 4, 1923

HIRASAWA KEISHICHI

Hirasawa was born in 1889 in Niigata and adopted into a blacksmith's family at the age of four. He moved to Ōmiya, became a trainee at the Japan Railway Company's Ōmiya factory, and began to write seriously as a teenager. He moved to Hamamatsu, near Nagoya, in 1912 and joined the Yūaikai while working at a railroad factory. In 1914 he moved to Ōjima in Minami Katsushika County and became a leader in the Yūaikai in the Nankatsu region, encouraging literary and cultural activities among workers, writing and performing plays with labor themes and editing the Yūaikai magazine. He left the Yūaikai in October 1920, founded the Pure Laborers' Union, and in December formed a theatrical group. His union became involved in several disputes in Nankatsu, and he had been arrested once before the earthquake. On the evening of September 3, he was arrested by foot patrolmen.

KAWAI YOSHITORA

Kawai was born in 1902 to poor farmers in Nagano. His father became a miner, working at the Ashio copper mine and elsewhere, and he was fired for participation in the 1907 Ashio mine riot. Kawai graduated from elementary school in the mining town of Hitachi and became a lathe trainee at the mine's machine shop in 1918. He then met Kitashima Kichizō and Tanno Setsu and joined the newly formed Yūaikai Hitachi Federation in November 1919. That same month he was fired for his union activities. He moved to Tokyo in September 1920 and was introduced to the Gyōminkai study group in Nankatsu by a former elementary school teacher. He became active in labor and socialist organizing in Tokyo and was arrested and imprisoned for three months in the winter of 1921. During these years he held various jobs in Nankatsu factories. He joined the Communist Party in the summer of 1922 and was a founder of the Nankatsu Labor Association, which he served as secretary. He actively supported several strikes in the area, and in April 1923 he was among the founders of the Communist Party youth league. On September 3, as he was leaving to join a vigilante group night patrol, he was arrested at about 10 P.M. by Kameido police.

KATŌ KŌJU

Katō was born in 1897 to middling farmers in Tochigi Prefecture. He moved to Tokyo after graduating from elementary school and worked at a variety of jobs (newspaper boy, day laborer, retail clerk). He joined Watanabe Masanosuke's Celluloid Workers' Union in May 1919 while employed at a Nankatsu celluloid factory and took the lead in organizing a local at his factory. He was then fired in a unsuccessful dispute. Later, while employed at the Adachi Engineering Works, he was imprisoned for fourteen months for his role in an incident of machine-breaking during a dispute there in January 1921. He later became active in the Nankatsu Labor Association and Communist Party youth league. He was arrested at 10 P.M. on September 3 while napping after an evening patrol.

KITASHIMA KICHIZŌ

Kitashima was born in 1904 in a mining town in Akita, the son of a miner. He moved frequently as a youth, whenever his father changed jobs, and attended six elementary schools, graduating in 1918. He became a lathe trainee at the Hitachi Mines machine shop, befriending Kawai, Tanno, and others and joining the Yūaikai Hitachi Federation. He followed Kawai to Tokyo in the fall of 1920, began to work at the Hirose Bicycle Company and joined the Gyōminkai. He helped Watanabe with labor organizing and was a founder of the Nankatsu Labor Association, chosen one of its directors (*riji*) in April 1923. Active in the Communist Party youth league, he was leader of an antidismissal dispute at Hirose Bicycle when the earthquake hit. He was arrested by the Kameido police at 10 P.M. on September 3 at the Nankatsu Labor Association Headquarters.

KONDŌ KŌZŌ

Kondō was born in 1904 in Gunma Prefecture. He worked locally as a clerk in a fertilizer company after graduating from higher elementary school. He moved to Tokyo in 1922 and began to work at an electrical engineering factory in the Nankatsu area. When he was fired for arguing with a factory supervisor, his friends Watanabe and Kawai intervened and forced his rehiring. Kondō then became more involved in the labor movement. He joined the Nankatsu Labor Association and was selected head of Kameido Local # 2. On the morning of September 3, he was beaten by vigilantes for defending Koreans from attack. He sought refuge with Kawai and was arrested with him.

NAKATSUJI UHACHI

Nakatsuji was a member of the Pure Laborers' Union and was arrested near Kameido's Katori Shrine on September 3. He and Satō Kinji were probably killed separately from the other eight on September 4.

SATŌ KINJI

Sato was born in 1902, the second son of poor farmers in Iwate Prefecture. He graduated from elementary school and the Prefectural Middle School of Sericulture. He came to Tokyo in 1920, hoping to enter a university, but as he had no money, he began working at Minami Kiichi's factory in Azuma, taking a correspondence course from Waseda University. Satō befriended Minami's younger brother, Yoshimura Kōji, who influenced him to join the Nankatsu Labor Association in the summer of 1922. He worked at several other factories and became head of the association's Azuma local. After being detained on September 3 by army troops, who mistook him for a Korean, he was passed on to Kameido police and later killed.

SUZUKI NAOICHI

Suzuki was born in 1900 (place unknown). He worked at the Ashio and Jōban mines, met the socialist Katō Kanjū at the latter, and moved to Tokyo in August 1923 at Katō's request. He was staying temporarily with Kawai Yoshitora on September 3 and was arrested with Kawai at 10 P.M. upon his return from evening patrol.

YAMAGISHI JITSUJI

Yamagishi was born in 1903 to poor farmers in Nagano Prefecture. His family moved to Tokyo, where they lived in poverty. He left elementary school in second grade, worked for a waste-paper dealer at the age of eleven, and became a juvenile delinquent. He began to work as a lathe trainee in 1917. After meeting Kawai and Watanabe in 1922 while working at a factory in Azuma, he threw himself into the labor movement, joined the Nankatsu Labor Association, and became head of the Kameido Local # 1. He also joined the Communist Party youth league. He was arrested at 10 P.M. on September 3 upon return home from an evening vigilante group patrol.

YOSHIMURA KŌJI

Yoshimura was born in 1900, sixth of the eleven children of poor farmers outside Kanazawa City. Minami Kiichi and Minami Gen were his brothers. His name was changed when he was adopted at the age of two by the Yoshimura family. He apprenticed to a gold-leaf artisan in Kyoto in 1911, but he returned to Kanazawa to work at a bookstore in 1916. He moved to Tokyo in 1917 and worked at the factory owned by his brother Kiichi. Through his brother Gen, he met Kawai, began to study socialism, and joined first the

Gyōminkai and then the Nankatsu Labor Association. He headed the association's Azuma local, consisting mainly of rubber workers. In April 1923 he joined the Communist Party youth league. He and Gen also led a community group in petitioning for construction of a railway crossing gate along the Tōbu Railway Line in his neighborhood. He was arrested at home on the evening of September 3.

Bibliographic Essay

The numerous secondary sources that stimulated my thinking and provided the intellectual and empirical context for this work are cited in the footnotes. In addition, I explored a number of primary sources not well known to researchers outside Japan, in particular the collection of the Ohara Institute for Social Research. While the footnotes list the specific items from this and other collections, a general description of the most important sets of primary sources should prove useful to those interested in pursuing similar or related topics in the future.

SOURCES ON THE CROWD AND RIOTS

There is no single archive with particularly rich materials on the riots that are the subject of chapter 2. However, the library of the Tokyo Lawyers' Association (Tōkyō bengōshi kyōkai) contains at least one valuable resource, the record of the preliminary interrogations of the defendants in the Siemens incident of 1914. These were collected by the defense attorney, Hanai Takuzō, as "Taishō 3 nen sōjō jiken kiroku." The eight volumes include records of the extensive interrogation of the five men accused of conspiracy to riot, as well as of the unusual interrogation of roughly one hundred defendants facing nonpolitical charges such as arson. A similar document in four volumes offers interrogations of the 1905 Hibiya riot defendants. Titled "Kyōto shūshū hikoku jiken yoshin kiroku," it is less useful for the kind of study of the crowd undertaken here, as it focuses almost exclusively on the leaders charged with conspiracy. The only copy I was able to locate is in the Waseda University Library. Also in the Waseda collection is an unusual scrapbook of material on the Hibiya riot, "Meiji 38 nen yakeuchi jiken no shinzui" (call number Ka-2/3184/1-3), collected and donated to the library in 1924 by Muroi Hirazō, a Waseda alumnus, later an employee of the Bank of

Japan. The scrapbook contains a copy of *Tōkyō sōjō gahō* (Tokyo Riot Illus-
trated; no. 66, September 18, 1905). This is a special issue of *Senji gahō* (the
magazine has an English title, *The Japanese Graphic*). In addition to these
sources, newspapers and journals, especially the *Hōritsu shinbun*, offer extensive coverage of the riots.

SOURCES ON LABOR DISPUTES AND UNIONS

THE ARCHIVES OF THE JAPAN INDUSTRIAL CLUB (NIHON KŌGYŌ KURABU)

These documents are not open to the public, and I was unable to gain direct
access to this archive. As of 1985 the documents were stored in uncataloged
boxes at the club headquarters in the Marunouchi section of Tokyo. A graduate
student at the University of Tokyo's Faculty of Economics (Ueda Hiroshi), who
did gain permission to survey and make microfilm copies of a portion of the
collection, was kind enough to share his data with me. The collection is extremely valuable. Particularly important for this study were the extensive surveys carried out by the club as part of its drive to oppose the Labor Union Bill in
1930–31. The collection includes dozens of questionnaires completed by personnel managers at large and small companies concerning unions, disputes, and
management practices, as well as transcripts of interviews and speeches by owners of factories experiencing strikes. A few of these were published by the club's
Research Section (Chōsa Ka) in 1930 and 1931 as *Saikin ni okeru rōdō sōgi
no jirei* (4 vols.), but others are available only in the archive. I hope that the
club will eventually catalog its archival materials and make them available to
researchers or donate them to an appropriate archive.

THE OHARA INSTITUTE FOR SOCIAL RESEARCH

This is certainly the single most important repository of materials on prewar
labor history, as well as on the history of proletarian parties and tenant farmer
unions. In recent years it has added massive holdings from unions of the post–
World War II decades, particularly the documents of the Japan National Railway union. The prewar collection was only fully cataloged in the 1970s and
1980s, and scholars have yet to exploit its full potential. Three portions of the
collection were of particular importance for this study.

The Former Kyōchōkai (Kyū-kyōchōkai) Collection.
Acquired by the institute in the late 1940s after the Kyōchōkai was disbanded,
this collection includes the Kyōchōkai's own massive library of Western-
language and Japanese books in the social sciences, as well as roughly one
hundred bound volumes of Kyōchōkai staff reports on various labor disputes,
unions, and political parties of the left. These volumes are a particularly
rich source of analysis and information from a variety of perspectives. First,
Kyōchōkai staff members occasionally wrote reports of their firsthand observa-
tions of strikes, demonstrations, or rallies. Second, and most numerous, the
volumes contain police reports of labor disputes, political party activities,
union conventions, rallies, and so forth, prepared by the local police in mimeo-

graphed form and sent to the home minister, the governor of the prefecture where the event took place, and the Kyōchōkai. In the case of a lengthy dispute, one might find ten or fifteen police reports, written every other day or so. The structure and concerns of these reports offer valuable insights into the perspective of the government, and they occasionally supply relatively unmediated access to worker voices in the form of verbatim transcripts of speeches or negotiation sessions. Finally, the volumes also include copies of leaflets prepared by unions or strike groups, as well as company announcements issued in the course of disputes.

Documents of Prewar Labor Unions.
In the 1930s the Ohara Institute purchased the office records of a number of financially strapped labor unions. The institute has only recently cataloged these and collected them in loose-leaf note files. Included are records of Sōdōmei unions and some from the Hyōgikai, but documents of the centrist groups, especially Kumiai dōmei and, among its constituent unions, Kantō Amalgamated, are particularly numerous. As Kantō Amalgamated was quite active in Nankatsu, these records were invaluable for the analysis of Nankatsu unions and disputes from 1924 through the mid 1930s. The documents include records of union conventions, minutes of union executive committee meetings, reports on disputes and organizing efforts, and records of educational activities.

Documents of Proletarian Parties.
In similar fashion, the institute acquired documents from political parties, especially the Social Masses Party and its predecessors, Nihon taishūtō and Zenkoku rōnō taishūtō. Included are reports prepared for annual party conventions and analyses of election campaigns, as well as rare copies of leaflets, posters, and newsletters issued in the course of both national and local campaigns.

DATA BASE OF NANKATSU LABOR DISPUTES

The statistical analysis of labor disputes in Nankatsu, reported in various tables in chapters 6 through 9, was generated from data concerning 516 disputes that took place in Minami Katsushika County from 1897 to 1938. The data were culled from several sources: Aoki Kōji, *Nihon rōdō undō shi nenpyō*; Keishichō, *Rōdō sōgi junpō* (at the Ohara Institute); Kyū-kyōchōkai, *Rōdō sōgi* (all volumes, at the Ohara Institute); and Shakai seisaku jihō, *Shakai undō tsūshin*. To the extent that information was available, the following items were recorded for each dispute: dates and duration, address and name of factory or factories involved, total number of employees (men and women), number of participants in the dispute (men and women), unions involved, primary demands, tactic (strike, slowdown, lockout), result, and police intervention.

Index